VOYAGE TO JAMESTOWN

VOYAGE TO JAMESTOWN

Practical Navigation in the Age of Discovery

ROBERT D. HICKS

NAVAL INSTITUTE PRESS
ANNAPOLIS, MARYLAND

This book has been brought to publication with the
generous assistance of Marguerite and Gerry Lenfest.

Naval Institute Press
291 Wood Road
Annapolis, MD 21402

Library of Congress Cataloging-in-Publication Data
Hicks, Robert D.
  Voyage to Jamestown : practical navigation in the Age of Discovery / Robert D. Hicks.
      p. cm.
  Includes bibliographical references and index.
  ISBN 978-1-59114-376-5 (hardcover : alk. paper) 1. Navigation—History—17th
century. 2. Naval art and science—History—17th century. 3. Ocean travel—History—
17th century. 4. Seafaring life—History—17th century. I. Title.
  VK549.H53 2011
  623.8909'032—dc23
                    2011028655

∞ This paper meets the requirements of ANSI/NISO z39.48-1992
(Permanence of Paper).
Printed in the United States of America.

19 18 17 16 15 14 13 12 11   9 8 7 6 5 4 3 2 1
First printing

Dedicated to
JOCELYN R. GILL
Astronomer, Space Pioneer, Teacher

Contents

Illustrations

Foreword

An old navigation textbook explained that the stars are guides for people who know them. An astronomy course in college formed the basis of my interest in celestial navigation, at which I became proficient while flying aircraft in the Navy. I love celestial navigation and what is involved in using it. Although many years have passed since I was an aviator and astronaut, the science of celestial navigation remains fascinating to me. The fascination resides in the competence to use a sextant, lines of sight, almanacs, and other tools and reference books together with an understanding of and familiarity with the stars and their apparent motions.

When I flew a large aircraft with an eight-man crew, I was personally satisfied by being able to look at the stars and calculate where we were at night over the Pacific. To be able to do that, one must have the knowledge and equipment. Still, it is not easy to take a sight that is valuable for navigational purposes. If we do not have the experience of taking and reducing celestial observations to obtain a position, we do not understand the difficulty of the problem.

Once I failed at navigating on a flight from the Philippines to Guam during daytime because I did not think I needed to bring a sextant to read the sun. We got lost. We had to give up trying to find the island and had to fly a square search to find it. I was lazy and underestimated the difficulty of the problem. That was a good lesson to this young aviator: do not

forget the power of celestial observation; it is always of value.

Museums are excellent places to explain the principles behind celestial observation and navigation. Most people do not understand how to look at the position of a star and find out exactly where they are. These principles are rarely explained well except to navigational students in the classroom. It is difficult for museums to display a sextant, the icon of celestial wayfinding, a fascinating and versatile tool. It is not an easy instrument to explain through a demonstration, but museums should take on this challenge to educate people in a very interesting science. It takes time and is not easy. Museum staff should personally help visitors to understand; personal instruction is a requirement to capture their attention and imagination.

Celestial navigation is a disappearing talent because of the march of technology. Current technology has allowed us to navigate in a very lazy fashion; we do not have to work for it. We have lost this skill of looking skyward to find our way. Based in astronomy, celestial navigation, once learned, is a technique that a person does not lose. And it is a technique that should not be lost. Pre-electronic methods of navigating should be preserved because they are beyond failure except by the failure of the navigator himself.

Navigators in the era discussed in this book employed much guesswork. Still, they needed reference books. Celestial navigation demands study, and books on astronomy remain recommended reading. Even recreationally, celestial navigation with its computations is a fascinating thing to be able to do. As a memento of my flying days, I still have my E6B, a hand-held mechanical computer used for various calculations, a tool I used in naval aviation training and one still admired and used today. This instrument recalls to my mind with pleasure many observations made with an aircraft sextant. Celestial navigation remains a technique very dear to me.

CDR. M. SCOTT CARPENTER, USN (Ret.)

Acknowledgments

This book evolved from several years of interpreting early modern navigation at museums and historic sites, mostly in Virginia. In fact, this book's voyage began at The Mariners' Museum, Newport News, Virginia, and Historic Jamestowne, Virginia, and in a doctoral dissertation at the University of Exeter, United Kingdom. Many museum exhibits examine the social milieu of European voyages to North America but few have the space or resources to show how ships navigated, or to use navigational challenges as a window to explore the mental world of seafarers. Navigation can appear forbidding in museums when visitors confront tools that embody mathematical applications and require some conceptual background.

I aim to place readers within a mental seascape of the early seventeenth-century navigator. Years of interpretation have convinced me that people best respond to the topic of navigation through storytelling. Captain Tristram Hame, through whose practice navigational tools and methods become clear, may be a fictional character, but his words all derive from primary sources, now seldom read by anyone except scholars. The primary model for Captain Hame is Captain Tobias Felgate, who made multiple trips to Virginia from Bristol. I was delighted to discover an exuberant extended family of Felgates in the United Kingdom who have recovered much of their ancestor Tobias' life and circumstances. I thank Don Felgate for copies of many primary sources on Tobias that

have been cited here. Finally, to make seventeenth-century discourse more appealing, I have modernized spellings and removed the most obscure usages and turns of phrase.

Over the past few decades, I have been privileged to know, correspond, and meet with other devotees of this subject, some of whom have read and commented on parts of the manuscript. Thanks are due to Captain Søren Thirslund, retired merchant mariner of over a half century, the navigational authority at the Danish Maritime Museum and an investigator of Viking navigation. In the same category is Captain José Manuel Malhão Pereira, retired from the Portuguese Navy, a tireless researcher and promoter of an understanding of early modern navigation. He has published important research that illuminates early navigational tools and criticizes grandiose claims about the putative achievements of Chinese navigation of the early modern period. Similarly, I thank Alan Stimson, former Curator of Navigation, National Maritime Museum, and Dr. Willem F. J. Mörzer Bruyns, former Senior Curator Navigation, Nederlands Scheepvaartmuseum, Amsterdam, both of whom commented generously on my various navigational essays, incorporated in this book, saved me from embarrassing errors, and suggested other avenues of research.

I would not have written this book or, indeed, gotten very far in the interpretation of navigation, without constant reference to the research and writing of Lieutenant Commander D. W. Waters,

Royal Navy, former Deputy Director of the National Maritime Museum, United Kingdom. About a half century ago, he put Elizabethan navigation on the scholarly map and created a framework for the study of early instruments and texts. I am indebted to the many conversations we had at his Gloucestershire home.

Notes on Text

This manuscript has traveled among publishers, many of whom expressed difficulty reconciling historical discourse with fiction (Hame's hypothetical voyage). Along the way, the text benefited from—and I here express thanks to—anonymous reviewers for the University of Virginia Press and Boydell & Brewer, Ltd. I am grateful to the United States Naval Institute Press for taking it on, particularly to Tom Cutler, Director of Professional Publishing at the Press, who nurses his own interest in marine navigation and has edited the current version of the venerable *Dutton's Nautical Navigation*. Evi Numen, indefatigable and talented exhibits manager for the Mütter Museum in Philadelphia, prepared the diagrams and scanned and improved almost all of the illustrations.

Some of the text borrows from my other publications on historical navigation. I am indebted to Wiley-Blackwell for permission to quote from "The Interpretation of Measuring Instruments in Museums," *Curator: The Museum Journal* 44.2 (April 2001); to Taylor & Francis for permission to quote from "What Is a Maritime Museum?" *Museum Management and Curatorship* 19.2 (2001); and to the Mary Rose Trust for permission to quote from my essay, "Navigating the *Mary Rose*," in Peter Marsden, editor, *Mary Rose: Your Noblest Shippe, Anatomy of a Tudor Warship*, The Mary Rose Trust, Ltd., 2009.

This book's dedicatee, Joceyln Ruth Gill (1916–84), visited my family in South America in 1966, which launched a correspondence that lasted until her death. An astronomer, she served as chief of in-flight sciences for the early manned spaceflight program at the National Aeronautics and Space Administration. At NASA, she devised science experiments for the Mercury, Gemini, and Apollo space missions. A graduate of Wellesley College, she pursued postgraduate studies at Yerkes Observatory, University of Chicago, and earned a doctorate from Yale University. Dr. Gill provided a conduit to the adventure of space science and the excitement of astronomy. Throughout our acquaintance, while multiple sclerosis gradually reduced her physically, it never inhibited her intellectual pursuits. She was, as Henry Adams put it in his *Education*, one of those teachers who "affects eternity; he can never tell where his influence stops." I am most grateful to a former associate of Dr. Gill's, Commander M. Scott Carpenter, USN (Ret.), one of the original Mercury astronauts, the fourth American in space and the second to orbit the earth, for contributing a foreword. Commander Carpenter, a proficient navigator who promoted the scientific study of the space "ocean" during Project Mercury, discusses Dr. Gill's NASA work in his own fascinating memoir, *For Spacious Skies: The Uncommon Journey of a Mercury Astronaut*.

To Kathleen R. D. Sands, my wife, I owe a supreme debt for proofreading, editing, and ceaseless supportive conversations that improved this work:

> A grateful mind
> By owing owes not, but still pays, at once
> Indebted and discharged.
>
> —MILTON, *Paradise Lost*

VOYAGE TO JAMESTOWN

CHAPTER 1

INTRODUCTION:
The Haven-Finding Art

How beneficial the art and exercise of navigation is to this realm, there is no man so simple but sees, by means whereof we being secluded and divided from the rest of the world, are not withstanding as it were citizens of the world, walking through every corner, and round about the same, and enjoying all the commodities of the world.

—ROBERT NORMAN, *The Newe Attractive*, 1581

The Haven-Finding Art

A popular Cole Porter song from the 1920s proclaims that birds and bees fall in love, as do, among others, Cape Cod clams, electric eels, and kangaroos.[1] Porter might have substituted "let's navigate" for "fall in love," for all of the beings included in the lyrics must also find their way to food, shelter, and rest. As for birds, each year the Arctic tern navigates from pole to pole, a round trip of 40,000 kilometers; when first exploring a new food source, honeybees rely on landmarks, while experienced ones use the sun's changing position as a datum; as for fleas, the beach flea, *Talitrus saltator*, educated or not, relies on celestial referents to time its movement with the tides.[2] To navigate, insects, animals, and people require a sense or awareness of space, direction, distance, and the time necessary to reach a destination.[3] Animals may rely on visual cues for direction finding but genes have

afforded them mechanisms not available to people's unaided senses: echolocation, olfaction, magnetic fields, and even atmospheric pressure. People, however, have few innate navigational mechanisms and must be taught how to navigate. Navigators of all cultures and eras have acquired acute sensitivity to environmental phenomena for wayfinding, sometimes augmenting their own senses with tools. Even in the twenty-first century with electronic navigational tools such as Global Positioning System (GPS) and inertial guidance in submarines, the sailor has not been relieved of learning environmental (including celestial) cues to aid wayfinding.

Most westerners have little contact with seafaring. Many of the commodities that we buy arrive through seaborne commerce, an invisible process indispensable to modern life. Navigational tools, too, are unfamiliar to most people, except for those who choose maritime vocations. Whether taught at naval or merchant marine academies, yachting schools, or museums, navigation is presented too often as a specialized scientific endeavor borne of mathematical astronomy, with arcane nautical almanacs of celestial data, dense sight-reduction forms, and computer-assisted models. Students at many naval academies no longer learn celestial navigation. Still, where *celestial* navigation is still taught, students have no time to absorb the conceptual basis of the subject and instead try to memorize rules for adding or subtracting data to obtain longitude and latitude. Navigation becomes an abstract exercise based on calculation rather than one that heightens the ability of the student to "read" the natural environment or visualize the celestial sphere with its apparent motions of the sun, moon, and stars.

Geoffrey Chaucer described one of the most famous literary navigators of the late Middle Ages in "The General Prologue" of *The Canterbury Tales*. Chaucer's description attests to the ability to "read" nature. Acute knowledge of tides and currents, sensitivity to celestial phenomena, and a healthy respect for the apparent whims of the ocean has defined, and continues to define, the apprenticeship of the navigator:

> A shipman there was, dwelling far to the west—
> For ought I know, he was of Dartmouth . . .
> But of his craft, to reckon well his tides,
> His harbor and his moon, his lodemenage [pilotage],
> There was no one such from Hull to Cartagena.
> Hardy he was and wise in his undertakings;
> With many a tempest had his beard been shaken;
> He knew all the havens that there were
> From Gotland to the Cape of Finisterre,
> And every creek in Britain and in Spain.
> His barge was called the *Maudelaine*.[4]

The good Dartmouth captain of *Maudelaine* exemplifies the accomplished navigator of any era or culture: he had to have empirical, predictive knowledge of winds, currents, and other environmental phenomena; he had to be competent at seamanship; he had

to recognize landmarks as seen from the sea; he had to know his *havens*. Chaucer's pilot does not just seek a port or a harbor; he seeks a *haven*, a place of protection and safety for himself, his crew, his ship, and his cargo. The pilot, without reference to a chart, could relate from memory the soundings as he approached his haven even before it was visible; he could describe the nature of the seabed underneath his ship; he knew local tidal patterns; he could describe from memory the location of shoals or reefs; he could identify the direction and strength of predominant winds for different seasons[5]; he could reckon the lateral movement of the ship over water, leeway, by visual estimate; for his own notes and papers, he drew an outline of coastal features visible from a distance at sea such as a church steeple, prominent hill, or fortress; he knew where to moor his ship or careen his ship's hull for repairs; he knew the victualers, the port reeve who supervised many quayside legal affairs, local pilots (taken on board if the anchorage was difficult or heavily trafficked), and innkeepers; he knew the factors who arranged for lading and discharging of cargo. The pilot carried with him, at any moment, a mental *seascape* charged with all of this information, which he could recall at will.[6] Thinking about navigation was inseparable from thinking of the ship's safety, the timely completion of business, the urgency to manage tempestuous and contrary weather, the exploitation of favorable winds and tides, and the satisfaction of completing a successful voyage by reaching a haven. In 1599, Simon Stevin published a navigation manual entitled, *The Haven-Finding Art*, the title attesting to the importance of finding the place of completion, safety, and rest. Only in a haven is the navigator free of buffeting, jarring, swelling movement that pulls, bends, tears, and slaps his vessel.

This book explicates the navigational art through a hypothetical voyage of a merchant galleon, *Guyft*, from Bristol, England, to Jamestown, Virginia, in 1611. The voyage is a composite of many voyage

1. GUYFT — Guyft under way. A small merchant galleon, Guyft is typical of ships engaged in the English trade with Virginia. The ship carries cargo and passengers, and can defend herself. Credit: Ann Berry

narratives of the era, most found in compilations of exploration accounts little read today, Richard Hakluyt's *The Principal Navigations Voyages Traffiques & Discoveries of the English Nation* and Samuel Purchas' *Hakluytus Posthumus or Purchas His Pilgrimes*. The reader experiences the voyage through the hypothetical persona of the ship's master and navigator, Tristram Hame. Hame, in turn, is a composite of several skilled contemporary navigators. This book is not a novel. Firmly anchored in historical sources, the hypothetical voyage by a hypothetical master and crew presents factual information to aid the reader in developing an historical imagination. The aim of this imaginary exercise is the construction of Hame's worldview, his perception of the sea and the world,

and the solution of navigational problems within the perspective of the early seventeenth century when the Western Hemisphere was still the New World. Some navigational practices and tools common to ships in 1611 have an ancient pedigree far from England; some methods are new and presage the geometry- and trigonometry-based methods of following centuries. The early texts of the art of navigation still impress with their confidence, direct engagement with the reader, and experience. Many of these texts as quoted throughout this book clearly explicate the necessary conceptual background to navigation (which still applies), offer logical rationalization of observational techniques and data reduction, deliver an engaging style of presentation, provide long-forgotten rules of thumb or mnemonic devices to ease calculation, and resonate with heady anticipation of commercial success in Asia and the Americas. The method of this book follows the advice of Captain John Davis, the first professional English navigator to write a text on the subject, who defends the unvarnished language of his instruction: "Therefore I omit to declare the causes of terms and definition of artificial words, as matter superfluous to my purpose, neither have I laid down the cunning conclusions apt for scholars to practice upon the shore, but only those things that are needfully required in a sufficient seaman."[7]

Learning navigation as practiced in 1611 encompassed both mastery of mathematical calculation and a keen sensitivity to the marine environment. Early texts by practitioners sharpen one's perception in apprehending the shape of a coastline, the nature of the seabed underneath a ship, the changing sky view as one traverses a range of latitude, the apparent motions of the sun and moon, the smell and texture of the sea. Navigation as an art requires more than taught knowledge: it embraces apprenticeship, experience, skill in application. Samuel Purchas, particularly, infused his vision with the language of destiny, unbridled expansion, and unlimited possibilities in an exuberant paean to the benefits of navigation:

> Now for the services of the sea, they are innumerable; it is the great purveyor of the world's commodities to our use, conveyor of the excess of rivers, uniter by traffic of all nations; it presents the eye with diversified colors and motions, and is as it were with rich broaches, adorned with various islands; it is an open field for merchandise in peace, a pitched field for the most dreadful fights of war; yields diversity of fish and fowl for diet, materials for wealth, medicine for health, simples for medicines, pearls and other jewels for ornament, amber and ambergris for delight, the wonders of the Lord in the deep for instruction, variety of creatures for use, multiplicity of natures for contemplation, diversity of accidents for admiration, compendiousness to the way, to full bodies' healthful evacuation, to the thirsty earth fertile moisture, to distant

friends pleasant meeting, to weary persons delightful refreshing; to studious and religious minds a map of knowledge . . . the sea yields action to the body, meditation to the mind, the world to the world, all parts thereof to each part, by this art of arts, navigation.[8]

Relevant to the era of concern to this book, the Elizabethan polymath and genius, Dr. John Dee, rehabilitated in recent years from an image of a wizard, a panderer of occult mysticism, applied his mathematical talents to furthering the navigational abilities of his countrymen. In an influential essay promoting mathematics that prefaced an English translation of Euclid, he stated that the "1st 'Art of Navigation' demonstrates how, by the shortest good way, by the aptest direction, & in the shortest time, a sufficient ship, between any two places . . . may be conducted: and in all storms, & natural disturbances chancing, how, to use the best possible means, whereby to recover the place first assigned."[9]

Dee defines navigation within an elaborate model of mathematically based arts. Most practitioners of navigation wrote of their craft to promote its stature among the mechanical arts as beneficial to national prestige, but also as divinely merit-worthy. Very little has changed from Dee's day. A modern definition places navigation within the practice of seamanship as both an art and science for getting a vessel from here to there. A subcategory to navigation is pilotage, which is navigation close to land and within shallow waters.[10]

Stephen Borough, chief pilot of the Muscovy Company during the sixteenth century, arranged for the translation from Spanish and publication of the first navigation manual in English. Martín Cortés' *The Arte of Navigation*, published in England in 1561, survived in many editions through the following decades and became "one of the great formative books of the English nation."[11] Cortés offers a view of navigation not only as an art to be mastered, but also as a practice amounting to Christian virtue: "What

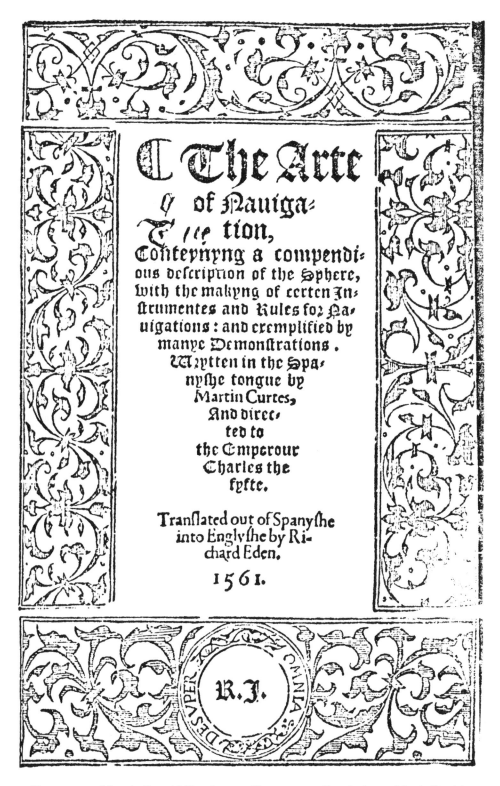

The Arte
of Nauiga-
tion,
Conteynyng a compendi-
ous description of the Sphere,
with the makyng of certen In-
strumentes and Rules for Na-
uigations: and exemplified by
manye Demonstrations.
Wrytten in the Spa-
nyshe tongue by
Martin Curtes,
And direc-
ted to
the Emperour
Charles the
fyfte.

Translated out of Spanyshe
into Englyshe by Ri-
chard Eden.
1561.

R.J.

2. FRONTISPIECE, MARTÍN CORTÉS' THE ARTE OF NAVIGATION ⁓ Frontispiece to Martín Cortés' *The Arte of Navigation*, 1561, one of the most important books published in English during the **early modern era and an essential text for Captain Hame.** Credit: Courtesy of the John Carter Brown Library at Brown University, shelf mark B561 C828a

can be a better or more charitable deed, than to bring them into the way that wander: what can be more difficult than to guide a ship engulfed, where only water and heaven may be seen."[12]

Essential ingredients to navigation include a sense of place, directionality, distance to be traversed, and the time required to traverse it.[13] To a contemporary of Hame, "the six principal points in navigation" were "Card, Compass, Tide, Time, Wind, Way."[14] A "card" is a chart. The magnetic compass presents the mariner's lingua franca of directionality, a template dividing the horizon equally into thirty-two points, a framework with deep antiquity. The parlance of naming directions provided the means of articulating tide, wind, and way, and even "card." Observing the tides and winds requires a visual skill grounded in mnemonic techniques and some tools, including the chart, methods of accounting for distance covered and in what direction, and the sandglass to measure the passage of time. Without clocks on board ships in 1611, shipboard life was measured and regulated by sandglass in parcels of half hours. As we shall see, various tools aided the recording of distance and direction.

Navigation subdivides into piloting, dead reckoning, and celestial techniques, categories that also apply to insects, fish, and animals. Because piloting concerns navigation near shorelines or in shallows, it generally employs landmarks and other topographical features. Dead reckoning involves keeping a running track of direction and distance covered; celestial relies on the sun, moon, and stars. For Tristram Hame, however, navigation represents a complex whole: he and his contemporaries did not make the distinctions common to modern people with our fetishes for classification and delineation. The ocean could not, and cannot be partitioned or segmented. When Hame peered down over the gunwale at the ocean, he did not view an undifferentiated medium surrounding and supporting his ship. He was at once aware of the current, a wind-induced movement; the tides, a daily, recurrent cycle of movement related

to the moon's position relative to the earth and sun; and leeway, a movement of the ship forced by wind or tide.[15]

With navigation defined within its early seventeenth-century context, we must outline the other important perspectives that govern the narration of this voyage: an interpretive lens, an archaeological framework, the place of an account of navigation within maritime history, and the view of the seascape.

Interpreting the Navigator and His Worldview

Tristram Hame is based mainly on Tobias Felgate, an actual navigator known to have captained five merchant voyages to Virginia during the early years of the colony following its permanent establishment at Jamestown in 1607. Hame and his ship, *Guyft*, are introduced in Chapter 2. Engaging the art of navigation through Hame's worldview, a form of personalizing the past, the reader becomes an historical anthropologist visiting another era to observe human behavior. We shall construct Hame's universe through the narrative of a voyage with its obstacles, hazards, problems, and successes. Note that *all* quotations in this book, including any words uttered by Hame or his fellows, come from sixteenth-or seventeenth-century sources. Readers intrigued to read the original materials will find sources listed for all quotations.

This book must equip the reader to enter a psychological framework common to Hame and his contemporaries, a framework in some ways foreign to us.[16] Exploiting Hame in order to fathom the past has a parallel in visits to historic sites. Most museums and historic sites make some use of personal methods of interpretation. The most popular personal method is the guided tour, followed by interpreters trained to engage people through storytelling.[17] In other words, most visitors to historic sites and museums first encounter history through a person, an interpreter of the past.[18] Similarly, most readers of history seek information about *people* of the past for implicit comparison with themselves in the present.[19] Good personal interpretation militates against a view of the past as linear and progressive. It reminds people that inhabitants of the past did not simply seek to reach the future, but that their universe was in most ways no less complicated than our own. The reader can readily empathize with Hame's fears, uncertainties, and difficulties. My hope is that readers will come to see Hame's worldview as compelling and unifying on its own terms.

An Archaeological Framework

To aid the reader in entering this psychological framework, we shall adopt the approach of historical archaeology, a way to appreciate how people thought and behaved as inferred from their artifacts, in this case, their navigational tools. Readers will learn to use Hame's tools as he was taught to use them. Historical archaeology uses artifacts, documents, oral history, and folklore—indeed, all relevant evidence—to form a broad picture of how people behaved in the past. This approach fosters experiments with replica or reconstructed artifacts and the testing of hypotheses.[20] Historical archaeology, then, often emphasizes complex relationships, all in flux.[21]

Most people encounter navigational tools, if at all, in museums. Maritime and other museums that exhibit navigational instruments frequently give them only cursory attention. The best archaeological displays explore how people shape, think about, adapt, or respond to tools or techniques.[22] Navigational tools, particularly, fare poorly in most museums, which implicitly denigrate early ones by denoting them as "simple" or "crude," thus communicating to visitors that the instruments are not worth their study. Many museums depict early navigational instruments as mere precursors to more sophisticated versions, not as practical problem-solving tools in their own right. Museums convey a twentieth-century bias toward pinpoint accuracy in measurement by presenting navigational tools as evolving in a linear sequence from simple to complex. The assumption is that any tool with an extra millimeter's precision must certainly have replaced its forebear. This book aims to militate against these assumptions by showing that apparently simple instruments were clever, useful constructions in their own right, tools that aided wayfinding, some of which required a geometrical frame of reference.

In archaeology, artifacts are simply human-made, -modified, or -used, very distinctively the result of *human behavior*.[23] Archaeology texts define artifacts in terms of patterns of behavior, as things made or manipulated by people. When examining artifacts, archaeologists not only examine their context and provenience, but also seek to infer meaning through inductive questioning: what raw materials were used, how the materials were combined to produce the artifact, what tools were required to produce it—a form of "cultural investigation."[24] During Hame's voyage, readers will obtain measurements with navigational tools and reduce observations to obtain essential wayfinding information. Most importantly, readers are invited to view artifacts as historical documents or texts in their own right. They are documentary sources that embody a worldview, or in the case of Hame's tools, a geometrical frame of reference.[25]

The terms "tool" and "instrument" are used interchangeably throughout this book. Some museums categorize navigational tools as scientific instruments, but the term "scientific" first appeared in English in 1649, and "scientific instrument" in the United States in 1847, too late to apply to the instruments considered in this book.[26] Further, "science" had a different meaning in 1611 than it does to modern readers: it referred to all knowledge, not a label for a method of enquiry.

Maritime History

This book is a form of maritime history, a field defined as "a humanistic study of the many dimensions in man's relationship with the sea."[27] Readers might infer that maritime history concerns ships and sailors, which is true in that the field examines the lives of those who make their living from the sea, at the same time contending with a very hostile natural environment.[28] Maritime history is not just seagoing sagas of heroes and pirates, but looks at a larger dimension of actions, choices, and contexts, from the political and religious, to the economic and environmental.[29] Maritime history encompasses all human activities.[30] While history still features narratives of great exploits by great men, it cannot ignore the many voices of those whose lives shaped or were shaped by the sea: the shipwright, the sailor's wife, the victualler, the smuggler, the African or Native American who contended with European newcomers.

We portray Hame's tiny ship against a backdrop of overwhelming natural forces. Hame's ship is a microcosm of his society, and all the activities and lives on board her embody the politics, economy, religion, and early science of the time.[31] Maritime history is very much a social labor history. In our voyage, we aim to set the practice of navigation within wider contexts while emphasizing the daily hard work of running a ship. Hame's seascape encompasses the Atlantic from Bristol, down the Avon into the Severn and then into the Atlantic. "Atlantic" derives from the Atlantides, daughters of Atlas, otherwise known as the Hesperides, those that lived in the Garden of the Hesperides far from the Pillars of Hercules, the gateway west from the Mediterranean for ancient mariners.[32] Some maritime historians argue that "Atlantic" is a cultural construct: before the English, Iberian voyages created in the expanse of water now called Atlantic a zone of connections—political, social, and economic.[33] Voyaging within this zone, *Guyft* does not sail forth into limitless expanse; rather, she follows mileposts to reach the New World. The Atlantic does not pose an absolute water barrier that separates continents; as we shall see, Hame voyages from island to island between Old and New Worlds, thus making the crossing easier.[34] In fact, *Guyft* plies a route common to merchant and naval voyages to the Americas of Hame's era.

Like Iberian ships of Hame's day, *Guyft* makes for the Azores and Madeira, then south to the Canaries before she runs the latitude toward New Spain, and then northward to Virginia. Island-hopping affords Hame the opportunity to replenish stores and repair damage. *Guyft* is no lone occupant of the Atlantic waters; her crew and passengers are acutely aware that their voyage is an assertion of national right and will to compete commercially and militarily. A maritime trade and colonization network only exists as long as it is used. The voyage is indeed a projection of power. The physical, political, and economic seascape for the hypothetical Hame, then, includes well-plied trading routes for Portuguese, Spanish, Dutch, French, and English ships, complex networks that transcend landward national boundaries.[35] Despite the absence of national borders, by Hame's era, the mastery of maritime trade networks was indispensable to the idea of statehood. The sea was essential to state economic and political power.[36] Ironically, despite intense state competition at sea, the European nationalities who set out over the Atlantic employed common technologies and exhibited common cultural traits and even some common sea-language. In some ways, European mariners who crisscrossed the Atlantic shared some common cultural features of a "maritime system," owing to similar means of exploiting the sea. Cultural features of the seascape Atlantic littoral in 1611 had two foci in Europe, one confined between Portugal and Morocco to the south, and a northern one roughly from Ireland to France.[37] Hame's voyage is a microcosm of this shared maritime system, embodying the complex whole of national power, economic competition, religious belief, and the evolving mathematical frontier of measuring instruments to extend and augment man's senses to better exploit the shared system.

The Seascape

The ocean that Tristram Hame traverses, in most physical aspects, has not changed since his era. The sea is a dramatis persona in any maritime history. It allows triumphs but also arbitrarily consigns seafarers to oblivion, its unpredictability and omnipotence imposing humility. People romanticize seafaring because they think of it as physically isolating and consequently free from social and political constraints, somehow removed from the larger world picture, a view promoted by popular fiction.[38] We must be mindful that the sea is not a blank book to be written in by historians; the sea has "a lively and energetic materiality of its own."[39] Our relationship to and perception of the sea, however, differ from that of Hame. Most readers of this book have had little direct experience of the ocean except for seaside vacations. Some readers will have taken island-hopping cruises. The idea of a pleasure cruise would have been unthinkable to Hame and his contemporaries. As we shall explore, for Hame, the sea furnishes providential lessons about English commercial destiny and mortality. The largest maritime museum in the world, the National Maritime Museum in Greenwich, England, presents a seascape by emphasizing characteristics that differ from the landscape common to our experience. The museum's new guidebook observes that "the sea is remote from the ordinary citizen": "However, the sea has a major impact on modern lifestyles. Over 95% of all world trade goes by sea, and in 1996 international merchant ships carried 20 trillion 'ton/miles' of goods. World fish stocks diminish with catches of 90 million tonnes a year destroying 20 million tonnes of unwanted fish and other ocean life in the process. We burn carbons and worry about sea-level rise, not surprisingly, since 70% of the world's population lives within eighty kilometres of the coast."[40] The quoted statistics construct an image of a vast human enterprise that exploits and is shaped by the sea. The statistics outline some features of the seascape, the most important context to any narrative of seafaring, and the most difficult to implant in the reader's mind.

The seascape, then, is a cultural lens through which we experience the sea. Unlike a landscape,

the seascape is not a unit or jurisdiction of territory. Its characteristics include mutability, connectedness, timelessness, and the closest approximation to perceptible eternity available in the natural world. The sea is both changing and changeless and therefore appears without boundaries, eternal. Decades after Hame's voyage of 1611, Hugo Grotius, the early seventeenth-century legal theorist, characterized "the OCEAN, that expanse of water which antiquity describes as the immense, the infinite, bounded only by the heavens, parent of all things . . . the ocean which . . . can neither be seized nor enclosed; nay, which rather possesses the earth than is possessed."[41] Many modern writers have described the tug of ancient beliefs that give the seascape a personality, equal parts primordial energy, limitless power, a realm untamable by humans, but at the same time furnishing sustenance and inspiration.[42] Within the seascape, people are among many inhabitants; they are not the central, defining feature. Further, understanding ships within the seascape means adopting a "waterview," a perspective from sea rather than land.[43] For example, today's visitors who travel to Jamestown, Virginia, to see the remains of the first permanent colony of English-speaking peoples, do so by car. Arriving Europeans, however, came by ship, and carried on commerce by boat. To truly see Jamestown as Hame saw it, visitors ought to arrive by water. Hame and his contemporaries, then, filtered the world through an "oceanic mentality."[44] The seascape, then, has a natural or physical component, and also a conceptual or cognitive dimension (the waterview) as well as an archaeological one with definable material components, the evidence of maritime cultures on land and underwater.[45] The human, or material and cultural dimension of the seascape includes port architecture, the technology of ship construction and fishing, and other evidence of human activity involving the sea.[46] To glimpse the seascape as experienced by Hame includes examining a sailor's will, shipboard medicine, the use of a magnetic compass as a clock and counting device to predict tides, maritime iconography, funerary customs, and even colloquialisms such as maritime proverbs and figures of speech. Our exploration of Hame's seascape goes beyond navigational tools to examine, for instance, medical practice and religious discourse involving the sea.

Voyages are made by the central artifact of the seascape—the ship, the largest conveyance built by man—a floating microcosm of society that challenges and exploits the sea but is ultimately controlled by it, an environment simultaneously effacing, mutable, overpowering, and menacing.[47] Hame's little ship negotiates this environment as a concentrated essence of his civilization. To voyage safely requires a complex organization of work shaped by rituals. Rituals govern all social endeavors, but shipboard rituals circumscribe a working life at sea. Ritual "is a symbolic, conscious, and voluntary form of repetitive behavior that links an individual to a community."[48] Rituals serve to guide people from adolescence to adulthood, from apprentice to master, from unredeemed to redeemed sinner, in our case as members of a maritime community.

The linguistic aspect of the seascape is our way of talking about it. We have the language of sea narratives of discovery and exploration. The sea sagas narrated by Hakluyt or Purchas hold suspense, conflict, crisis, and climax, the essence of any good story. In our case, we shall add Christian themes of redemption and salvation.[49] In fact, all of these themes occur in English promotional literature of the early seventeenth century, designed to encourage emigration to Virginia. The attribute of language encompasses two phenomena, sailors' argot and the metaphors of seafaring. Sailors' argot impresses non-sailors with its sometimes impenetrable technical jargon and the richness of the vocabulary. The metaphors of sea voyages have widely pervaded vernacular speech.

Shipboard language constituted a precise technical dialect that served to organize and execute cooperative tasks to control the sea environment.[50] For example, Captain John Smith, the early leader of Virginia's Jamestown colony, wrote *A Sea Grammar*

because no formal, written instruction existed for novice mariners in the language of ship construction and operation, particularly during wartime when quick, coordinated responses were imperative. Smith gives a dense example of the language a sailing master of Hame's day must employ to get a ship under way: "Boatswain fetch an anchor aboard, break ground or weigh anchor. Heave a head, men into the tops, men upon the yards; come, is the anchor a pike, that is, to heave away? Yea, yea. Let fall your foresail. Tally, that is, haul off the sheats; who is at the helm there, coil your cables in small fakes, haul the cat, a bitter, belay, loose fast your anchor with your shankpainter, stow the boat, set the land, how it bears by the compass."[51] Many nautical terms or phrases have entered the vernacular. We *chart a course through dangerous shoals*; we see a project through to *the bitter end*; we describe an *aloof* personality; we are *taken aback* with surprise; we maintain honest relationships by remaining *above board*; politicians conduct a *filibuster*; we *embark* on an undertaking; we *pilot* a new program; we dispose of *junk*; we *rummage* through the attic; we *average* test scores; we give others *leeway*; and we look to mother as the *mainstay* of the family. In short, common talk includes many unconscious maritime references, artifacts of the past influence of seafaring on mainstream culture.[52] Nautical etymologies furnish fossils of our links to the sea. Some terms show up in the languages of many European littoral cultures that share the same working environment. For instance, the pilot had been the *lodesman* or *lodeman* of earlier centuries, evincing a Norse or Norman French origin. The Old English *lādman*, or guide, serves also Breton, Spanish, Galician, and Portuguese terms for the same concept.[53]

For Hame, language has another role. Contemporary narratives of exploration include metaphors of ships and seafaring that highlight spiritual self-discovery and collective destiny. Purchas and Hakluyt chronicled the voyages of their contemporaries but placed them in the context of national destiny, the sea as a road to conquest and colony. The trials imposed by the marine environment—storms, hurricanes, buffeting seas—appear in Christian motifs of God's favor or displeasure, inscrutable providence, sacrifice, punishment for sin, and redemption. Samuel Purchas writes in his "Preface: Commendations of Navigation":

> Man that has the earth for his mother, nurse, and grave, cannot find any fitter object in this world, to busy and exercise his heavenly and better parts then in the knowledge of this earthly globe, except in his God . . . there is no way by land alone to the top of human felicity . . . but as God has combined the sea and land into one globe, so their joint combination and mutual assistance is necessary to secular happiness and glory. The sea covers one half of this patrimony of man, whereof God set him in possession when he said, replenish the earth and subdue it, and have dominion over the fish of the sea, and over the fowl of the air, and over every living thing that moves upon the earth. And when the sea had, as it were, rebelled against rebellious man, so that all in whose nosethrils [nostrils] was the breath of life, and all that was in the dry land died, yet then did it all that time endure the yoke of man, in that first of ships the ark of Noah. . . . Thus should man at once lose half his inheritance if the art of navigation did not enable him to manage this untamed beast, and with the bridle of the winds, and saddle of his shipping to make him serviceable.[54]

Sea narratives within a Christian framework not only propelled natural events into the realm of the exceptional and divine, they functioned as cautionary tales and as theater for a large reading (and listening) public. Narratives such as those found in Hakluyt and Purchas allowed readers to participate in God's historical epic for English peoples.[55] Sailors who survived disasters at sea had survived God's trials and had answered the call of the faithful. One of the sources for our composite voyage, the 1619 voyage of *Margaret* to Virginia from Bristol, not only exemplifies the consciousness of sea deliverance, but in gratitude its passengers celebrated America's first Thanksgiving.[56] In these narratives, the ship functions as the primary metaphor by posing as an emblem of aspirations, intellectual triumph, struggle, and freedom. Once a medieval religious symbol, the ship became a metaphor for national pride and Christian destiny.

Method of the Hypothetical Voyage Narrative

This book's simulated voyage may be hypothetical, but it is based directly on primary accounts of wills, charter parties, legal proceedings, contemporary texts on navigation, cosmology, and seamanship, and narratives to illuminate the mental world of early modern English seafarers who journeyed to explore, exploit, and colonize North America. The strength of this approach lies in its reliance on primary sources: all events, circumstances, narratives, and navigational problems and their solutions come from contemporary accounts.[57] Even the names of Hame and his passengers and crew, while hypothetical, are composites of names drawn from lists of mariners from the region in the early seventeenth century. The voyage is a focus for historical enquiry with an emphasis on defining and solving navigational problems from the perspective of a master mariner.

Our chapters join the ship at several critical milestones. First, the ship lades cargo and takes on passengers in Bristol and navigates the temperamental Avon into the Bristol Channel. Second, *Guyft* approaches the Azores to take on fresh water but also engages a French ship. Third, the ship reaches the Canary Islands before setting a course west for North America. At the Canaries, *Guyft* lays over for repair and to replenish food and water supplies. Fourth, the ship reaches the Caribbean and briefly explores some islands before heading north to Virginia. The fifth milestone has the ship about midway to the Chesapeake Bay from Hispaniola as the weather worsens into a hurricane. Finally, the ship arrives at Jamestown.

The chief objective of the voyage of *Guyft* is to navigate safely to Virginia from England. In the process, the reader will learn to do the following:

Name the thirty-two points of the compass and
describe their utility to navigation.
Define dead reckoning.
Define the purpose of the traverse board and
explain its use.
Describe the purpose of obtaining soundings
and the tools and methods involved, both in
coastal areas and in the open ocean.
Define latitude and longitude and their importance to navigation.
Describe the log and line and describe how they
determine the speed of the ship.
Describe compass variation and describe its
importance to navigation.
Describe early modern methods of determining
longitude based on magnetic variation (and
explain why this method did not achieve its
intended result).
Identify and describe the celestial sphere and its
major components, the equator or equinoctial, the ecliptic, the meridian, the north and
south poles, zenith, nadir, horizon, their earthly
counterparts, and explain the relevance of the
celestial sphere to navigation.

Define declination and explain its importance to
determining ship's latitude.
Describe the apparent motion of the sun.
Explain the difference between celestial and dead-
reckoning navigation. Describe some methods
and limitations of each.
Obtain altitude measurements of the sun and
polestar with a cross-staff and reduce the data
to obtain the ship's latitude.

Readers should not find this list daunting.
Tristram Hame would have endorsed the learning of
all of these objectives; through his apprenticeship,
Hame would have mastered the same syllabus. Our
voyage, then, presents a narrative through which we
cross the Atlantic, aware of background political and
economic circumstances, sensitive to the sociologi-
cal and anthropological dimensions of belief, hope,
fear, and the role of technology and mathematical
thinking.

We first explore Hame's background and circumstances, and inspect his important responsibility: his
ship, crew, cargo, and passengers.

*Read with the eye of reason, and labor to understand with judgment that which
you read.*

—John Davis, *The Seamans Secrets*, 1607

CHAPTER 2

"SEA CHARIOTS AND HORSES OF ENGLAND":
Guyft, Her Master, and the American Enterprise

We are not born for ourselves only, but . . . those that traffick in the deep, and have their business in great waters, those that are unto this island as a wooden wall, the sea-chariots, and the horses of England; these, I say, may claim justly to the fruits of their own labors.

— JOHN ASPLEY, *Speculum Nauticum*, 1624

Who is Tristram Hame and what is his background? What circumstances of politics, national pride, and world geography form his thoughts and opinions? In this chapter we examine these circumstances.

Ships' Masters

Hame's persona derives from Tobias Felgate and incorporates the known facts about him, listed below, but also includes some characteristics of other master mariners such as Captain Christopher Newport, the admiral of the three-ship flotilla that settled Jamestown in 1607. Hame's sailing master persona has several attributes, borrowed from Newport and others, which are manifested throughout our voyage. First, Hame represents a new breed of seagoing professional, highly skilled and experienced as now required for the distant

Virginia, Baltic, East Indian, and Mediterranean commercial voyages.[1] Masters such as Felgate succeeded not just because of navigational skills, but because of commercial ones as well. Masters sought likeminded merchants and vice versa: these partnerships shaped the global economy through wide-ranging, inventive, and diverse export and import strategies.[2] Hame understands how to mediate risks through diversified investment. Captain John Davis, whose writings furnish much of the navigational text of our voyage, epitomized this new professional. Second, through accounts and letters, Hame, as a successful master mariner, is a self-promoter whose success encourages others to invest in or support overseas ventures. The masters themselves became spokesmen for empire and fostered a sense of national identity. Third, Hame consults with and is supported by leading mathematicians or other theoreticians who together refined navigational practice, as in the examples of Richard

Chancellor and master pilots Stephen and William Borough. Fourth, Hame is a successful privateering sailor in the mold of Newport, an activity that converges with piracy.

Successful privateering required not only an aggressive spirit but also adroit piloting skills. Settlements were not founded by plucky mariners who relied on luck rather than foresight. The original Jamestown voyages have been presented by most popular histories as sui generis colonizing, without accounting for the previous reconnaissance of the Chesapeake Bay of the eastern coast of North America to better appreciate its hazards and benefits to navigation for future commercial exploitation. Newport, before guiding the ships that founded the Jamestown colony, may have known some New World coastlines better than his contemporaries, particularly the Florida coast.[3] Newport, too, exemplified the social mobility possible in the seafaring economy. His first appearance in the record dates to 1581 when he was a common sailor, yet he died in 1617 as a shipowner in command of squadrons of the East India Company and Virginia Company.[4] While his adventures were noteworthy, Newport's ascendancy from a hired hand to privateering master to investor in further exploits was not unusual.[5] In fact, the perquisites of the master mariner encouraged speculation: masters could carry private cargoes, earn commissions, and even claim exemption from some duties.[6] Newport may have been unusually successful, for William Bourne observed during the 1570s that most masters were coasters who relied on rule-of-thumb techniques and had no interest in sophisticated navigation.[7] These old coasters, however, were not in the employ of the prosperous merchant adventurers.

What is the status of a ship's master, and what are his responsibilities? Captain John Smith says that the master "is to see the conning of the ship, and trimming of the sails. The master and his mates are to direct the course, command all the sailors, for steering, trimming, and sailing the ship."[8] In previous voyages, Hame, as master, was subordinate to the ship's captain (not necessarily a person of seafaring skills) and sometimes the owner or part-owner of the ship which Hame commanded. Generally, ships' masters of the early modern period were responsible not only for navigation but also for the safety and general well-being of the ship and crew, over whom they exercised disciplinary authority; a successful voyage may very well depend on the experience and character of the master.[9]

Hame as master is an adept navigator, proficient in the skills and knowledge of pilotage and open-ocean sailing. John Dee outlines the requisite background:

> What need, the master pilot, has of other arts . . . it is easy to know, as of hydrography, astronomy, astrology, and horometry [and] the common base, and foundation of all: namely arithmetic and geometry. So that, he be able to understand, and judge his own necessary instruments . . . whether they be perfectly made or no; and also can . . . make them himself. [Requisite instruments include:] quadrants, the astronomer's ring, the astronomer's staff, the astrolabe universal. An hydrographical globe, charts hydrographical [and] true (not with parallel meridians). The common sea compass, the compass of variation; the proportional, and paradoxal compasses. . . . Clocks with springs; hour, half-hour, and three-hour sandglasses, & sundry other instruments. And also, be able, on globe, or plane [chart] to describe the paradoxal compass, and duly to use the same, to all manner of purposes, whereto it was invented. And also, be able to calculate the planets' places for all times.
>
> Moreover, with sun, moon, or star (or without) be able to define the longitude & latitude of the place, which he is in, so that, the longitude & latitude of the place, from which he sailed, be given, or by him be known. Whereto, appertains [pertains] expert means, to be certified ever, of the ship's way. And by foreseeing the rising, setting, noonsteading [noon meridian passage of the sun], or midnighting of certain tempestuous fixed stars, or their conjunctions, and angling [taking angles of] with the planets, &c., he ought to have expert conjecture of storms, tempests, and spouts, and such like meteorological effects, dangerous on sea.[10]

In the next chapter, we examine the specific texts and technology that Hame employs. Dee has emphasized the need for the master to have a thorough grounding in arithmetic and geometry, skills necessary to work courses on various kinds of charts and globes. The various astronomical instruments he cites—the ring, quadrant, astrolabe, and staff (a cross-staff)—are intended for latitude determination by measurement of the sun's altitude. Note, too, that Dee cites the master's ability to fashion instruments himself. Dee may be ambitious, however, in claiming that the master ought to be able to calculate planetary positions and carry a clock at sea. Hame's seagoing contemporaries did not calculate planetary positions. *Guyft* carries no clock; none were seaworthy in 1611, their errors rendering them useless for any precise timing of phenomena, astronomical or otherwise. Glasses, or sandglasses that measured several intervals from a half minute and longer were carried in multiples. Multiples insured against the inevitable losses. Further, glasses timed phenomena and regulated all shipboard life.

Dee identifies several course-plotting and visualization tools including the globe, and charts "plane," "paradoxal," "hydrographical," and "true." With the advent of long-distance voyaging, masters had to cope with navigating three-dimensionally while conceptualizing courses two-dimensionally. We are accustomed to various map and chart projections, but in Dee's day—and in 1611—long-distance plotting was hampered by the recognition that as one sailed north or south, as represented on a two-dimensional chart, something went wrong. To sustain the course as a straight line, the shape of the landmasses and their relationship to latitude, longitude, and even the orientation of the chart went awry. Plotting a course on a globe created its own problem: as meridians converge near the poles, a course that cut meridians at the same angle was no longer a straight line but a spiral. The mathematical challenge to reconciling the two resulted in the Mercator projection, commonly used today as the basis for maps in classrooms the world over, which enabled courses to be plotted on charts as straight lines as they crossed meridians, no matter how northerly the voyage. Dee also describes the intimate awareness of celestial movements and meteorological phenomena requisite in the navigator. He also highlights the importance of understanding compass variation.

Despite the knowledge and skills proclaimed by Dee as essential for any master, surprisingly, England had no system of licensing for pilots and masters. Reliable pilots were undoubtedly hired based on personal recommendations. Guild-like institutions, however, that served mariners did arise through which pilots were examined orally, such as Trinity House, Deptford. By contrast, Spain had a *piloto mayor* who oversaw a rigorous testing procedure. In Spain, masters and pilots had to be examined and certified by the *Casa de Contratación*. Richard Hakluyt documented this process, which included the following procedure:

> First, [new masters and pilots] make suit unto the pilot major . . . that he would admit them to examination, because they are all natural Spaniards, and sufficient for the same. Hereupon the pilot major commanded the party to be examined, to give information that he is a mariner, and well practiced in those parts, about which he desires to be examined. And then immediately he brings five or six pilots before examined to give testimony that he is a good mariner, and sufficient to become a pilot, that he is a Spaniard born, and that he is not of the race of the Moors, Jews, or Negroes.[11]

For two months the masters and pilots attend lectures by the pilot major, not failing to be present twice a day. Following this period of instruction:

> They resort then unto the hall of examination which is in the *Contratación* house, where there are assembled the pilot major and diverse other pilots, to the number of 25 at the least; who are all sitting there in order, the pilot major demands of him that would be examined, of what part of the Indies he desires to be examined: Whereto the examinate answers, that he would be examined

concerning New Spain, or of Nombre de Dios and Tierra Firma. And others that are not experienced in those parts, crave to be examined of Santo Domingo, Puerto Rico, and Cuba.

The pilot major commands the examinate to spread a sea chart upon the table, and in the presence of the other pilots to depart or show the course from the bar of Sanlúcar de Barrameda to the Canary Islands, and from thence to the Indies, till he come to that place whereof he is to be examined, and then also to return back to the bar of Sanlúcar in Spain, from whence he departed. Also the pilot major asks him, if when he sails upon the sea, he be taken by a contrary wind, what remedy he is to use, that his ship be not too much turmoiled upon the sea? And the examinate answers as well as he can.[12]

Questions and answers continue, some of which concern matters of astronomy and the tides: "Others ask him if a pirate should take him and leave him destitute of his chart, his astrolabe, and his other instruments serving to take the height of the sun and of the stars, what course he would take in that extremity?"[13] Licensing pilots in Spain was a complex business at the center of a political debate between practical pilots and academic cosmographers over authority versus experience.[14]

Despite the lack of a similar formal examination for navigators in England, sponsors of long-distance trading voyages hired pilots and navigators by reputation: Hame claims to possess the same knowledge as required in Spain. The financial sponsors who supported voyages to Virginia employed navigators with current piloting knowledge in foreign waters and who also proved adept at mathematical skills in cartography and astronomy (for latitude measurement) in the open ocean.

The Geometrical Seaman

A signal characteristic of late Tudor voyages that set them apart from all seafaring before this period was the marriage of seafaring practice with the theoretical contributions of mathematicians and astronomers and the innovations in ship design that improved their handling under the advanced navigational techniques being developed, evident in the construction of *Guyft*.[15] Mathematical reasoning, much championed by Dee, would have been part of the intellectual milieu of navigation for sailing masters such as Tobias Felgate and Hame. Felgate would have had some mathematical skills for his repeated voyages serving the Virginia Company investors. Mathematics as a body of knowledge was relatively new, yet by Hame's era cartographers, surveyors, and instrument-makers would have been adept at some mathematical skills, and would have viewed this knowledge as essential.[16] Further, the reliance on mathematics in 1611 did not mean an art of navigation that was scientific in the modern sense, a discipline bounded by mathematical formulae and tabulated data. Mathematics occupied a niche shared by other mechanical arts, jointly practiced by university scholars and tradesmen. Mathematically informed disciplines in the twenty-first century do not reflect the blend of scholarly traditions, craft lore, and the various contexts of knowledge, from academic to self-taught, so characteristic of the acquisition of knowledge in 1611.[17]

Hame's mathematics is strongly grounded in practical geometry.[18] John Dee had promoted mathematical study through an elaborate argument for its application to most realms of knowledge.[19] Although universities were central to the articulation of mathematical theory, practical schooling came from two sources, primarily other mariners and their mentors (such as Dee), and perhaps Gresham College in London. Sir Thomas Gresham, the founder of the Royal Exchange, created his college in 1597 through a legacy that provided for resident scholars to give lectures in English for a broad public. The public, who paid to attend lectures, consisted largely of merchants and their associates. Gresham, in fact, intended merchants as the audience for his college's twice-weekly scheduled lectures in astronomy, divinity, geometry, medicine, law, music, and rhetoric, given in both English and Latin.[20] We cannot be sure if Hame's contemporaries valued these lectures: we have no diaries or letters to tell us. Gresham was more a meeting place than a college in the traditional sense, with open lectures, no degrees, and no student records.[21] The few mariners who wrote about navigation cite many of the practical mathematics and astronomy texts of use to their trade, reflecting learning acquired outside of universities, possibly at Gresham.

Hame practices navigation following John Davis or William Bourne, and he attends Gresham when he has the opportunity. Hame heard lectures on a published schedule. Astronomy lectures were given on Friday, geometry on Thursday, beginning at eight o'clock in the morning, Latin first, then English in the afternoon.[22] Specifically, lectures were to follow a different format than those at universities. For the lecture in law, for example, "it is thought meet . . . for the quality of the hearers, who, for the most part, are like to be merchants and other citizens, that the said law lecture be not read after the manner of the university; but that the reader cull out such titles and heads of law, that best may serve to the good liking and capacity of the said auditory."[23] Topics were rotated. The geometry lecture treated arithmetic in Trinity Term, theoretical geometry in Michaelmas and Hilary Terms, and practical geometry at Easter Term. Similarly, the astronomy lecturerer was "to read in his solemn lectures, first the principles of the [celestial] sphere, and the theories of the planets, and the use of the astrolabe and the [cross-]staff, and other common instruments for the capacity of mariners; which being read and opened, he shall apply them to use, by reading geography, and the art of navigation, in some one term every year."[24]

Modern readers must bear in mind the nature of learning in the early seventeenth century. Much religious instruction, for example, was delivered through sermons that drew huge crowds, may have lasted a few hours, and required a rhetorical skill virtually absent from modern public discourse. Further, without the modern reliance on recording technology,

audiences simply remembered more, and remembered it easier. The possible influence of Gresham for engendering an interest in mathematical skills is an open question, but it was English universities that first endowed a professorship in mathematics. It was also a place of mathematical innovation.[25] Gresham's history displayed educational successes and failures as the institution grew, but mathematics furnished a reliable core topic, thanks to the geometry professor at Gresham from 1597 to 1620, Henry Briggs. Briggs, in fact, lectured on new developments in mathematics such as logarithms and worked with Edward Wright in developing tabular data for his influential work on navigation, *Certain Errors in Navigation*, which, among other achievements, explicated the method of producing a Mercator chart, a breakthrough technique.[26] Hame fit Gresham's intended audience, for a mathematically literate Hame advances his trade for the benefit of the country. The Gresham lectures also encourage Hame's use of mathematical instruments for navigation. The place of instruments in mathematical education was in some debate: some thought that grounding in theory should precede the practical application of mathematics through instruments.[27] Hame has found particularly useful the Gresham lectures on Euclid's *Elements of Geometry*, which advanced methods of reasoning found in many contemporary navigation texts. In fact, most mathematical problems were presented and solved by geometrical representations, a characteristic teaching method.[28] Gresham teaching will become evident in subsequent chapters as Hame calculates latitude and estimates his ship's position on a chart.

Although Gresham's innovation marked an English ascendancy in practical navigation, Hame's English milieu for navigational improvement, the application of mathematics, and oceanic trading would not have been possible had the Portuguese, Spanish, and Dutch not been there first. Before Elizabeth I became the great Protestant icon and patron of English sea dogs, Spain had pioneered geometrical navigation, established American colonies,

created a state body to regulate navigational training and practice, state-sponsored cartography, and
developed instruments that the English ships' masters would soon take in hand. The Portuguese, a century before Hame, had established the link between
altitude measurement, solar position, and declination
tables to find latitude.[29]

Tobias Felgate

Tobias Felgate is a suitable model for Hame because
of the confidence and status he enjoyed within merchant trading circles as a successful master, and
his apparent eye for opportunity and good fortune.
We know nothing of the circumstances of Felgate's
upbringing. We do not know when he went to sea,
how he was apprenticed to navigation and other shipboard skills, and how he was selected for his documented voyages. These unknowns are common to
most navigators who show up in the historical record
for our period. The limited facts about Felgate's life,
all related to Virginia, are detailed here.

An exemplar of the new breed of master mariner, Felgate represents a suitable model for Hame.
Tobias Felgate was born around 1585–7, possibly in
Pettaugh, Suffolk.[30] A stained-glass Felgate coat of
arms, dated 1593, can be seen in St. Mary's parish
church, Yaxley, Suffolk. He had three elder brothers, William (b. 1572), John (b. 1574), and Robert
(b. 1578), all of whom became investors and gentlemen planters in Virginia. Between 1601–11,
Tobias worked as an apprentice to William, a skinner, in London, but evidently went to sea shortly
thereafter.[31] By 1617 "Toby Felgate of Lymehouse,
Stepney, Middx. mariner aged 32" is recorded as a
mate aboard *Edwin* on a voyage to Virginia from
London.[32] He next appears as the sailing master who
sailed *Margaret* from Bristol to Virginia in 1619 with
colonists who founded the Berkeley Plantation. An
account of the 1619 voyage survives, penned by
a colonist-investor, Ferdinando Yates.[33] Surviving
documents of the voyage include the agreement

composed by the sponsors of the colony (including
the contract for the hire of the ship as well as wages
paid "to Toby Felgate pilot"), the charter party, a certificate of the Bristol mayor that attests to the cargo
and lists the colonist-passengers (Felgate first), correspondence between the colony's backers, and a certificate of the ship's safe arrival in Virginia, attested
to by Jamestown's governor.[34] The voyage of *Guyft*
makes use of these. From the surviving accounts,
we can infer that Felgate negotiated his contract
astutely, judging from the numerous references to
his pay, and that, like Newport, he invested in the
Virginia venture as a speculation. The Virginia voyages were evidently remunerative: the Virginia quarter court for July 17, 1622, records the testimony of
"Tobias Felgate" who went "M[aste]r and Mate of
ships 5 times to Virginia."[35] In any event, Felgate also
speculated through his own private cargo, a common
practice and perquisite of sailing masters. Returning
to Virginia aboard *Supply* in 1620, Felgate apparently
brought and possibly sold two "barrels of Irish beef."[36]
Tobacco in 1620 was becoming Virginia's cash crop,
a commerce in which Tobias Felgate participated.
Felgate shipped tobacco "aboard *Defence*" in 1623.[37]
On another occasion, Felgate transported goods
for an investor, and another investor reimbursed
Felgate £17 in freight charges.[38] Once Felgate's
brother Robert was established in Virginia, Tobias
acquired 150 acres on the Pamunkey River adjacent
to his brother's land, a 1632 transaction in which
Tobias was noted as an "adventurer" in the colony.[39]
Felgate's sphere of activity seemed to concentrate
on the Virginia enterprise as a family interest, but
he also participated in other maritime business as he
is named in government warrants for issuing letters
of marque dated 1626 through 1628 to take pirates
preying upon English commercial traffic.[40]

Felgate's family embraced Virginia for its possibilities, perhaps because of Tobias' experience. The
commercial interests that drew Felgate's brothers to
Virginia resulted in successes: the brothers beat the
odds in surviving and prospering in Virginia, rather

uncharacteristic of most emigrants because of high mortality. The surviving records attest to vigorous commercial activities, most apparently stemming from Tobias Felgate's profession. As readers observe Hame's management of his voyage, they may consider that he, like Felgate, would have embraced profitable opportunities. Tobias Felgate may have induced his brother "Mr. William Felgate citizen and skinner of London" to invest in Virginia, for another Virginia court for 1622 records a transfer of a company share in Virginia from William "unto Toby Felgate of Ratcliffe mariner his brother."[41] Another court for the same year categorizes William Felgate as one of the "adventurers and planters [who] have undertaken with their associates to transport great multitudes of people to Virginia," affirmed at the next quarter court, which records "Mr Wm Felgate" as one of many "Adventurers."[42] William and Tobias traded with one another. Records of the London Company include a reference to William signing over to Tobias a share in the Virginia adventure in 1615.[43] A petition of 1629 to the Lord Keeper of the Great Seale of England, Thomas Lord Coventry, reveals the nature and complexity of the Felgate brothers' business interests, listing William and Tobias as part-owners of James, with William identified as the chandler: "William Felgate was victualler for peas, butter, cheese, oatmeal, candles, powder, shot, match, and all manner of other provisions at his own rates and prices and the said Tobias Felgate went always as master in the said ship and so had the sole managing and ordering of all business concerning the same."[44] Possibly Felgate not only became an investor but, like his brother, also sponsored colonists under the headright system by which he would have accrued land grants.

The colonists voyaging to Virginia with Hame are indentured to an investor, who gains land via the headright system, that is, based on the number of colonists. Another Felgate brother, Robert, evidently emigrated to Virginia in the 1620s or early 1630s, and settled not far from Yorktown where he owned land

bounded by two streams known as King's Creek and Felgate's Creek.[45] Robert received a grant of 400 acres in 1639 for transportation of eight new colonists to Virginia.[46] Doubtless the Felgates carefully managed and protected their investment in Virginia. Tobias would have moved within an intimate circle of investors and contractors, participating in speculation through joint investments with his brothers. William Felgate signed a petition to the Privy Council concerning trade in Virginia, dated August 14, 1633, which argues for the necessity of a strong trading monopoly based on a discussion of creating surpluses, managing markets, and exploiting opportunities: "All of which benefit to his Majesty's kingdom and people [who] are wholly lost if strangers be permitted to trade and transport the commodities of that plantation into foreign parts as now they do."[47]

William, Robert, and Tobias Felgate married and died in Virginia. When Ralph Hamor, an influential planter and administrator of the Virginia colony died in 1626, his widow, the former Elizabeth Clements, married Captain Tobias Felgate, then listed as captain of Defiance.[48] Felgate subsequently married again, a woman named Sarah, and died at Westover, Virginia, in December 1634, leaving a son, William, and a daughter, Sarah.[49] William Felgate married a widow, Mary Bassett, and died near Felgate's Creek in 1660.[50] Robert married a woman named Margaret, his first wife, and had a son, Erasmus, and a daughter, Judith, but their survivorship at his death is not clear, for a record of 1655 has Mary Bassett inheriting Robert Felgate's estate following his death.[51] Robert evidently had had a will drawn up in England before he came to Virginia, a will superseded by the 1655 one. Robert Felgate died in debt to his brother, William, and his will provided a payment of £60 to William.[52] Robert had died by 1646, for a bond dated 1646 refers to his widow, Sibella. Robert had apparently achieved some status and prosperity in Virginia, for by 1633 he was serving as a justice at the quarterly court, a burgess at the General Assembly, and by 1639 the General

Assembly authorized payment to Robert for "his employment as Muster Master."[53]

The brief record about Tobias and his family attests to energy in exploiting the opportunities presented by the Virginia colony. Tobias handled the shipping but, together with his brothers, invested in land, ships, cargo, and, atypically for early English Virginians, Tobias and his three brothers all prospered, influenced the affairs of the colony, and established families.

Readers may imagine a similar background for Hame in some respects, particularly in aspirations for success in voyaging and investing in the American enterprise. Hame was born in 1560 in Exeter, Devon, where he grew up in the coastal and riverine trade. Traffic along the River Exe led to the growth of a community of shipowners and merchant traders in nearby Topsham, where Hame would have made many useful contacts. Shortly after 1580, Hame moved to Staines, near London, where his skills and aptitude came to the attention of Muscovy Company investors and master mariners. Hame participated in two great episodes of Elizabethan maritime history: in July 1588, Hame served under Martin Frobisher on board *Triumph* in action against the Spanish Armada, greatly outnumbered but boldly fighting the Spanish fleet off Portsmouth. Ten years earlier, Hame first served under Frobisher, sailing to the Canadian Arctic under George Best, captain and master of *Anne Francis*, in a voyage to seek the Northwest Passage and to deposit miners to search for precious metals. Through Frobisher, Hame met Dr. John Dee, who tutored him in astronomy and navigation. In 1611 Hame is well connected both in London and Bristol. Major shareholders in trading companies know and trust him. Hame is part-owner of two ships and although he has been hired to master *Guyft*, he will pay close attention to what he sees in Virginia for investment possibilities.

Ships and Seafarers

Our vessel for the Virginia voyage represents a convergence of navigational technique and ship design. Navigational abilities link to the design of the ship: ships capable of carrying significant cargoes under all sea conditions require navigational skills (and therefore tools) beyond those needed for ships adapted to a coastal trade. Ships, for example, that are highly maneuverable and can sail close to the wind just as effectively as beat before it require navigational tools that enable the sailing master to best match the ship's capabilities to achieving a desired course.

The prototype ship for our voyage is the armed merchantman of 120 tons, *Susan Constant*, built in 1605 and used as the flagship of the original 1606–7 voyage to Jamestown, Virginia.[54] While no record of the ship's appearance survives, the replica at the reconstructed Jamestown Settlement in Virginia is based on contemporary records of like ships and on archaeological evidence (particularly that of *Sea Venture*, which sank in 1609 off Bermuda).[55] The comparatively heavily armed and manned merchantman represented a specialized cargo carrier developed to handle the distant, vulnerable Levant trade and competed well in shipping costs with Dutch and Venetian rivals.[56] *Susan Constant* and other merchantmen of high tonnage, called galleons, featured two planked decks with artillery, a low forecastle, and a quarterdeck and poop with an overall distinctive profile, as Illustration 1 shows.[57] The three-masted merchant ship was maneuverable because of its tacking ability and capability of close sailing to windward, which, with its arrangement of sails, gave the master many options for exploiting variable winds in the Atlantic.[58] As for sailing characteristics, in a light breeze a merchant galleon of this type made two knots, four knots in a fresh breeze, and six in a strong one. While sailors had no practical method in 1611 to measure the speed of ocean currents that affect the speed of the vessel, they did measure leeway, which for *Guyft* involved 1.5 to 2 points on the compass, translating to between 15 and 25 degrees on the compass unless the wind was abaft the beam.[59]

Shiphandling and seamanship for *Guyft*'s voyage are based on Henry Mainwaring's *Sea-mans Dictionary* (1644), Captain John Smith's *Sea Grammar* (1627), the experiences of sailors of replica ships such as *Mayflower II*, and merchant seamen on late nineteenth- and early twentieth-century sailing ships.[60] Abundant contemporary records note the hazards of long-distance shipping, including lack of watertightness, broken masts, lost rudders, lost anchors, and lost small boats.[61] *Guyft*'s voyage may include these happenstances with a lack of English standardization in shipboard training, shipping, or safety rules.[62] By comparison, a deposition of 1627 cites Tobias Felgate's experience in 1625–6 with a comparable ship, *James*, of between 120 and 140 tons, with a crew ranging between 15 men and a boy to 18 men and a boy, the crew size about double that of *Susan Constant*.[63] The same deposition refers to *James* as having carried "fifty thousand weight" of tobacco and on another occasion as transporting from Mallaga 120 tons of wine and raisins, and 137 tons of wine from Bordeaux, typical business of a galleon.[64]

For purposes of *Guyft*'s voyage, the crew comes from southwest England, particularly Devon and Cornwall, where privateering seemed to be a major lure for seafaring. Apart from the latter sixteenth-century exploits of John Hawkins and John Davis, little Devonian interest in North America existed, yet Sir Walter Ralegh's two captains for the first Roanoke voyages were Devonians.[65] In fact, a national survey of 1582 revealed that over 10 percent of the country's master mariners resided in Devon.[66] Contrary to the claims of Hame's contemporaries that population expansion constituted a reason for overseas colonization, no surplus population characterized Devon or Cornwall and, in fact, ships arriving at ports in these areas sometimes brought plague, which further reduced the population.[67] After farming, woolen cloth production, and tin mining, seafaring occupied fourth place in the Devon and Cornwall economy. Occupational censuses of mariners in 1619 and 1626 in Devon and Cornwall, which named over six thousand men and more than six hundred vessels, identified eleven types of seafaring professions from master, master's mate, and cooper to less familiar types such as seineman, bargeman, and sounder, or other variants such as trumpeter and the sailor for coal.[68] The surveys showed that men often pursued land occupations alternating with sea employment. Devon and Cornwall seafarers spanned a surprisingly wide range of working ages, with men in their forties and fifties prominent in the censuses. Similarly, a study of thirty-six master mariners of the early modern period revealed a range of men from their early twenties into their sixties, the age distribution paralleling that of modern industry.[69] Owing to Hakluyt's propagandizing and other popular literature that featured accounts of fights with the Spaniards, the Devon and Cornwall seamen became privateering heroes.[70]

Studies of seamen's wills probated in ecclesiastical courts have provided important evidence of the social world of Tudor sailors two generations before Hame's voyage.[71] The existence of the wills with their detail and their regular presentation to the courts for probate attests to a community of mutually dependent sailors that militates against the view of seamen as undisciplined, unruly boors. Instead, the wills show that some seamen were literate, many had more than a few possessions and some changes of clothes, some had their own beds, and their food and drink were not as vile as many assume.[72] Insights from the study of wills inform our voyage to help avoid caricature in constructing sailors' personalities. While studies of Tudor mariners reveal no predominant reasons why men went to sea, social mobility must have been a strong motivator. Seamen not only could advance in rank, but the perquisites of sea voyaging permitted an opportunity to trade on their own or through joint privateering.[73] Outside of legal methods to capture

---

other ships, piracy was widely practiced.[74] Further, crew members had an incentive for success: they received shares.

Although the Devon and Cornwall information indicates that seafarers may have lived within complex economic circumstances that dictated the pursuit of multiple trades, we have relatively little information on how they learned seafaring. Sea apprenticeship, apparently, resembled any apprenticeship to a trade on land, with its combination of technical learning and discipline.[75] Apprenticeships would have lasted at least seven years, as stipulated by the Statute of Artificers (1563), or as many as twelve, although exceptions were many. Without a supporting guild, too, seamen observed few common standards of performance characteristic of other trades. Borne out by seamen's prerogatives in making some shipboard decisions (see below), sailors acted as individual, contracting agents.[76] Information from other port cities indicates that sailors were very clannish ashore, marrying into the families of other sailors, and relying on other sailors for favors, loans, and other

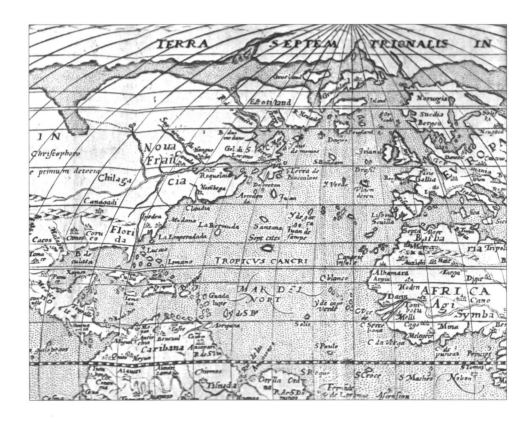

3. MAP OF THE ATLANTIC WORLD IN 1611 — This map of the Atlantic, a foldout from Richard Hakluyt's *The Principal Navigations*, represents the geographical understanding of Captain Hame's era. The Atlantic Ocean—a name not in common use in 1611—appears well populated. Hakluyt supplies sailing directions for many islands, while other islands are rumored to exist or represent wishful thinking. Off the east coast of Ireland, for example, a pair of islands can be seen denoting Brasil. Not to be confused with the South American country, the island Brasil derives from a Gaelic myth representing a blessed isle of enchantment. It appeared on charts into the nineteenth century, attesting to the power of the marine environment over the human imagination. Credit: The Rosenbach Museum & Library, Philadelphia, shelf mark A589p

assistance. The very nature of seafaring life with long absences from home necessitated a dependence on other sailors. Some sailors desired to be buried at sea regardless of the conditions of their death.[77]

The portrayal of seamen in our voyage offers glimpses into the hierarchy of shipboard duties and the culture of a working ship. The caricature of the slavish life of Tudor mariners does not account, for example, for the exercise of the seamen's collective prerogative in making decisions about the business of the voyage. In many cases, ships' crews were consulted on what had to be cast overboard in emergencies, whether to accept extra freight, or they could decide whether to continue or return to their port of origin during extremes of weather or other trying experiences.[78] Martin Frobisher's list of "articles . . . to be observed for the fleet," in effect for his 1587 voyage to North America, probably reflected the disciplinary difficulties faced by Tudor masters in handling crews but also provides a contextual snapshot of shipboard life incorporated into our voyage. Not surprisingly, the orders forbade swearing and dicing and "filthy communication" but they also described watch discipline and emphasized the need for ships to keep station.[79]

Voyaging in 1611

What is happening in Hame's world in 1611? What recent events have shaped the circumstances of his present voyage? In Europe in 1611, the Kremlin is under siege by Polish soldiers who have overrun Smolensk. Gustavus II Adolphus, of later fame during the Thirty Years' War, becomes the Swedish king. Denmark and Sweden go to war. In France, Henry IV had been assassinated the year before. In America, in New France, a vigorous fur trade develops that lasts for centuries and stimulates European investment. Dutch seafarers begin trade with Japan. Two years earlier, Johannes Kepler published *Astronomia Nova*, which held that the orbit of Mars is elliptical, not circular. In 1611, Galileo travels to Rome to demonstrate the telescope to the Vatican. Within the past two years, with a telescope Galileo has observed sunspots, Jupiter's brightest moons, and Saturn's ring. Beyond Hame's day, these astronomical discoveries will affect new navigational methods and technologies. In England, James I continues to experience conflict with Parliament. He creates the title of baronet, thus requiring those elevated to the title to pay a patent fee of £1,000. William Shakespeare writes *Winter's Tale*. Britain also continues its eastern exploration by sending its first envoy to the Great Mogul of India. In Virginia, a new governor, Sir Thomas Dale, has instituted martial law in a colony desperate for survival following the "starving time" in which hundreds of colonists have died. Hame knows of Henry Hudson's voyages, but does not know that his latest voyage to find the Northwest Passage has ended in mutiny, and that Hudson has been abandoned in Hudson's Bay.

In 1611, *Guyft* under Tristram Hame, master, sails from Bristol to Virginia with colonists and supplies. Hame has matured professionally as England has intensified maritime activities. Hame's country has been aggressive at sea, infused by a militant, Protestant nationalism that pressured Spain and her possessions, in reaction to the counter-Reformation.[80] *Guyft* sails not as a tiny emissary to an unknown continent, but as the spearhead of a highly organized effort of statesmen and merchants, relying on the best available technology of exploration and colonization. Many of the authors of navigational texts cited throughout this book, their patrons, and their masters, occupied a tight network with like-minded, driven scholars, statesmen, and investors. John Dee, Henry Briggs, and Edward Wright—already cited—and their circle who promoted westward expansion, were members or trustees of trading companies. Mathematician Henry Briggs, for instance, was a member of the Virginia Company.[81] Hame claims an English seat at the global seafaring table, and in support cites Sir Francis Drake's and Thomas Cavendish's circumnavigations in 1577–80 and 1586–8, respectively, which

invigorated maritime expansion, and the defeat of
the Armada in 1588 (followed by formal peace in
1604), which encouraged North American colonization. Hame has read Richard Hakluyt's propaganda
efforts through the compilation and dissemination
of voyaging narratives in *The Principal Navigations*,
which furnished empire-building propaganda. The
circumnavigations strengthened English confidence
by showing how adroit seamanship (and navigation)
could ensure an English presence wherever Spain
and Portugal had already established trading outposts.
The popularization of Drake's ventures strengthened
English self-confidence, exploiting Spanish navigational achievements against the country of their
originators: Drake probably used as navigational handbooks the *Arte of Navigation* by Martín Cortés and
Pedro de Medina's *Arte de Navegar*, and to find his
way from Cape Verde to the Pacific Ocean he relied
on the Portuguese pilot Nuño da Silva.[82]

Drake's achievements must also be viewed within
the context of piracy. His 1585–6 foray into the West
Indies, certainly viewed by the Spanish as piratical, had political ends, that of acquiring war funds
for the British treasury and destabilizing the Spanish
empire.[83] Piracy and privateering in the Caribbean,
an important prospect for the voyage of *Guyft*, continued despite formal peace with Spain, a contest
with the freewheeling involvement of the Dutch,
French, as well as English.[84] In the absence of a universally accepted law of the sea, for *Guyft* to attack
another European ship is not privateering; it is
piracy.[85] The ends of piracy and privateering frequently blended, and the people involved gave piracy
an ambiguous status, exemplified by Drake. Hakluyt's
publication of piratical accounts legitimized them
before the British public.

Providence and Propaganda

Drake's audacity may have excited Hame's imagination, but the Armada victory stimulated and
shaped national self-esteem, and fueled a florescence

of British geographical and navigational writing.[86]
Narratives of new voyages were readily absorbed
into the emerging propaganda, which disseminated accounts to a wider public.[87] Hakluyt's first
edition of *The Principal Navigations* appeared the
year after the Armada. These events—circumnavigation, the Armada defeat, privateering successes
(which during the period accounted for up to 15
percent of England's imports)—for Hame's contemporaries, define a new English identity. English
Protestantism abets this identity and its providential view of history and English pre-eminence in it,
promoted vigorously by John Foxe, that the entire
English nation was God's elect polity with a special
destiny.[88] Further, copies of *The Principal Navigations*
had begun to appear on board voyages of exploration;
ships' officers were reading the reports of their contemporaries.[89] Hame has read propaganda promoting Virginia colonization. Colonial promoter Robert
Gray's 1609 tract, *A Good Speed to Virginia*, argues a
parallel with Joshua and the journey to the Promised
Land, quoting Joshua 17:14: "And Joshua spake unto
the house of Joseph . . . saying, Thou art a great people, and hast great power, and shalt not have one
lot. Therefore the mountain shall be thine, for it is a
wood, and thou shalt cut it down, and the ends of it
shall be thine."[90] Gray explains, "I thought good to
handle this conference between the tribe of Joseph . .
. & Joshua a faithful and godly prince over the whole
commonwealth of God's Israel: which to my seeming,
is much like that plot which we have now in hand for
Virginia; for here the people of Ephraim and of the
half tribe of Manassas, are a great people, and so are
we."[91] Hame has certainly heard talk from the pulpit
and in the streets about providential destiny, opportunity in Virginia, and achieving pre-eminence over
the Church of Rome.

Hame and the senior passengers of his voyage
have been immersed in this propaganda. Hakluyt's
volumes have influenced Hame and his sponsors
to promote maritime expansion and the increasing reliance on navigational methods that Hakluyt

advocated.[92] Hakluyt's promotion of voyage narratives not only helped form the British identity as a maritime world power, but also ensured that the language of seafaring became common parlance with its navigational appurtenances of maps, charts, and instruments. Ships became metaphors for a national identity.[93] Thanks to Hakluyt, whose vast contacts included literati, statesmen, and merchant adventurers, in short, the national elite, and therefore all facets of national trade, the English voyage became the epic narrative of the age, creating a continuing appetite for voyage narratives that has not ceased.[94]

The Business of Empire Is Business

Hame participates in a very specific niche within the Hakluyt world. The demand for imports is an impetus for *Guyft's* voyage, particularly if imports could be obtained directly from foreign sources (such as Virginia) in order to keep costs minimal (without intermediate trading partners) and profits high. Creating an English-populated North America was less important than establishing a network of trading centers to ship raw materials or manufactured commodities using native materials. *Guyft's* colonists aimed to fulfill this mandate, as the voyage's charter asserts. The challenge is high: even in 1611, Virginia is not turning a profit.

In Hame's era, Bristol and Plymouth carry overseas trade, but London predominates. Britain was unique in Europe in that one city, London, overpowered others in trade. London conducts four-fifths of England's foreign trade.[95] One trading company, the Merchant Adventurers of London, soon managed virtually the country's entire overseas trade. London-based financiers and government ministers have assumed control of domestic and foreign markets, a merging of state and economic interests.[96] As an example of these merged interests, Sir Thomas Smythe, an early treasurer of the Virginia Company, served as lord mayor of London.[97] *Guyft* departs from Bristol, showing support from both local and

London-based investors.[98] The convergence of growing trading monopolies and the state's facilitation of their growth led to the colonial policy that guided the Virginia voyages of the 1580s through the early seventeenth century. The new trading companies developed investment capital unlike anything previously available, and marshaled their colonizing efforts around the production of profit.[99]

Richard Chancellor's pioneering visit to Moscow during the reign of Edward VI led directly to the founding of the Muscovy Company, based in Bristol.[100] The Muscovy Company actively stimulated an intellectual interest in furthering navigational knowledge by having Richard Eden translate Spanish navigational texts and employing pilots sophisticated in navigational methods, such as Stephen and William Borough and mathematicians Robert Recorde and John Dee. Indeed, in planning his voyage Chancellor consulted with Dee and Thomas Digges, another influential mathematician.[101] Chancellor, indeed, played a pivotal role in solving navigational problems to aid long-distance trade. Hame is aware of the importance of these men and their work, and inherits their legacy.

British expansion has occurred in surges of maritime energy. The discovery of North America led to the first surge, followed by the Chancellor voyages of the 1550s, then the anti-Spanish expansion of the late 1570s, and finally English empire-building through trading companies, beginning around 1600, which defines the purpose of Hame's voyage.[102] These bursts or surges had direction, as the discovery of North America occurred incident to a European search for a route to the Far East. An evolving European economy, the character of religious devotion, and the rise of nation-states fueled a convergence of explosive interest in maritime expansion, characteristic not only of England but also of other European states.[103] A half century before Hame was born, France and Spain competed globally with England situated on a strategic knife edge, alternating between war with one and then the other, or officially allowing if not encouraging privateering ventures against both.[104] Internal conflict in France following the treaty with England at Cateau Cambrésis in 1559, and the death of the Holy Roman Emperor Charles V in 1558 and subsequent instability in Habsburg affairs, affected Elizabeth I's foreign policy: from this point until the end of the century England was in the ascendant as a major, competing, centralized European power.[105]

With trading monopolies organizing American exploitation, all of the people involved from major investors to members of ships' crews manage their risks. Navigational techniques and tools, also, serve risk reduction, as we will discuss. We have noted that Devon seamen pursued land occupations, a diversification that reduced risks of penury. Seafaring trade must have been one of the most risky endeavors for small traders, the high risks partly explaining the need for trading monopolies. Many master mariners were part-owners of the vessels they sailed, the part-ownership a method of distributing risk with another part-owner.[106] Tobias Felgate participated in this method. A 1629 record lists six owners of a merchant ship, *James*, including his brother "William Felgate, chandler," although each owner did not necessarily possess an equal portion of the ship's worth.[107] Many master mariners owned land, doubtless in part an insurance against the risk of losing a ship, a huge capital investment. Most maritime merchants were small, independent but diversified traders. Long-distance trade required joint ventures, usually involving many small merchants who pooled their resources, evolving into a system of shares through speculative loans.[108] Italians in the fourteenth century had developed marine insurance, but the concept was slow to be adopted in England and insurance pools were therefore rare in Elizabethan times.[109] In the absence of banks and merchant houses (which existed in Spain), English trading companies relied for capital on the joint-stock system, which became the prevalent risk-reduction

method.[110] Joint-stock companies pooled investment capital exclusively, which enabled almost anyone with disposable income to invest.[111]

By 1600, the Merchant Adventurers of London turned their attention from trade with Russia, Turkey, the Levant, and the East Indies, to the Americas.[112] The Virginia colonization, however, was not funded to the same degree and required several investment and, hence, risk strategies. The Virginia colonizing ventures largely relied on joint-stock backing.[113] Shortly after the first Jamestown voyages, English merchant adventurers employed a joint-stock program to lessen risks by offering anyone the opportunity to own an equal share in the colony. The 1609 voyage of *Sea Venture* and its fleet for the relief of Jamestown was supported by joint-stock funds.[114] The sale of Virginia shares became for some a patriotic mission, inspiring a national effort that attracted investors of every rank and class. The Virginia trade, however, proved unstable so eventually the Virginia Company tried a lottery. The lottery was followed by offering land to colonists who had served their indentures, and, finally, investors implemented a headright system by which individual investors sponsored others to emigrate in return for land.[115] *Guyft*'s voyage reflects this financial arrangement.

Navigation and the Management of Risk

To his sponsors, Hame's navigational expertise is an asset, one which lessens their risks. The reader of our voyage can examine the rationale for the Virginia expedition, see the cargo manifest, scrutinize the charter party, and review the sponsors' agreements and expenses, and may also see how increasing sophistication in navigational technique functioned as a form of risk management. Profits increased when trading voyages became repetitive; repetition lessened risks owing to better knowledge of the seas, advanced navigation, and innovative ship designs.[116] Charts imposed a two-dimensional abstraction onto the seascape over which the master guided the ship from one point of intersecting reference lines to the next, enabling ships to sail anywhere.[117] The flexibility of ship design plus navigational expertise allowed more choices and hence more managed risks.

The Portuguese development of latitude sailing by *altura* furnishes an example of the parallel development of navigational techniques and ship design and the management of risk. *Altura* meant the altitude or height of the polestar. Fourteenth-century Portuguese mariners sailing westward into the Atlantic to the Canaries or Azores returned by observing the changing altitude of the polestar until it equaled its height as viewed from the desired port, and then steered eastward until making landfall. Clearly, ships that navigated by *altura* had to be able to handle the wind and sea adequately to make a return journey by this method. The sailing abilities of the Portuguese ship allowed the master to steer toward a latitude equal to that of the port of departure, and then sail eastward. Navigation by *altura* preceded latitude navigation as practiced on *Guyft*.[118] Alternating between direct observations of the seascape for navigational clues and the employment of a mathematical model based on texts—charts, sailing directions, almanacs—the master could decide courses based on several alternatives. The alternatives were viable only if the ship was capable of realizing them. Between the fourteenth century and Hame's day, the navigator could determine latitude by measuring the movement of the polestar about the celestial north pole and making corrections, and by solar altitude measurements; and his charts increasingly showed land forms oriented to true, not magnetic, north. A "better" representation translated into sailing reliability: with an increased reliance on accurate charts, errors were minimized and risks reduced in repeated voyaging.

The early attempts to plant colonies in Virginia illustrate the connection between risk management and the improvement of navigational technique. John Smith's early efforts as a Jamestown leader included charting the Chesapeake Bay and its rivers

to promote the exploitation of inland areas and to find a way to reach the South Sea. Smith recorded piloting information of soundings and impediments to navigation: his work was intended to help secure an English shipping base.[119] Risks were reduced not only by enlarging the number of investors but also by constructing a reliable and methodical process of trade for which a refinement of navigational knowledge was critical. During the Roanoke voyages, the refinement of mathematical navigation formed part of Thomas Hariot's assignment (Hariot may have been England's foremost mathematician at the time). Numerous and influential subscribers and sponsors carefully planned and supported the first Roanoke voyage, including Thomas Cavendish and Sir Richard Grenville. Sir Walter Ralegh, who held the patent for the colony, received an endorsement and backing from Elizabeth I, and with Hakluyt's active involvement in planning the voyage, the Roanoke voyages became one of the best conceived and organized efforts to colonize America, despite their failure.[120] Further, Ralegh had employed two competent captains to navigate the first colonizing voyage, Philip Amadas and Arthur Barlowe, one of whom wrote an account, probably at Ralegh's instigation, of the reconnaissance of the outer banks of present North Carolina to the Chesapeake Bay, a description that helped form the basis for future sailing directions (familiar to Hame) to reduce risks.[121] Hariot was specifically charged with refining navigational technique, again to provide a guide for the future reliable and safe piloting of ships to Roanoke, to England, and back again.

Bristol

Two major roadways skirt Bristol today, the M4, an arterial east–west corridor just north of the city, and the M5 to the west, a north–south corridor. The intersection of these roadways is an overpass. Motorists less intent on their driving, heading south on the M5, might notice the Severn River in the distance to the west and, if attentive, see much closer a mini-city of pipes, cylindrical storage tanks, overhead cranes, and cargo containers, the modern Port of Bristol, which manages collectively the docks at Avonmouth and nearby Portishead, and those in Bristol. This city within the city is remote from the experience of most people. Containerized shipping has reduced the human infrastructure of cargo handling. Now, large machines perform the work. Port facilities feature buildings and machines that have no counterpart elsewhere, that resemble nothing else, and which exist on a scale apparently indifferent to human actors. Invisible to outsiders, modern ports operate according to a world clock: computers control cargo lading, the departure and arrival of ships, and coordinate international traffic to a rigorous schedule. Removed from the milieu of urban life, even from their parent cities that evolved from waterborne trade, modern ports nevertheless retain a communication between land and sea, a place of cultural and economic "interpenetration."[122]

Today's tourist might exit the M5 at the Bristol port and, leaving it behind, drive east into Bristol. A different world appears almost immediately as the driver passes through a gorge, hugging the stone cliff, the River Avon to the right, then under Isambard Kingdom Brunel's Clifton Suspension Bridge, a monument to Victorian large-scale exuberance in iron, and into the city. The river loops through the city, which arose at the confluence of the Frome and the Avon. Victorian and Georgian buildings on steep hillsides front both the Avon and the Floating Harbor, an inner basin, now the scene of marinas and the berthed SS *Great Britain*, Brunel's first modern ocean liner (and first iron ship), launched in Bristol in 1843. From the appearance of the modern marinas alongside superannuated warehouses and chandleries now converted to other purposes, the tourist can perceive that the area once supported the intense, serious business of creating an empire. Ports are unusual places, simultaneously maintaining reference to

landward architectural history, and a seaward trajectory of economic and social history. The port is truly a "venue of arrival and departure."[123]

Today, the quayside is quiet compared with the noisy roadways that bound the river and harbor, the shipbuilding industry having faded decades ago. The re-creation of John Cabot's fifteenth-century *Matthew*, the ship that conducted the earliest known English exploration of North America, stimulated tourist interest in maritime Bristol in recent years as it was built in a temporary shipwright yard in the shadow of St. Mary Redcliffe, a church indeed atop a reddish stone cliff, once visited by Elizabeth I who described it as "the fairest and goodliest parish church in all England."[124] The church, which presided over a parish, Redcliffe, abutted merchants' homes and storehouses. Today, the church's north porch, which faces a traffic roundabout, leads to an inner porch, the oldest feature of the church, where merchants and mariners prayed at the shrine of Our Lady for safe voyages.[125] Bristol reveals glimpses of its seventeenth-century past here and elsewhere; we can imagine *Guyft* at the quayside.

In 1611, seafarers may have spelled "Bristol" as "Bristowe," a clue to the pronunciation of the name. Given the Brunel bridge plus the others that have spanned the Avon over the centuries, not surprisingly Bristol's etymological origin is "Brygstowe," the "Place of the Bridge."[126] Two centuries before Hame's voyage, Bristol had become, second to London, England's major seaport. As Bristol grew as an inland port city about seven miles up the Avon from the River Severn, it occupied a crucial link to inland and European commerce. Bristol ships left for Spain or Iceland, equidistant destinations, in fact, while some exited the Severn but instead of sailing south, headed north for the coastal and riverine trade with the Cotswold country. For centuries, Bristol ships conducted a thriving export trade in wool and stockfish (dried cod), or perhaps returned from Iberia with wine and olive oil, or from Bordeaux with wine and woad (used for blue dye). Woad, other dyes, even iron and spices passed through Bristol on the way north. The wool which Bristol exported to Europe may have included varying qualities of fineness from as far away as Lancashire or the Midlands, or closer, from Shrewsbury. To Bristol, the inland coastal trade delivered timber from the Forest of Dean, butter from Tewkesbury, or malt, wheat, apples, and pears from Gloucester and Worcester.[127] As London grew in economic importance, so did Bristol assume significance as the "metropolis of the west" in its quick-profit ventures with the prospect of immediate financial returns.[128]

Conclusion

We have circumscribed Hame's professional character by examining his background and upbringing, his possible motivation to go to sea and practice navigation, and the ambience of late Elizabethan England. Hame has matured during an era of an intense revival of trade between Spain, France, Italy, the Baltic countries, and England.[129] The later, prolonged war with Spain in which Hame participated, inspired the evolution of well-equipped merchant fleets conducting oceanic trade, in an aggressive pursuit of overseas exploration.[130] Where do we place Hame's voyage in a larger context of English exploitation of North America? Despite contemporary claims about England's seagoing destiny, colonizing efforts in North America have been few, on a small scale, and reflect a relative poverty of supporting resources

that could be invoked to support voyages and foreign outposts.[131] Nevertheless, Hame's 1611 voyage to Virginia to land colonists to exploit America's natural resources connects to a widening sphere of economic and political circumstances. Against this background, after 1600, merchants and backers have created trading companies based on joint-stock investments, of which the Virginia colony was one in 1611.[132] Despite these economic realities and the economic arguments for American colonization as promoted by Hakluyt, those who most vigorously promoted the American enterprise were those who had fought the Spanish and pressured for further governmental anti-Spanish policies.[133] Hame, a veteran of the war with Spain, may have this attitude. Guyft's voyage reflects these circumstances by providing in the ship's cargo not only the tools to build a plantation but also those necessary to cultivate Virginia's natural resources as vendible imports to support a growing consumer economy, grounded in a steady awareness of a potential threat from Spanish-controlled territories to the south.[134] Hame has opinions on relationships with Spain and other rival countries and on how best to exploit American opportunities, and doubtless his motives for entering his profession and participating in colonizing voyages include some distillation of propaganda, national and personal identity, and the goals of his employer.

The port of Bristol demands our attention as Guyft prepares to voyage to Virginia. Hame supervises the lading of cargo and passengers, then he prepares to get under way.

The first rule is of a good Navigator. Of all sciences that is used with us in England, navigation is one of the principal and most necessary for the benefit of our realm and native country and also most defensible against our enemies, because we lie environed round about with the sea.

— WILLIAM BOURNE, *An Almanacke and Prognostication*, 1571

CHAPTER 3

"BREAK GROUND OR WEIGH ANCHOR":
Getting Under Way to Virginia

A ship that will try, hull, and ride well at anchor, we call a wholesome ship.

— John Smith, *A Sea Grammar*, 1626

Master Tristram Hame and his servant arrived in Bristol almost a fortnight ago on September 9, 1611.* They took lodgings near the quayside; Hame has attended to the lading and outfitting of his ship daily. Much work has to be done: Hame has assigned Roger Coopy, the ship's carpenter, to supervise the repair of *Guyft*'s gudgeons, essential to holding the rudder steady, but damaged during a recent storm. Gudgeons are the rings into which pins, or pintles, fit to create the hinge that secures the rudder to the sternpost and allows the rudder to move from side to side. The ship's owner, Nicholas Sheers, has visited the ship almost daily, and some of the financial backers including Sir Peter Fayrewether and Josias Quick Esq. of Hascombe have seen to the business details firsthand. Hame negotiated his wages at four pounds ten shillings monthly, with an additional eighteen shillings for his servant.[1] Further, Hame has seen to the stowage of his private cargo, "two barrels of Irish beef."[2] Captain James Lynnis, the appointed colony leader, has located most of the people traveling to Virginia under indentures, and has secured testimonials from their parishes to their good character. Time is critical: Hame intends to depart tomorrow on September 24. To a visitor at the wharf, *Guyft* might be hard to identify: merchant ships are berthed so close to one another that their masts present a thick copse obscuring the view of the city. Some of *Guyft*'s sailors assist with unloading cargo from another ship for which they will be paid an extra fee, windage, work that is supervised by the cape merchant, under further oversight of the port reeve.

Charter Party

The two busiest and most tightly regulated economic spheres in England were found in the town

---

* Hame and his contemporaries observed the Old Style calendar; its dates lag behind the modern one by about 11 days. Further, Easter in 1611 fell on March 24, which set the calendar for the year. At this time, too, the year advanced to 1612. For an explanation of the calendar change, consult C. R. Cheney and Michael Jones, *A Handbook of Dates for Students of British History*, new edition, Royal Historical Society Guides and Handbooks, no. 4 (Cambridge, 2000).

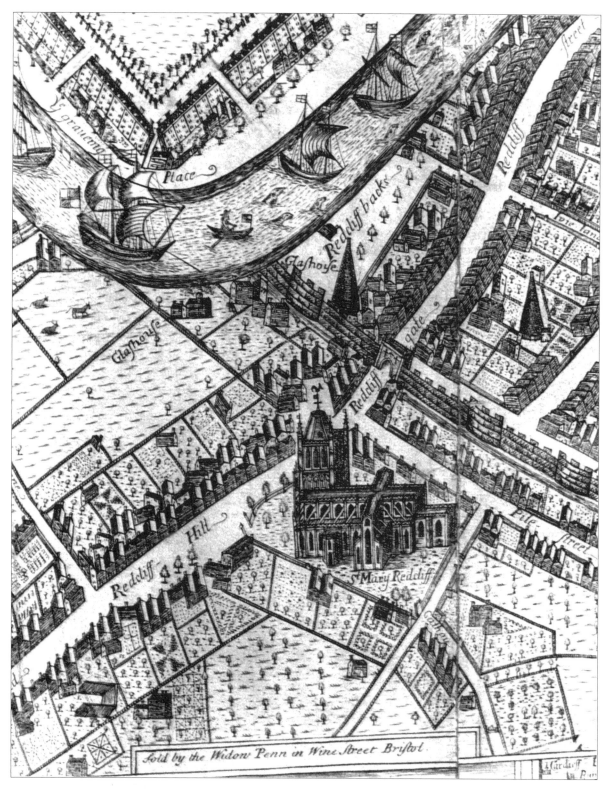

Within the map: *Graueing*, *Place*, *Redliff.*, *Street*, *Redcliff backs*, *Glashoye*, *Glashoye*, *Redcliff gate*, *one lane*, *Redcliff*, *File Street*, *Redcliff Hill*, *St Mary Redcliff*, *Gallow*, *Sold by the Widow Penn in Wine Street Bristoll.*

4. MAP OF BRISTOL SHOWING ST. MARY REDCLIFFE CHURCH — James Millerd, *An Exact Delineation . . . of the Citty of Bristoll*, a 1673 map of Bristol showing St. Mary Redcliffe Church at center. Since the early seventeenth century, the church has been a prominent landmark. Overlooking the quay where *Guyft* readies for a transatlantic crossing, for centuries St. Mary Redcliffe has received hopeful mariners praying for protection. Credit: Bristol Museums, Galleries & Archives, shelf mark Mb 6690

marketplace and at the quayside. In the marketplace, law regulated where and when a merchant could sell, proscribed monopolies in trading and price gouging, and appointed several law enforcement officers to patrol the market to ensure that goods had not been cheapened or corrupted, that poultry, fish, and meat were fresh, that merchants could not secure an advantage over their competition. Similarly, waterborne commercial traffic met the same oversight and control. As the most highly paid hired hand, Hame was given charge of *Guyft*, his role delineated along with that of the cape merchant (now called a purser or supercargo) on a legal writ called the charter party.[3] Through this instrument, the cape merchant hired the ship and described the freight arrangements (including freight charges), allotted shares to named investors, and stated the conduct of the voyage from the point of departure to the ship's destination. The charter party specified applicable charges, including Hame's pay, any local taxes or harbor fees, and the costs of unloading cargo, even the cost of the local pilot who would guide *Guyft* to the Severn. Each participating merchant or investor placed his seal upon the charter, removing it once the freight had been paid.[4] Once the cargo had been stowed, a bill of lading would be drawn up, a copy left with the merchant-investor, one taken by Hame, and, if applicable, another copy delivered to the cape merchant at the destination. Further, once the bill of lading had been written, a customs declaration had to be signed and delivered to the appropriate authority. Bureaucratic controls clearly are not a modern invention.

Guyft's charter party reads as follows:

> In the name of god Amen. This present charter party indented and made the 28th day of August in the ninth year of the reign of our sovereign lord James by the grace of God of England, France, and Ireland, King, Defender of the Faith &c. and of Scotland the 35th [year of his reign as James VI of Scotland]. Between Nicholas Sheers of the City of Bristol, merchant owner of the good ship called *Guyft* of Bristol, of the burthen of 100 tons or thereabouts, whereof under God Tristram Hame

is appointed to go master this present voyage of the one part. And James Lynnis of the Town of Staines, Esq., merchant lader [the merchant shipping cargo] in the said ship this present voyage of the other part. Witnessed that the said owner for the consideration hereafter in these presents expressed has granted and to freight the said ship unto the said merchant lader, his factors, and assigns for a voyage with her to be made by God's grace in manner and form following, viz.

> To sail by the grace of God from the port of Bristol called Hungrode with the first fair wind and weather that God shall send thereunto after the 25th day of September next with all such men, goods, provision, and other things as the said merchant lader, his factor, or assigns shall think fit, as directly as wind and weather will permit unto such port, place, or harbor or ports, places, or harbors in the land of Virginia as the said merchant lader, his factors, or assigns shall think fit. And to be there discharged, reladen and recharged when and as often as occasion shall serve at the wills and pleasures of the said merchant lader, his factors, or assigns. And when the said ship shall be so discharged, reladen, and recharged in Virginia aforesaid, then (by the grace of God) she shall return and sail about again with the next fair wind and weather that God shall send unto the said port of Bristol called Hungrode for the end of the said voyage, there to be discharged of all her charge, goods, wares, and merchandise. In consideration whereof, the said merchant lader for himself, his heirs, executors, and administrators do hereby covenant, promise, and grant to and with the said owner, his executors, administrators, and assigns by these presents that he, the said merchant lader or his assigns, shall and will within fifteen days next after the return and arrival homewards of the said ship at the said port of Bristol called Hungrode, for the end of the said voyage, well and truly pay or cause to be paid unto the said owner or his assigns for every month that the said ship shall continue and be in her said voyage the full sum of 33 pounds sterling of lawful money of England, accounting twenty and eight days to every month, beginning to enter into pay from the day that the said ship shall sail out of Kingrode to proceed in her said voyage. That if it shall happen (which God forbid) that the said ship shall be robbed or spoiled on

the sea of any manner of goods, wares, provisions, or merchandises belonging to the said ship or merchant lader, that then the said owner shall stand to his own loss (if any be).

In witness whereof &c—[5]

The reference to "Hungrode" concerns an anchorage not far from the mouth of the Avon about three miles west of Bristol. South of Avonmouth along the Severn lies another road near Portishead, known to Hame and modern mariners as Kingroad or King Road.[6] The suffix "rode" refers to "road," which in 1611 means, "[A]ny place where a ship may ride near the land and yet cannot ride, land-locked for all winds. A good road is, where there is good ground for anchor-hold, shoal water, and so as however the wind blow, there can no great sea gate come in, being the land . . . on one side, and some sands, rocks, or the like, to break of the sea on the other."[7] Not surprisingly, "A bad road is the contrary to the good," and any "ship that rides at anchor in a road, is a roader."[8] In 1611, Bristol merchants are proud of their secure port, and a few years earlier they claimed to the Privy Council that its harbor was large enough to handle virtually any kind of ship or boat. The choice of a late September departure is unusual because the colonists to be transported will arrive during winter, but doing so will allow them to prepare for spring planting.

The Crew and Passengers

Guyft sets sail with the following crew complement and passengers.[9] All of the colonists go to Virginia under contracts of indenture to investors. Most of the indentures apply for seven years, after which the colonists who survive may receive acreage of their own for cultivation. Investors who paid travel expenses for indentured colonists reaped benefits in real estate: the "headright" system, the latest incentive announced by the Virginia Company to elicit more interest in Virginia, rewarded investors with acreage for sending colonists.[10] The land grant reward for those people who survived their indentures effectively began

around 1614, and was followed by other schemes to promote investment, such as the headright system. In 1611, tobacco plantations are a phenomenon of the future, so indentured servants either pursue their trades, or apply their labor to other industries from the production of lumber, to silk harvesting, to glass manufacture. Captain and Master Tristram Hame musters the following crew followed by a list of his passengers:

Crew
Gerard Chilson, barber surgeon from London
William Horwood, boatswain from Southampton
Roger Coopy, carpenter from Greenwich
Robert Pyke, sailor and boatswain's mate from
    Topsham, Devon
George Brasye, from London, cook; in charge of
    food stores
Thomas Blunt, sailor and master's mate from
    Dartmouth, Devon
John Carter, sailor from Plympton St. Mary,
    Devon
Silvester Heale, master gunner from Torbay,
    Cornwall
William Norrys, gunner's mate, sailor, from
    Plymouth

Passengers
Captain James Lynnis, designated captain of the
    plantation at which all the passengers will
    work, from Staines, near London
Ferdinando Morgan, gentleman and "ancient,"
    from Coberly, Gloucestershire
Thomas Davye, gentleman, from Bristol
Walter Flick, indentured colonist (blacksmith)
    from Bristol
Christopher Hills, indentured colonist
    (shipwright) from Sidmouth, Devon
Thomas Marks, indentured colonist (cooper)
    from Taunton, Somerset
Adria Marks, indentured colonist, wife of
    Thomas Marks
William Tollye, indentured colonist (farm
    laborer) from Bristol

Joane Tollye, indentured colonist, wife of
    William Tollye

Ellis Coursey, indentured colonist (farm laborer)
    from Tavistock, Cornwall

Margaret Coursey, indentured colonist, wife of
    Ellis Coursey

John Collyns, indentured colonist (sawyer and
    carpenter) from Exeter, Devon

John Jones, indentured colonist (gardener and
    smithy) from Glamorgan, Wales

Lewis Walkey, indentured colonist (sailor) from
    Clopton, Somerset

Richard Hine, indentured colonist (laborer) from
    Bristol

William Couch, indentured colonist (laborer)
    from Barnstaple, Devon

Nicholas Denn, indentured colonist (laborer)
    from Padstow, Cornwall

John Bickford, indentured colonist (stonemason)
    from Hascombe, Gloucestershire

Richard Haywood, indentured colonist (laborer)
    from Bradford, Somerset

Thomas Tapley, indentured colonist (fisherman)
    from Cockington, Devon

William Sheere, indentured colonist (laborer)
    from Newton, Somerset

George Whitcow, indentured colonist (laborer)
    from Barnstaple, Devon

Lewis Taylor, indentured colonist (laborer) from
    Glamorgan, Wales

Ellis Michell, indentured colonist (fisherman)
    from East Teignmouth, Devon

Crew's Responsibilities

During the days and weeks preceding departure, *Guyft*'s crew assembles. Since their last voyages, some of the crew have returned to their home parishes, and some may even have resumed land occupations as farmers or in some trade. Others naturally seek the company of mariners, perhaps lodging with

friends or relations in a part of Bristol known as a mariners' quarter. On Marsh Street, for instance, many mariners' families had lived for generations, and infirm sailors may have sought on this street a home, founded in 1445, which supported a dozen old, sick, or disabled mariners. On Nicholas Street in the same proximity, John Cabot once rented lodgings following his epochal voyage.[11] During the last weeks before departure, *Guyft* has resembled a queen bee attended by drones and workers. Not only has the ship been laded with supplies and cargo, but passengers brought on board their belongings and tools, and the mate and boatswain kept busy managing the sea hive. Ships are under incessant repair. Most of the workers attending to the ship are not crew or passengers, but dockyard laborers and vendors: caulkers, carpenters and joiners, sailmakers, painters, riggers, assistants, and apprentices. These workers repair damage—in our case, the gudgeons and pintles of the rudder—and perform necessary maintenance. Cargo handlers and some crew lade supplies. Various local officials ensure that good order is maintained, that the slips are not damaged, and that trash is not dumped in or near the quays. Further, joiners, carpenters, and wrights have their workshops and homes in the vicinity, and merchants maintain warehouses by the quay, particularly victuallers.[12]

Narratives of voyages in early modern England say very little about the crews, much less give the names of common sailors. Scholars surmise that merchant ships voyaging to Virginia carried one man for every 9.8 tons in 1686, with more manning earlier in the century. *Guyft*'s prototype, the somewhat larger *Susan Constant* of 120 tons, possibly carried a crew of 14. By comparison, during one voyage in 1602 on a similar vessel, Captain Bartholomew Gosnold sailed with 32 colonists as passengers and a crew of eight.[13] In addition to the captain and two mates for administering the crew, *Guyft* has a few skilled mariners along with some general hands. The skilled jobs are that of the gunner, carpenter, boatswain, and cook.

Persons with skilled jobs have subordinate trainees called mates.[14]

By comparison, the career path for Spain's sailors at this time began with long years at sea as a boy page, to youthful apprentice, to designation as sailor for a man in his mid- to late twenties. This long sea service required learning many skills, which included navigational ones, from administering the turning of the half-hour sandglass to regulate shipboard activities, to heaving the lead and quickly determining the nature and depth of the sea bottom.[15] In England, apprentice sailors were released from indentures during their mid-twenties and perhaps, like Spanish sailors, acquired some navigational skills. Throughout their careers, English sailors had few institutions to advance their social standing, or assert their rights.

Cargo and Provisions

Hame relies on a similar system for handling cargo in Bristol as at other ports. On previous voyages, Hame was visited by the water bailiff, who collected dues on particular goods including fish, corn, and salt, but also maintained shipping and cargo records, directed shipping within the port, and watched merchants and customers. The water bailiff arrests transgressors of customary law.[16] Bristol, however, presents certain challenges. The long, narrow gorge that borders the Avon into the city, and the steep tidal range that prevails along it, contrasts with the more serene journeys along the Avon and Frome from the city into the country. Hame has encountered smuggling in these waters. A 1559 statute forbade ships from lading or discharging cargo at all English ports during darkness to reduce smuggling. Bristol's tidal circumstances, however, necessitate a legal exception. Letters Patent from Elizabeth I, dated 1563, stated that "the port of Bristol is so dangerous and low of water, except it be at spring tides, that great ships laden cannot come nearer than four miles, because the water ebbs and flows suddenly for loading and unloading;

whereby ships that before the statute might have been unloaded in four days cannot now be unloaded within 15 days."[17] Consequently, local authorities permit lading in Bristol between 4 a.m. and 8 p.m. but only in designated areas.

Provisioning a ship takes careful planning, negotiation with victuallers, judicious selections of what could be safely stored, how long food might last, and the projected rate of consumption. What and how much does a seaman eat during the day? Hame's sponsors set the food allowance as follows:

A proportion for the diet of one man for seven days at the sea and on land:
In biscuit bread for seven days seven pounds
Beer at three quarts the day for seven days five gallons one quart
Beef, for four days in the week four pound
Habardine or stockfish one fish & eleven for three days
Cheese for three days in the week three quarters of a pound
Butter for three days in a week eleven pound
Peas for seven days, two quarts
Oatmeal for seven days, one pint
Sweet oil after the rate of a pint for a month
Vinegar, after the rate of a pint for a month
Salt, after the rate of eleven pint for a month
Mustard seed, after the rate of a pint for a month[18]

The following list of *Guyft's* stores is not all-inclusive but suggests the scope and diversity of stores.[19] A businesslike accounting of stores does not reflect the work required in their stowage. Boatswain William Horwood and his mate, Robert Pyke, work tirelessly and imaginatively to take advantage of limited space to stow supplies and cargo: by experience, they perform their work with consideration of spoilage, contamination, dangerous shifting of weight that could imperil the ship's stability, and ready access to victuals.

Weapons

muskets, gunpowder, slow match [for the muskets], bandeliers [leather shoulder straps from which are suspended containers with gunpowder, each container constituting a charge]

swords

pikes and halberds

Food

seeds: fenugreek, cumin, aniseed, "garden seeds," mustard

spices: salt, pepper, ginger

almonds

cheese and butter

oatmeal

aqua vita [an alcoholic beverage made from potato or grain mash, formerly distilled from wine]

beer

bacon

peas

dried fish

onions

biscuits

Clothing

thread, buttons, beads, belts, points (decorative metal trimmings), handkerchiefs, falling bands (collars), canvas, thimbles, cloth of various kinds including taffeta, silk, and buckram, frieze

shoes

stockings

shirts

caps

Containers, building materials, and tools

construction tools: copper, glue, brimstone, hatchets, hammers, wedges, axes of various kinds, screws, pairs of compasses, adzes, nails of various kinds, saws, chisels, carpenter's tools, shears, carpenter's lines, squares, files, whetstones, pliers, punches, bits, chalk, planes

food utensils: platters, bowls, dishes, spoons, trenchers, horn cups, kettles, frying pans

knives

padlocks

andirons

rope of various sizes, materials

barrels, casks of various sizes

lanterns

pothooks and iron pots

caulking irons

needles

spades

gridirons

bellows

Other

church bibles

copies of Arthur Dent's *The Plaine Man's Pathway to Heaven*, 1610

paper and ink

candlesticks

materials for making sheets and bolsters

bread and wine for communion

soap

Navigational Texts and Instruments for the Voyage

One of Hame's possessions is a book of copperplate engravings of charts of European coastlines from the Zuider Zee to Cadiz, accompanied by navigational and astronomical instruction. This book, originally titled *Spieghel der Zeevaerdt*, by Lucas Jansz. Waghenaer, was translated into English as *The Mariners Mirrour*. The book's primary innovation, a compilation of the first printed charts for use at sea, became much emulated, creating an eponym of its author: such books became known as "waggoners."[20] The preamble to *The Mariners Mirrour* contains "An Exhortation to the Apprentices of the Art of Navigation," advice which Hame has read frequently and applied:

The first and chiefest way to attain to the perfect skill and science of navigation, is whensoever any shipmaster or mariner shall set forth from land out of any river or haven, diligently to mark, what buildings, castles, towers, churches, hills, vales, downs, windmills, or other marks are standing on the land. All which, or many of them, let him portray with his pen, how they bear, and how far distant: but upon the true and certain points of the compass, upon which he first set sail, and shaped his course, whilst yet every mark on the land may be clearly and evidently perceived, to the end the true arising thereof may be the better had. He must also very often cast the lead, that he may most exactly note in his compt-book [account book], how far off, all the shoals and sands lie from the shore. . . .

Any mariner that will diligently, and with understanding practice these precepts, shall attain the true skill and science of navigation. For that which any man either young or old exercises, searches out and observes himself, sticks faster in memory, than that which he learns of others. Notwithstanding let him not neglect, nor shame to enquire of the master of the ship . . . the situation of countries, the courses upon several points, the depths or soundings, and the elevations of the pole [altitude of the polestar]: and practice with the cross-staff, and astrolabe. The which two, are the principal instruments (next the compass) that belong to safe and skilful seafaring.[21]

The texts and instruments that furnish Hame's navigational kit for the voyage reflect Waghenaer's advice. Hame apprenticed to pilots and masters who had accompanied Frobisher—indeed, Hame himself served under one of Frobisher's captains—and Dee tutored Hame. Dee, in fact, selected the instruments and navigational texts and instructed both Frobisher and his pilot Christopher Hall on their use.[22] The Frobisher voyage is significant not only for his explorations but also because it was one of the earliest voyages in which the testing of navigational and cartographic methods was paramount. Hall, the master of *Gabriel* during the 1576 voyage and chronicler of the expedition, revealed himself a keen and prescient navigator in his careful observations of the sun's and

polestar's altitudes for latitude determination coupled with his piloting notes on soundings, winds, bearings and courses made good, and compass variation, duly recorded in Richard Hakluyt's *Principal Navigations*.[23] The voyage of *Guyft* is selective in appropriating instruments and texts from Frobisher's bill that reflect navigational "basics" and to eliminate instruments not in common use. Globes and treatises on their use have been eliminated because Hame does not possess nor has he yet used them successfully. From Frobisher's bill Hame takes the following:

> A great instrument of brass named Compassum Meridianum.
> An instrument of wood, a staff named Balestella.
> A very great cart [chart] of navigation.
> A cosmographical glass & castle knowledge.
> Compasses of divers sorts.
> Hour glasses.[24]

The "Compassum Meridianum" is a meridian compass that compares a magnetic compass bearing to the bearing of true north as shown by measuring the shadow cast by the sun. It is used for determining magnetic variation. The "Balestella" is a cross-staff, a tool also recommended by Waghenaer. A "great cart" is a chart of the ocean with compass roses and rhumb or bearing lines superimposed. The "cosmographical glass" is *The Cosmographical Glasse* (1559), an influential treatise on the organization of the visible universe and the behavior of celestial phenomena by William Cuningham, a Tudor physician. "Castle knowledge" refers to one of four popular treatises that promoted practical mathematical knowledge by "the father of English mathematics," Dr. Robert Recorde, *The Castle of Knowledge*, published in 1556.[25] Intended for Muscovy Company navigators, *The Castle of Knowledge* explicates the terrestrial and celestial spheres.[26] We shall return to these instruments and texts in subsequent chapters.

Captain John Smith also recommends a suite of navigational tools and texts. Smith's *Sea Grammar*, based on an earlier text by Sir Henry Mainwaring,

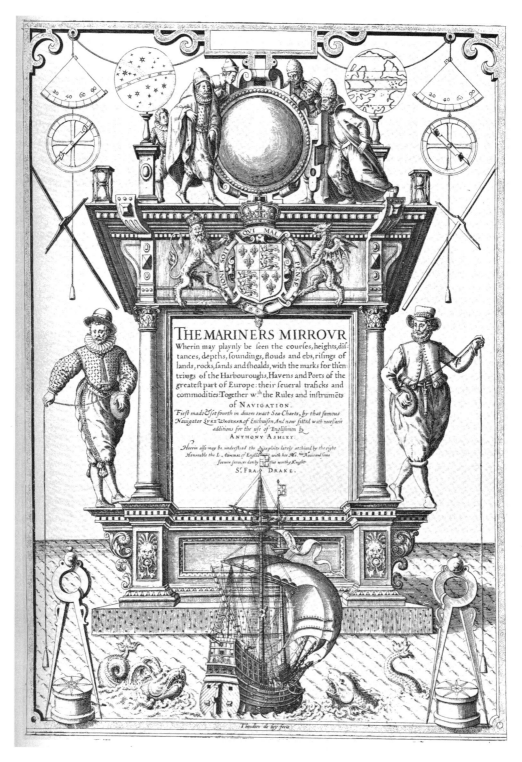

5. FRONTISPIECE, LUCAS JANSZ. WAGHENAER'S *THE MARINERS MIRROUR* ⁓ Waghenaer's *Mariners Mirror* is the first comprehensive atlas of the sea, appearing in English in 1588, the year of the Spanish Armada. Its exquisite and detailed charts still excite readers for their artistry combined with utility. Theodor de Bry's engraved frontispiece has become an icon of Elizabethan seafaring. It depicts several navigational tools including a magnetic compass, lead and line, mariner's astrolabe, cross-staff, celestial and terrestrial globes, sandglasses, and cartographic tools, and also shows what the well-dressed navigator wears. A Dutch pilot himself, Waghenaer was a highly experienced sailor and cartographer. Credit: Courtesy of the John Carter Brown Library at Brown University, shelf mark [R] 2-SIZE Z.W131 1588

represents the first English publication (in 1627) of a manual on seamanship.[27] Doubtless the seafaring lexicon and the descriptions of shipboard evolutions reflected common practices for several decades before the seventeenth century, and some of the texts and instruments Smith names had been in circulation for at least that long. Smith's summary of the navigational abilities requisite for "young sea-men" describes the skills at which Hame is adept:

> For to learn to observe the altitude, latitude, longitude, amplitude [angular distance at rising or setting of the sun from magnetic east or west, measured along the horizon, used for gauging compass variation], the variation of the compass, the sun's azimuth and almicanter [circles of altitude or height, parallel to the horizon], to shift the sun and moon, and know the tides, your rooms [rhumbs or lines of bearing on a chart], prick your card [measure on a chart with a pair of dividers], say your compass [know the thirty-two compass directions], and get some of these books, but practice is best.[28]

"These books" include:
Master Wright's Errors in Navigation.
Master Tapp's Sea-Mans Kalendar.
The Arte of Navigation.
The Sea Regiment.
The Sea-mans Secret.
Waggoner.
The New Attracter for Variation.

Edward Wright's *Certaine Errors in Navigation* (1599), an early scientific text designed for practical application, identified errors and their correction in instrumental use and showed for the first time how to create a Mercator-projection chart.[29] The "Calendar" refers to *The Sea-Mans Kalendar* (1602), a nautical almanac by an early professional teacher of navigation, John Tapp.[30] The *Arte of Navigation* by Martín Cortés, translated by Richard Eden (1561), was the single most influential navigation manual of the era and the first published in English.[31] William Bourne's *A Regiment for the Sea* (1574) was the first navigational text written and published by an Englishman.[32]

Bourne presents an interesting authority for navigational technique and instrumentation. He was a native of Gravesend, near London, and worked variously as a gunner, surveyor, innkeeper, and portreeve; he also created almanacs. *The Seamans Secrets* by John Davis (1607) introduced an important new altitude-measuring instrument, the backstaff.[33] A "waggoner," as mentioned earlier, refers to a compilation of sailing directions and charts, the name derived from Waghenaer's *The Mariners Mirrour*. "The New Attracter" refers to two texts originally published in tandem, Robert Norman's *The Newe Attractive*[34] and William Borough's *A Discourse of the Variation of the Cumpas*[35] (both 1581), influential early treatises on magnetic variation. All these texts were republished (and usually enlarged or revised) several times before Smith published his list. These and other texts will show up repeatedly throughout our voyage. Collectively, they communicate excitement in recommending the application of mathematics to practical ends.[36] While Gresham College becomes an innovation center for mathematics, universities at Oxford and Cambridge witness an influx of practical men from the merchant class. By 1611 geography, as a topic of study, has taken on a mathematical dimension. University mathematician-geographers are orienting their work to the solution of longitude determination and the challenge of northern navigation with converging meridians and magnetic variation.[37]

Smith does not neglect to list the "Instruments fitting for a sea-man" of relevance to *Guyft's* voyage: "Compass so many pairs and sorts as you will, an astrolabe quadrant, a cross-staff, a backstaff, an astrolabe, a nocturnal."[38] Hame takes an astrolabe and a cross-staff to determine latitude. He does not have a backstaff, but Hame emulates some of the principles of its design and use by employing the cross-staff as a shadow-casting instrument, as we shall see. The nocturnal is a device for determining the local time at night, based on an observation of the configuration of the constellations Ursa Major and Minor (the Big and Little Dippers, or to Hame, wains, not dippers) with respect to Polaris, the polestar. In addition to the texts and instruments recommended by Frobisher and Smith, Hame relies on two other works commonly cited by late Tudor mathematicians and experts on navigation: William Barlow's *The Navigators Supply* (1597) and Thomas Blundeville's *M. Blundeville His Exercises* (1594). Barlow, a cleric who tutored James I's eldest son, Prince Henry, on mathematics, may have been the first to devise a compass with a graduated rotating ring for taking accurate bearings, and invented a traverse board for plotting the course of a ship without a chart.[39] Blundeville, a gentleman enthusiast of applied mathematics, wrote his *Exercises* as a compendium of mathematical and navigational knowledge at the close of the sixteenth century, including the first explication by an Englishman of the use of trigonometric tables.[40]

As the embodiment of cosmological and mathematical ideas, navigational manuals and instruments constitute the key primary sources of Hame's worldview. The texts and instruments are models superimposed on nature, lenses through which we can peer at the early modern seascape "where only water and heaven may be seen."[41] As we will discover, Hame regards his texts and instruments highly; in 1611 even as significant a port city as Bristol does not have abundant instrument makers. As evidence of the value of instruments, a will reveals that a local Bristol merchant, one Nicholas Thorne, bequeathed to the Grammar School an astrolabe, charts, maps, and instruments belonging to astronomy.[42] Some of Hame's instruments would have been made by engravers, craftsmen whose livelihoods were not made from ships' masters. Brass instruments are not easy to come by as England had a fledgling brass manufacture by 1611.[43] Some of the texts described above, however, contain templates for laying out instruments with tools no more sophisticated than a straightedge, paper, and pairs of compasses.

Under Way to Virginia

On September 24, as *Guyft* prepares to get under way, the character of shipboard work changes as sailors enter into the watch cycle of work. Under the watch system, each crew member performs assigned duties for a designated part of the day. Sir Henry Mainwaring explains how the watches operated:

> At the sea, the ship's company is divided into two parts, the one called the starboard watch, the other the larboard [now called the port] watch. The master, is the chief of the starboard, and his righthand mate of the larboard. These are in their turns to watch, trim sails, pump, and do all duties for four hours, and then the other watch is to relieve them. Four hours they call a whole watch. In harbor, and roads, they watch but quarter watch, that is, when one quarter of the company do watch together.[44]

While a ship was in port, perhaps a quarter of the ship's company was required for watchstanding. When a ship got under way, the entire crew would have been involved. Hame, William Horwood, or his mate supervises the watches in turn, or they divide the crew for simultaneous duties. Once under way, the crew performs tasks according to a system of four- and two-hour watches, or "whole watches" and "half watches." When the ship leaves the dock and heads seaward, Hame's mate, Robert Pyke, sets the internal clock of the ship: beginning at noon, he inverts a half-hour sandglass. This timer regulates shipboard life for the coming months. At the conclusion of each half hour throughout the voyage, Pyke (or another) strikes a bell (an additional bell struck at each subsequent half hour, up to eight bells or four hours), monitors the compass, and records data on the heading and speed of the ship (as we shall see). The crew's watches are therefore timed by the glass; courses are set by it; navigational computations rely on it. Beginning the cycle, the starboard watch takes "first watch" from 8 p.m. until midnight; the larboard

6. St. Mary Redcliffe Church, north porch — Before setting off on their voyage, *Guyft*'s crew and passengers walk a short distance uphill from the quayside and enter the north porch of St. Mary Redcliffe to pray in the small mariners' chapel **just inside.** Credit: Author's collection

watch takes "second watch" from midnight until 4 a.m.; the crews alternate, the starboard watch taking "day" or "morning watch" from four until eight. The next two watches, one before and one after noon, bear names now lost to us. Afternoon and evening watches may have been subdivided into two-hour watches, as the 4 to 6 p.m. watch is termed the "lookout watch." A final two-hour watch (original name unknown) brings the cycle to a close. When the cycle resumes, the larboard watch begins the first watch. With small crews, ships may have maintained two watch sections of equal strength, the starboard and larboard watches.[45] The term "watch" therefore refers both to a team of crew members as well as a block of time. This nomenclature persists today where the American Navy refers to "port" (larboard) and "starboard" watches.

Before getting under way, Tristram Hame and *Guyft*'s crew and passengers hike uphill to the north porch entry to St. Mary's Redcliffe where they pray in the small sailors' chapel for a safe crossing to Virginia. Walking to the church where the previous Sunday he and his crew took communion, Hame passes Marsh Street, where his predecessors established a home to support a dozen old sailors. Sailors' wives go about their business of sustaining families with absent fathers, yet some impoverished sailors' widows and children are begging this morning outside the church precinct. Hame enters the church where he sees votive ships, made by sailors eager to secure a blessing on their voyages, small models perched just beyond reach. Hame also notices a large narwhal tusk, brown with age, brought back by John Cabot's crew over a century earlier and placed within the church. Hame's gaze drifts along the nave to artifacts of local achievements, wars, notable people, some objects intended as *mementi mori*, some simply placed within the church because no other institution exists to accept or display them, while others are meant to inspire awe or devotion. Hame looks to the altar and says a short prayer for the safety of his ship. His devotions ended, Hame departs and returns to *Guyft*. Even at the last instant

before departure, cargo and personal effects continue to be stowed, and friends, well-wishers, and peddlers clamor for the attention of passengers and crew.

Even at the ship's departure, administrative and legal paperwork require completion. Before *Guyft* departs Bristol, the mayor signs a certificate listing the passengers and crew:

> To the Treasurer, Company and Counsel of Adventurers
> and Planters of the City of London, for the first Colony in Virginia.
>
> These are to certify that in the good ship of Bristol called *Guyft*, this present 25th day of September, 1611, were shipped from our port of Bristol for the plantation in Virginia, at the charges of Sir Peter Fayrewether, knight and baronet, Thomas Gould, and Josias Quick, Esquires, under the conduct of James Lynnis, Esq., appointed captain and governor over them, the persons whose names ensue, who forthwith proceeded in their voyage accordingly.
>
> [The names listed appear under "The Crew and Passengers" above.]
>
> /s/ John Swye mayor[46]

Just as the future settlers aboard ship emigrate to Virginia under contracts of indenture, the entire voyage is under an indenture regarding ownership of the venture to protect investments and minimize liability. A part of the indenture reads as follows:

> This indenture made the third day of February in the years of the reign of our sovereign lord James, by the grace of God of England, Scotland, France, and Ireland, king, defender of the faith &c. That is to say, in the year of his reign of England, France, and Ireland the eighth and of Scotland the 34th. Between the treasurer and company of adventurers and planters of the City of London for the first colony in Virginia with the advice and consent of the counsel of the same of the one part, and Sir Peter Fayrewether of Tewkesbury in the County of Gloucester knight and baronet, Henry Briddick of Gloucester, Thomas Gould of Gloucester, and Josias Quick of Huntley in the said County of Gloucester, Esquires, free of the said company of Virginia and who have severally adventured for

7. PHOTO OF RIVER AVON AND GORGE AT LOW TIDE ⁓ To reach the Bristol Channel, *Guyft* must negotiate the Avon River with one of the most extreme tidal ranges in the world. *Guyft* passes through this gorge with the Avon at a higher tide.
Credit: Author's collection

their several shares hereafter mentioned and for every of the said shares, either they or those whose estates they now have or shall have, have paid or are to pay within one year after the date hereof twelve pounds ten shillings.[47]

Hame employs a local pilot to take *Guyft* through the Avon, into the Severn where Hame may have to hire additional pilots to clear the Bristol Channel. The pilots are regulated, even though Hame's skills as navigator are not. Local pilotage affords a decent living, and Bristol, along with London, Hull, and Newcastle, license and examine pilots per royal charter.[48] Pilotage is highly competitive; the Bristol town council appoints its own, as do neighboring shires, with very specifically defined boundaries of operation.

Even in modern times, Bristol pilots operate with an intense consciousness of their heritage. While most British ports employ pilots, Bristol ones are today self-employed; their pilotage district, which encompasses waters just as formidable now as in 1611, spans eighty miles.[49] For centuries, Bristol Channel pilots came from families who resided in Pill, formerly Crockerne Pill, a village near the M5 motorway close to Avonmouth.[50] Hame pays his pilot based on a strictly regulated scale, as the local pilot receives 6s 8d for guiding a ship between one hundred and two hundred tons.[51] Pilots also assign moorings, the mooring posts themselves having been carefully placed to avoid impeding the river flow. Localities that provide moorings inspect them frequently for reliability,

8. CHART OF GREAT BRITAIN AND IRELAND, FROM WAGHENAER'S *THE MARINERS MIRROUR* — Crisscrossed by rhumb lines, Waghenaer's chart of England, Scotland, and Ireland depicts only the key coastal towns, landmarks, and features important to navigators. Credit: Courtesy of the John Carter Brown Library at Brown University, shelf mark [R] 2-SIZE Z.W131 1588

and to ensure an adequate depth for anchorage. Concerned to reduce or prevent silting, local officials require ships' masters to apply for permission to remove riverbed rocks or sand for ballast.[52]

Hame depends upon a reliable local pilot to getting *Guyft* into the Bristol Channel. Not only does the ship have to pass through a long, narrow gorge with steep cliffs, but the stretch presents one of the largest tidal ranges in the world, a range of twenty-one feet at the neap tides, forty feet at the spring tides, with a six-knot tidal current.[53] Hame depends on the pilot not only to recognize hazards but also to convey an acute knowledge of the tides. As the tidal range is wide, the tidal strength can be formidable. At Avonmouth, and southward into the Bristol Channel, *Guyft* is not safe from tidal fury. Even modern coastal guides for yacht sailors emphasize the dangerous and powerful tidal streams: if not taken into account, no yacht can hope to oppose them.[54] Hame fears the jolt in his ship's forward momentum: the sensation of his keel hitting sand or mud, a sure sign that he has miscalculated the time of high tide or high water. The three knots that *Guyft* might make good depend entirely on being with the tide. As it happens, Hame plans to sail southwest on the ebb to take his ship out of the Bristol Channel and south into the Atlantic. A rutter (a sailing guide with piloting information) of 1605 describes the behavior of the tidal streams near Avonmouth: "In the Channel of Bristol, the flood sets east northeast, and the ebb west southwest."[55]

Hame takes the ebb to proceed southwest. Even so, the Bristol Channel presents another set of difficulties with its hazardous sands or reefs, beset by furious gales, and additional tidal surprises.[56] Hame does not study the tidal direction and strength of flow, but he considers the totality of environmental circumstances: he must view the tidal current, its direction and force, in tandem with the behavior of prevailing winds. Mindful of the direction of flood and ebb tides as described in 1605, the prevailing winds alternate between southwest and northwest. The southwest ebb, which lasts for just over six hours, propels *Guyft* at between one or two knots in addition to the speed she makes good under sail.[57] In managing a difficult passage to the open sea, Hame does not pass all responsibility to the local pilot; an observant master, Hame learns from his hired pilots and makes his own notes and observations on local conditions, just as did his navigator forebear, Christopher Hall who, decades earlier, guided one of Frobisher's ships, *Ayde*, along the same route. Without detailed charts of the region, Hall sketched his own views of coastlines and features, annotated with observations on local conditions, particularly noting the depth of the water by frequent soundings, a practice Hame also observes.[58]

Hame may, for several hours, have the strength of the tide with his southwesterly heading, sailing with the wind from the southwest. Tidal flow and the wind's direction and force, then, determine the speed of his travel. Further, leeway, the action of the wind and tide that imparts movement to the ship, may counter the ship's progress. In heading to windward (the direction from which the wind is blowing), Hame will have to sail one or more compass points to the wind, depending on characteristics of the ship. That is, he will head at least 11 degrees to either side of the wind, alternating course first to one side of the wind, then the other. Sailing to the wind is difficult because of the strain to the rigging and the crew.[59]

Hame annotates his card, or chart, of coastal features and sounding datums, probably a rutter more than a chart, paying strict attention to his compass directions, not only for gauging the heading of his ship, but also to observe the tide, its direction of flow, to take advantage of its extra push or plan for its hindrance. He has an ingrained sensitivity to the wind's strength and direction in making way. He runs his ship by the sandglass reckoning of time, which, when *Guyft* reaches the ocean, determines the watch schedule, but also becomes essential for his astronomical navigation. Hame notes in his log, "And so with a good north wind we held our course southwest & south, purposing to pass the Canary Isles."[60] One of Hame's passengers, Ferdinando Morgan, gentleman, has agreed with Captain James Lynnis, military leader of the colonizing expedition, to maintain an account of the voyage and, upon arrival in Virginia, to record the construction of a plantation. When *Guyft* departed Bristol, Morgan records that the ship's sponsors and the shipowner,

> took their leave, whom with tears we commended to God, bequeathing both them & all other our owners, his Majesty and our selves to the protection of the Almighty & so according to the poesy of our ship: *Under the conduct of Christ we furrowed the seas*. We last set eye on the Lizard of England: wherefore not without tears in our prayers, we commended the safety of his Majesty, the merchants, & all our friends to Almighty God, desiring that after the honest dispatch of our business, we might on our return find them in safety. Which God grant.[61]

Conclusion

From the rivers Avon and Frome, nexus between England's rural interior and the larger world reached via the Severn and the Bristol Channel, *Guyft* traverses three maritime spheres of influence, from riverine to coastal to oceanic. These spheres attest to an interdependency between waterborne trade and traffic by the largest man-made structures ever devised for moving goods and people: ships.[62] The character of shipboard work alters as the ship passes through these environments; after all hands get the ship under way, a watch system settles in as the crew begins to perform other duties, and passengers create their own small territories for the coming months. The shift in environments is also reflected in a change in Hame's navigational methods and instruments. Pyke inverts the sandglass at noon on the day of departure to signify the beginning of the nautical day that will not expire until noon the next day. Initially, a hired pilot dictates the orders given to helmsman and crew.

Hame stations Thomas Blunt in the chains for the delicate task of navigating the Avon to its mouth: from his station, Blunt heaves the lead frequently to obtain soundings (by chains "is meant those chains to which the shrouds are made fast, on the ship-sides").[63] As *Guyft* enters the Severn and the Bristol Channel, Hame consults his chart and compass more frequently while he continues to take soundings. As he enters the ocean and landmarks recede, Hame ceases to take soundings as the continental shelf can no longer be reached by hundreds of fathoms of line. For the first time, he employs altitude-measuring instruments to take the height of the sun at noon and thereby obtain his latitude. Away from a coastal view, which always gives Hame (in good weather) a navigational referent, on the open sea environmental cues may deceive. He has an intended compass heading, but Hame knows that his true course is a convergence of circumstances: drift, an imperceptible movement due to currents pushing his ship one way or another, and winds from any direction except astern, which create a movement called leeway. In the Atlantic Ocean, Hame must perform his navigational skills with confidence and an intuitive feel for the limits of his ship's performance. Maritime historian and archaeologist Barry Cunliffe describes the experience. The ocean's "savage energy and remorseless rhythm cannot fail to make a deep impression on anyone who comes within its presence. The ocean dominates. There is also the sense of limitlessness—of being on the edge of the world looking out across an infinity of ever-changing sea. These simple realities are part of the experience shared by all those who have faced the ocean."[64] Hame is very much the Dartmouth navigator that Chaucer described. Hame is certain of his navigational tools and methods; he has attended to the stowage of cargo and the embarkation of passengers; and he has acquitted all legal and administrative tasks. Now he is absorbed with the winds, currents, and next landfall.

The master and company being aboard, he commands them to get the sails to the yards, and about your gear or work on all hands, stretch forward your main halyards, hoist your sails half mast high. Predy, or make ready to set sail, cross your yards, bring your cable to the capstan.

—John Smith, *A Sea Grammar,* 1626

CHAPTER 4

OCTOBER 8, THE AZORES

For except there be a uniting of knowledge with practice, there can be nothing excellent:
idle knowledge without practice, & ignorant practice without knowledge, serve unto
small purpose.

— WILLIAM BARLOW, *The Navigators Supply*, 1597

Azores

A few weeks have passed since *Guyft* departed Bristol. Hame has steered the ship in a southerly direction to its first replenishment stop in the Azores. Following a common route to the Americas that takes his ship south to the latitude of the Canary Islands in order to pick up prevailing trade winds westward, Hame stays alert to dangers as well as opportunities. "Opportunities" translates into privateering or piracy. Piracy is aggressive theft; privateering, technically allowed only in wartime under some circumstances, required a license from one's country to prey upon ships of an adversary. In fact, the term "privateering" was not yet in common parlance. Privateering relied on an ancient principle of securing "the right of reprisal."[1] Although in 1611 England is at peace with Spain and France, respect for sovereignty at sea sometimes differs from its landward counterpart. Merchant ships, which are armed, may employ their guns to beat off the competition or to prey upon them without serious risk of their

respective countries going to war with one another. Hame has harbored a grudge against the French for the past few years. Even after peace with Spain (1604), piracy has remained an ever-present threat. French pirates robbed Hame himself on board a merchant vessel in English inland waters. Hame seeks personal retribution.

Hame writes the log entry (see next page).[2] Note that "38G 20M" gives the latitude in degrees (G) and minutes (M). The modern degree (°) and minutes (') symbols were not in use in 1611. The hypothetical voyage follows the 1611 convention. Log-keeping was by no means common. Log books, variously known as traverse books or brief journals, became common during the first quarter of the seventeenth century, originally a narrative summary of each day's sailing, and later in a columnar format.[3] Masters of sailing vessels in expeditions of discovery, sponsored by merchant adventurers or trading companies, kept them for good business reasons: if a voyage proved successful, its sponsors would be keen to send subsequent voyages as a going concern. Trading

Months and days	Latitude	Course	Leagues	Winds
October 7, 1611	38G 20M	SW & by S	15	NW

The Discourse

Sighted I. of Tercera in the morning. Chased and overtook a French ship from Calais with pepper and cinnamon. William Norrys wounded by French cannon. In the afternoon, anchored in 6 fathoms at Tercera. We were forced to depart from thence by reason of a great tempest that suddenly arose in the night.

Almanac

Monday, Eighth Day of Feast of Sts. Marcellus et Apuleius, Martyrs. Saturn is southeast at sun setting, Jupiter is southeast at sun setting, Mars rises and sets with the sun, Venus is yet our bright morning star, Mercury is now our evening star. Full moon the 11th day at 5 a clock 53 minutes in the evening. Today is an evil day for undertaking an idle journey.

companies relied on logs to reduce risks, develop a predictable trade cycle whereby ships embarked on voyages at the same time each year, reached their destinations after a reliable interval of time, and returned with profitable cargoes before environmental circumstances (winter, hurricane season) required ships to be laid up for months. Hame's log or traverse book follows the format devised by Captain John Davis, exemplified in his *Seamans Secrets*.[4] The "Almanac" text is not part of the log as such; rather, the text is an extract from a published almanac for 1611, included here because almanacs were ubiquitous guides to predicting natural phenomena, used by sailors and landsmen alike. The data in three categories—course, leagues, and winds—relate to Hame's dead-reckoning tools, the compass, chip log, log and line, sandglass, and traverse board. In this chapter, we explore all of these except for the compass.

9. KEEPING A LOG — The ship's master prepares his log of the day's sailing. He records the date, course or heading, distance (in leagues) made good, wind direction, and latitude. Credit: Science Museum of Virginia

Dead-Reckoning Tools and Methods

The etymology of "dead reckoning" remains obscure, despite the efforts of some to ascribe it to colloquialisms such as "dead on" or "deduced reckoning." The term has come to refer to techniques that provide a running account of the ship's course and distance covered from the last measured position. Hame's essential dead-reckoning tools include the compass, log or chip log, sandglass, and traverse board, the device for recording speed and direction. According to a sixteenth-century source, "The quantity of the ship's way, to wit, how many leagues she sails in an hour, or a watch . . . they term the dead reckoning, and is learned by often experience."[5]

Lead and Line

Hame's most ancient navigational tool, and his most valuable, is the lead and line. Described as "a long plummet at the end, made hollow, wherein is put

10. TRAVERSE BOARD, COMPASS, SANDGLASS — The tools of dead reckoning. In the foreground is a boxed compass. Balanced on a pin pivot, the rotating compass card showing thirty-two winds bears a magnetized piece of iron underneath. Above the boxed compass is a traverse board. The board's upper portion depicts the compass rose of thirty-two wind directions. The navigator places a peg in a hole aligned with a compass direction for each half hour of a four-hour watch. At the end of four hours, the navigator infers the average course made good during the watch, records the information, and clears the board for the next watch. Pegs in the lower section of the board record the ship's speed. At right is a half-hour sandglass. Credit: Science Museum of Virginia

11. LEAD AND LINE ⟶ Captain Hame holds a lead and line. By casting it overboard, the navigator ascertains the depth of the water as the line, marked in fathoms, pays out. The lead weight contains a recess at the bottom into which the navigator plac-es a wad of tallow. When the lead hits the sea bottom, debris adheres to the tallow. When the navigator hauls in the lead, he can "read" his location by the combination of depth and type of debris underneath the ship. Credit: Science Museum of Virginia

tallow, that will bring up any gravel," this tool is a conical or cylindrical lead weight affixed to a line marked at intervals representing fathoms.[6] With it, Hame not only takes soundings but uses the depth measurement in conjunction with the nature of "the ground that sticks upon the tallow of the lead" to reckon his position in coastal or riverine waters.[7] Before "heaving the lead," Hame or his mate arm it by placing a small amount of tallow in the recess in the bottom of the lead. The tallow collected debris from the sea floor so that Hame observes the sam-ple's color, consistency, smell, and taste, and com-bines these data with the depth in fathoms to locate his ship. Hame and his contemporaries memorized thousands of locations based on a combination of soundings, observations of coastal features or land-marks, and the nature of the sea floor. Hame carries two kinds of leads, a hand lead weighing approxi-mately seven pounds (lbs) for shallow waters (up to 20 fathoms or so), and a deep-sea or "dipsie" lead

of between 10 and 14 lbs, used for deeper waters of 150–200 fathoms.[8]

Convention and tradition dictate how the line supporting the lead ought to be marked to indicate different depths. Captain John Smith instructs on how to mark a line:

Fetch the sounding line . . . [that] is marked at two fathoms next the lead with a piece of black leather, at three fathoms the like, but slit; at 5 fathoms with a piece of white cloth, at 7 fathoms with a piece of red in a piece of white leather, at 15 with a white cloth, etc. The sounding lead is six or seven pound weight, and near a foot long, he that do heave this lead stands by the horse, or in the chains [a small platform secured to the outside of the gunwale on which the mate stands to heave the lead; this plat-form secures rigging shrouds to actual chains], and does sing [shout] fathoms by the mark 5.0 and a shaftment less, 4.0 this is to find where the ship may sail by the depth of the water. Foul water is when she comes into shallow water where she

12. CHIP LOG ⤙ Captain Hame holds the chip log. The mate throws the chip—a weighted panel of wood—astern. Once it hits the water, the mate or another hand inverts a half-minute sandglass as the line pays out. The line is knotted at 47-foot intervals. The chip drags upright in the water, held vertically by a crowfoot attachment. Once the sandglass has run out, the navigator notes the number of knots that have passed overboard in the half minute. **The number of knots equates to speed of the ship in nautical miles per hour.** Credit: Science Museum of Virginia

raises the sand or ooze with her way yet not touch the ground, but she cannot feel her helm so well as in deep water.[9]

Sounding lines traditionally have been marked with an assortment of leather and colored cloth flags. The pilot "must also very often cast the lead, that he may most exactly note in his compt-book [account book], how far off, all the shoals and sands lie from the shore."[10] Hame records these data in his "compt-book."

Chip Log and Distance Measurement

The chip log, traverse board, and sandglasses supply the tools for determining and accounting for speed and distance. The determination of speed and distance covered require measurements with respect to a unit of time. As we have seen, the sandglass times all shipboard work. Glass-timed events range from a half minute to four hours, the length of a watch. To determine the ship's speed, the pilot employed the log and line. William Bourne provides the earliest description of this technique in English:

> They have a piece of wood & a line to veer out overboard, with a small line of a great length which they make fast at one end, and at the other end and middle, they have a piece of a line which they make fast with a small thread to stand like unto a crowfoot: for this purpose, that it should drive astern as fast as the ship do go away from it, always having the line so ready that it goes out as fast as the ship goes. In like manner they have either a minute of an hour glass, or else a known part of an hour by some number of words, or such other like, so that the line being veered out and stopped just with that time that the glass is out, or the number of words spoken, which done, they haul in the log or piece of wood again, and look how many fathoms the ship has gone in the time: that being known, what part of a league soever it be, they multiply the number of fathoms, by the portion of time or part of an hour. Whereby you may know justly how many leagues and parts of a league the ship goes in an hour.[11]

The "piece of wood," the chip, was secured to the line in three places, the line splayed like a "crowfoot" to afford maximum drag behind the ship. The knots are strands of light line spliced into the longer one. When Thomas Blunt throws the chip into the water, another sailor holds the reel as the line pays out, and a third sailor counts the knots in the line as they pass over the taffrail or gunwale. This requires finesse: the chip must hit water undisturbed by the ship's wake. Extra stray line must be paid out to get the chip clear of the ship.[12]

Bourne suggests that a glass may not always be available, and the mate would have had to count out the intervals. To avoid the need for computation, Hame knotted his line at about 42–47-feet intervals or about 6 or 7 fathoms so that, by timing according to a half-minute glass, he could translate, say, 3 knots into 3 nautical miles per hour, or one league per hour. Although a nautical mile represents one minute of latitude, during Hame's day no international agreement obtains about the precise length of a degree, and even Bourne notes that an English league consists of 2,500 fathoms, a Spanish league 2,857 fathoms.[13] Further, not all of Hame's contemporaries trust the chip log.

To record the ship's progress, Blunt resorts to a traverse board, a wooden panel showing a large compass rose, with eight small holes radiating from the center along each wind. He places a small wooden peg into the hole nearest the center to denote the ship's heading during the half hour. At the turning of the glass a half hour later, Blunt repeats the procedure, placing a peg in the second hole away from the center along the appropriate wind direction. A contemporary seamanship guide describes the use of the traverse board:

> Is a board which they keep in the steerage, having the 32 points of the compass marked in it, with little holes on every point, like a noddy-board, that is for him at the helm, to keep (as it were) a score, how many glasses they have gone upon of the compass, and so strike a pin on that point; this is to

save the master a labor, who cannot with so much curiosity, watch every wind and course so exactly as he at helm, especially when we go by a wind, and the wind veers and hulls.[14]

At the end of four hours, Blunt will have inserted eight pegs into the board. Hame then determines the average course made good during the previous four hours and uses this information to direct the helmsman. To William Bourne, the old coasters—"those ancient masters of ships"—within his acquaintance disdained the use of charts, preferring to "keep a better account upon a board."[15]

Hame's traverse board has another use: Blunt inserts a peg into a numbered hole below the compass rose to record the ship's speed. Measuring the ship's speed enables Hame to determine distance run: distance equals speed multiplied by time. If speed measurements over, say, a four-hour watch show that the ship has maintained a constant speed, then Hame multiplies the measured speed by the four hours to obtain distance made good. Aside from the direct measurement of the ship's speed, the lateral movement of the chip log astern in the ship's wake gives Hame a rough indication of leeway, a sideways motion of the ship owing to the wind: a compass reading of the direction of the tug on the chip in the ship's wake, compared to the ship's heading, gauges leeway.

Rutters

Long before recognizable charts came into existence, pilots relied on oral transmission of sailing directions. Early written sailing directions have been known since antiquity, attesting to an ancient pedigree for the observational skill of the seaman and the imperative to share practical knowledge with fellow sailors. Sailing directions have formed a common vernacular of seafaring peoples from the Byzantine *peripli* to the Italian *portolani* (evolving into an early chart, the portulan or portolan), by the thirteenth century

the German *seebuch*, by the fourteenth century the Dutch *leeskaarten*, Portuguese *roteiros*, and Spanish *derrotas*, the latter term giving rise to the French *routier* or English rutter, or route guide. Hame and his contemporaries all possessed rutters. In the previous chapter we quoted from a rutter regarding the Bristol Channel. Hame's waggoner (also described in the previous chapter) might have absorbed information from an early rutter. North Atlantic sailors shared the vernacular and technology of pilotage, and early sailing directions identified phenomena and features crucial to navigation, now systematically found on modern charts with common, international symbols. The nature of the information contained in rutters, and the expression of this information, attest to the practice of dead reckoning with the instruments described in this chapter.

Tercera

After the morning's action with the French vessel, *Guyft* reaches the Azores at the Island of Tercera. Today, October 8, Hame decides to reconnoiter the island's coastline before returning to the anchorage: mindful of the French presence, Hame wants to ensure that no threat lurks nearby. Further, yesterday's anchorage was not ideal: Hame prefers a broad bay with an anchorage close to shore. Last night, a sudden, violent rainstorm forced Hame to make for open sea to protect the ship, but almost immediately the storm abated, and *Guyft* returned to its anchorage. Early this morning, *Guyft* weighed anchor and under a northeast wind coasted a few miles to find a better anchorage and a place to take on provisions. By midday, the wind shifted to north-northeast, and by early afternoon, northeast by north. Unsettled conditions took *Guyft* into evening, the wind shifting to north-northwest in the late afternoon, and by evening northeasterly again, accompanied by more rain. Hame's coasting has an urgent purpose: he needs to obtain fresh victuals and repair leakage that has worsened because of the rain. Ferdinando Morgan describes the Azores, and the Island of Tercera in particular. We include Morgan's descriptions of the islands visited along the way to Virginia because, like Virginia, these places represent part of the Atlantic world familiar to Hame and his crew. For passengers who have not yet seen anything outside of England, the islands are no less exotic than their destination:

> The Isles of Azores, or the Flemish Islands, are Tercera, Saint Mary, Saint George, Gratiosa, Pico, and Faiael. There are yet two islands called Flores and Corvo, which are not contained under the name of Azores: but yet at this day are under the government of the same islands. They are called Azores, that is to say, sparhawks or hawks, because in their first discovery, many sparhawks were found in them, whereof they hold the name, although at this day there is not any there to be found. They are also called the Flemish Islands, that is, of the Netherlanders, because the first that inhabited the same, were Netherlanders.
>
> The principal island of them all is that of Tercera, called Insula de Jesus Christus of Tercera. It is between 15 or 16 miles in compass, and is altogether a great cliff of land, whereby in it there is little room, for it is walled round about with cliffs, but where any strand or sand is, there stands a fort. It has no good havens for the security and safety of the ships, but only before the chief town called Angra, where it has an open haven, which in form is like a half-moon. This town of Angra is not only the chief town of Tercera, but also of all other towns within the islands thereabouts. Therein is resident the bishop, the governor for the king, and the chief place of judgement, or tribunal seat of all the Islands of the Azores.
>
> The island is likewise very fruitful and pleasant, it has much corn and wine. It abounds in flesh, fish, and all other necessaries and meats for man's body, wherewith in time of need they might help themselves. For fruits they have cherries, plums, walnuts, hazelnuts, chestnuts, but those not very good; of apples, pears, oranges and lemons, with all such like fruits there are sufficient.
>
> The principallest traffick of this island is their woad, such as we use for dying, whereof much is made in that island, and is fetched from thence by Englishmen, Scots, and Frenchmen, in barter for clothes and other wares, who continually traffick into that island.
>
> The island has not any wild beasts or fowls, but very few, saving only Canary birds, which are there by thousands, where many birders take them, and thereof make a daily living, by carrying them into divers places.
>
> All those islands are inhabited by Portugals [Portuguese]: but since the troubles in Portugal, there have been divers Spanish soldiers sent thither, and a Spanish governor, that keep all the forts and castles in their possessions. The Isle of Tercera stands in 39 degrees [latitude].[16]

The incident with the French merchant ship yesterday has troubled Hame. He has taken on extra cargo that he did not anticipate as a result of his piracy, but a fragment of shot fired by the French ship injured a key member of his small crew, William Norrys. As we noted in Chapter Three, the master gunner, in company with the ship's master, carpenter, and boatswain, is a skilled member of the crew. Sylvester Heale, the master gunner, possesses a skill similar to that of the navigator with its combination of apprenticeship, craft ability, and formal early scientific knowledge.[17] Norrys had been learning this skill, and had expectations of greater remuneration for his service in coming years with expanded opportunities among the trading companies.

Further, Captain Lynnis is concerned that Hame jeopardized the safety of his passengers and their supplies by diverting *Guyft* instead of making for Tercera and fresh victuals. No one on board ship debates with Hame, however, the legitimacy of taking a French prize: at this time, all merchant vessels are armed, and for good reason. As we have seen, privateering permits the confiscation of cargoes in wartime or in reprisal, say, for a robbery suffered during peacetime. Hame, though, has no license to plunder French ships, but English ships compete with French ones, particularly in the New World where both England and France have made territorial claims, and merchant masters of both countries take liberties with the law. Admiralty officials stand to gain a percentage

13. The Azores, from Richard Hakluyt's *The Principal Navigations* — Although not identified on this Atlantic map, the Azores group (lower left) marks a halfway stop for voyages to North America along a northern route. For Captain Hame on a southern route, however, the Azores mark the first of three stops before heading west across the ocean to the New World. This map shows the mythical Isle of Brasil to the north. Credit: The Rosenbach Museum & Library, Philadelphia, shelf mark A589p

of the sale of Hame's confiscated cargo.

Hame recounts yesterday's piracy:

> On the morning of October 7, we had sight of the island towards which we sailed all that day. The same day we had sight of a little ship, which we chased towards Tercera, the weather being calm, and we overtook her to descry whence she came. Approaching near, some shot passed betwixt us, whereby, their captain putting forth his flag of France, we perceived that some fight was likely to follow.
>
> Having therefore fitted ourselves for them, we made what haste we could towards them with regard always to get the wind of them. But after some few shot, and some little fight passed betwixt us, they yielded themselves and the master of their ship came aboard us, showing their passport from Calais. They had certain bags of pepper and cinnamon, which they confessed to be the goods of a Jew in Lisbon, which should have been carried by them into their country, to his factor there.
>
> And so finding the ship and its commodities by their own confession to be lawful prize, the same was soon after taken and divided among our whole

company, the value whereof was esteemed to be about 4,500 pounds at two shillings the pound.

> We then came to the Island of Tercera where we determined to take in some fresh water and fresh victuals, such as the island did afford. We sent our boat to the road to sound the depth, to see if there was any anchoring place for us, where we might lie without shot of the castle and fort.[18]

Norrys' Wound

Whereas Morgan describes the new environments he discovers, Hame enters his record with a merchant's eye, emphasizing matters of navigation and safety. During the fray, a French cannonball struck and splintered the gunwale, sending fragments of metal and wood into seaman William Norrys' thigh. Fortunately, *Guyft* counts a surgeon among ship's company, Gerard Chilson. Many merchant ships carried no trained medical professionals, but in any case, crews would have had the use of a surgeon's or an apothecary's chest. Medical professionals of Hame's era belong to a hierarchy of fraternities, with, at the most prestigious end, physicians, university-educated practitioners, people who prescribe medicine and diagnose illness, although they may or may not have examined the patient.[19] Lower on the hierarchy, surgeons, or barber-surgeons, perform surgery on patients, the skill learned through apprenticeship under guild oversight by the Chartered Company of Barber-Surgeons. The icon of the barber-surgeon is the red-and-white striped pole, still seen at barber shops today, which symbolizes blood and bandages.[20] Finally, at the lower end of the medical hierarchy is the apothecary who mixes and provides the physic or medicine. Because apothecaries import medicinal ingredients, they are classed with grocers. In 1606 apothecaries were combined with grocers into a single guild, but they separated by 1617.[21] Although at the lower echelon of the medical professions, apothecaries suffer no mean reputation; rather, they act independently within a wide network, providing medicines to physicians, or directly administering to the population at large.[22] Importantly, apothecaries enjoy a monopoly on the provision of medicinal chests on board navy ships.[23]

We can infer much about medical practices on board merchant ships thanks to John Woodall (1569–1643), dubbed the "Father of Sea Surgery" owing to his 1617 treatise, *The Surgions Mate*, the first textbook published specifically for surgeons at sea.[24] Woodall was particularly qualified to promote standards in medicine at sea as he first apprenticed as a London barber-surgeon, and later was appointed surgeon-general to the East India Company, under which office he directed the appointments of surgeons' mates and the furnishing of medicine chests on ships. *The Surgions Mate* was intended as a manual to supplement the chests. The text systematically inventories necessary surgical instruments and describes their uses, lists medicines and their applications, outlines first-aid procedures, contains the first discussion of scurvy and its treatment in English, and concludes with a lesson on medicinal chemistry.[25]

Gerard Chilson has examined Norrys' wound but at first could not locate any shrapnel. Woodall advises caution in entering the wound:

> The use of a probe can no way be forborne in the surgeon's chest, for no chirurgical [surgical] work is well and artificially effected without some occasion of the use thereof . . . oftentimes it is to be armed with dry soft lint to cleanse a wound: sometimes again . . . armed with dry lint and dipped into some lotion, oil or liquor, therewith to . . . corrode or heal the grief . . . sometimes to inquire the depth of a wound
> . . . in which work many times great wrong is done by unconscionable or ignorant surgeons, to their patients by forcing too far the probe, thereby to make the grief appear deeper, which I advise young surgeons to make a conscience of, for by such abuse the patient is many times greatly endangered of his life.[26]

Chilson knows the advice that Woodall will later publish as common practice. He agrees with Woodall's dictum to "take away whatsoever is besides nature, as iron, wood, lead, or ought else with fit instruments, and that without pain, if it may be . . . that consolidation may the better be affected."[27] On the specific type of wound that afflicts Norrys, however, Woodall cautions, "Wounds made by gunshot are always compound, never simple, and are the more difficult of cure by reason of a certain humor without the veins found near them inclining to corruption, the quality thereof being changed by the sudden violence of the blow. The composition of which wounds for the most part consists of loss of substance, contusion, fraction of many sinewy fibers, veins, arteries, membranes and bones, yea often shivered into divers pieces."[28] Alarmed at the complexity of Norrys' wound, Chilson follows Woodall's advice and aims to prevent hemorrhaging and the onset of gangrene. To this end, Chilson observes the wound frequently, applies salves that resist putrefaction "and which are grateful to the vital faculties," administers a little wine or barley water, and keeps Norrys' bowels "loose

Months and days	Latitude	Course	Leagues	Winds
October 8, 1611				

The Discourse
We anchored and sent the boat to shore for water, bartering with our own goods.

Almanac
Tuesday, Feast of St. Pelagia the Virgin. Today is a good day to get the start of him.

with glisters [enemas], or suppositories," allowing him to bleed a little "lest poison or venom [settle] in the outward parts [and] be thereby drawn in back into the more noble parts."[29]

Chilson has not organized the medicinal and surgical chest to any standard. Although he possesses his own surgical kit, the ship's chest contains drug jars or bottles in an upper tier, with salves or ointments in pewter containers underneath. Other components of the chest include vinegar (to use as an antiseptic), splints, cupping glasses, chafing dishes, probes of various sizes, lengths, and materials, with clean cloth, lint, or lawn (linen cloth) to attach to probes for applying medicines.[30]

Today, October 8, Ferdinando Morgan continues his narrative as *Guyft* drops anchor at a promising inlet, deploys the pinnace, and sends a contingent of sailors and colonists to obtain provisions. The crew members proceed tentatively, cautiously, uncertain of the response they will evoke in the islanders: "So we manned our boat and rowed to the shore. Whereto when we approached, the inhabitants that were assembled at the lading place, put forth a flag of truce, whereupon we also did the like. We gave them to understand that we meant only to have some fresh water and fresh victuals of them, by way of exchange for some provision that we had, as oil, wine, or pepper, to which they presently agreed willingly, and sent some of their company for beefs and sheep."[31]

Hame's crew was fortunate, and after taking on victuals, in the afternoon *Guyft* made its way back to its original anchorage, the wind having now shifted.

Hame considers the events of the day and begins the log with this summary observation on the wind:

> October 8: We had the wind at north and by east with a very strong gale the which we prayed God to continue to his will and pleasure.[32]

Hame's version of the forage for supplies pays attention to the rain and its consequences, a matter overlooked by Morgan in his account:

> On the evening of the seventh, we were forced to depart from our anchorage by reason of a great tempest that suddenly arose in the night, in so much that soon after midnight our men were raised out of their cabins to weigh anchor, and after cheering them up with wine, all officers together with them hauled at the capstan.
>
> Tuesday, the eighth day. We sent our boat for fresh water, which by reason of the rain that fell the former night came plentifully running down the hills. The ship was now very foul, and much grown with long being at sea. When the rain fell, the raindrops were carefully saved. Some hanged up sheets, tied with cords by the four corners, with a weight in the midst, that the water might run down thither, and so be received into some vessel set or hanged underneath. And that water which fell down and washed away the filth and soiling of the ship, trod under foot. At every scup-hole and other place where it ran down, with dishes, pots, cans, and jars, whereof some drunk hearty draughts even as it was, mud and all, without tarrying to cleanse or settle it.[33]

During the recent rainy weather, *Guyft* developed a leak: "We stopped a leak on the larboard bow betwixt wind & water or rather under water. Got in some water and repaired other things decayed in the ship. . . . Wednesday, the ninth day, about four of the clock in the morning we weighed not able to ride any longer under the island, and not long after it became calm and so continued until 12 of the clock. Then we cast about and went SW 3 leagues and from thence till 12 the next day SSE 10 leagues."[34] A leak on board a sailing vessel in 1611 is no anomaly: preserving watertightness is an ever-present objective of all crew. A wooden vessel at sea for weeks is a study in decay. The oakum between planks rots and disappears; the seams between planks open; leaks develop and may go undetected for days, even weeks. In certain climates and seas, the *teredo* shipworm can perforate and reduce timbers just as termites can weaken and destroy house frames.[35] In 1611, the crew plugged a major leak with the same technology as in modern metal warships in battle: with whatever works. Crew on a modern naval vessel might shore a hole with a mattress, for example. On *Guyft*, Hame's carpenter, Roger Coopy, takes charge, aided by passenger John Collyns, himself a sawyer. Coopy has directed that a sail, or portion of a sail be prepared to enclose a wad of oakum. Under Coopy's direction, the crew positions the plug over the hull until an inflow of water sucks the bag into the opening.[36] At the next opportunity, perhaps days later, when the ship makes an anchorage, Hame will order that the hull be careened and examined, whereupon Coopy and his assistants will fix it. Today, however, Coopy has found the leaks annoying and troublesome, but not major.

Charts

The last tool in Hame's non-astronomical instrument kit, alongside his glass, lead and line, chip log, and compass, is his chart. Maps display cities, roads, and topographical information, all land fixtures. Charts reveal the seascape. Charts are unconcerned about cities and roads: the only landward features they contain are those visible from the sea. A modern chart conveys the direction and prevailing force of winds and currents; depth; navigational hazards; commercial shipping routes; and a frame of reference, longitude and latitude. We are so accustomed to relying on maps that we are unconscious of the assumptions we share about the representation of distance and space.

Hame carries multiple charts. Charts are not benign products of scientific endeavor and empiricism about the seascape: they are political tools, emblems of power. Charts are works in progress: mariners are expected to correct or complete them during voyages. Hame and his contemporaries share methods of representing the natural world and the foreign peoples they encounter through a complex whole of technological power that includes navigation and writing and charts, gunpowder and ships.[37] The geometric conception of space familiar to us is not that of Hame. Hame's fraternity of mariners—whether Spanish, English, French, or Dutch—view maps and charts as a new way to conceptualize space. Europeans "were only beginning to think cartographically."[38] Hame represents the seascape not through images but through text. In requesting details of the West Indies, early Spanish colonial managers asked for narratives, not pictures.[39] Before charts, the first treatises on navigation, rutters or sailing directions, were written texts. Portolan charts derived from them, at first as a visual accompaniment to written sailing directions and later as a device for plotting courses, concomitant with the development and refinement of globes.[40] The rediscovery of Claudius Ptolemy's *Geography* in the fifteenth century, a text that represented the earth as a two-dimensional map contained within a grid, provided a visual model that has informed geography and navigation ever since. "Better to delineate all on a card rather than a globe," writes William Cuningham, "because we can see all at once."[41] In time, the portolan evolved from a visual record of coastlines and the distances and bearings between

14. Measuring distance on a chart: Caribbean to Virginia — Chart work in 1611. The navigator uses a pair of dividers to estimate the number of leagues that he will sail along a rhumb line (lines emanating from compass roses) from the West Indies to the Chesapeake Bay. The navigator places the dividers, spanned to the distance between these two locations, against a scale of leagues (at right on the chart, underneath the image of open dividers) for a rough gauge of distance. The dots on the scale of leagues are one hundred leagues apart. Here, the navigator aligns *Guyft's* course from the Indies to the Chesapeake with the nearest rhumb line that approximates his intended course. Working that rhumb line back to the compass rose, Captain Hame can tell at a glance what course to instruct the helmsman. Credit: Science Museum of Virginia

them, to a true chart, with, initially, a latitude scale.

Although a Cartesian coordinate system for fixing and describing locations in space is years away, the notion of a geographical grid had become common in navigational cartography and in terrestrial mapping to fix places within space. The depiction of motion, however, was not a component. The English visual imagination had moved quickly from the concept of a closed to an open space in nature with no absolute barriers to exploration.[42] Professional surveying was in the ascendancy during the last half of the sixteenth century, in no small part due to the needs of landowners following the dissolution of the monasteries under Henry VIII. Surveying and linear perspective, in fact, produced a "secular topography" that proved very popular in the proliferation of maps.[43] Hame's mathematical learning informs many practical activities, including cartography, a subject evolving rapidly with its "complex pageant of geographical ideologies."[44] William Bourne argues that "those people that are able to benefit their country by their travail [travel]," ought to go abroad with an informed mathematical judgment built of practical methods to apply John Dee's argument for applied mathematics in all human endeavors.[45] In navigation, Euclidean geometry and its linear perspective

15. DETERMINING POSITION ON A CHART ⸺ A method of determining position on a chart by using two pairs of dividers. At far left, the navigator places one foot of the dividers at the ship's estimated position (A), and the other foot on the rhumb line which represents *Guyft's* course (B). At right, the navigator places one foot of the second pair of dividers on the vertical latitude scale at the latitude he has calculated for the ship (C), and the other foot on an east–west line nearest the latitude calculation (D). Ensuring that compass feet (B) and (D) stay on their rhumb and east–west lines, he then draws the compass feet to one another. When the measured latitude and course meet, the navigator reckons that the intersection point represents his location. This method is detailed in Martín Cortés, *Arte of Navigation*, **1561.** Credit: Science Museum of Virginia

expressed a ship's movement through a grid "that [the ship's pilot] may set down the prick thereof upon his card."[46] In time, geometric order came to be associated with a moral order.[47]

For a marine chart, however, applying a geometrical grid in order to depict journeys in straight lines led to gross error as a ship entered extreme northerly or southerly latitudes, owing to the convergence of longitude lines and the changing measure of a degree of latitude near the poles. The most significant navigational insight of late Tudor times was to create a chart in which a ship's course crossed meridians at the same angle in a straight line. Flemish cartographer Gerard

Mercator's projection, the basis for maps hung in classrooms around the world, solved this problem by allowing a ship's track to be shown as a straight line cutting each successive meridian at the same angle. The stunning virtue of this projection was to depict, on a plane, longitude and latitude lines at right angles to one another, no matter how northerly or southerly, so that the ship's path could be plotted linearly. The Mercator projection was perhaps the most crucial navigational achievement since the Portuguese practically invented nautical astronomy.[48] Ironically, just as the Mercator projection fixed one problem, the landmasses, recognizable by sight, were necessarily

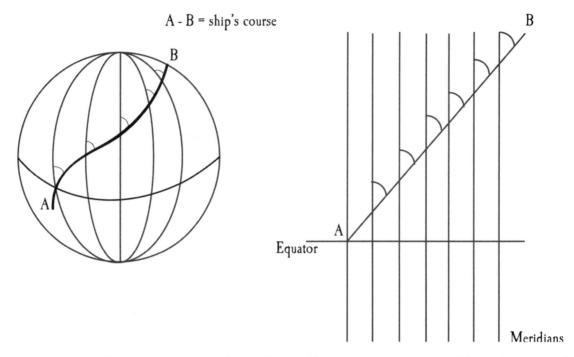

A - B = ship's course

B

B

A

A

Equator

Meridians

16. RHUMBS AND THE MERCATOR PROJECTION ⁓ Captain Hame and his contemporaries experienced frustration in reconciling course finding on a chart and a globe. Crossing meridians on a globe at a constant angle produces a spiral path as the ship voyages north. Further, plane charts did not enable straight-line plotting over long distances. To ease plotting so that great circles cross meridians at the same angle on a chart, Gerard Mercator stretched the separation of parallels of latitude to enable loxodromes (lines of constant bearing) to be plotted as straight lines. Credit: Evi Numen

distorted beyond recognition on a Mercator chart. On a globe, crossing meridians at a common angle created a spiral path toward polar regions, owing to the convergence of meridians. Because of this, John Davis dubbed "the true motion of the ship upon any course, . . . neither circular nor straight, but concurred or winding lines," as "paradoxal navigation."[49]

The depiction of motion remains a challenge. Hame has no language to express nor means to measure motion except for fixing the ship's position as successive intersections of reference circles on celestial (declination or right ascension) or terrestrial (latitude and longitude) spheres. To John Davis, three forms of navigation on a chart co-exist, all related to the depiction of motion, each of which the mariner must recognize and reconcile. First, horizontal navigation "manifests all the varieties of the ship's motion within the horizontal plane superficies," where a plotted ship's course is a straight line; second, paradoxal

navigation, already noted, with the ship's course being a spiral; and third, great circle navigation "upon a great circle drawn between any two places assigned," which involves elements of the other two.[50]

Hame embraces all available tools and techniques to understand and exploit charts, immediately conscious that, taken as a whole, they combine to reduce errors and produce an overall acceptable result. With additional voyages, Hame and his contemporaries find that the discrepancy between dead-reckoning techniques and reliance on compass bearings and measured distances, on the one hand, and astronomical methods on the other, are growing. This discrepancy owes to the translation of the earth's oblate spheroid onto a plane chart with the attendant distortions. As we shall see, Hame employs some geometrical methods to obtain longitude from a chart, but they require rules of thumb alongside calculation. His techniques work best near the equator, and it is within the tropical equatorial zone that *Guyft*'s track is easier to gauge and manipulate.[51]

Conclusion

Hame must now turn his attention to the next leg of the journey to the Canaries. The Canary Islands will furnish the last opportunity to replenish the ship's stores with fresh food before crossing the Atlantic. Hame's navigation has relied on an interdependence of compass, glass (sandglass), chart, log and line, and celestial techniques to reckon latitude. After *Guyft* departs the Canaries for the New World, we will consider Hame's methods of obtaining his latitude (Chapter 7). Hame pays particular attention to the variation of the compass (discussed in Chapter 6), a phenomenon that has engendered much speculation and anxiety, referred to by him and his contemporaries simply as "the variation." He and his contemporaries try to understand the phenomenon and harness it into predictability. Hame's navigation is tied to the performance of his ship: storms and leaks threaten to delay arrival in Virginia, and he worries about the wounding of sailor Norrys. The master's thoughts must encompass all of these challenges.

To manage all of the astronomical and dead-reckoning measurements, Hame heeds Captain John Davis, who instructs that successful navigation consists of three components:

> The pilot, in the execution of navigation, do with careful regard consider three especial things, whereupon the full practices are grounded.
>
> 1. Of which the first is, the good observations of his latitude . . .
> 2. The second is a careful regard unto his steerage, with very diligent examination of the truth of his compass, that it be without variation or other impediments.
> 3. And the third is a careful consideration of the number of leagues that the ship sails in every hour or watch, to the nearest estimation that

possibly he can give, for any two of these three practices being truly given, the third is thereby likewise known.[52]

As *Guyft* leaves Tercera, Ferdinando Morgan, with Hame's permission, offers a prayer in thanks for the voyage's safe passage thus far, and in hope for continued good fortune. Morgan worries about the rain and the leaks, fearing a dilapidation of the hull and a long interruption to repair it. He reads from a printed sermon, one of a handful in his personal papers. The sermon uses maritime imagery to assail the fair-wind religiosity of his shipmates:

> Then we will cry, convert thou us, O Lord, and so shall we be converted indeed. Then discouragement will seize upon us in an unseasonable time, and our sure foundation will be to lay when the rain falls, and the floods come, and the winds blow. A great part of men when they fall sick, are like them which commit themselves to the raging seas in a riven ship. Their religion and their faith is not the strong operation of the Lord within them, but a bare conceit of faith and a conceit of religion. And many professors are like fresh-water soldiers which brawl in taverns before they come to true employment, but after in due season do show neither courage nor hardiness. Much talking there is and much disputation of religious matters: but let us take heed that our courage fail us not then, when we must either stand fast or stick fast.[53]
>
> As David said, One thing have I desired of the Lord, that I will require, and will not alter this petition into another, that I may dwell in the house of the Lord all the days of my life to behold the beauty of the Lord, and to visit his temple. For as he said Mount Zion is the joy of the whole earth, to wit, as far as God has any people in the earth belonging to his election. For in it (says the prophet) he speaks forth all his glory. This is the ark, out of which there is no salvation: all else is a flood 15 cubits above the highest mountains.[54]

The sermon reminds the passengers and crew of their humility before forces that dwarf them and can consign their ship to oblivion. *Guyft* voyages on.

And since navigation is the means whereby countries are discovered, and community drawn between nation and nation, the word of God published to the blessed recovery of the foreign offcasts [outcasts] from whence it has pleased his divine Majesty as yet to detain the brightness of his glory: and that by navigation commonweals through mutual trade are not only sustained, but mightily enriched, with how great esteem ought the painful seaman to be embraced by whose hard adventures such excellent benefits are achieved, for by his exceeding great hazards the form of the earth, the quantities of countries, the diversity of nations and the natures of zones, climates, countries, and people, are apparently made known unto us.

—John Davis, *The Seamans Secrets*, 1607

CHAPTER 5

"BEHOLDING THE DIVERSITY OF DAYS AND NIGHTS": The Universe of 1611

The heavens declare the glory of God, and the firmament shows the work of his hands. Day unto day utters the same, and night unto night teaches knowledge.

—Psalm 19, quoted in Charles Turnbull, A perfect and easie Treatise of the use of the coelestiall Globe, etc., 1585

For segments of the voyage, days resemble other days. The weather conditions may change little, and shipboard tasks are performed according to the prescribed routine. When the sameness of days begins to yield subtle differences, Tristram Hame takes notice. The comparative monotony of long-distance voyaging forces attention on details. The color, texture, and smell of the ocean, distant clouds that form over land, the hue of the western sky at sunset all offer cues to location, to distance run, to changes in wind direction that may require a course change. To better harness a change in wind direction while heading into it, Hame may order the ship to tack or maneuver through a broad reach. The arc of the apparent trajectory of the sun each day alters as *Guyft* voyages south, the sun appearing higher in the sky. At night, a faint sky glow demarcates the sea horizon from the starry dome. Without obstructions to obscure the sky and without interference from sources of light, Hame watches the apparent fixed stars move around the earth. He requires no provocation to imagine a Ptolemaic universe centered on his ship: while at sea, everything in nature happens around *Guyft*. The celestial dome surmounting his ship gives Hame the local time, the direction to true north, and his latitude. It also reveals celestial wayfarers, the planets, in their zodiacal courses, their apparent direct and retrograde movements furnishing ocular proof of the frictionless character of the crystalline spheres that contain their observed movement. To navigate, Hame matches his acquired mathematical models of the seascape and heavens to a cognitive map based on experience and observation.[1] Hame's navigational tools function as mathematical models that impress a new order of measurement onto an older one of correspondences and hierarchies of being.[2] Mathematical models require a new observational discourse that absorbs an older moral order. In this chapter, we explore Hame's universe and glimpse how he learned the cosmology and astronomy that shape it.

Moral and Geometrical Order

Through his apprenticeship and attendance at Gresham College lectures, Hame has learned to comprehend his observable universe as consisting of tiered domains, from the mutable and decaying sublunar sphere, the quotidian world of life and death, to the immutable and fixed celestial hierarchies of stars and angels. Hame's navigational instruments and associated texts may serve practical ends, but they also attest to a moral order in the universe. In this moral order man—and an Englishman, particularly—occupies the pinnacle of earth's natural life with all else within the sublunar realm subordinate to his interests.[3] As Samuel Purchas writes, "This our earth is truly English, and therefore this land is justly yours O English. Thus we have discovered the English right by discovery, possession, prescription."[4] The consequence of this subordination is a universe created for man's disposal but hostile to him because of Adam's sin. God resides beyond the sublunar sphere, above the crystalline spheres that propel the planets and contain the stars. The geocentric model of the universe, theologically important, persisted for navigational use. Robert Recorde writes that the "liquid heavens not only govern time itself, but utterly stand clear from all corruption of time. Oh worthy temple of God's magnificence," a common view.[5] The convergence of religious doctrine, ancient explanations of cause and effect in the cosmos, and the persistence of the Ptolemaic universe of sub- and superlunar spheres reinforces Hame's notions of correspondences between the macro- and microcosmos. God heads the hierarchy of celestial beings over man just as man heads the hierarchy over beasts.[6] The use of navigational instruments is proof of nature's subordination to man's intellect. God gave man the facility of invention to make tools. Correspondences present

in nature mean that phenomena in the seascape, including the apparent motions of celestial bodies, reflect God's heavenly order, made visible for man's use through measurement. To William Barlow, God directs international commerce, having provided navigational tools for the purpose: "I perceived that God . . . had ordained the sailing compass to be the notable means and instrument of this intercourse . . . to join dispersed nations."[7]

Correspondences are correlations of bodily phenomena with external phenomena. Modern astrology is a vestige of this once-pervasive belief that the cosmos has a direct relationship to the health, appetites, and thoughts of human beings.[8] Because God's purposes are enigmatic, hidden meanings lurk behind appearances, and explanation means a language redolent of allegory and analogy in order to decode the world.[9] Nature provides a text, an encyclopedia of meanings and interpretations.[10] The prevalence of misfortune and ill luck, particularly dramatic when voyaging over oceans, fuels a preoccupation with elaborate explanations for causality in earthly affairs, the ultimate cryptogram of life.[11] William Barlow states that the sea must be understood as an instrument of God's will, that God "alone is the lord of the seas, that all storms and tempests do but fulfill his will and pleasure, that all the waves of the sea are continually at his commandment."[12] The seascape and its attendant meteorological phenomena assume moral importance: a thunderstorm, a gale, or even a calm sea might betoken a prodigy (a natural phenomenon that reflected spiritual malaise due to sin), a reflection of man's moral state, or a portent of divine judgment.[13] Hame and his shipmates may impute divine intervention to many phenomena as the working of providence, for God was the instrument of all earthly happenings, no matter how apparently trivial. Providence was a code word for God's unalterable plan, which means that every accident, success, failure in one's life was divinely decreed. There is no random occurrence, no true accident of fate.[14] To Samuel Purchas, the seascape was less significant as a natural phenomenon than as a prodigy: "But at sea . . . no earth is seen, only the Heaven (the walls of our Father's palace) and the inconstant shifting elements, which constantly put us in mind of our pilgrimage, and how near in a thin ship, and thinner, weaker, tenderer body we dwell to death, teaching us daily to number our days, and apply our hearts to wisdom."[15] To Purchas, navigation enables man to assert supremacy over the sea:

> And when the sea had, as it were, rebelled against rebellious man, so that all in whose nosethrils [nostrils] was the breath of life, and all that was in the dry land died, yet then did it all that time endure the yoke of man, in that first of ships the ark of Noah. . . . Thus should man at once lose half his inheritance, if the art of navigation did not enable him to manage this untamed beast, and with the bridle of the winds, and saddle of his shipping to make him serviceable.[16]

The prodigal or providential role of the sea might get in the way. William Barlow found the ocean odious, an interference with his interest in navigation: "Even when I was young and strongest, I altogether abhorred the sea: howbeit, that antipathy of my body against . . . so barbarous an element, could never hinder the sympathy of my mind, and hearty affection towards so worthy an art as navigation is."[17] Perhaps for Barlow's reasons, no romantic literature of the sea exists in Hame's day, and virtually no literature of the sea characterizes the period.[18] Aristotelian notions of the currents and tidal theory constitute the only literature on the causes of oceanographic phenomena. To John Flavel, "The sea produces nothing memorable."[19] Hame and his fellow English or northern European navigators perceive the ocean as a space of ambiguous legal status ripe for exploitation.[20] The sea's characteristics also render it unpossessible.[21]

Hame's observations with a cross-staff or astrolabe confirm the moral order of the universe by demonstrating celestial phenomena as predicted.[22] True to Purchas' view of the seascape, Hame thinks of his sea road as a brutish and menacing fluid element,

which imposes a trial on man. His altitude-measuring instruments, however, promise mastery by projecting geometrical models onto the sky and sea. The oceans presented a generalized, unified space, but they also afforded a space to test these altitude-measuring instruments, thus linking ocean and sky into a mathematically defined space.[23] Therefore, as John Dee observes, the "master pilot" needs to be versed in "hydrography, astronomy, astrology, and horometry" [time reckoning], he must know "the common base, and foundation of all: namely arithmetic and geometry" in order to make and use instruments, plot courses, and "have expert conjecture of storms, tempests, and spouts."[24] Hame's charts encapsulate ideas about how best to represent the world, an intersection of observational and theoretical knowledge.[25]

Motion and Space

Today, locating anything in any space, and moving through any medium, whether the vacuum of space or underwater, can be depicted in any number of ways, aided by photography and computer imagery. In Hame's day, a fired cannonball is the fastest moving object. Speed is something people experience on horseback. The movement of celestial objects and the ocean currents, however rationalized, require a theory of motion. Hame's universe conforms to a Ptolemaic moral order with limited movement: celestial orbs move along tightly regulated paths with little superfluous motion. A cross-staff or astrolabe does not capture the motions of celestial objects. Rather, the motion of the sun and moon can only be fixed instrumentally by locating them along a succession of points, each point an intersection of reference circles within the celestial sphere. Does Hame make a conceptual leap in thinking that his geometrical models represent a reality, and that the models coincide with observed phenomena? This coincidence leads to standardized reference points or datums, the basis for more measurement. In later centuries, mathematical predictability will furnish other insights into the nature of the earth's topography. In our world, all observations, all discourse about the relationship of places, lands, and oceans are mathematical. Numbers reign.[26] We cannot assume, however, that Hame thinks that his mathematical models represent a reality. His instruments, to us, may model the observable universe, but Hame did not perhaps share this view. For him, instruments did not embody a philosophy. Instead, Hame applies a prescribed technique to measure a phenomenon, and then reduces (a modern term) the data to achieve an answer. His instruments are made for doing, not knowing.[27]

In the absence of a practical coordinate system to locate celestial phenomena in space (the familiar Cartesian system decades away), Hame employs non-mathematical descriptions of motion, dividing all forms of movement in the sublunar realm into the categories of natural and violent.[28] "The heaven's contrary ways have such a natural motion that never rests . . . [or] can be stayed by any violence," observes Dr. Recorde.[29] Aristotle held natural motion to be a quality inherent in the moving object, striving to help the object reach its correct place within the universe, whereas violent motion was imparted by an external force. Hame has absorbed these notions of Aristotelian movement from the writings of his contemporary, Captain John Davis. Violent motion adds to the disorder and decay of the sublunar realm. The sea is certainly in motion and is occasionally violent. To Aristotle, oceanic movement owes to the shifting moisture enveloping the earth, alternating between flowing water (to and from the earth's center) and evaporation.[30] The sea's violence reduces and corrupts, "the sufferings of the bellows of the seas [having] beaten away the feet of those hills, that are by the sea coasts."[31]

John Davis concerns himself only with the motions of the sun and moon, the objects of his cross-staff and tidal computer. He finds Aristotelian explanations barely adequate in light of his experience, yet frames the motions of the sun and moon in Ptolemaic terms. Lunar and planetary motion,

however, are not simple and easily predictable. He describes lunar motion from east to west as "caused by the violent swiftness of the diurnal motion of *primum mobile* [Prime or First Mover]."[32] However, the moon's "natural motion" is comprised of three subsidiary movements, "a swift motion" [of the perigee, or nearest point to earth], "a mean motion" [an average 13-degree daily motion], "and a slow motion [of the apogee, or farthest point from the earth, which moves], all which are performed by the divine ordinance of the Creator in 27 days and 8 hours nearest."[33] The Ptolemaic model remains in use in navigation today. The model is mankind-centered in a pre-ordained order.[34] The exigencies of navigation, the concern for exactitude, requires a recognition and understanding of lesser motions, the grand Ptolemaic scheme remaining intact. These additional movements beyond the east-west and west-east motions of the celestial sphere due to the Prime Mover show the elasticity of the Ptolemaic cosmos.

Climates

Richard Hakluyt espouses the cosmology of the day that divides the globe into zones or climates, the peculiar environments of each determining the cultures of the inhabitants and their commodities for trade. An ardent champion of America, Hakluyt posits an equivalence between Mediterranean and Virginian climates, observing that "between 30 and 63 degrees in America," an English plantation might realize: "spices and drugs, as pepper, cinnamon, cloves, rhubarb, musk called castor . . . silk worms, fairer then ours of Europe . . . salt for fishing; excellent vines . . . the soil apt to bear olives for oil; all kinds of fruits, as oranges, almonds, filberts, figs, plums."[35] In the "epistle dedicatory" of the 1600 second edition of the compilation of his voyages, Hakluyt writes to Sir Robert Cecil, "principal secretary" to Elizabeth I, of his economic arguments in support of his "western Atlantis or America," which were based on climate theory.[36]

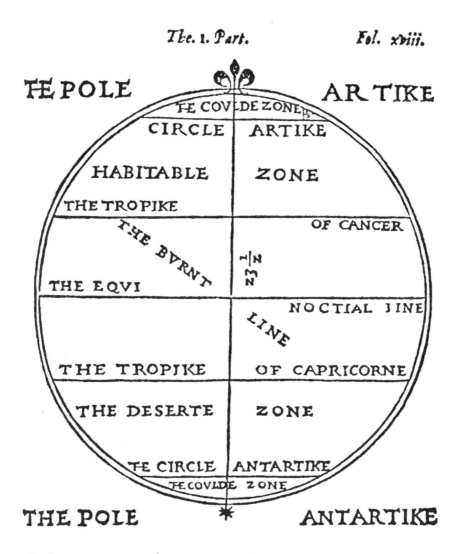

The. xvii. Chapter of longitude and
latitude: and of the proportion whiche
the lesse circles haue to the
great Circle.

17. CLIMATES AND ZONES — This diagram from Martín Cortés, *The Arte of Navigation*, 1561, represents an ideology about the earth's climate accepted by most authorities. Zones were classified based on temperature, nature of sunlight, flora and fauna, the environmental qualities determining the character of what peoples and cultures could survive within them. The zones embodied racial determinism in that environments of extreme cold and heat, for instance, determined the intelligence and aptitude of the inhabitants. Credit: Courtesy of the John Carter Brown Library at Brown University, shelf mark B561 C828a

In lectures at Gresham College and through his apprenticeship, Hame has learned a geographical paradigm, derived from classical authors, that the earth is divided into five climates or zones, two polar and two temperate regions and an equatorial torrid zone (a scheme not universally recognized). Each zone dictates a peculiar combination of flora and fauna: what flourishes in, say, Asia at a particular latitude should flourish in North America at the same latitude. The model of zones and climates forms a discussion in any cosmographical text, yet empirical evidence has begun to suggest flaws in the model. Despite the flaws, the paradigm remains and dictates the choice of settlement sites in North America. Navigating ships to America has generated data about magnetic variation, which complicates climates and zones. The new data have stimulated debate and new theories to account for variation, in turn leading to new instruments to measure it, as we will explore in the next chapter.

Before the voyage of *Guyft*, the idea of climates and zones influenced where the English thought they would settle, find precious commodities, and engage in trade.[37] Others have told Hame that both spices and precious metals should flourish in the torrid zone, including part of North America.[38] Hame suspects that climate theory relates to the origin and movement of ocean currents and winds, but so far his contemporaries have not articulated a coherent theory of currents, winds, and tides and their influence on climates.[39] Climate theory has an astrological frame of reference since each zone is governed by a triplicity of zodiacal signs, three signs for each of the four elements, which, set against planetary movement, influence the behavior of the zones' inhabitants.[40] As regions of like latitude correspond with one another astrologically, thermally, and seasonally, they also exhibit religious characteristics: south, a warm region, is associated with the Passion of Jesus; east, originally associated with the Holy Land, links to Eden.[41] These notions nestle within Hame's mind mixed with the empirical observations of his fellow seafarers. While some of Hame's contemporaries use "climate" and

"zone" interchangeably, William Cuningham distinguishes the terms: a zone "does in it contain the fifth portion of the earth, and a climate but only so much of the earth, and longest day in that place, do differ from the equinoctial 30 minutes, or half an hour."[42] By this system, the earth divides into five zones, subdivided into seven climates on each side of the equator. Each hemisphere, between the equinoctial and polar zones, divides into 21 parallels, every 4 degrees 15 minutes apart. The space between two parallels is a clime, based on Ptolemy's determination that the longest day of the year within each parallel was between 15 and 30 minutes longer than in the preceding one, measured north or south from the equator.[43] The ancient cosmographers had determined that seven climes in each hemisphere encircled the habitable regions. Hame's contemporaries disagree, however, about the number of climates.

North America for a long time presented only an obstacle to get around to reach sources of spices and metals. In time, however, merchant adventurers began to consider the middle Atlantic coast of North America as a Mediterranean equivalent. Hame recalls the French Huguenot settlement in Florida, established in 1562 and wiped out by the Spanish in 1565, which sought to replicate tropical agriculture.[44] Hame's sponsors speculate about what commodities might prosper in North America. They acknowledge climate theory but express doubts about its validity. John Davis's northern explorations convince them that the polar regions exhibit much local variation in climate.[45] Martín Cortés, too, describes the supposedly desolate polar and torrid zones and the habitable northern zone and concludes that the ancient authors erred because voyages of discovery have shown people living where they theoretically should not.[46] Hakluyt used George Best's narrative of Thomas Wyndham's 1553 voyage to Guinea to show the habitability of all of the earth's climates, thus refuting climate theory: "We . . . in England have black moors, Ethiopians, out of all parts of Torrida Zona, which . . . can well endure the cold of our country, and why should not

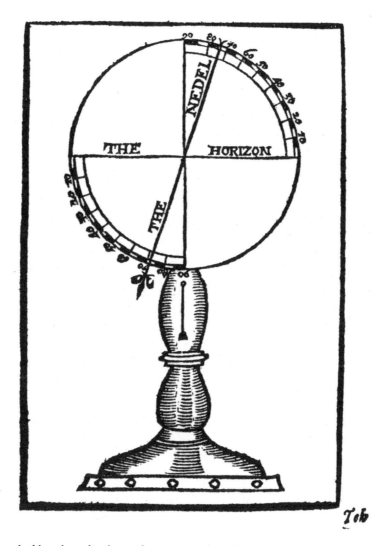

18. Dɪᴘ ᴄɪʀᴄʟᴇ ⁓ Mariners had long been familiar with a magnetized needle acting as direction finder. The magnetic properties of the earth, however, work in three dimensions. Magnetism can force the needle downward. The dip circle measures magnetism in a vertical plane. Many of Hame's contemporaries suspect that a catalog of magnetic variation for key places on the globe could aid in wayfinding. **This illustration appears in Robert Norman, *The Newe Attractive*, 1581.** Credit: Beinecke Rare Book and Manuscript Library, Yale University, shelf mark BEIN Taylor 170

we as well abide the heat of their country?"[47] Hakluyt expresses his belief that because God caused "all things in this lower world be given to man to have dominion and use thereof," then surely mankind can flourish in places thought uninhabitable, such as the polar regions during the summer.[48]

In the four decades between Cuningham and Thomas Blundeville, oceanic voyaging had upended the model of zones and climates for cartographic purposes, if not ideological ones. Blundeville finds the model explicated by Cuningham to be obsolete as it

no longer matches experience, and he suggests that the Mercator projection ought to replace the inexact system of parallels and climes because: "with Mercator . . . the best and most exact way of dividing the earth to serve all purposes is to be made by degrees and minutes, wherein is less error than in climes and parallels, neither can climes or parallels be so well described when you draw nigh to any of the poles, for that the spaces as well betwixt the parallels as betwixt the meridians do grow continually straighter and straighter."[49] In short, the cartographer's dilemma of proportionally adjusting degrees of longitude to those of latitude as the meridians converge at the poles required a mathematically exact solution, namely, the Mercator projection, which has lessened the hold of ancient zonal notions. Despite two reasons for abandoning the classical zonal system—that supposedly uninhabited regions were inhabited and that cartographic necessity required a Mercator projection based on mathematics—the system continued to be influential because of its symmetry and utility as an explanation for the distribution of the earth's commodities and peoples. Hame has read Hakluyt and the cosmographers and maintains a perspective that retains some climate theory with awareness that his fellow navigators are voyaging to places where, theoretically, no people are supposed to live. Magnetic variation and its implications, however, very much vex him. Complicating matters for Hame, zonal theory influenced a theory of magnetic variation.

In Hame's day, William Gilbert's researches into magnetism, following Robert Norman and William Borough closely, draws an analogy between the magnetic earth and the geographical one of climates and zones. Although Hame is ignorant of Gilbert's assertion that the earth is magnetic, his treatise, *De Magnete,* which built on the works of Norman and Borough, "was the first thoroughly experimental treatise."[50] It ranks with the works of Galileo and Kepler. Hydrographer Norman discussed the discovery of magnetic dip in his *The Newe Attractive,* co-published in 1581 with Borough's *A Discourse of the Variation,* which featured the first discussion in English of methods to measure compass variation. Both books—and that of Gilbert—stress reason, experience, and experiment as the key to understanding variation: Borough constructs a geometric model of magnetism while Norman had discovered magnetic declination (or dip) and invented an instrument for its exploration, the dip circle. Norman, over twenty years a navigator himself, was an instrument maker to Borough. Borough's book remained a standard work into the eighteenth century. Gilbert's investigations of the

terrella, a globular magnet, leads him to hypothesize that the earth itself is a massive lodestone with lines of magnetic force aligned with the meridians and parallels of latitude, "for the bodies [northern and southern hemispheres of the *terrella*] are equal distances from the poles and have equal changes of declination, and are attracted and held and come together under the action of like forces; just as regions of the earth on the same parallel, though they may differ in longitude, are said to have still the same quantity of daylight and the same climate."[51] Gilbert matches the cosmography of climates with his model of a magnetic earth. Mathematical cartography with its newfound reliance on Mercator's projection may be rendering climate theory obsolete, but zones still retain predictive value: some merchant adventurers still select the sites of their colonies based on what other regions of similar latitude were like. Further, Gilbert concludes what his predecessors have suggested, that the magnetic qualities of the earth are analogous to climates or zones. Magnetic variation, therefore, might vary according to climate, indirectly offering a way to determine one's location at sea. If this supposition is true, then observations with altitude-measuring instruments should be compared with compass readings.

Dr. John Dee, Tutor

Hame has attended lectures at Gresham College to learn navigation and related subjects, but he has also learned from fellow mariners, and has conversed with a few scholars who sought to apply their knowledge to the practical arts, especially the application of mathematics. When in the service of Martin Frobisher, Hame, among other pilots, learned astronomy, cartography, and navigation from John Dee. While Dee dies a few years before *Guyft* makes its voyage, and while Dee's active involvement with merchant ventures abroad was decades before 1600, as a young man Hame was fortunate in meeting this university-educated, mathematically adept scholar who tutored him in cosmography. Dee influenced the rise of mathematical navigation during the mid- to late sixteenth century and his multitudinous interests, contributions, acquaintances, and patrons set him within the center of European intellectual life. Further, Dee's own library, *Bibliotheca Mortlacensis*, one of the best in Europe, furnished a meeting ground for scholars, the court, seafarers, and independent inquirers, a place to which Hame was drawn. Hame also heard Dee argue for American colonization, for which he advocated strongly.[52] Dee understood the potential of mathematical navigation, and particularly sought to educate his country's seafarers. Dee's mathematical preface to the first English edition of Euclid, which Hame has read, has been celebrated in its own right for propelling the growth of navigation as a modern science. The translation of Euclid was remarkable as it came about through collaboration between Dee the scholar and Henry Billingsley, a merchant, "an informative connection between theory and practice."[53] Dee founded mathematical navigation in England.[54]

As teacher and adviser, Dee earns this credit. The Muscovy Company employed him to instruct its navigators in mathematical arts. His earliest known pupil was Richard Chancellor, later the two pilot brothers, Stephen and William Borough (who wrote the treatise on magnetic variation), and the last known pupil was John Davis, whose discussion of the types of navigation in his *Seamans Secrets* reflects Dee's teaching.[55] Dee's role as professional tutor, then, encompasses all of England's navigational achievements from the first tentative steps under Edward VI to the end of Elizabeth's reign. Aside from his responsibilities as a teacher and scientific adviser to the Muscovy Company, Dee contributed materially to the development of navigational instruments. His sojourn in Continental Europe ended with his return to England with celestial and terrestrial globes made by Gerard Mercator and an astronomical cross-staff made by Gemma Frisius, mathematics professor at Louvain, instruments much studied and emulated by the English.[56]

Further, Dee invented an early form of azimuth compass—a "sea compass"—consisting of a magnetized compass rose but with the innovation of a superimposed scale of degrees.[57] Dee also wrote what would have been the first, original navigational manual in English, now lost, with the planned title *The British Complement of Perfect Navigation*.[58] Dee's major cartographic achievement may have been his "paradoxal compass," a chart on a polar projection developed to help navigators search for the Northwest Passage. The pole occupies the center of the chart, the meridians of longitude radiating outward. Alas, Dee's paradoxal compass does not survive, although a circumpolar chart he prepared does. The paradoxal compass, however, may have been an independent invention of a Spanish device. Even Hame, however, is aware that Dee, despite skill in astronomical computation, had no practical experience at sea.[59] In modern cartographic terms, Dee's innovative chart, which may represent a major English achievement, shows a zenithal equidistant projection still used for sailing in Arctic waters. Dee perhaps intended his "sea compass" for use with this chart. About fifty years before Hame, the English imported all charts; no English chart-making center existed. Unlike Spain, England had no chart-making authority, no state apparatus to monitor or control the advance of cartographic knowledge. By Hame's voyage to Virginia, the situation had changed, yet Hame may have carried with him English charts, and also Dutch, Spanish, or French ones.[60]

Dee's preface to Euclid posits mathematics as the key to God's mind, the code of the Creation, the means God employed.[61] Dee begins his preface by asserting a "triple diversity" in all things, deemed supernatural, natural, or things mathematical, the latter exhibiting "a strange participation between things supernatural, immortal, intellectual, simple and indivisible."[62] This unity in Creation is accomplished through mathematics, which becomes the language of correspondence between the macrocosm and microcosm. Dee defines "cosmography" as "the whole and perfect description of the heavenly, and also elemental part of the world, and their homolo-gal [homologous] application, and mutual collation necessary."[63] Dee defends both the spiritual and prac-tical value of mathematics as interdependent: "No man, therefore, can doubt, but toward the attaining of knowledge, incomparable, and heavenly wisdom: mathematical speculations . . . are means, aids, and guides."[64] As the "principal example or pattern in the mind of the Creator," however, arithmetic reigns supreme: "Who can remain, therefore unpersuaded, to love, allow, and honor the excellent science of arithmetic? For, here, you may perceive that the little finger of arithmetic, is of more might and contriving,

then a hundred thousand men's wits . . . are able to perform . . . without help thereof."[65]

Where Hame is concerned, Dee has commit-ted his command of arithmetical knowledge to the improvement of artisanal skills and abilities.[66] Dee is an ideal scholar to tutor Hame; he can quote with facility from Recorde or Cuningham to teach his stu-dent "how, by the shortest good way, by the aptest direction, and in the shortest time, a sufficient ship . . . may be conducted."[67] Conversations between Hame and Dee mimic some of the pedagogical methods of the texts on navigation and cosmography that furnish the basis of Hame's instruction, particularly the mock dialogues between master and student.

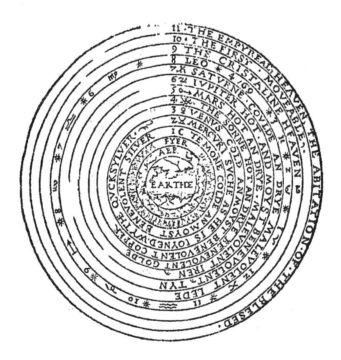

19. THE PTOLEMAIC COSMOS ⁓ This diagram, from Martín Cortés, *The Arte of Navigation*, 1561, shows the cosmos as Captain Hame has learned it. The celestial realm consists of concentric, circular zones within which heavenly bodies move around the earth. For Hame, the crucial barrier is that between the sublunar sphere—within which earth and its inhabitants are found—and the supralunar one of the planets, stars, sun, and moon. Credit: Courtesy of the John Carter Brown Library at Brown University, shelf mark B561 C828a

Cosmography

Texts on navigation have taken a common approach since they were first published. Readers first learn the conceptual basics of astronomy, cartography, and mathematics before making sense of the navigational tools and methods. The exposition on cosmography that follows offers an essential grounding in cosmography that Hame has to master. Cosmography for Hame and his contemporaries describes and explains their place in the universe. By contrast, navigation today relies on machines, instruments, and electronics to obtain one's position at sea (or on land, for that matter). For Hame, printed texts on cosmography use a customary didactic approach in conveying information through a dialogue between master and student. This dialogue is the pattern for Hame's private tutorials. Here, Hame recalls his basic instruction in cosmography and the celestial sphere.

Dee poses questions:

What is cosmography and how did it come to be so called?
Cosmography is the description of the world; that is, of the *cosmos*, the Greek for world, and *grapho*, for description. Cosmography is thus a description of the world.

What is the world?
The world is the universe of men made up of heaven, earth, the sea, and other elements. It is called "world" because it is always in motion and no rest is ever granted to it. This world is divided into two parts or regions, to wit: the celestial region and the region of the elements.[68]

The geocentric (earth-centered) model of the cosmos prevails in 1611. Copernicus had posited a mathematical model that included a heliocentric (sun-centered) cosmos over fifty years before, but in 1611 Galileo in Italy was beginning to tangle with church authorities over this issue. Hame and his contemporaries believe the geocentric or Ptolemaic cosmos, originated by Greek philosophers, to be a "true" depiction of the heavens. Modern readers may wonder how anyone could have believed in a geocentric

cosmos, but the reader should pause to consider proofs of the geo- or heliocentricity of the observable universe. Whatever proofs one may advance probably depend on technological innovations available only during the last few centuries. The geocentric cosmos was one of the most long-lived scientific models in history. In fact, most practical demonstrations or experiments—without telescopes or rocket travel—confirm the geocentric model, not the heliocentric one.

The diagram of the Ptolemaic cosmos shows the geocentric cosmology of early modern Europeans. Concentric circles move outward from the earth (which occupies the bottom of the cosmos more than its center), each circle containing a planetary orbit. In order of their appearance in the diagram, moving outward from earth, are *luna*, or moon; Mercury; Venus; Sol, or the sun; Mars; Jupiter; Saturn; the firmament of fixed stars (thought to be immutable); the crystalline sphere; the *primum mobile*; imperial heaven, where God and the angels reside. The planets shown are those known in Hame's era, all visible to the naked eye. The remaining planets (Uranus, Neptune, and Pluto) were discovered in later centuries. Beyond the planets, the crystalline concentric sphere encloses the fixed stars (as they were denoted during the Renaissance). Beyond the starry shell are two additional concentric spheres that make everything else move. The *primum mobile* imparts movement to the inferior spheres, and moves in the direction opposite to their courses. Below, Dee explains the other crystalline sphere, the second mover. Change and decay characterize the sublunar domain, which we inhabit. Comets and meteors are both viewed as disturbances of the upper air, still within the sublunar domain. The four elements—earth, air, fire, and water—account for the constitution of the earth and all life and non-life.

To resume Dee's instruction:

How is the world constituted?
The world is divided into two regions: celestial and elemental. The region elemental, which is

continually subject to alterations, is divided into four elements, earth, water, air, and fire. The heavenly or ethereal region contains the elemental world within it. The earth is a prick or point in the middest, called the center, to which they assign the lowest place. Next unto the earth and about it, the water occupies the second place, and the air the third. The fire is higher than any of the other elements. The four elements constitute all of nature in the sublunar realm.[69]

What is beyond the planets?
The knowledge of the planets was had by their sundry motions and by their courses not uniform to that of the stars in their heaven. The crystalline heaven compasses about or contains within it the heaven of the stars. This crystalline heaven is as transparent as clear water or glass. This crystalline heaven reaches to the first moveable heaven called the *primum mobile*. And this reaches to the empyrean heaven, so-called because of his clearness and resplendence. This does not move, and is most perfect. We believe by holy scripture that such a heaven is the habitation of angels and spiritual creatures.[70]

Dee links the four elements to bodily humors, a switch from macro- to microcosm. The discussion of humors bears on attitudes toward the health and diet of seamen. Further, these principles form the background to shipboard medical first aid, as we shall see. The four elements correspond with the humors, which constitute the essence of life; the humors derive from the elements and display qualities of hot and cold, warm and moist. Humors can be thought of as essences that make the body work. Proper health requires a balance of humors; injury or sickness requires medicine to restore the balance of the humors. Dee instructs in the key features of humoral theory:

Explain the elements and their qualities.
Earth is the most gross and ponderous element, and of her proper nature is cold and dry.
    Water is more subtle and light than earth, but in respect of air and fire, it is gross and heavy, and of her proper nature is cold and moist.

Air is more light and subtle than the other two, and being not altered with any exterior cause, is properly hot and moist.
    Fire is absolutely light and clear, and is the clarifier of other elements, if they be out of their natural temperance, and is properly hot and dry.[71]

How are the elements combined in man?
Complexion is a combination of two diverse qualities of the four elements in one body, as hot and dry of the fire; hot and moist of the air; cold and moist of the water; cold and dry of the earth. But although all these complexions be assembled in every body of man and woman, yet the body takes his denomination of those qualities, which abound in him, more than in the other.[72]

What are the different complexions among men?
Here are examples of two complexions. The body, where heat and moisture have sovereignty, is called *sanguine*, wherein air has pre-eminence, and it is perceived and known by these signs: hair plenty and red, the visage white and ruddy, and given to anger.
    A melancholic complexion is cold and dry, over whom the earth has dominion, as is perceived by these signs: hair plain and thin, dreams fearful, stiff in opinions.[73]

Once body types can be identified by their complexions, it follows that good health can be maintained by eating foods with qualities (hot, cold, moist, dry) that correspond with the complexions. Illnesses can be diagnosed and treated by balancing the humors.

What is the cause of sickness?
In the body of man are four principal humors, which continuing in proportion, that nature has limited, the body is free from all sickness. Contrary wise, by the increase or diminution of any of them in quantity or quality, unequal temperature comes into the body, which sickness, follows more or less, according to the lapse or decay of the temperatures of the said humors, which be these following: blood, phlegm, choler, and melancholy.
    Blood has pre-eminence over all other humors in sustaining of all living creatures, for it has more

conformity with the original cause of living, by reason of temperatures in heat and moisture.

Phlegm is a humor cold and moist, white and sweet, or without taste, engendered by insufficient decoction in the digestion of the watery or raw parts called *Chilus*.

Choler is the essence of blood wherein fire has dominion, and is engendered of the most subtle part of matter decocted, or boiled in the stomach, whose beginning is in the liver. Melancholy or black choler is the dregs of pure blood, and is known by blackness, and is very cold and dry.[74]

The active ingredients of life, however, which manifest themselves in complexions, are three "powers," animal, spiritual, and natural. While animal and natural powers "ordain, discern, and compose," spiritual powers make the body work.[75] Dee again:

What is spiritual power? How does spiritual power affect the body?
A spirit is any substance subtle, stirring the powers of the body to perform their operations, which is divided into three kinds. Natural spirits begin in the liver and spread unto all the whole body. Vital spirits proceed from the heart, and by the arteries are sent to all the body. Animal spirits, engendered in the brain, are sent by the sinews throughout the body and make sense or feeling.[76]

The source of Dee's teaching, Thomas Elyot's *The Castell of Health*, is popular because it combines formal medical education with practical observations. Elyot proposes that sound health requires proper diet, clean living, moderation in consumption, and exercise.[77] Following practices introduced decades earlier, Hame promotes a clean ship, encourages changes of clothing, and when he makes for a safe haven to careen the hull for maintenance, he fumigates the ship. Despite his lesson in a conservative framework of humoral theory, Hame is aware of other schools of thought on the nature of health and remedies for disease and illness, particularly stimulated by Paracelsus, whose influence extended to correlations, correspondences, and sympathies between things in nature. These relationships led to the promotion of chemical

treatments and remedies. Paracelsus (1493–1541) enjoys today fame for a spectrum of achievements and insights, but his influence in Hame's day includes the promotion of chemical medicines and the advancement of botany. Hame, as we shall see, however, like his seafaring contemporaries, will try anything that works or which experience has proved reliable.[78]

The Celestial Sphere

Hame has learned the conceptual basis for navigation within the context of a whole: the workings of the human body, the microcosmos, are reflected in the structure of the macrocosmos, the observable universe. To master astronomical navigation, Hame recognizes the invisible benchmarks that are essential to measurement. Dee acquaints Hame with the celestial sphere.

What shape hath the earth?
The earth is round, although some believe, more due to sight than to reason, that it is flat. But this is not so, because if the earth were flat, the waters of the rain which fall on the earth and rivers would no longer run to join and form lakes or pools in one place. Also there are stars which appear in one zone and not in another. The Egyptians see a star called Canopus which we do not see, and that would not happen if the earth were flat. We also see that an eclipse of the moon does not appear simultaneously to everyone.[79]

What are the poles of the earth?
The celestial poles are two points which we imagine to exist as they are the end points of the earth's axis.

What are the zones of the earth, and how are they found in the heavens?
Between the poles we divide the earth into five zones, just as we can imagine the whole of the round heavens likewise to be divided into zones. The first zone is that of the Arctic reaching from the Arctic Pole to the Arctic Circle. The second goes from the Arctic Circle to the Tropic of Cancer, the third extends from the Tropic of Cancer to the Tropic of Capricorn and through

A plaine Treatise of the first

principles of Cosmographie, and specially of the Spheare, representing the shape
of the whole world:
Together with all the chiefest and most necessarie vses thereof, written by M. *Blundevill* of
Newton Flotman, *Anno Dom.* 1594

The heauens declare the glory of God, and the
firmament sheweth his handy worke. Psal.19.

LONDON
Printed by *John Windet.* 1594

20. CELESTIAL SPHERE — This grand frontispiece to Thomas Blundeville, *His Exercises Containing Six Treatises*, 1594, depicts an armillary sphere with the celestial referents essential for navigation. The dark globe at center is the earth. Except for the zenith, nadir, and horizon, all of the circles must be inferred from angular measurements of the sun and stars. The horizontal ring rests on the heads of the lions. The zenith is marked at the top of the circle, directly overhead for anyone standing on the earth in a plane parallel to the horizon ring. The tropics of Cancer and Capricorn mark the extreme northerly and southerly points (solstices) on the sun's apparent path around the sky. This path, the ecliptic, is marked by alternating black and white squares. The axis capped by the fleur de lis extends the earth's poles to their heavenly counterparts on the celestial sphere.
Credit: Beinecke Rare Book and Manuscript Library, Yale University, shelf mark BEIN QB41 B55 1597

the middle passes the equinoctial line. The fourth zone reaches from the Tropic of Capricorn to the Antarctic Circle. The fifth zone reaches from the Antarctic Circle to the Antarctic Pole.[80]

To visualize the celestial sphere, we imagine the entire sky as a giant globe encircling the earth. The stars have different distances from the earth, of course, although in Hame's era, people imagined the stars as occupying a single concentric sphere around the earth, as shown in Illustration 19. For reference and navigational purposes, this model continues in use. As Dee instructs, just as the earth is represented as a globe with an equator and north and south poles, so is the sky. Hame imagines that the sky is one great shell with poles, an equator, and celestial latitude and longitude. Hame sees that the stars appear to move about the pole: does he conclude that the earth rotates on its axis, as the celestial sphere does? Historian Stephen Pumfrey describes the Elizabethan conception: "Because the Earth was stationary, these points or poles had no geophysical significance. It was the heavenly spheres, or rather space itself, that had physical polar points, joined by an axis with the centre of the universe as its mid-point. Any natural motion could therefore be classified in terms of straight-line motion to or from the centre, or a circular motion around the celestial axis. This concept of space is very different to our Newtonian concept that space is the same in all directions."[81] Although the celestial sphere consists of projections of the earth's poles and equator, these features do not correspond with bright, easily identifiable stars. The modern polestar, Polaris, is actually very close to the celestial north pole, but in 1611 it was almost 1.5 degrees from it. On the other hand, projecting the south pole does not lead to a star, just an apparently empty place. For modern navigational and astronomical purposes, the same scheme obtains, the celestial sphere is mapped by declination (analogous to latitude) and right ascension (analogous to longitude).

What is the meridian?
The meridian is a great circle extending through the poles and traversing the zenith, thus cutting the sphere into two parts. Wheresoever a man stands and at whatsoever time of year, when the sun shall come to the meridian, to him it shall be high noon. There are as many meridian lines as there are differences of habitations by longitude. "Meridian" comes from the Latin *meridianus*, meaning "of the moon, southern."[82]

What is the equinoctial?
The equinoctial is a great circle that divides the sphere into two parts, so that every part is equally distant from the poles. We imagine the equinoctial as the equator of the earth placed onto the heavenly sphere. For equality and regularity, the equinoctial is more noble than the zodiac.[83]

What is the zodiac?
The zodiac is a great circle that divides the sphere into two parts, and cuts the equinoctial by an oblique angle. This circle is divided into 12 parts, whereof every part is called a sign. The breadth of the zodiac is 12 degrees, and the zodiac divides along the middest line by the ecliptic, under which the sun and moon traverse the heavens. The signs of Cancer and Capricorn, about 23 degrees north and south of the equinoctial, show the places reached by the sun farthest from the equinoctial, the solstices. The sun is closest to us in June, which brings the hot and dry season. In December, when the sun is in Capricorn, it is farthest from us and brings cold and wet. The term "equinox" means "equalizer" because on the days when the sun crosses the equinoctial, day and night are of equal length.[84]

What is the horizon?
The horizon is a great circle that divides the heavens in two equal parts. The one half above the horizon is always in sight, for where the heavens and seas join together, that is the horizon. The horizon is not fixed in the firmament, but there are many horizons for each inhabitant of the earth. The horizon is the beginning of all altitude, for whatsoever is above the horizon has an altitude.[85]

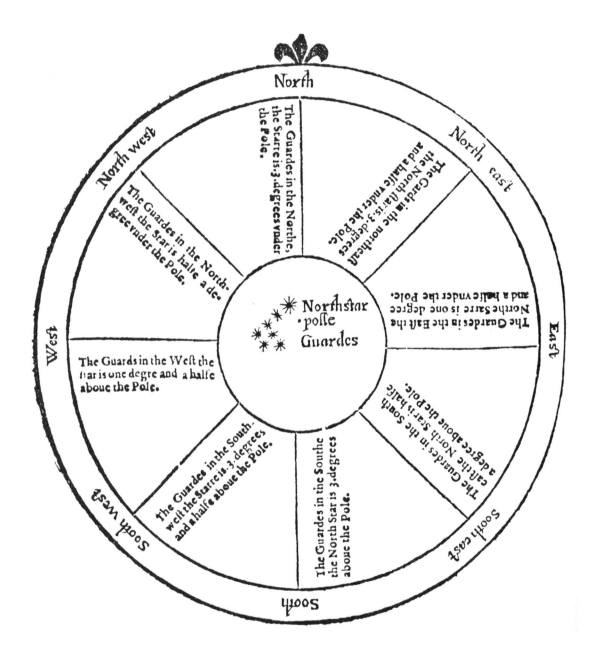

21. REGIMENT OF THE NORTH STAR — During Captain Hame's day, Polaris, the North Star did not occupy a point in the heavens at the celestial north pole. Polaris circumscribed a small circle about the pole each day with a diameter of about three degrees. The circle at center shows the constellation of the Little Dipper, the polestar, and the celestial north pole. The diagram instructs the user on correcting for the separation based on the configuration of the "guardes" about the pole. The guard stars are the two stars at the opposite end of the dipper from the polestar. When making observations of the polestar's altitude to reckon latitude, Hame uses this diagram from William Bourne, *A Regiment for the Sea*, 1574, to correct for the separation of the star from the celestial pole. Credit: William Bourne, *A Regiment for the Sea*, 1574. Reprint, introduction by E. G. R. Taylor (Cambridge: Cambridge University Press, 1963), 230. Reproduced by kind permission of the Syndics of Cambridge University Library, shelf mark 694:01.c.4.121

From the horizon, what are the points directly
above and below?
The zenith is that prick or point directly over your
head, and the point opposing, directly beneath
your feet, is the nadir.

What is latitude?
Latitude is that arc of the meridian between the
parallel of any place and the equator, or that part
of the meridian contained between the equinoctial
and the zenith, reckoned in degrees.[86]

What is longitude?
Longitude is that portion of the equator contained
between the meridian of Saint Michael, one of the
isles of the Azores, and the meridian of the place
whose longitude is desired.[87]

Today, longitude is measured from Greenwich,
England, but this datum did not become the convention until long after Hame's voyage. Contemporary
texts impose a system of *celestial* longitude and latitude. Dee, however, confines his discussion to terrestrial longitude. As John Davis explains, longitude
was reckoned from the datum of the island of Saint
Michael because magnetic compasses were thought to
show no magnetic variation there.

Declination is of great purpose in navigation.
What is it?
Declination is the distance of any body from the
equinoctial, or that part of the meridian that passes
through the center of any celestial body and the
equinoctial.[88]

Although measurements of celestial altitudes
are accomplished in degrees and segments of longitude are reckoned in degrees and minutes, true also of
declination, the application of degrees to computations is not straightforward. To John Davis, "a degree
is the 360 part of a circle, how big or little soever
the circle be," but he points out that there are several sorts of degrees, "to the equator, to the meridian, to the horizon, to the vertical circle, to measure
to time."[89] As applied to time, the sun apparently
moves through the sky 15 degrees for every hour, so

an arc of movement, in degrees, can be converted
into time, a principle essential to reckoning longitude with a chronometer about 150 years after Hame.
The application of degree scales on charts, however,
poses problems as a ship sails to extreme northerly
or southerly latitudes. As a globe reveals, all meridians of longitude converge at the poles. For a seafarer,
this presents obstacles to planning courses: does the
60-degree north latitude circle contain 60 minutes for
each degree, as opposed to latitude zero, the equator?
If so, does each degree, then, contain fewer minutes
at a northern latitude as opposed to a southern latitude? Fortunately for Hame, his transoceanic navigation is confined within a small span of latitude not far
from the equator.

Understanding the celestial sphere is essential for
Hame to visualize his location on earth and for com-
prehending the relationships between the equinoctial, meridians, the zodiac, and the poles for celestial
navigation. With this understanding, Hame knows
that the height or altitude of the north star above the
horizon, for any place on earth, *roughly* equates to his
latitude. The sun's altitude over the horizon also gives
latitude, but only after a few calculations that rely on
obtaining the sun's declination. Hame deems the sun
the more reliable indicator of latitude because the distance between Polaris and the celestial north pole
is more difficult to ascertain accurately. In his calculations, Hame must transform the visual into the
abstract, as he must determine the location of the
equinoctial. Any mariner can determine the location
of the zenith, directly overhead, and can see the sun.
With these two visible referents, the observer calculates the sun's height in order to arrive at the invisible
referent, the equinoctial. Later in the voyage, we shall
take Hame through an altitude observation and his
calculation to achieve latitude.

At night, Hame is particularly interested in the
circumpolar stars that never rise or set owing to their
proximity to the polestar. The celestial north pole,
occupied by the polestar, Polaris in Ursa Minor, the

22. NOCTURNAL — A nocturnal in use. For time-telling at night, Captain Hame first adjusts the extended tooth of the inner, serrated disk until the tooth matches today's date (note the months graduated along the circumference). Next, he holds this instrument against the sky so that he can view the polestar through the tiny hole at center. He then rotates the large arm ("y Index y Hora y Noctys") until its longer edge aligns with two pointer stars at the far end of the Little Dipper (Ursa Minor). He reads the local time on the serrated disk. The local time shown here is about 3:50 a.m. Another version uses a much longer arm to align with the pointer stars of the **Big Dipper.** Credit: Science Museum of Virginia

Little Dipper (known in Hame's era as the Lesser Bear), today appears as a fixed point in the sky, a pivot around which the entire celestial sphere seems to rotate. Polaris has been variously known as Stella Maris, the Loadstar or Lodestar, or the Steering Star. The polestar was more distant from the pole for Hame than now, necessitating rules of thumb to determine the location of the celestial pole given the configuration of the circumpolar constellations. To find Polaris, Hame locates the most prominent stars of Ursa Major (or the Great Bear) in the Big Dipper, always a circumpolar constellation in northern latitudes. Hame finds the two "guard" stars of the dipper's bowl, Dubhe and Merak, which point almost directly to Polaris. Once Hame locates the polestar, if he intends to use its height to determine his latitude (a check on latitude determined from the sun's height during the day), he has to introduce a correction as at any given moment the polestar might be 1.5 degrees above, below, or to the side of the celestial north pole. Martín Cortés describes the Big Dipper as a horn, and provides "common rules" for reckoning the location of the celestial north pole with respect to one of the guard stars and the polestar: "And as the guard is to the north according to the placing of these positions, so shall it be higher or lower from the pole."[90] In an earlier era, sailors memorized rules of thumb based on the figure of an imaginary man in the sky with outstretched arms, a "sky man," each limb superimposed on selected stars. When the sky man's left foot or right hand was in a given position, the mariner could determine the position of the polestar with respect to the true pole. Cortés, however, offers less evocative rules:

> The guard being in the north, the [pole]star is three degrees under the [celestial north] pole.
>
> The guard in the northwest, the star is half a degree under the pole.
>
> The guard in the west, the star is one degree and a half above the pole.[91]

Hame knows the circumpolar sky as a vast clock face. The local hour can be reckoned by the relative position of the Big Dipper (or Little Dipper) with respect to Polaris. Dubhe and Merak have been used as clock stars for at least 4,500 years. Two faint stars in the Little Dipper—beta and gamma Ursae Minoris—have also been used as guard stars or pointers, but they are fainter than Dubhe and Merak. Hame has a device, a nocturnal, to determine the local hour of night by the configuration of the Little and Big Dippers.

Conclusion

Guyft makes its way confidently toward its destination, master and crew having placed their fates in God's hands, the small ship not just a mechanical contrivance bearing cargo and humanity, but an organic whole in which the human actors work the vessel with wind and sea, sun and stars. Hame surveys the lone human contrivance within view, his ship, and meditates on the relationship between the macro- and microcosmos. Hame and his crew maintain intimacy with ocean currents, winds, and celestial movements outside of the experience of readers of this book. The safe passage of *Guyft* requires environmental alertness that informs action. At the same time, Hame guides his ship based on a vernacular of navigation that appropriates the sum total of what northern European and Mediterranean sailors have learned through their exertions over millennia. Submerged in histories that recount kingly rivalries and national ambitions, Hame, his crew, and passengers are easily overlooked. Hame's cosmography affords an understanding of his natural environment, locates him within its hierarchy of beasts, angels, and planets, and presents a universe as a unified whole no less mysterious and fascinating as that made possible by radio telescopes and space travel.

Historian Ursula Lamb, in her translation of a sixteenth-century Spanish text for pilots, asks: "Who were these . . . prestigious professionals, who, reduced to the democracy of common suffering aboard their ships, would walk ashore to deliberate with kings? These stargazers who would catch the movement in the heavens on a small scale or bronze ring and reduce the New World to lines on a chart?"[92] Tristram Hame belongs to a community of navigators, some of whom did indeed "walk ashore to deliberate with kings." We can be sure that Hame captured celestial phenomena with his scales engraved on boxwood or brass, confident that God placed him at sea and equipped him with His methods to exploit man's dominion for the prosperity of his country.

For albeit that men read or hear never so much of cosmography or astronomy, yet without practice and experience it is unperfect: and how can perfection be attained, but by sailing, and transporting from place to place, thereby beholding the diversity of days and nights, with the temperature of the air in sundry regions, whereby the whole course and revolution of the sphere is made apparent to man's capacity?

—JOHN TAPP, *The Sea-Mans Kalendar*, 1631

CHAPTER 6

OCTOBER 27, MADEIRA

The Magnes or Lodestone's Challenge

I guide the pilot's course
his helping hand I am,
The mariner delights in me,
so doth the merchant man.
My virtue lies unknown,
my secrets hidden are,
By me the court and commonweal,
are pleasured very far.
No ship could sail on seas,
her course to run aright,
Nor compass show the ready way,
were Magnes not of might.
The lodestone is the stone,
the only stone alone,
Deserving praise above the rest,
Whose virtues are unknown.

⸺ Robert Norman, *The Newe Attractive*, 1581

Madeira

Before crossing the Atlantic, *Guyft* makes for the Canary Islands by way of the island of Madeira, about 375 miles to the northeast. We are visiting the island way stations en route to the New World for three reasons: first, to illustrate the importance of the Atlantic islands to ships on long voyages for replenishment; second, prize-taking opportunities may materialize; third, the islands visited were colonized by Europeans a few centuries earlier, important steps in creating a global economy and thus remain places of interest

and fascination. Atlantic islands also gave many
European travelers important firsthand experience in
confronting foreign habitats. Transatlantic voyaging
means island-hopping. As the voyage enters the third
week of October, storms slow the ship's progress, caus-
ing damage and worry. Ferdinando Morgan records:

> We were tossed and turmoiled with such horri-
> ble stormy and tempestuous weather, that every
> man had best hold fast his can, cup, and dish in
> his hands, yea and himself too many times, by the
> ropes, rails, or sides of the ship, or else he should
> soon find all under foot.
>
> Herewith our main sail was torn from the yard
> and blown overboard quite away into the sea with-
> out recovery, and our other sails so rent and torn
> that hardly any of them escaped whole. The rag-
> ing waves and foaming surges of the sea came row-
> ling [roiling] like mountains one after another,
> and overraked the waist of the ship like a mighty
> river running over it, whereas in fair weather it was
> near 20 foot above the water. Thus it is writ in the

scripture, Psalms 107 vers. 26, "They mount up to
heaven, and descend to the deep: they reel to and
fro, and stagger like a drunken man, and all their
cunning is gone."

> With this extremity of foul weather the ship
> was tossed and shaken, that by the cracking noise
> it made, and by the leaking which was now much
> more than ordinary, we were in great fear it would
> have shaken asunder, so that now also we had just
> cause to pray a little.
>
> Notwithstanding it pleased God of his great
> goodness to deliver us out of this danger. Then
> forthwith a new mainsail was made and fastened
> to the yard, and the rest repaired as time and place
> would suffer.[1]

But no sooner had the new mainsail been fas-
tened to the yard, than fierce winds returned. Hame
now records:

> We made what sail we could, it blowing a very
> stiff gale of wind until eight in the evening of the
> 24th, then it began to blow fiercely, and we took in

23. MADEIRA, FROM RICHARD HAKLUYT'S *THE PRINCIPAL NAVIGATIONS* ⸺ Hakluyt's map shows but does not label Madeira,
almost due north of the Canary Islands. About five hundred miles from Portugal, the Romans knew the small Madeira
island group, rediscovered by the Portuguese in the fifteenth century. In Hame's day, two islands were inhabited. Credit: The
Rosenbach Museum & Library, Philadelphia, shelf mark A589p

our topsails, and stood under our two courses and bonnets. At nine, it blew a violent storm at SSE, so that we took in our foresail, and let her drive northwest. All the night it continued an extraordinary storm, so that we heaved the lead every half watch, but the ship did drive so fast, that she would be past the lead before there was twenty fathom of line out.[2] The sea was all in a breach, and to make up a perfect tempest, it did so rain and blow, all the night long, that I was never in the like. We shipped many seas, but one most dangerous which racked us fore and aft, that I verily thought I had sunk the ship. It struck her with such violence. The ship did labor most terribly in this distraction of wind and waves, and we had much ado to keep all things fast in the hold, and betwixt her decks.[3]

By the 25th, the ship began to experience fair wind and weather, and with a full gale, *Guyft* held its course southeasterly to within sight of Madeira, passing it to larboard, before coming about northward in a broad reach. Tristram Hame discovers, however, that the storm has aggravated the leak that *Guyft* developed near the Azores: "Friday, the 25th day, in the morning we put over a bonnet [a section of sail] with oakum [hemp roap fibers] to search for our leak but found it not. By midday we went having little wind and rummaged in the hold to search for our leak but could not find it, albeit we had a weeping of water in the larboard quarter abaft about the biscuit room. At midday we went till 12 the next day S[outh] 15 L[eagues]."[4]

Madeira had been a Portuguese dominion since the fifteenth century, but Spain now owns the island. Madeira provides a convenient replenishing spot en route to Virginia from England; it furnishes a stepping-stone between the Azores and the Canaries. Charts show Madeira as a fleck of land in the vast Atlantic, an appearance that does not reckon with its importance. At first, the island provided fresh supplies to Portuguese ships voyaging south along the African coast, and later for ships of several nations crossing the Atlantic. From the island's exploitation by the Portuguese through Hame's era and into the eighteenth century, the island occupied the nexus of a burgeoning Atlantic economy that created and long influenced international markets.[5] Sugarcane, under European control of the island, became the foundation of Madeira's wealth, along with wheat and wine. Madeira's export of sugarcane to Flanders, Italy, Tuscany, Portugal, England, France, Brittany, and even the Ottoman Empire, constituted an early Atlantic trade that provided the structure for Europe's New World trade. Brazilian sugar plantations, which superseded Madeira ones, were a product of the commercial structure that was built from Madeira westward.[6] Until sugar production began in Madeira, Europeans had imported it from the Islamic world, an eastward commercial focus. Hame not only obtains sugar and wine in Madeira, but he saw his first African slaves there, a key component to Atlantic trade.

Hame records his arrival in Madeiran waters in a log entry.

Months and days	Latitude	Course	Leagues	Winds
October 27, 1611	31G 12M	NNE	26	Strong NW

The Discourse
Made for Madeira, first coming S and E of the island, then making for it E & by N, then NNE, NE & by N, and NW into anchorage. Strong fresh winds swinging N to NW.
At midday we cast about being within 2 leagues of the shore, the land trending NE & by N, & SW & by S.

Almanac
Sunday. An evil day to rise up and fall.

Ferdinando Morgan describes Madeira:

> The Island of Madeira stands at 32 degrees dis-
> tant from the equinoctial line, and 70 leagues from
> the Isle of Tenerife northeastward and southwest
> from the Pillars of Hercules [Strait of Gibraltar].
> This island was conquered and inhabited by the
> Portugal nation. It was first called the Island of
> Madeira, by reason of the great wilderness of sun-
> dry sorts of trees that there did grow, and yet do,
> as cedars, cypress, pine trees, and divers others. It
> has one fair city called Fouchall, which has one fair
> port or harbor for ships, and a strong bulwark, and
> a fair cathedral church, with a bishop and other
> dignitaries. There are also sixteen sugar houses
> called Ingenios, which make excellent good sugar.
>   Besides goodly timber, the isle has great store
> of divers sorts of fruits, as pears, apples, plums, wild
> dates, peaches of divers sorts, melons, batatas [West
> Indian sweet potato], oranges, lemons, pomegran-
> ates, citrons, figs, and all manner of garden herbs.
> But chiefly this land produces great quantity of sin-
> gular good wines which are laden for many places.[7]

Madeira has a companion island, Porto Santo, and
both islands have been characterized for centuries as
mostly uncultivated in their interior. Hame enters
the harbor of Madeira carefully, as he would any harbor or road because he does not want to risk running
aground in shallow waters. He writes:

> At midday and for a few hours after we sounded
> at 12, 11 and 10 fathoms, finding white sand, and
> trending along the land 1 league NE, & 2 L. by E
> & ENE, and went till 8 of the clock at night SE 3
> L. & SE & by E 1 L, then we came to anchor, the
> wind being at SE & ESE till 9 the next day, at what
> time we set sail. In weighing our anchor we broke
> our cable a foot from the anchor, and so lost our
> anchor.[8]

The past few days have created misery: storms, leaks,
and a lost anchor. As he prepares to create the log
entry for October 28, Hame considers the events
of the previous night, when high winds came to his
anchorage:

> In the evening of the 27th, after surveying the
> coast, it was calm, and we came to an anchor. The
> tide set. There we rode all that night, and the next
> day: by reason the wind was contrary. There went
> a chopping short sea, and the ship did labor at it,
> exceedingly leaping in spritsail yard, forecastle,
> and all; for as yet we had not trimmed her well,
> to ride. About 9 at night on the 28th, it was very
> dark, and it did blow hard. We did perceive by the
> lead the ship did drive, wherefore bringing the
> cable to capstan, to heave in our cable (for we did
> think we had lost our anchor), the anchor hitched
> again, and upon the chopping of a sea, threw the
> men from the capstan. A small rope in the dark
> had gotten foul about the cable, and about the leg
> of Robert Pyke, but with the help of God he did
> clear himself, though not without sore bruising.
> The two mates were hurt, one in the head, the
> other in the arm.[9]

On the 29th, however, *Guyft* took on supplies of
fresh food and water, and despite the annoying leak,
Hame decides not to risk more chopping seas and
contrary winds that may delay the voyage. The wind
blew from the northwest in the morning, and as the
ship left its anchorage and coasted to reach a nearby
trading village, the wind shifted to west by north,
then west, west by south, and finally west. The westerly wind seems auspicious, so Hame decides to proceed south by west immediately to the Canaries.
"The wind shifted to W & by S contrary to our
course and in the afternoon we had a shroud storm
and we struck our sails and topmast but in the evening the wind came fair and so the storm ceased and
we set our main course half mast high."[10]

Acute observation of wind and clouds offers
Hame important clues to his location that he considers along with his periodic soundings and measurements of celestial altitudes. Although Hame does
not possess tools to give measurements of humid-
ity and the force of wind, he can sense changes in
these characteristics, the temperature, and type of
clouds to ascertain where the wind originates. For

instance, as the air temperature changes from day to night, a change in wind direction might betoken the direction to land, the source of a fresh breeze. The air immediately over the sea takes longer than air over land to heat during the day, but, once heated, it retains the heat longer than over land. As land cools while adjacent sea air remains warmer, cooler land air moves seaward as warm sea air rises. The direction of the cool breeze, then, indicates land; further, the breeze might bear the scent of trees or vegetation.[11] Hame combines his observation of wind with that of the swells that slap the ship's hull. Wind changes affect the superstructure of the ship, as yards are positioned to control and channel winds to best advantage. Even in modern sailing instruction, knowing the direction of the wind is paramount. Despite the

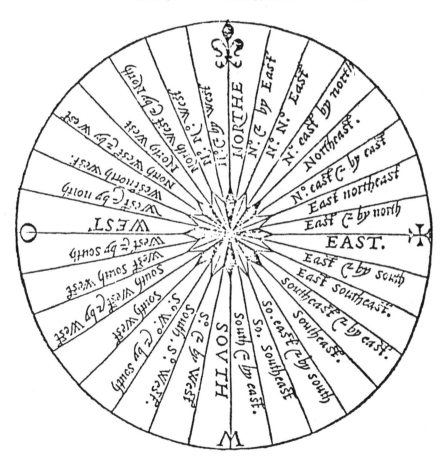

24. WIND ROSE ⌐ One of the first tasks requisite in a would-be navigator was the ability to "say" the compass. The compass rose became the vernacular of sailing. Captain Hame recognized the division of the horizon into thirty-two named directions as shown by the wind rose here, from Martín Cortés, *The Arte of Navigation,* 1561. Credit: Courtesy of the John Carter Brown Library at Brown University, shelf mark B561 C828a

movement of the wind, swells buffet the ship with little respect to the wind direction. Swells obey their own momentum, and only a prolonged, consistent change in wind alters their direction. Their direction, though, gives clues to the location of land. Swells may parallel a sustained wind toward land. As a ship approaches an island, swells begin to arc to the shape of the island coast.[12]

The Compass

Hame's notes reveal close attention to the compass. His magnetic compass consists of a box containing a circular piece of wood or cardboard, the fly, with a depiction of the wind rose, a diagram of thirty-two winds including the eight prime ones in black, half winds in green or blue, and quarter winds in red. Martín Cortés describes this color scheme in his *Arte of Navigation*, which had become, and remained, the convention.[13]

North is represented with a fleur de lis and east marked with a small cross (denoting the Holy Land), chart-making conventions possibly established by the Venetians about two centuries earlier. The fly, pivoted on a brass pin, rotates due to the magnetic quality of the wire or needle glued underneath. Hame keeps a

25. COMPASS HOUSED IN A BITTACLE ⟶ Captain Hame consults a compass at the binnacle or bittacle, which houses a candle and a sandglass. This compass, unlike the one shown in Illustration 10, is set within interlocking rings called gimbals. A gimbaled compass compensates for the motion of the ship. Credit: Science Museum of Virginia

piece of magnetite, a lodestone, in a case for periodic refreshing of the needle (by rubbing it). Rubbing the needle is a navigator's ritual: Hame has multiple compasses and he periodically strokes their needles with the lodestone to freshen them. Still, to Hame's consternation, his compasses do not always agree. Their needles might even change direction.[14] This essential configuration of the magnetic compass—the rotating fly, the wind rose, the magnetized needle—has been established in Europe for at least four centuries before 1611. Sophisticated compasses contain the fly within gimbals, or two rings of brass, "annexed the one within the other: which serve that the compass . . . hang not toward the one side or the other, although the ship sway."[15] Ships carry spare compasses and sandglasses as insurance against breakage or loss, but also for simultaneous use in several areas of the ship. Although he has no systematic understanding of the phenomenon, Hame knows about compass variation, the difference between magnetic and true north, and refers to it as "northeasting" or "northwesting" of the compass. Some of Hame's contemporaries, however, think that compass variation might be a key to determining longitude at sea.

Variation and Its Measurement

Hame and his contemporaries view the magnetic compass as indispensable to navigation, an instrument that eliminated the uncertainty of relying on clear days and nights to measure the height of the sun or polestar. Most importantly, the compass, "that moveable instrument with a fly, whereon are described the 32 points or winds by which we direct . . . our courses at sea," meant that trading voyages were uninhibited by season or weather, in some places taking place year-round.[16] Although the phenomenon of variation had been observed earlier in the East, by the late fourteenth century, Portuguese navigators were investigating magnetic variation, and the Spanish and Portuguese were first to develop a theory about it. By the early sixteenth century,

Iberian scholars had linked variation to longitude determination.[17] Portuguese efforts came into the hands of Dutch mathematician and engineer Simon Stevin who published *The Haven-Finding Art*, which advanced variation's relationship to longitude. Peter Plancius, a Dutch cartographer, devised a longitude finder, an instrument to determine longitude based on measured characteristics of variation.[18] For oceanic navigation, this discovery was vital, as during a long voyage, cumulative errors in variation might produce a deviation from true of 20 or more degrees.[19]

William Borough defines magnetic variation as "the arc of the horizon contained between the true meridian of any place and the magnetic meridian of the same, and is dominated to be easterly or westerly, according to the position of the magnetic meridian to the eastwards or westwards of the true meridian," hence the terms "northeasting" or "northwesting."[20] This mode of discourse probably derives from a common method of ascertaining variation. Observations of variation became an indispensable part of the pilot's work, for by the mid-seventeenth century, Henry Mainwaring describes three kinds of compasses as common to piloting practice: the "plain meridian compass," described above as the simple 32-point fly or compass card; the "dark compass," so called because it eliminated colors on the compass card for night use; and the "compass of variation," probably an azimuth or bearing compass with a 360-degree circle.[21] Magnetic variation also occurs in a vertical plane called dip. Some of Hame's contemporaries hold that magnetic north resides in the *sky*, a place called the "virtue attractive."[22]

To Hame and his contemporaries, the precise nature of variation remains elusive, however. The magnetic earth remains to this day a partially understood phenomenon. The earth's core is solid iron surrounded by a shell of molten metal, encased in solid matter once again. Complex chemical and physical processes produce a magnetic field, which, at the earth's surface, may change weekly or over millennia.[23] The behavior of a magnetized needle is also

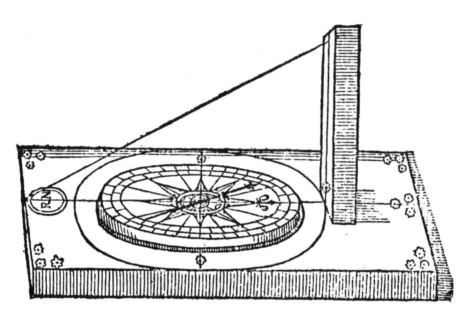

26. AZIMUTH COMPASS ↜ This woodcut from William Borough, A *Discourse of the Variation of the Cumpas*, 1581, shows a sighting mechanism atop a magnetic compass. Captain Hame notes where the shadow of the string, cast by the sun, falls on the compass card. Credit: Courtesy of the John Carter Brown Library at Brown University, shelf mark D581 B736d

complex, even though on Hame's compasses it moves solely within a horizontal plane. In modern terms, the earth has a dipole—the magnetic pole–inclined 11 degrees to the earth's axis. Magnetic *declination*—Hame's variation—is defined as the angle between geographic and magnetic meridians at any point on the globe.[24] In Hame's day, however, despite proliferating theories about magnetic rock, most navigators believe that magnetic variation exists, that a magnetic pole or center also exists, which rules all compass needles, whether terrestrial or celestial, and that some relationship links variation at a given location with longitude.[25]

Hame may enjoy confidence in his altitude measurements of the sun to determine latitude, but he is less confident when trying to mesh altitude observations with compass bearings and the attendant problem of variation. Importantly for the voyage of *Guyft* is the interdependence of terrestrial and celestial observations for position finding. Hame's contemporaries assume that variation is fixed for specific

locations, and on the assumption that a measurement of variation might help a pilot determine his position, the compass has undergone adaptation. The variation or azimuth compass evolved to allow the simultaneous reading of a magnetic bearing and an observation of a celestial body, usually the sun, which casts a shadow from a gnomon onto the compass face: the difference between the shadow alignment and the compass bearing showed the difference between magnetic and true north and hence the amount of local variation.[26]

William Borough's azimuth compass consisted of a perpendicular style with a single string to cast a shadow onto the compass face, to be used for equal-altitude measurement.[27] (Without clocks for timing celestial events, Hame uses the azimuth compass by the equal-altitude method, whereby he observes the sun ascending to some height before noon, then descending to the same height during the afternoon. A line bisecting the two observations gives true north, easily compared with magnetic north by the compass reading.[28] Say that in the morning the sun is 20 degrees altitude at the southeast point of the compass. When the sun is at 20 degrees again in the afternoon, you find that the compass indicates west-southwest. Notice that the southeast and west-southwest bearings are ten points apart. The midpoint between the two is south by west. If there is no variation, due south would be the halfway mark. Today, however, the variation is one point to the west. A related instrument, the amplitude compass, measured the sun's amplitude, or its azimuth at rising and setting, and a comparison between observations and published data yielded the difference between true and magnetic north or variation. Both variation compasses require the superimposition of a graduated 360-degree circle onto the traditional compass rose. In a short time, pilots combined the functions of an azimuth and amplitude compass by taking a simultaneous observation of the sun's altitude and azimuth in the morning and repeating the observation in the afternoon when the sun again occupied the same altitude, the mean of the two azimuths giving magnetic north and therefore variation.[29]

Publication of Norman's *Newe Attractive* and Borough's *Discourse of the Variation of the Cumpas* fueled interest in the dual observations of magnetic compass readings with solar altitudes.[30] Borough's book remained a standard work into the eighteenth century. Further, experiments with variation were tied to the rise of mathematical astronomy.[31] The azimuth compass blended celestial and terrestrial observations in a single instrument.[32]

If latitude can be reckoned by observations of celestial altitudes, then the possibility exists that variation might furnish the key to longitude determination. The major investigators—William Gilbert, William Bourne, William Borough, and Edward Wright—are skeptical. If variation can be proved to be idiosyncratic to a specific place, then longitude could be measured.[33] By the end of the sixteenth century, the English had tried to integrate variation into cartography with the Mercator projection and the

consequent adjustment of polar longitudes and latitudes to facilitate course plotting.[34] Just as zonal theory imposed an irresistible symmetry on the earth's topography, magnetic variation made sense as a geometric grid system: all that remained was to map the magnetic grid as analogous to latitude and longitude.

Among Hame's fellow navigators, no consensus exists on how best to reckon variation and make practical use of it. Norman expresses frustration about the superficial knowledge available about variation, its nature and behavior: "I wish the mariner to have a great regard unto this, as a principal point in navigation, and not to sail by a compass of one parish, and a plat [chart] of an other: I mean, that they have a respect . . . to sail by a compass of that country, where his plat was made."[35] In his publications, William Bourne discusses opinions about variation and agrees with Martín Cortés that it involves a proportional change.[36] Bourne thinks that magnetic compass readings can compensate for the effects of variation by offsetting the magnetic wire glued underneath the compass card.[37] Norman, though, argues against any proportion or uniformity in variation and asserts that any locale exhibits fixed, unchanging variation, therefore relevant to longitude determination.[38]

Borough proposes a better understanding of variation by close comparison of compass readings with solar altitude measurements. For instance, he recommends taking a solar altitude reading with an astrolabe to the nearest degree while simultaneously adjusting the shadow string on his azimuth compass so that the shadow falls upon a north–south line on the compass. He then compares the reading to that indicated by the north-pointing needle, the angle between the needle and the north–south line giving variation.[39] Thomas Blundeville takes a similar approach by proposing that the mariner compare meridian altitude observations of the sun as taken with a cross-staff and astrolabe, to compass bearings by the equal-amplitude method.[40] Dual observations using a shadow device on the compass itself compared with cross-staff or astrolabe measurements probably constituted the most common method for gauging variation. Borough introduced some geometric elaboration on this technique by showing how to use two solar observations to find the height of the pole, the local meridian, and variation simultaneously, working the solution on a globe.[41] Blundeville and his contemporaries clearly favor an experimental approach.

Hame has read Norman's pamphlet but could not make much sense of the companion essay by Borough because of the spherical trigonometry. Norman's experimental findings impress and distress Hame: impress, because of the arguments based on experiment; distress, because Norman introduces a new dimension in magnetic variation, dip (not to be confused with a correction to altitude observations of the sun, also called dip, detailed in the next chapter). Norman's pamphlet "set down a late experimental truth found in this [lodestone], contrary to the opinions of all them that have heretofore written thereof." He defines his discovery of dip as "the north point thereof would bend or decline downwards under the horizon," pointing to the "point respective."[42] So in addition to a needle responding to magnetism in a horizontal plane, Hame now considers that magnetism induces movement in a vertical plane as well. Hame does not carry a dip circle for observing this behavior. If he read Latin, he would find an experimental elaboration on dip in Gilbert's *De Magnete*.

Edward Wright and Simon Stevin weighed in with the last word on interpreting and measuring variation in the sixteenth century. Wright's *Certaine Errors in Navigation* signaled English supremacy in the navigational art.[43] In assessing the state of navigational practice, Wright bemoans the instruments commonly used as "much stained, with many blots and blemishes of error, and imperfection."[44] In particular, Wright articulates several related sources of error: faulty sea charts based on poor projections, coupled with the neglect of compass variation "as by some it . . . may cause you err an whole point or two in the courses of diverse places: and not rightly used has bred much confusion in many parts of the

chart."[45] Wright notes that charts commonly feature "an inextricable labyrinth of error" where variation is most pronounced, such as the Florida coast, Newfoundland, or "Nova Francia" (Canada).[46] His own published variation tables and his experiments with instruments of his own design, a variation compass (a compass within a 360-degree circle) and a mariner's ring, led him to articulate a way for mariners to apply a simple ruler and compass to determine the sun's true azimuth where the sun's altitude, declination, and therefore local latitude are known.[47] Wright, though, fresh from a seafaring venture to the Azores, cautions his readers about the best measurement one could reasonably achieve: "Exact truth amongst the inconstant waves of the sea is not to be looked for. . . . Yet with heedful diligence we may come so near the truth as the nature of the sea . . . will suffer us."[48] By the second edition of his *Certaine Errors*, Wright had begun to retreat from his opinions about the worth of variation studies to position finding.[49]

Stevin was one of the first investigators of magnetic phenomena to recognize the instability of variation, what became known as secular variation: "the magnetic needle touched with the lodestone . . . does not always point out the same part of the world, but without any respect of that magnetic pole . . . sometimes indeed it shows the true place of the north: but for the most part it declines either towards the east or west."[50] Stevin nevertheless advocates a study of variation for position finding and states in *The Haven-Finding Art* that if the pilot knows his latitude and his variation, then he can plot a course to a location of known variation.[51]

Tristram Hame's observations of variation are necessary for navigation, although the precise nature of the phenomenon and its utility for position finding remain elusive. Because studies of magnetic properties remain a part of experimental investigation, Hame hopes that his observations, as recorded in his log, will be of some value to others who are investigating the idea of a geometric magnetic grid superimposed on the earth, analogous to longitude and latitude that with further study may become a fruitful navigational tool. Many of Hame's contemporaries perceive variation to be part of symmetry in nature rendered intelligible through geometry. For our voyage, Hame records measurements of variation and employs an azimuth compass for direct measurements of the phenomenon. Hame knows key navigational texts of the period, has weighed various opinions about variation, and finds merit in the nexus between a magnetic grid system and the determination of longitude. Meanwhile, he must conduct observations of variation in tandem with observations of celestial altitudes as a way of independently determining his latitude if not longitude. This optimism about the use of variation will persist for decades among navigators.

William Barlow designed a compass that was the first for sea use with a graduated ring to take accurate bearings. His dedication to the Earl of Essex in *The Navigators Supply* includes the following anecdote about variation, which reveals an awkward moment for Sir Francis Drake, overconfidence in navigation by the compass, and the acrimony that could arise among ship's company at sea over the not insignificant matter of knowing precisely where they were:

> In the rude beginnings [of navigation] of former times, men were drawn by [variation] into many perplexities, yet in the settled experience of these our days they rejoice therein . . . as in a thing greatly concerning their good and welfare. But [variation] is a principal secret, only known unto those that are of greatest skill among them.
>
> A memorable example hereof fell out *Anno* 1586 when Sir Francis Drake, a gentleman of famous memory, in his West Indian victorious voyage, departing from the harbor of Cartagena, arrived some small time after at the westernmost point of Cuba, called Cape St. Antony, and having stayed there some few days, put to sea for Virginia, for the relief of our countrymen that were there in great danger and distress [the Roanoke colony]. Having continued at sea 16 days tossed with variable winds, they came at last within sight of land, but by no means could they discern, or give any probable guess what land it should be. So it was,

that one of Southampton, being an expert and skillful navigator . . . for his forwardness, having received disgrace before, was notwithstanding upon this necessity called unto conference, where, after Sir Francis had bestowed on him some part of his eloquent persuasions and fair promises, at length he undertakes to do his best. And having made his observations according unto art, he pronounced in laughing and disdainful manner (because his advise was not taken in the setting of their course) that look what land they had been at 16 days before, the very same precisely was the land that now they were at again. Which assertion of his being rejected, as a thing impossible, by all those of skill in the company, and especially by Sir Francis himself not without reproachful words, he still persevered therein, and assured them, that upon his life they should find it so, and in the end they did.

> This could never have been done without his knowledge of the variation of the compass. . . . Yea besides the particular knowledge of places, the expert navigator stands in great hope hereby to attain unto good helps [from variation] for the finding of longitudes. . . . But this is a matter somewhat dainty among the chief of them all. As for the rest, in all their conclusions about the variation, they may as yet . . . be well likened unto chapmen, who are merchandizing for the skin of a wild beast, before the beast be taken.[52]

Time and Tide

The compass serves not only to find direction, but the thirty-two equispaced points on the fly, the winds, provides the vernacular of navigation. Hame describes every movement of the ship in terms of the wind or compass bearing: he instructs the helmsman to steer along a particular wind, and all phenomena external to the ship, whether sunrise, an approaching storm, or a visible coastal feature, Hame describes by wind direction. To Captain John Davis, knowing one's compass (or boxing one's compass, in today's parlance) is the first task of any navigator.[53] In addition to wayfinding, Davis outlines the other important uses of compasses that Hame practices: expressing time and reckoning the tides. As Davis

27. TIDE COMPUTER ⚓ This tide computer is the reverse side of the nocturnal shown in Illustration 22. The long pointer shows the position of the sun along the ecliptic. Note the 360-degree graduation of the outermost part of the instrument, against which the sun's position can be shown. The middle disk with the smaller pointer represents the position of the moon. Using information from an almanac, the navigator adjusts the instrument to show the time of high water or high tide from a given location. As almanacs only gave this information for a few days in each month, the navigator must count forward to find the time of high tide for the current date. The computer therefore shows the relative positions of the sun and moon. Instead of giving the time of high water, the instrument gives the compass bearing of the moon at high water, which is more useful as Captain Hame does not have a reliable clock. Credit: Science Museum of Virginia

explains, "It has been an ancient custom among mariners to divide the compass into twenty-four equal parts or hours, by which they have used to distinguish time, supposing an east sun to be six of the clock, a southeast sun nine of the clock," and so on.[54]

Dividing twenty-four hours by thirty-two winds means that forty-five minutes separate each point. Once Hame understands the use of a compass template as a clock, then he can "know the alteration or shifting of tides, that thereby he may with the greater safety bring his ship into any barred port, haven, creek, or other place where tides are to be regarded."[55] To reckon tides with the compass, Hame understands some characteristics of lunar motion. Although ignorant of the causes of the tides, he knows that the spring tides (with the largest range between high and low water) occur within a few days of full moon or change (new moon), when the moon and sun are in conjunction, and that the neap tides (with the smallest range) occur within a few days of first and last quarter, when the moon and sun are 180 degrees apart. Each month contains two springs and two neaps.

To make use of the compass bearings for tidal prediction, Hame requires certain information from an almanac. If he does not have an almanac, he has to compute the moon's age by determining the epact and the prime. John Davis defines the prime (also known as the golden number) as "the space of 19 years, in which time the moon performs all the varieties of her motion with the sun, and at the end of 19 years begins the same revolution again, therefore the prime [which always begins in January] never exceeds the number of 19."[56] Computing the prime means adding 1 to the year and dividing by 19. The remainder after the quotient is the prime. Next, the epact (which always begins in March in Hame's era) is "a number proceeding from the [additional days] of the solar [over the] lunar year, which number never exceeds 30, because the moon's age never exceeds 30."[57] To compute the epact, multiply the prime by 11 and divide by 30. Eleven days approximates the

difference between the solar year of 365 days and the lunar year of 354 days.

Example: With an electronic calculator, assume that, applied to the year 1611, the prime, by these rules, is 15 (1611 + 1, or 1612, divided by 19 gives 84 and a decimal. Nineteen multiplied by 84 gives 1596, or 15 years short of 1611). For the epact, 15 multiplied by 11 gives 165, and divided by 30 gives 5 and a decimal. Multiply 5 by 30 to obtain 150: the difference between this and 165 is a remainder of 15 days. Fifteen is the epact. These calculations enabled the mariner to determine the moon's age. To obtain the moon's age, the mariner adds the day of the month, the number of months "there are between the said month and March, including both months," and the epact. For example, for October 28, add 28 + 6 (six months between October and March following, including both months) + 15 = 49, and subtracting 30 gives 19. The moon is 19 days old.[58] Although multiplication and division are easy for us to perform, the calculations were laborious in 1611 and Hame obtains them from tables in an almanac.

An almanac recorded the times of high water for given ports expressed as the compass bearing of the moon and the lunar phase (or age of the moon).[59] These times later came to be called the "establishment of port." For example, Waghenaer's *Mariners Mirrour* contains tide tables listing "What moon makes full sea on all the coasts of England, Scotland, & Ireland." Bristol and the Severn show the following entry: "Within Bristol to the shore, with an E. and by S.M. In the Sea of Wales or Severn, with a W.S.W.M."[60] For both references, the final "M" means "moon." The establishment of port at Bristol is east and by south on days of "full and change," or on days of the full or new moon, when the spring tides are at their highest. At Bristol, then, high water occurs when the moon's bearing is east and by south, or, translating the bearing into time, at 6:45 a.m. (recurring at about 6:45 p.m.). Six hours after the first high water, low water occurs, and then six hours later, it returns. To be astronomically precise, the two high

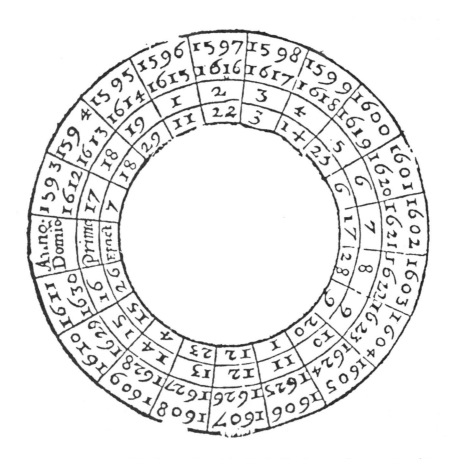

28. COMPUTING THE PRIME AND EPACT ‿ This diagram, from John Davis, *The Seamans Secrets*, 1633 edition, provides Captain Hame with two significant numbers, the epact (difference between a lunar and solar year) and the prime (a 19-year cycle through which the moon completes its peculiar motions). This diagram for 1611 gives a value for the epact of 26, the prime 16. By John Davis' rules for calculation, however, one arrives at values of 15 for both epact and prime, as listed in the diagram for the year 1610. Hame uses these figures for arithmetic calculation to determine phases of the moon and the times of high and low tide. See text for discussion. Credit: Courtesy of the John Carter Brown Library at Brown University, shelf mark D633 D268s

and two low tides occur within the moon's revolution about the earth in 24 hours and 48 minutes. As William Bourne describes it: "For the course of the tides is nothing else, but to put for every day of the age of the moon one hour, pulling back the fifth part of an hour, being 12 minutes, and by this account you may at all times know what that it does flow, by putting to every flood and ebb 24 minutes, and two floods and two ebbs, putting to 48 minutes."[61]

Hame knows this cycle. After timepieces came into common use, later mariners reckoned a tidal retardation of 48 minutes daily. High water occurs today at 6:45 a.m., tomorrow at 7:33 a.m. Without a reliable clock, however, Hame uses another method for expressing time, the bearing of the moon by the compass. Hame imagines a 24-hour clock face superimposed on a compass rose. To use the compass rose in this way, Hame rounds off 48 minutes to 45, the interval between compass points. Second, he predicts high water tomorrow at Bristol when the moon's bearing is one point southwestward of the establishment of port, or east-southeast (7:33 a.m.).

Hame has no means to reckon or measure the passage of forty-eight minutes. Away from land, where time is sounded in public places by clock bells, if at all, Hame has only the sandglass and the sundial to measure time. Hame relies on an almanac for tidal data translated into the bearing of the moon as the expression of local time. Hame will have to interpolate because almanacs only give the establishment of port for certain benchmarks, such as when the moon was at change or full. If, say, the moon on October 28 is four days old, then Hame counts with his compass rose clock four days forward to determine the bearing (and hence local time) of the moon at high water (using our example, southeast by south, or 9:45 a.m. or p.m.) at a particular location. To complicate matters, the tidal current does not change from flood to ebb and back again at the precise times of high and low water; knowledge of the local change, and the force of the ebb and flood currents, resides with the observant local pilot. In between the high and low tides, then, Hame has to know the local circumstances of the direction and force of the tidal flow. The importance of tidal understanding cannot be underestimated. Hame's capacity to reckon the tides is of crucial importance: he needs some understanding of contemporary tidal theory; he must memorize the vagaries of local tidal flows; he must integrate lunar and solar time; and he must understand how to use his compass rose as a clock, a "cognitive schema" that functions simultaneously as a recording device and a calculator.[62]

The Canary Islands

After almost eight days of fair sailing, Hame reaches the Canary Islands—also known as the Fortunate Isles—as he sights the island of Lanzarote. About a week's sailing from the Iberian Peninsula, the Canaries, with Madeira and the Azores, effectively mark the western boundary of the Old World. As the early Portuguese began to exploit the islands, and assigned them the virtue of zero magnetic variation, they discovered that the islands' location also demarcated major changes in prevailing winds. Currents in the vicinity tend toward the south, but sailing westnorthwest from the Canaries allowed Portuguese ships to recover winds to expedite a homeward voyage.[63] Hame records his arrival, and notes the islands of Fuerteventura and Gran Canaria: "Monday, the 4th day of November by 4 of the clock in the morning we discovered Lanzarote, one of the Islands of the Canaries. Sailing SSW and the island bearing SSE of us, cast about and went E for 2 glasses, then ran SW & by S & SW all the day long to fetch up Fuerteventura bearing 30 L long, and so to run betwixt it & Gran Canaria, spending all the night in very foggy and hazy weather."[64] The fog is typical for this time of year, along with much rain throughout the fall. The most important port for *Guyft* is at Lanzarote, followed, in order, by Gomera, Gran Canaria, and Tenerife (La Palma and Hierro, or Ferro, are other islands in the archipelago, but not of particular interest to Hame).[65]

The Canaries had become, by the mid-sixteenth century, a common way station for the Spanish silver

29. CANARY ISLANDS, FROM RICHARD HAKLUYT'S *THE PRINCIPAL NAVIGATIONS* — About three hundred miles south of Madeira, this island group must have enchanted explorers because of the diverse environments they present, from extreme dryness to lush rain-soaked regions. Navigators can rely on finding northeast trade winds in this region. The Canaries furnish the last replenishing stop before voyaging to the New World. Credit: The Rosenbach Museum & Library, Philadelphia, shelf mark A589p

treasure fleet. Outbound fleets left Seville in June, arrived in the Canaries by July, and then voyaged to Panama, whereas returning ships, laden with silver and now prey to piracy, left Panama in the spring, arriving at the Canaries in June.[66] For Hame, the Canaries supply fresh water and some other provisions. Although relationships between local authorities and the English are cordial, they have not always been, and Hame hastens to accomplish his business and get under way across the ocean sea to the New World. From the Canaries, Hame will try to "run his latitude," that is, maintain a constant, westerly course within a narrow range of latitude. Hame plans to voyage south to 20 degrees latitude north, and then turn west. During this time of year, Hame can expect fairly constant northeast winds as he sails south to find his latitude, but as he turns west, he expects easterly winds to propel his ship. In fact, Hame will mimic Christopher Columbus who, on his voyages following the first one, sailed south to find the prevailing trade winds that took him to the Windward Islands, and later to Trinidad.[67] For this, Hame will rely on the cross-staff and astrolabe. Hame consults his rutter, published in Richard Hakluyt's *Principal Navigations*, for the best advice on shaping a course for New Spain and Virginia:

> If you be at the Canaries and would sail to New Spain, you shall sail four and twenty hours south because of the calms of Hierro. And from thence you shall go west southwest, until you find yourself in twenty degrees. And then go west and by south, which is for the Isle Deseada [now La Désirade, just east of Guadeloupe in the Leeward Islands]. And from Deseada go west and by north, because of the variation of the compass.
>
> And if you are going for *terra firma*, go west and by south until you come to Dominica, and there on the northwest side is a river, where you may water. The marks to [look for are] a certain high land full of hills. And seeing it when you are far off to the seaward, it makes in the middle a partition; so that a man would think it divided the island in two parts. And this island stands [at] 14 degrees and a half [latitude].[68]

Hame makes for the West Indies from the Canaries with confidence: "The 10th of this month being Sunday, we were up betimes. And I caused our ship to be adorned the best we could, the King's colors in the main top. To all, I provided a short brief of all the passages of our voyage to this day, and I likewise declared in what state we were at present, and how I did intend to prosecute the voyage to the westward and to Virginia. This brief discourse I concluded, and then we read morning prayer."[69] Despite Hame's optimism, the leak of almost two weeks ago has damaged supplies and food has spoiled. Several passengers have fallen ill. Surgeon Gerard Chilson, who also became ill, decides to keep a record of this circumstance:

> Divers of our men were sick and I had neither skill nor medicine so yet I would advise such as shall hereafter appoint such a voyage to prepare good provision of wholesome comforts and ordinary salves. Let the surgeon be prepared to use the salve when there is need. All this while I was seasick, and no marvel, having changed at once both air, exercise, and diet. Rheumatic I was and exceedingly costive and troubled with heartburning which be appendixes [consequences] of the sea. Wherefore I could advise him that is to appoint such a voyage that he have of violet flowers, borage flowers, rosemary flowers and such like, which he may gather in England, caphers [pickles or conserves] made, to comfort him, and barberis [barbery, a shrub with sour berries] seed and rosemary and thyme to make a little broth in an earthen pipkin [baking pot]. Others have told us that plenty of bonitos [a large fish related to tuna] and dolphins we should have all this way but hitherto we smacked no bite of fresh fish. The like they told of gurnet [or gunard, a fish with a large, spiny head] and whiting in the west but our hooks could catch none, and therefore I perceive men must not go to sea without victuals in hope to have flying fishes break their noses against the bunt of the sail.[70]

Chilson recommends the use of violets, borage, and rosemary for apothecary use, plants associated with relief of inflammation or swelling, expulsion of poison, and easing pain, respectively.[71] Chilson's emphasis on fresh herbs, flowers, and fish for good health was a common plea, but difficult to effect given the problems of food preservation at sea. He refers to a practice, known to oceanic sailors, of catching flying fish when they crash into sails.

Chilson has other problems. William Norrys was injured in the exchange of gunfire with the French ship near the Azores. A French cannonball splintered a section of *Guyft*'s gunwale, and pieces of shot and splinters drove into Norrys' thigh. Chilson examined the wound at first but could not locate the tiny fragments of wood and iron. Now, a few weeks later, the wound has caused great pain and inflammation. Upon inspecting the wound, Chilson notes to himself that the wound has caused burning heat and watchings. This wound is near a joint and he fears that the slivers lie in the tendon and the wound will not digest. If he removes the pieces, doing so may bring on a mortification. The splinters and threads of clothing that entered the wound and reside there have made apostemations and will delay a cure.

"Watchings" refers to sleeplessness owing to pain or fever; "digest" refers to the process or a substance that aids suppuration in a wound; "mortification" usually means gangrene; and "apostemations" are abscesses.[72] Chilson decides to treat the wound superficially in hopes that the inflammation will cease. With multiple persons aboard suffering from illness, including himself, Chilson fears that Norrys may worsen.

Hame delivers his morning sermon. He invokes a nautical image from a Roman coin to draw a moral: "Vespasian's emblem on his coin did well moralize the meaning of zeal's moderation. There was a dolphin and an anchor: the dolphin outstrips the ship; the anchor stays the ship. If [steadfastness] and swiftness, earnestness and peacefulness did go together, then were zeal, that true zeal that the holy prophets and servants of God had."[73] Not at all to his surprise, Hame has heard some murmurings from sick passengers that Virginia plantations, where they will work through their indentures, may fall far short of expectations. Hame has always tried to suppress indications of discontent during his voyages. Ferdinando Morgan, however, encouraged by Captain Lynnis, made a short speech to his fellow passengers following the mid-afternoon service:

> Give me leave to examine the lying speeches that have injuriously vilified and traduced a great part of the glory of God, the honor of our land, and joy of our nation, I mean in the plantation of Virginia. When the descry [promise] of the Indians was offered to that learned and famous prince, Henry the Seventh, some idle, dull, and unworthy skeptics moved the king not to entertain the motion. We know our loss by the Spaniards' gain. Surely, if the prayers of all good Christians prevail, the expectation of the wisest and noblest, the knowledge of the most experienced and learned, the relation of the best traveled, and [most observant] be true, it is like to be the most worthy voyage that ever was effected by any Christian.[74]
>
> Virginia may in time prove to us the barn of Britain, as Sicily was to Rome, or the garden of the world as was Thessaly [Greece], or the argosy of the world as is Germany. And besides the future expectation, the present encouragement is exceeding much, in that it is a voyage countenanced by our gracious king, consulted on by the oracles of the council, adventured in by our wisest and greatest nobles, and undertaken by so worthy, so honorable, and religious a Lord, and furthered not only by many other parties of this land, both clergy and laity.[75]
>
> Whosoever has a hand in this business shall receive an unspeakable blessing, for they that turn many to righteousness, shall shine as the star forever and ever.[76]

Following the service, the crew returns to their duties, and passengers linger to peer at the horizon, left to their own thoughts. Over coming weeks, during which no land will disturb an even horizon, Hame and his crew will remain alert to the navigational clues of the sea environment. The sea may appear featureless and disturbing to some of the passengers, but it supplies many clues to location. In the open ocean, no birds will appear. When *Guyft* nears land, seabirds appear as clues to direction and location. Within a day or two of land, Hame may spot the greater shearwater, a bird that breeds in the South Atlantic and migrates in huge flocks along the coastlines of Europe and America.[77] As *Guyft* departs the Canaries, Hame spots the herring gull taking up winter residence.[78] As with the greater shearwater, when Hame spots the gull again, he knows he is nearing the American coast. Early morning sightings of boobies and gannets portend land, as these birds visit fishing areas for food and then return to their nests. Farther from land, Wilson's storm petrel signals the proximity of the Gulf Stream.[79] Distant clouds, too, form over land, thus providing a directional indicator. The next oceanic milestone for *Guyft*, however, will be a traverse through the Sargasso Sea, a region of calm characterized by floating islands of seaweed.[80]

For the next month, *Guyft* voyages westward out of sight of land, following the route pioneered by the renowned Genoese navigator who led three ships in Spanish service just over a century earlier.

Time (said the philosopher) is a measure of moving according to first and last, or before and after. Although by accident . . . time may be a measure of rest or quietness: as measures of habits are measures of privations. Or time may be a measure of the moving of the first moveable called primum mobile, *and cause of generation thereby, and of corruption by accident.*

—MARTÍN CORTÉS, *Arte of Navigation*, 1561

CHAPTER 7

"HE SETTETH FOR THE SUN": Finding Latitude

The cross-staff, the compass, and the chart, are so necessarily joined together, as that the one may not well be without the other in the execution of the practices of navigation.

— JOHN DAVIS, *The Seamans Secrets*, 1607

Shooting the Sun

After a few days of difficult weather, today promises sunshine. Around mid-morning, Tristram Hame assembles the transversary, a sliding cross-piece, onto a graduated staff. As he stands on the main deck midships, he braces himself against the gunwale and levels his cross-staff in the direction of the sun. Morning haze still hovers over the ocean, partially obscuring the horizon. With the staff placed against the notch next to his left eye, he loosens the tightening screw on the transversary and moves it toward his eye until he can see the lower edge almost flush with the horizon. Squinting because of the sun's morning glare, he blinks and upon opening his right eye glances along the upper edge of the transversary: it does not quite align with the sun's upper limb, so he moves the transversary slightly toward his eye. With each blink, he alternately glances along the transversary's lower edge to see the horizon, and then to the upper edge, moving the transversary again until the upper edge just covers the solar disk. Unlike Hame who uses the

transversary to cover the solar disk, William Bourne recommends aligning the transversary's upper edge with the center of the sun.[1] Bourne's measurement may be the truer, but Hame saves his eyes. The diameter of the sun is about a half degree, so errors can arise if the navigator takes measurements inconsistently. The correction for semidiameter in the computation of latitude reconciles the disk of the sun to a consistent datum for measurement. With the alignment set, Hame tightens the screw to clamp the transversary in place. He glances upward only momentarily because of the intense solar glow. When the sea calms, it becomes a mirror, too, producing an intense, bright shimmer. Hame's mate, Thomas Blunt, continues to invert the sandglass each half hour; Hame knows that noon approaches when the sun reaches its maximum altitude.

Hame sets the staff down and retrieves another instrument, a heavy brass circle suspended from a ring. The cross-staff is a direct reading instrument that uses a scale of unequal graduation; the astrolabe, also a direct reading instrument, has a scale

30. Captain Hame uses the cross-staff (above) ⌐
Captain Hame measures the altitude of the sun on a partly
cloudy day using a cross-staff. One end of the instrument
is buttressed against the notch next to Hame's left eye. He
moves the transversary or crosspiece back and forth until
the lower edge appears set on the horizon, the upper edge
aligned with the solar disk. Hame then reads the graduated
scale of the staff to get the sun's altitude at noon. Credit:
Science Museum of Virginia

31. Cross-staff aligned with sun and horizon
(right) ⌐ A Hame's-eye view along the cross-staff. The
lower edge of the transversary is flush with the horizon.
Hame uses partial cloud cover to diminish the glare of the
sun along the upper edge of the transversary. Credit: Science
Museum of Virginia

constructed on an arc, a semicircle of 180 degrees, marked in two 90-degree segments.[2] The circle, an astrolabe, hangs true despite the gentle movement of the ship, and the instrument's four apertures around a central pivot allow wind to pass through. John Davis describes an astrolabe as "the representation of a great circle containing four quadrants, or 360 degrees, which instrument hath been in long use among seamen, and is an excellent instrument being rightly understood and ordered."[3] Braced against the mainmast, Blunt holds the astrolabe as Hame adjusts the rotating alidade to allow sunlight to pass through two pinnules to align with the sun. Once he has achieved the alignment, Hame reads the degrees indicated by the alidade along the upper semicircle. Hame has become adroit in the use of both instruments: he deftly switches from his staff to the astrolabe. In fact, after he takes his astrolabe reading, he reverses the instrument 180 degrees and takes another sun sighting. He does this to correct for any error inherent in the construction of the astrolabe in case the pivot is off center.

Minutes later, Hame repeats the process with both tools. He places the cross-staff against his eye again, the transversary still clamped into place. *Guyft*'s deck gently heaves as Hame stiffens against the gunwale. Holding the cross-staff as he strives to frame the horizon and sun is difficult with the transversary held vertically, but over the past few minutes the sun has gained altitude. Hame releases the clamp and draws the transversary slightly nearer to his eye. Quickly changing the staff for the astrolabe, Hame finds that the sun has indeed risen slightly from the previous sighting. Moments later, he tries again: this time, the sun has apparently lost altitude as Hame unclamps the transversary and moves it away from his eye. Within the last few minutes, the sun has crossed the meridian, its highest point in the sky, signifying local noon, and now moves toward its daily setting. Hame notes the degree measurement on the staff as

shown by the transversary moments ago when it was closest to the eye: this moment must have occurred close to the meridian passage. Local noon is not easy to gauge: Hame turns his eye away from the sun frequently, and the precise moment of local noon cannot be fixed: the sun does not reach an apex during its altitude climb. Rather, during the minutes preceding and following the noon meridian passage the sun's apparent motion resembles that of a straight east–west line. Throughout this process, Blunt monitors the compass. When the sun crosses the meridian, its compass bearing must be due south, with allowance for variation. Watching for the compass' "southing" helps determine the time of noon. Hame notes the degrees of altitude reached by the sun as shown on the staff. Opposite the altitude scale is a separate, parallel set of numbers, co-altitude or zenith distance, degrees measured from the zenith as zero, downward to the horizon. The zenith distance will be necessary for the calculation of latitude. The astrolabe has been graduated with zenith distance in mind as the zero measurement is right under the suspension ring, and 90 degrees aligns with the horizon. Hame returns to his cabin, consults a declination table, and on a slate computes his latitude.

A few days ago, Hame measured the sun's altitude with a cross-staff, but he used it differently. Using the cross-staff as a forestaff, Hame braced himself against the gunwale but with his back to the sun. Holding his cross-staff vertically, Hame sighted along the lower edge of the transversary to see across the deck to the opposite horizon. The end of the staff that normally marks the eye end has a small shoe attached that acts as a foresight to align with the horizon. Hame adjusted the transversary until the upper edge cast a shadow that fell upon the shoe, while he simultaneously had the horizon aligned with the lower edge. Hame took his degree reading and computed his latitude.

Two Instruments with One Moving Part

Now that *Guyft* is poised to head west to the Indies, Hame's primary celestial navigation tools, the cross-staff and astrolabe, embodiments of practical geometry, become important in "running the latitude." Coastal landmarks have disappeared, and the lead and line, the indispensable tool of coastal navigation, will not help *Guyft* as she no longer sails over the continental shelf. Celestial referents are necessary, invoking a few centuries of Portuguese maritime energy in exploring the African coast southward and around the Cape of Good Hope. "Running the latitude" refers to a technique of more or less maintaining a course within a very narrow range of latitude. The navigator finds his latitude and then tries to steer due east or west to a desired landfall. The cross-staff is a deceptively simple instrument: easily constructed from two pieces of wood, one of which slides over and at right angles to the other, the longer piece bears an incised scale, which enables the calculation of the ship's latitude. The navigator aims the staff at the sun, buttressing the staff next to his eye, trying to peer along the upper edge of the transversary to see the sun while quickly glancing along the lower edge to align with the horizon. The astrolabe, by contrast, does not require Hame to look through it to find the sun, and its use does not require finding the horizon. Deceptively simple, too, is the measurement of latitude. Many museum exhibits describe latitude measurement as easy and simple because the altitude of the polestar today almost equates to the observer's latitude, true today but not the case in Hame's day. Recent popular works on the history of longitude measurement, with emphasis on John Harrison's famous chronometers of the eighteenth century, have relegated latitude to a lesser category of interest. Latitude measurement, however, occupies no less a category of insight and originality as the much-celebrated methods of longitude measurement. Latitude measurement precedes accurate longitude measurement by over two centuries, and truly marks an intellectual achievement in locating a ship's position astronomically.[4]

Hame competes with other navigators for work: oceanic navigation promises long-term contracts with potential rewards in exploiting overseas commodities through trading monopolies. With the acquisition of astronomical navigation as a marketable skill, Hame can attract investor-employers.[5] Hame, practically speaking, is an empire broker and a reducer of investment risk. Astronomical navigation promises to reduce risks by surer, dependable wayfinding. Favored navigators make repeated voyages with minimal losses. Hame combines his empirical piloting skills with instrumental navigation, supported by published texts and almanacs. His employers have hired him in the expectation that he owns a suite of charts and instruments appropriate for the voyage. Decades before 1611, Martín Cortés listed the knowledge and abilities requisite in a mariner: "The making and use of instruments, to know and take the altitude of the sun, to know the tides or ebbing and flowing of the sea, how to order their cards and compasses for navigation, [determining] the course of the sun and motions of the moon [and] the making of [sun]dials both for the day and for the night [and] the secret property of the lodestone, with the manner and causes of the northeasting and northwesting (commonly called the variation of the compass) with also instruments thereunto belonging."[6] Geometrical knowledge had become increasingly important to performing these functions. To this list, another contemporary writer, John Tapp emphasizes that mathematical exercise plus sailing practice yield navigational expertise, a dictum Hame strives to realize: "Of which arts, namely, mathematical, navigation being a principal member, as having participation in arithmetic, geometry, geography, cosmography, and astronomy, or rather to say the truth; being the quintessence of them all . . . for albeit that men read or hear never so much of cosmography or astronomy, yet without practice and experience it is unperfect:

32. CROSS-STAFF USED AS A FORESTAFF (above) ⁓ Hame positions the cross-staff for use as a backstaff. He sights the horizon along the lower edge of the transversary and the opposite end of the staff, also aligned with the horizon. He moves the transversary until the sun casts a shadow from the upper edge of the transversary onto the horizon end of the staff. This process can be made easier by the attachment of a shoe to the end of the staff that supports a horizon sight. Credit: Science Museum of Virginia

33. CROSS-STAFF TRANSVERSAL AND CLAMP (left) ⁓ A close-up of the transversary and the staff of a cross-staff. Note that the staff is graduated in two ways: it shows degrees of altitude of the sighted object, from zero degrees at the horizon to 90 degrees at the zenith. It also shows co-altitude, which registers the horizon at 90 degrees, the zenith at zero. This conversion saves a computation as Captain Hame, in determining latitude from his altitude measurement of the sun, needs to know zenith distance, the location in the sky of the sun measured down from the zenith toward the horizon. This photograph shows how the transversary is constructed. Hame is shown tightening a screw to secure the transversary to the staff. Credit: Science Museum of Virginia

34. CAPTAIN HAME DEMONSTRATES A KAMAL ⌐ Hame illustrates the use of a *kamal*. He places the knotted cord between his teeth and stretches it taught so that he sights the polestar along the top edge of the tablet, the horizon along the lower edge. Instead of a numerical graduation, the cord shows irregularly spaced knots. The pilot fixed knots to correspond with specific locations. For instance, a pilot placed the knot representing Bristol between his teeth and framed the tablet between the horizon and polestar as seen from Bristol. If the pilot intended to navigate a ship to Bristol, he would sail north or south until he obtained the "fit" with the polestar appropriate for Bristol. Then he would sail east or west to reach the port. Credit: Science Museum of Virginia

and how can perfection be attained, but by sailing and transporting from place to place . . . whereby the whole course and revolution of the sphere is made apparent to man's capacity?"[7]

When we speak of the evolution of the astrolabe or cross-staff, we refer to their increasing mathematical elaboration and their progressively more complex relationship to other tools and methods. Hame's altitude-measuring instruments represent more than just an early technology: their extensive use and elaboration over time contributed to the rise of early modern science.[8] Readers who examine the astrolabe or cross-staff in museum collections will find variations and permutations: these instrument designs did not remain static.

Instrumental Histories

The origins of the astrolabe and cross-staff are murky; devices to gauge angular distances between objects or features had been known for many centuries. The earliest documentary reference to the use of a cross-staff at sea dates to the Portuguese in 1481, and the first solar declination tables (necessary to reduce cross-staff observations) appear in a Portuguese text of 1509, by which time the instrument apparently entered common maritime use.[9] Other Portuguese accounts have the cross-staff in maritime use by 1529 or 1537.[10]

The origin of the cross-staff for maritime use probably owes to multiple, simultaneous developments: maritime experimentation, the spread of university

learning, the European interest in Islamic scholarship, and European observation of Arab navigation in
the Indian Ocean. On the last point, the Portuguese
found the Arabs employing a distinct *altura* (altitude) technology of their own: the *kamal*. The *kamal*
consisted of a string, knotted at intervals, connected
to a wooden tablet or tablets. The string was held to
the eye or between the teeth; the tablet, attached to
the other end, held outward until the cord became
taut. The observer simultaneously sighted the horizon along the lower edge of the tablet and the polestar along the upper edge.[11] The observer made knots
in the cord to correspond with locations, or graduated
the cord, so to speak, in a unit of measurement known
as the *isba*. Most scholars of navigation presume that

the Portuguese discovery of the *kamal* stimulated the
adaptation of the cross-staff for sea use in imitation
of the Arab instrument, although this remains conjecture.[12] The contribution of the Muslim world to
altitude-measuring instruments, particularly those
that employ indirect observation of the sun through
shadow measurement, remains little investigated.

Several developments contributed to the adaptation of the staff for sea use. Early Portuguese ships
on the return trip from the Azores were forced to sail
west and then north, a course known as the *volta*,
but when sailing north pilots needed a method of
determining when to turn east to make landfall.
Portuguese pilots learned to observe the *altura* of the
polestar with a quadrant, a triangular piece of wood

35. CAPTAIN HAME USES A QUADRANT ⚓ Hame demonstrates the use of a quadrant. He sights the polestar through two sighting holes and notes where the weighted cord falls over the degree scale along the arc. This instrument, known as a Gunter's
quadrant, consists of a printed paper template glued to a wooden back. The cord suspended from the apex of the quadrant has
a small sliding bead that can be set against the section of crisscrossed arcs in order to make additional computations, such as
determining local time. Credit: Science Museum of Virginia

with a curved arc. In use, the observer sighted the polestar through two small peepholes or apertures on one straight side of the instrument. A weighted cord suspended from the apex of two straight sides fell over the lower arc. When his quadrant sighted the polestar at the same height as it appeared from, say, Lisbon, then the pilot sailed due east to reach the desired landfall.[13] Early quadrants were not marked in degrees but denoted the *altura* of specific ports. When quadrants began to show scales in degrees, portolan charts began to show meridians graduated in degrees as well.[14] The early pilot did not need to measure latitude (which did not appear on charts before 1505), only *altura*.

Some historians and museums offer a linear evolution of instruments: instrument B is more precise than instrument A, therefore, users tossed out A when B appeared. This is rarely the case. Instruments were not conceived or designed as inferior precursors to other tools; the instruments under discussion here were designs in their own right.[15] Altitude-measuring instruments did not march steadily from the quadrant to the astrolabe to the cross-staff. These tools may have been used in tandem, and even the quadrant saw continued reinvention into more complex instruments well into the seventeenth century. The astronomical, surveying, and mariner's staffs, though often confused, underwent concurrent development, each tool experiencing distinct evolution.[16] In fact, the cross-staff did not evolve anywhere in a linear fashion. Dutch East India Company (VOC) ships finally discontinued carrying astrolabes by 1670, long after cross-staffs had been introduced at sea, decades after the supposed successor instrument appeared, the backstaff. Even when the VOC discontinued backstaffs in the 1730s, as octants and sextants began to appear, the cross-staff continued as standard equipment until 1747.[17]

The English in the late sixteenth century adapted the astronomical cross-staff to a precise instrument, probably inspired by the instruments John Dee brought back from France in 1547, including a cross-staff given by Gemma Frisius.[18] Frisius, an influential professor at the University of Louvain, articulated mathematical ideas that were quickly disseminated in England, including the principle of triangulation. Frisius, a teacher not only of Dee but also of Gerard Mercator, advanced the idea that precise time measurement might be a key to longitude determination, a principle not translated into successful practice until the late eighteenth century.[19]

Dee and Leonard Digges collaborated on observations with the astronomical staff, possibly the most accurate staff in existence, and Danish astronomer Tycho Brahe studied their measurements of the great supernova of 1572 to compare with his own.[20] Digges, an astrologer and almanac writer, in collaboration with his son, Thomas, published navigational aids including tide tables and their *Prognostication Everlastinge* of 1576 featured a sympathetic, succinct summary of the Copernican theory. By 1556, Leonard Digges had published the first treatise in English on the surveyor's cross-staff, and five years later the first English description of a mariner's cross-staff appeared in the translation of Martín Cortés' *Arte of Navigation*.[21] The same scholars applied the staff to a variety of uses. Digges' use of the surveying staff fostered the recognition that instrumental error required corrections that Edward Wright, John Davis, and Thomas Hariot applied to the mariner's staff. These three men formed an ideal group. Davis was the practitioner with sailing experience from the Arctic almost to the Antarctic. Wright, an academic mathematician at Cambridge University, applied his talents to improving the navigation of his countrymen. His participation in a raiding expedition to the Azores furnished some sea experience, and he later wrote the first practical treatise on how to construct a Mercator projection chart, incorporated in his *Certaine Errors*.[22] Also noted for his incisive analysis of common errors in the use of a cross-staff, Wright says that it is more "profitable to be a fault mender, then a fault finder."[23]

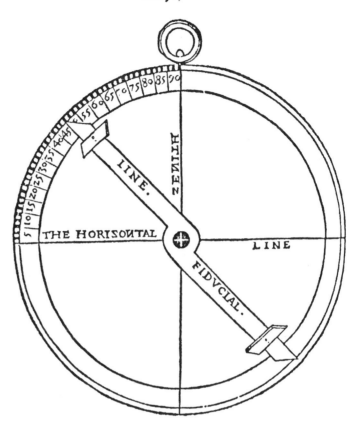

36. MARINER'S ASTROLABE (right) ⚊ This image of an astrolabe from Martín Cortés, *The Arte of Navigation*, 1561, shows the graduation with 90 degrees at the zenith and zero at the horizon. Compare this image with the astrolabe in Illustration 37, which shows the reverse. In computing latitude, Captain Hame will require the sun's zenith distance, the measurement in degrees from the zenith at zero, "down" to the sun. The graduation of the astrolabe in Illustration 37 saves Hame a step. Credit: Courtesy of the John Carter Brown Library at Brown University, shelf mark B561 C828a

37. ASTROLABE SHOWING SUNLIGHT ON ALIDADE (below) ⚊ Hame holds a mariner's astrolabe to obtain a noon determination of solar altitude. Suspending the instrument by the thumb ring, he rotates the alidade so that sunlight passes through the upper pinnule into the lower one. A dot of sunlight can be seen next to the lower pinnule. Once Hame has obtained the sun's altitude, he may reverse the instrument and take another measurement, averaging the two results. Note that the astrolabe is graduated to give zenith distance (the horizon gives 90 degrees, the zenith zero). Credit: Science Museum of Virginia

Hariot, a mathematician of exceptional ability, sailed with Sir Walter Ralegh's fleet to what became known as the failed Roanoke Colony in what is now North Carolina, in part to refine observational techniques for latitude measurement. Hariot introduced several innovations including ways of determining and correcting compass variation.[24]

The mariner's astrolabe doubtless mimics the cross-staff's varied history. Derived from the planispheric astronomical variety (a complex observational and computational tool), the astrolabe may have had Greek, Byzantine, or Muslim origins, appears a few decades earlier than the cross-staff, and receives its first published description by Martín Cortés.[25] Although the idea of determining latitude by the sun's altitude at meridian passage—the primary use of both tools—had been known for centuries, the first two decades of the sixteenth century saw the publication of Portuguese texts with rules for calculating latitude.[26]

In Hame's world, the cross-staff has excited more interest among fellow navigators: it can be produced relatively cheaply; one can either graduate it by means of dividers or copy the design from a full-scale paper template; and the astrolabe on a ship can produce errors upward of 4 or 5 degrees, whereas the cross-staff's errors are perceived as comparatively fewer and more easily corrected.[27] What Hame does not know is that the future elaboration of altitude-measuring tools will be based on the cross-staff and Hame's contemporaries' analysis of its errors. Our discussion examines the application of the cross-staff more extensively than the astrolabe.

Construction

In late sixteenth-century England, instrument makers were few, their surviving tools indicating skills in metalworking, but they may have worked in other media. Separate makers of wooden instruments also existed who may have provided Hame with his cross-staff.[28]

Makers of astrolabes and most cross-staffs probably came from the Low Countries and represented metalworking trades such as engraving.[29] Cross-staffs, though, were made of *lignum vitae* (*Gualacum* or "tree of life") and ebony. The oldest ones known are of ebony. Museum specimens are very rare; only a handful survive from the seventeenth century, and none are complete. Hame prefers close-grained hardwoods (possibly fruit woods) as they are easier to engrave with scales and resist warping under sea conditions. Engravers not only contributed to an evolving instrument trade, they also worked at printing. Printing enabled books with instrument templates to be produced. Woodworkers may have used paper templates as the cross-staff could be laid out geometrically from a diagram. In fact, a Dutch source records a box maker as having constructed a cross-staff.[30] A seaman or a ship's carpenter could make one. For Hame, the wooden raw materials are commonly available and cheap to obtain. Laying out an arc or degree circle involved no machinery but a firm hand with a pair of compasses. An early Spanish source instructs that the arc on a quadrant can be graduated by using dividers to "step off" up to 60 times.[31]

We have discussed many texts that taught Hame some astronomy and geometry. To Hame, however, no clear distinction exists between books on mathematics and his instruments, printed templates or diagrams—the latter either published as part of books or separately. Many mathematical instruments were related to others, as we have seen with the connection between navigation and surveying. Texts of the kind written by Bourne or Davis were a new phenomenon, "a new genre of text . . . which can be read as describing the instrument on the page just as easily and naturally as it might describe a brass example in a reader's hand."[32] The methods and tools of the engraver, the carpenter, the printer of maps, and the navigator shared mathematical practices.[33] Further, the images Hame sees in his books—whether illustrative of a principle, method, or tool, contributed to the making of new mathematically informed knowledge, and attested to the importance of observation in empirical knowledge.[34]

Other tools of the instrument maker besides compasses included a straightedge, a variety of scribing tools, and letter and number stamps, possibly the same as used in metalworking.[35] Over time, the cross-staff accumulated embellishments such as a smoked glass attachment for affixing to the upper edge of the transversary to reduce solar glare. As we have seen, a brass shoe could be added to the eye end of the staff when the instrument was used as a forestaff (early backstaff). Navigational tools underwent much adaptation by sailors for many reasons. Practitioners with the cross-staff noticed errors such as parallax, which they tried to correct by modifying the instrument (shortening the staff, for instance).

Metalworkers used pattern or technical notebooks to record tools, innovations, practice designs, or other engineering information including that related to navigational instruments. In fact, technical illustrations may owe their origin to such notebooks; books showing machines were becoming popular during the sixteenth century.[36] Metal- and woodworking artisans by the early seventeenth century were becoming conversant with geometry. Indeed, the technological revolution began with such artisans, their technical notebooks, discussions with one another, and the proliferation of books on mechanical and technical subjects. Metalworkers and allied artisans must have been as much a part of Hame's professional network as chandlers and victuallers.

Hame may have made some instruments himself or in collaboration with others. He is competent with the use of dividers and he knows some trigonometry. Mathematical instruments and the rules for constructing them, even rules of thumb, relied on the precursor to trigonometry, the "doctrine of triangles" with its axioms governing the relationships between angles, arcs, and chords, and its emphasis on linear functions because lines were easier to divide than circles or arcs.[37] These mathematical relationships

encouraged experimentation with the cross-staff (and other instruments), evidence of how the same template of the triangle with its internal relationships informed astronomy, navigation, and surveying.[38] Because these instruments measured angles in terms of ratios or tangents, only the linear components needed to be graduated, not the arcs and circles.[39] Easier to understand, linear scales became favored among artisans, and if craftsmen did not know the geometrical rules for laying out scales, they could obtain paper templates. Refer to Illustration 38 for laying out the cross-staff from Waghenaer's *Mariners Mirrour*. He describes a geometric method for laying out the instrument, probably much emulated, requiring no more than pairs of compasses and a straightedge. Indeed, Hame used the diagram as a template.

After Hame, mariners became more sensitive to the cross-staff's errors while the numerical scales evolved to enable measurements to fractions of a degree. While paper templates were popular, inexact methods of dividing arcs meant the inclusion of systematic errors in cross-staffs. The mariner who fashioned a staff from a paper template effectively made a third-generation copy. Errors of design were decried by critics of the cross-staff during the sixteenth century, but the contemporary literature did not address systematic errors in construction.

Even people today who shy from things mathematical unconsciously borrow from years of early mathematical education. We rely on everyday measuring instruments from rulers to speedometers to determine percentages, averages, and probabilities and base important decisions on them. Just as Hame learned to use a cross-staff and appreciate what a numerical scale can do, his contemporaries listened to lectures about, watched others practicing, or tried other mathematical applications in surveying, for instance, using theodolites, plane tables, and shadow squares.[40]

Both the astrolabe and the cross-staff helped to create dependability and predictability in transoceanic voyages. Celestial navigation with altitude-measuring instruments became the primary reliable

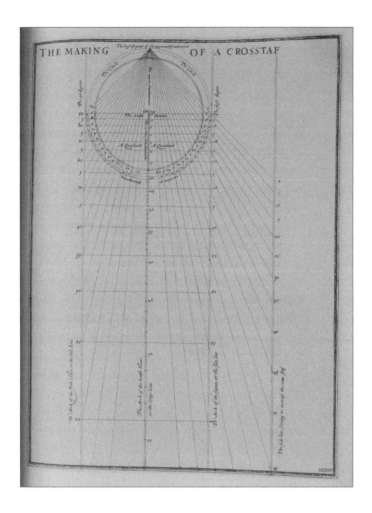

38. Constructing a cross-staff ━. Lucas Jansz. Waghenaer's *The Mariners Mirrour,* 1588, includes this template for laying out a cross-staff and its transversaries with paper and pairs of compasses. The mariner need understand no geometry to create the instrument. Credit: Courtesy of the John Carter Brown Library at Brown University, shelf mark [R] 2-SIZE Z.W131 1588

method of traversing oceans. William Borough confirms the quotation by John Davis at the beginning of this chapter by stating that the mariner need look no farther for altitude-measuring instruments than the cross-staff and its kin, maintaining that "a plain astrolabe exactly made, and a cross-staff, are sufficient," for with them "and the sailing compass and marine plat [chart] . . . the whole world may be traveled, discovered, & described."[41] Getting down to practical matters, whatever claims one might make about the utility of compass variation, the chief tasks requisite of any oceangoing pilot, according to Davis, are to determine latitude by measuring celestial altitudes, noting the compass bearing and correcting it to eliminate the effects of variation, and then carefully measuring the number of leagues the ship has sailed within a measured interval.[42]

The Polestar

Hame primarily relies on the cross-staff and astrolabe for the determination of latitude by the sun's altitude. He can use both instruments for observations of the polestar, the celestial datum that preceded the use of the sun. In our discussion of the compass and magnetic variation, we introduced the equal-altitude method. During the late fourteenth century and later, navigators applied a different kind of equal-altitude method to the polestar, which required calculation and interpolation. At the time, the polestar was about 3.5 degrees distant from the celestial north pole, which meant that the pilot using a quadrant might locate the polestar by this amount either below or above the celestial north pole, a span of about seven degrees.[43] To use the cross-staff with the polestar necessitated correction tables or a mnemonic system involving the visualization of a giant sky man whose feet and hands corresponded to relative positions of key circumpolar stars. By memorizing the orientation of the sky man, the pilot took *altura* sightings of the polestar by waiting until the sky man occupied a consistent configuration from night to night.[44] By the sixteenth century, the demands of increased precision in instrumentation meant the disappearance of mnemonic systems and the substitution of numerical tables. The sky man gave way to the Regiment of the North Star, a table of angular distances in degrees and minutes of the polestar from the celestial north pole.

Altitude-Distance Method

With increasing reliance on charts, the altitude-distance method became favored for computing distance run based on altitude observations. For this method, solar observations proved easier and universally applicable over polestar ones. Anyway, oceanic navigation below the equator rendered polestar observations impossible, so solar observations substituted, accompanied by the proliferation of solar declination tables.[45] The development of the altitude-distance method illustrates how navigational instruments influenced cartography and our understanding of the earth as a globe. Columbus and the early Portuguese had employed a system similar to Hame's "running the latitude." That is, they may have sailed north or south until they reckoned the altitude of the polestar to match that of the polestar's altitude at a desired port, at first relying on the sky man and later the Regiment of the North Star to correct the polestar's configuration about the celestial north pole. Once he observed the height of the polestar in the appropriate configuration, the navigator sailed east or west while maintaining the same latitude until he reached the desired landfall. Alternatively, the navigator used the sun's altitude at meridian crossing in lieu of the polestar.

It was a short step to creating the altitude-distance method. A ship, say, sails from point A at one latitude to point B at another. The navigator constructs a right triangle (a triangle including one 90-degree angle) on a chart with one acute angle representing the ship's measured latitude at the starting point, A, the opposite acute angle at the second latitude, B, reached after an interval, and the right angle (C) situated on the parallel of the desired or achieved latitude. The hypotenuse (side opposite the 90-degree angle), then, represents the ship's course. This triangle later became a nautical or sailing triangle on a globe, a configuration still used in celestial navigation.[46] At A and B, the navigator measures the altitude of the polestar when on the meridian. Over time, observations of the polestar for this purpose gave way to increased reliance on solar altitudes. Over time, however, the navigator will notice that his figure for the length of a degree along the meridian may not be correct, or may need adjustment as he travels north or south. To use this method successfully, then, Hame has to incorporate a cartographic referent, the length of a degree along the earth's meridian. In later years, cartographers, using navigational data, will refine this measurement and contribute to an understanding of the dimensions of the earth.

By about 1600, the mathematical relationship between longitude and latitude had been articulated so that a mariner could compute it by knowing some trigonometry, itself a new invention: the length of a degree of longitude varies as the cosine of a degree of latitude. (See the Glossary for an explanation of trigonometric terms.) Texts appeared with published tables that showed the length of a degree of longitude in different latitudes, along with rules based on the relationships of angles and sides in a right triangle, showing how far a ship must sail in each direction to raise or lower the ship's latitude by one degree.[47] Later in our voyage, we will re-visit the altitude-distance method as Hame constructs the sailing triangle on a plane chart and uses trigonometry to determine the distance between A and B. Readers should note the close connection between the sailing triangle, use of a globe or charts, and altitude observations with the astrolabe or cross-staff.

Calculating Latitude

John Davis outlines the method for reducing cross-staff or astrolabe observations to obtain latitude by pointing out that an altitude measurement required five considerations. These relationships are important because the difference between the zenith and the equinoctial equals the distance between the horizon and the celestial north pole, which equals latitude. Davis related latitude finding to what is now known as the nautical or sailing triangle, computing the relationship between the zenith, celestial north pole, and the location of the observer. Davis' five considerations are as follows:

> And in the observation of this altitude there are five things especially to be regarded: the first is, that you know your meridional distance between your zenith and the sun or stars which by your cross-staff or astrolabe is given: the second, that the declination be truly known at the time of your observation. And the other three are, that you consider whether your zenith be between the equinoctial and the sun or stars, or whether the equinoctial be between your zenith and them, or whether they be between your zenith and the equator [same as equinoctial], for there is several order of working upon each of these three differences.
>
> Latitude you must also know, that so much as the pole is above the horizon, so much is the zenith from the equinoctial, and this distance between the zenith and the equator is called latitude.[48]

So in addition to the altitude measurement and declination of the sun, the navigator must recognize which of the following relationships obtains for the day:

1. The zenith is between the equinoctial and the sun, or
2. The equinoctial is between the zenith and the sun, or
3. The sun is between the zenith and the equinoctial.

Again, latitude is equal to the height of polestar over the horizon, and the distance from the zenith to the

equinoctial.[49] *These relationships are important because Hame can see his zenith, the horizon, and the sun, but not the equinoctial, and the equinoctial's position relative to the zenith is the key to determining latitude.*

Davis' relationships can be summed up as follows:

sun - zenith - equinoctial	Latitude = declination − zenith distance
zenith - equinoctial - sun	Latitude = zenith distance − declination
zenith - sun - equinoctial	Latitude = zenith distance + declination

Hame's measurement (see the beginning of the chapter) yields a solar altitude of 52G. The correct celestial relationship that applies to today's calculation is *zenith - equinoctial - sun*.

In other words, Hame knows that the invisible equinoctial lies between his zenith and the sun. Hame's declination table furnishes the declination of the sun for the day. During its apparent annual path around the earth, the sun reaches a declination of just over 23 degrees north of the equinoctial at the summer solstice, the northernmost point reached by the sun, and six months later the sun reaches its southernmost point at just over 23 degrees south of the equinoctial at the winter solstice. By November 27, 1611, *Guyft* has arrived in the Caribbean. On this date, the sun's declination is 22G 42M south, so we know that the sun is situated south of the equinoctial. The latitude formula is:

> Latitude = zenith distance − declination
> Altitude of the sun = 52G
> Zenith distance = 90 − 52G = 38G

The altitude measures degrees upward from the horizon; zenith distance reckons zero at the zenith and counts degrees southward from it to the celestial object. Applying the formula:

> Latitude = 38G − 22G 42M = 15G 18M North

The distance between the zenith and the equinoctial is 15G 18M.

Hame knows that some angles are impossible or impractical to measure with a cross-staff. Bourne

Nouember.

First			Second			Third			Fourth		
1625			1626			1627			1628		
1629			1630			1631			1632		
1633			1634			1635			1636		
1637			1638			1639			1640		
1641			1642			1643			1644		
D.	G.	M.	D.	G.	M.	D.	G.	M.	D.	G.	M.
1	17	30	1	17	32	1	17	28	1	17	40
2	17	52	2	17	48	2	17	44	2	17	57
3	18	8	3	18	5	3	18	1	3	18	13
4	18	24	4	18	20	4	18	17	4	18	28
5	18	40	5	18	36	5	18	32	5	18	44
6	18	55	6	18	51	6	18	47	6	18	59
7	19	10	7	19	6	7	19	2	7	19	13
8	19	24	8	19	21	8	19	17	8	19	28
9	19	38	9	19	35	9	19	31	9	19	42
10	19	52	10	19	48	10	19	45	10	19	55
11	20	5	11	20	2	11	19	59	11	20	9
12	20	18	12	20	15	12	20	12	12	20	22
13	20	31	13	20	28	13	20	25	13	20	34
14	20	43	14	20	40	14	20	37	14	20	46
15	20	55	15	20	52	15	20	49	15	20	58
16	21	6	16	21	4	16	21	1	16	21	9
17	21	17	17	21	15	17	21	12	17	21	20
18	21	28	18	21	26	18	21	23	18	21	31
19	21	38	19	21	36	19	21	33	19	21	41
20	21	48	20	21	46	20	21	43	20	21	51
21	21	58	21	21	56	21	21	53	21	22	0
22	22	7	22	22	4	22	22	2	22	22	9
23	22	15	23	22	13	23	22	11	23	22	17
24	22	23	24	22	21	24	22	19	24	22	25
25	22	31	25	22	29	25	22	27	25	22	33
26	22	38	26	22	36	26	22	35	26	22	40
27	22	45	27	22	43	27	22	42	27	22	47
28	22	51	28	22	50	28	22	48	28	22	53
29	22	57	29	22	56	29	22	54	29	22	59
30	23	3	30	23	1	30	23	0	30	23	4

(Between each pair of year-columns is printed vertically: *South Declination.*)

39. Declination table — John Davis includes in *The Seamans Secrets* (1633 edition) a declination table computed for a several-year span. The table gives the sun's position along the ecliptic for any day of the year, showing the degrees north or south of the celestial equator, to a maximum of just over 23 degrees north at the Tropic of Cancer, to south at the Tropic of Capricorn. Extrapolated backward, the third column gives the degrees (D) and minutes (M) for the dates relevant to the computation discussed in the text. Credit: Courtesy of the John Carter Brown Library at Brown University, shelf mark D633 D268s

encourages the use of the astrolabe and cross-staff as complementary instruments, using the latter when the sun's altitude is below 50 degrees, the astrolabe for altitudes greater. Bourne gives two reasons for this. First, the wider the separation between horizon and sun, the more difficult to gauge the angle. Second, the graduation of the staff does not give accurate readings above that angle.[50] Thomas Blundeville's *Exercises* discusses the relative merits of the astrolabe over the cross-staff and concludes that when the altitude of the sun or the polestar exceeds 50 or 60 degrees, the pilot must use an astrolabe and not a cross-staff, "which astrolabe in mine opinion . . . is the best instrument of all others to take the altitude of the sun in the day, or of any star in the night."[51] Our example above requires Hame to exercise superb eye-hand coordination.

When shown a cross-staff in a museum setting, visitors inevitably ask how accurate it was. Accuracy is difficult to discuss in an historical sense because of our modern fetish for precision, and precision expressed numerically, even when a statement about precision might be meaningless. In an experiment, replicas of an astrolabe and a cross-staff were subjected to approximately two hundred tests at sea to examine characteristics of the instruments and their errors. To filter the sunlight, William Bourne's suggestion of using a smoked glass shade attached

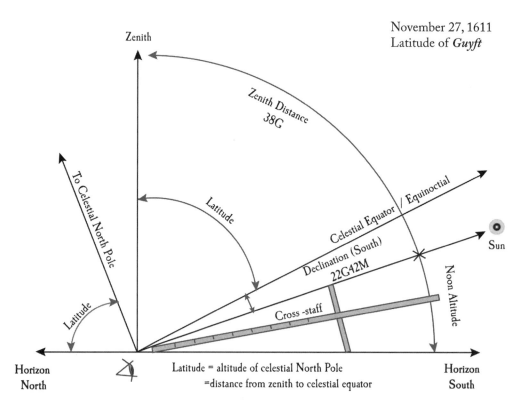

40. LATITUDE REDUCTION FROM SOLAR ALTITUDE OBSERVATION ⚊ This diagram shows the relationship between the observer, his measured altitude of the sun, the zenith, and the other components of the celestial sphere important to the computation of latitude described in the text. Credit: Evi Numen

to the upper edge of the transversary was followed, with certain corrections recommended by Edward Wright. Wright recommends adjusting a cross-staff measurement by considering the height of the eye above the earth's surface and parallax. In later years, these errors transformed into systematic corrections in reducing any altitude observations to obtain latitude. Nowadays errors corrected for sextants include dip (height of eye), refraction, the sun's semidiameter, and ocular parallax, although for most of the sixteenth century many of these corrections were not yet employed, or were employed inconsistently. The experiment with replica instruments revealed, however, that except for the semidiameter, ignoring the other corrections did not induce significant error, the cumulative error amounting to about a degree (or about sixty miles which might multiply throughout a voyage).[52] The trials with the replica cross-staff showed errors of between about 30 minutes and 1 degree. Some of the errors occurred randomly, some due to the difficulty of simultaneously viewing horizon and celestial object, and some because the precise moment of noon cannot be reckoned visually.[53] With practice, despite errors inherent in the manufacture of the instrument, a seaman could achieve an accuracy with the cross-staff to less than one degree, or about twenty to forty miles.

Hame has discovered errors in obtaining consistent results with the cross-staff. The most noticeable errors include the difficulty in gauging large angles, holding the staff vertically, and "eccentricity." To Edward Wright, the "eccentricity of the eye (that is to the distance wherewith the center or point wherein the sight beams concur within the eye is further backward then the end of the staff) may through neglect of this abatement cause error in taking the height observed to be greater then indeed it is."[54] As we have seen, Wright offers many corrections to charts and enumerates various common navigational errors, including these for the cross-staff. Wright's "eccentricity" is ocular parallax. For accurate observations,

sun- or starlight must fall directly on the retina, not on the exterior surface of the eye. To correct the eccentricity, William Bourne recommends paring down the end of the instrument to reduce parallax, a controversial measure.[55] Wright and Davis advocate the use of two transversaries simultaneously to locate and correct for ocular parallax.[56] Thomas Hariot even devised a foresight to attach to the cross-staff to reduce ocular parallax, and later constructed a table to correct for "surplus of the horizon" (dip), and tried to establish a correction for atmospheric refraction as well.[57]

Refraction, the apparent displacement of a celestial body near the horizon owing to the thickening of the atmosphere, did not become a systematic correction until much later, although Wright, too, recognizes this error. Even so, a correction for refraction is almost salutary as it can never be absolutely quantified. Wright's other parallax error is of the sun, or what we now term semidiameter. As the sun presents a disk (a half degree in diameter) and not a point source to an observer, a navigator can introduce an error by lack of consistency in his observational mark: does he reckon altitude according to the sun's upper or lower limb? Or center? At the beginning of this chapter, we saw how Hame handles the matter. Correcting for semidiameter allows the navigator to use the transversary to block the solar disk, taking a measurement on the sun's upper limb. This correction for semidiameter ensures that the observational datum will always be the sun's center. Bourne's smoked glass attached to the transversary to reduce solar glare may have enabled observations to be made when the sun was within 20 degrees of the horizon.[58] The glass, however, may exacerbate refraction. Because the sun presents a disk, Bourne cautions that the pilot needs to be consistent in using either a limb or the center of the sun for observations and suggests the use of the glass to view the upper edge of the sun's disk and allow a correction of 15 minutes of arc for the sun's semidiameter.[59]

Conclusion

With the introduction of the altitude-distance method and the reliance on solar observations, the cross-staff experienced rapid development through the latter sixteenth century, becoming the central, practical tool for determining latitude from a ship. The astrolabe became a complementary tool.[60] Inevitably, mariners and mathematicians sought to increase the accuracy of the cross-staff. Increased accuracy could be obtained with longer staffs, leading to the invention of multiple transversaries or crosspieces by the Dutch engineer and mathematician Michiel Coignet, an invention popularized in England by Thomas Blundeville.[61] The new design made systematic identification of the instrument's inherent errors possible, a task English pilots and mathematicians readily assumed. These corrections and developments transformed the cross-staff from an instrument with one transversary and one graduated side in the sixteenth century to a staff with four graduated sides with a corresponding transversary for each side by the mid-seventeenth. The instrument reached the pinnacle of its development around 1700, contradicting many texts and museum displays, which have the instrument disappearing in the early seventeenth century.[62] At this time, the cross-staff was the most reliable altitude-measuring instrument available, with an error reckoned at about 20', or about 20 miles.[63]

Tristram Hame may not have made all of the corrections recommended by his contemporaries to better his cross-staff results. Even experienced navigators disagree with the necessity to make some or all of them. Some navigators continue to dismiss magnetic variation as worth correcting. Hame, however, pays attention to current discoveries about variation. In his voyaging, he does not require or expect pinpoint accuracy. Twenty to forty miles constituted fair accuracy in the early 1600s. Making landfall reasonably close to his destination within an appropriate amount of time was the objective: he then sailed along the coastline until he reached his haven. A century and a half after Hame, Captain James Cook maintained that any instrument that could determine stellar altitudes within a half degree (thirty miles) was sufficient.[64]

Modern experimentation with replica instruments has afforded insights into the relative merits of the cross-staff and astrolabe, lending credence to the probability that navigators used multiple altitude-measuring instruments in tandem and adapted the instruments based on experimentation. In the 1970s during a voyage from Plymouth to San Francisco of a reproduction of Sir Francis Drake's ship, *Golden Hinde*, crew members made solar and stellar observations with replica cross-staffs and an astrolabe and compared readings with a modern sextant. Using sixteenth-century observational techniques, the crew found that even a slight wind upset the balance of the cross-staff, making observations of large angles particularly difficult. The astrolabe, though, provided an easier way of taking the sun's meridian transit at noon. While the astrolabe proved difficult to use at night with the polestar, the cross-staff proved surprisingly useful for this purpose, for when adapted to the dark, the crew could make out the horizon. Most of the solar meridian transits, however, were made with the cross-staff but with the instrument reversed and used as a shadow-casting forestaff.[65] In fact, the experimenters found that they achieved best results when they reversed the cross-staff and used it as a forestaff.

Despite the reliance on the sun, cross-staff observations had by no means abandoned stellar sights completely, as contemporary references indicate and as modern sea-trials with replica instruments have confirmed.[66] As noted, the *Golden Hinde* cross-staff proved useful for stellar observations at night, contrary to expectation, which held that the horizon would be invisible. The mariner's astrolabe, however, proved more useful for observations of the sun at a high altitude at noon, perhaps explaining the

41a. Captain Hame demonstrates a backstaff ⟿ Hame takes a noon altitude reading with a backstaff. The instrument has two arcs: the first, located at the far end of the instrument, supports a movable shadow bar and is graduated to 60 (or 65) degrees. The larger arc nearest Hame's eye is graduated to 30 degrees. Hame sets the shadow on the forward arc to within 10 degrees of yesterday's noon altitude reading for the sun. He then holds the instrument vertically and moves the sight vane on the 30-degree scale up or down until he can see the horizon through the sight vane pinhole aligned with the horizon vane slit at the far end of the instrument. Hame then notes the degrees indicated on both arcs and adds them and performs arithmetic (described in the text) to obtain his latitude. Note that unlike the cross-staff, Hame looks away from the sun: the sun is at his back. Credit: Science Museum of Virginia

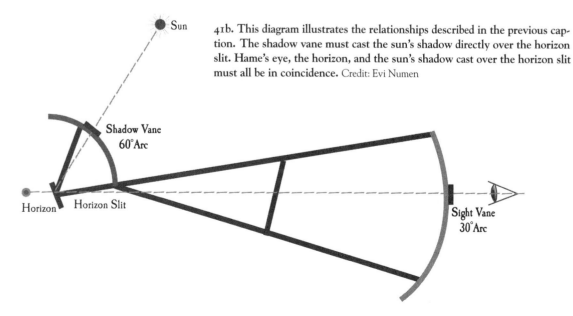

41b. This diagram illustrates the relationships described in the previous caption. The shadow vane must cast the sun's shadow directly over the horizon slit. Hame's eye, the horizon, and the sun's shadow cast over the horizon slit must all be in coincidence. Credit: Evi Numen

42a. DETAIL OF DIAGONAL SCALE ON A BACKSTAFF ⚊ A close-up view of the larger 30-degree arc on the backstaff. This is known as a diagonal scale. The diagonal lines intersect equidistant parallel arcs. This scale enables the mariner to reckon a measurement to a fraction of a degree. Credit: Science Museum of Virginia

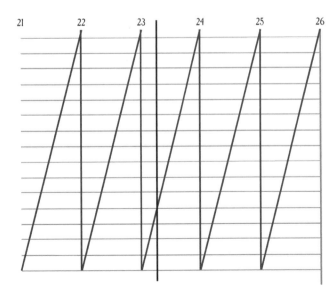

42b. An illustration of the diagonal scale on the 30-degree arc of the backstaff. The vertical numbered lines on the arc are individual degrees. The horizontal arcs denote fractions of a degree. This diagram shows 15 concentric arcs: each represents four minutes (15 x 4 = 60 minutes or one degree). To read the scale, the observer notes where the sight vane intersects a horizontal arc *and* the nearest diagonal line. The dark vertical line represents the position of the sight vane along the 30-degree arc. It shows 23 degrees 16 minutes. Captain Hame's backstaff has ten horizontal arcs: each denotes six minutes. Although the backstaff with a diagonal scale could mark fractions of a degree, the instrument did not necessarily supply this accuracy. Credit: Evi Numen

enduring use of the instrument even after the cross-staff had been improved.[67] Hame doubtless experiments with his tools and cleverly adapts them to suit his needs.

Tristram Hame's experience has proven the worth of the cross-staff when supported by altitude observations made with an astrolabe, but a new altitude-measuring instrument has appeared recently, the backstaff, which he does not possess for this voyage. The instrument contains a movable pinhole sight along a large arc (25–30 degrees), a movable shadow-casting bar along a smaller arc (65 degrees), and a fixed bar with a slit for viewing the horizon. To use the instrument, a navigator sets the bar on the smaller arc to within 10 degrees of the sun's altitude, turns his back to the sun and sights the horizon through the slit from the movable pinhole. The navigator lines up the pinhole with the horizon to coincide with the bar casting a shadow directly over the horizon slit. With the instrument set, the navigator adds the values of both arcs and then uses this altitude figure for calculating latitude (at the moment of noon, of course). When Hame uses his cross-staff as a forestaff, he is substituting an observation for the sun's shadow, cast by the instrument, for direct observation, essentially the principle of the backstaff.

Hame has read a text by Thomas Hood from the 1590s, which describes a cross-staff that does not require a simultaneous observation of the horizon, a work that argues the substitution of shadow-casting for direct observation.[68] The backstaff offers several innovations: unlike the cross-staff, the backstaff contains not linear but arc scales (although the first ones used linear scales to represent chords). Because the observer no longer peers at the sun directly, glare and eye strain are eliminated. The observer no longer has to view simultaneously the horizon and the celestial object.[69] While the 65-degree scale is calibrated in increments of 5 degrees, the 25-degree scale contains a remarkable innovation to enable readings of fractions of a degree, which the cross staff lacks: the

diagonal scale. In effect, the linear scale of the cross-staff transforms into a compressed scale of diagonal lines that cut across a number of equidistant parallel lines.[70] The diagonal lines either follow a zigzag pattern or parallel one another. The intersection of the diagonals and equidistant parallel lines (each parallel representing a concentric circle) pinpoint fractions of a degree, measured with a pair of dividers. The use of dual arc scales is clever and elegant. The earliest extant backstaffs, of the type illustrated here, date to the mid-seventeenth century. Hame will likely experiment with one in another decade or so.

We do not describe timepieces that may have found their way aboard Guyft. As we have noted, mechanical timepieces were not reliable for use at sea in 1611. Hame and some of the gentlemen may have carried portable sundials; however, they were of little practical use at sea. Many were made for specific latitudes and even if adjustable may only have given local time within fifteen to thirty minutes' accuracy. As shipboard life is regulated by the system of thirty-minute sandglasses and the ringing of bells to regulate a four-hour watch, Hame has little need for another timepiece.

When taken together, climate theory, compass variation, and altitude measurement of celestial objects combine empirical observation, the preoccupation with mathematical models to reveal God's methods, and the medieval cosmos of sub- and superlunar spheres to form the mental world of Tristram Hame's navigation. Importantly, as Davis and Borough advise, the cross-staff should be used in context with other tools: the navigator requires the cross-staff, a plane chart or a globe, and a compass to determine Guyft's location. The cross-staff and astrolabe, instruments with only one moving part, are artifacts embodying mathematical traditions of several cultures. The instruments can, indeed, be read as texts. Navigation with a cross-staff and astrolabe present a numerical way of looking at the seascape. This numerical vision transformed the seascape into a new space, one that supplanted an eternal sea with a mathematically contained, grid-enclosed world.[71] The imposition of trigonometry and geometry on the seascape, however, reduced error and uncertainty. The imposition of a geometric framework on nature made it possible to predict and forecast natural phenomena.[72]

Three new marriages here are made
One of the staff and sea astrolabe
Of the sun and star is another
Which now agree like sister and brother
And chart and compass which new at bate [did debate],
Will now agree like master and mate.

If you useth well in this your journey
They will be the king of Spain's atarny [attorney or agent]
To bring you to silver and Indian gold
Which will keep you in age from hunger and cold
God speed you well and send you fair weather
And that again we may meet together.

—Thomas Hariot, British Library, Additional MS 6788, fol. 490

CHAPTER 8

NOVEMBER 27, NEW SPAIN

Therefore the wise Christian mariner ought to have a clear conscience, and to call for the help of Almighty God, living by his eyes and hands unto heaven, and say with the Prophet . . . save me oh my God, for waters have entered even unto my soul.

— MARTÍN CORTÉS, *Arte of Navigation*, 1561

G*uyft* has crossed the Atlantic, conveyed by the seasonally reliable trade winds. By arriving during autumn, the ship has missed the hurricanes, which accompany the equatorial rainy summer. Tristram Hame planned a westward Atlantic voyage to reach the Caribbean, followed by island-hopping northward to Jamaica and Cuba, then Virginia. Absent the sight of land, Hame relies on many navigational clues, including the life beneath his ship. A sure sign of tropical waters is the blue shark, unique among its kind for ranging far from shore. Similarly, Hame's crew has found the ocean bonito far from land, a fish that competes with flying fish as sailors' food, and also provides a navigational hint of location. Flying fish, lured to the lanterns on board *Guyft*, fly into the canvas sheets, which function as nets.[1] Another tropical fish that feeds sailors and whose presence reveals a ship's location, skipper fish, are small, flat, and cluster in large schools. Triggerfish, particularly, gather in the ship's wake, amusing the sailors by turning over on their sides and appearing to stare upward.[2] The ocean's color also gives hints of Hame's location: generally,

the intensity of the ocean's color signifies depth, but the ocean's appearance as blue or green depends on several factors, including salinity and the abundance of microorganisms. Equatorial waters are usually blue, whereas greener seas are found in northerly and southerly regions. High salinity yields a blue tint, low salinity, green.[3]

During autumn, however, the Atlantic winds may blow from the south or west, producing unstable weather. The voyage thus far has not been without difficulties, particularly the torrents of rain and choppy seas that caused nagging leaks. Further, *Guyft*'s passage may not have been a solitary one. As the ship headed for Deseada, Hame might have encountered Spanish treasure fleets on their way to Veracruz.[4] In 1611, Britain and the Dutch Republic are at peace with Spain, but the Spaniards are wary about intrusions into their territory. Hame and his contemporaries routinely skirt areas claimed by Spain, but British, French, and Dutch ships search for opportunities to conduct contraband trade beyond Spanish military authorities. Dutch ships, particularly, eagerly sell linen, paper, and wine for pelts and skins.[5]

As Hame approached the West Indies, he consulted his rutter:

> If you set sail from any islands of the Canaries for
> the West Indies, you must steer away 30 or 40
> leagues due south, to the end you may avoid the
> calms of the Island of Hierro, and being so far dis-
> tant from the said island, then must you steer away
> west southwest until you find yourself in 20 degrees,
> and then sail west and by south until you come to
> 15 degrees and ½. And from thence steer away west
> and by north, and so shall you make a west way by
> reason of the northwesting of the compass, which
> west way will bring you to the island of Deseada.[6]

As certain kinds of land birds show increasing numbers, Hame reasonably concludes that his ship nears
land. Tropical birds do not travel long distances from
their breeding areas. We cannot be sure of what birds
were common in this region in Hame's day, but we
assume that, as now, he expects to encounter the
common noddy, which breeds on local islands, and
the laughing gull, which winters near South America
but at other times inhabits much of the eastern
American seaboard.[7] During late fall and early winter,
Hame might encounter the northern gannet, which

shifts between its breeding area in the north and the
American coast around 23 degrees north latitude,
or the masked booby that breeds year-round in this
vicinity.[8]

When *Guyft* approached the Indies, however,
Hame became very cautious to ensure that he was in
fact heading for Deseada. He records:

> We were in the latitude of 14 degrees, and hauled
> over toward the islands of the West Indies, and
> toward night we saw land. One of our company
> took it to be the Bermudas: being very near the
> shore we sounded many times and had no ground,
> at the last we found good ground in 14 or 15 fath-
> oms. There we cast anchor. In the morning we
> weighed, and sounded still as we trended by the
> shore: but after we were past a cable's length from
> our road, we had no land again in 40 or 50 fath-
> oms. We kept still by the shore not yet being cer-
> tain what island it was. Later, we espied people
> coming from the shore, who when they came near,
> cried out for barter or trade. When they came
> close aboard, they made signs and cried out to see
> our colors, which we presently put forth in the
> main top, and told them we were *Ingleses*, *amigos*,
> and *hermanos*, that is, Englishmen, their friends,
> and brothers. As soon as they understood we were

43. WEST INDIES, FROM RICHARD HAKLUYT'S *THE PRINCIPAL NAVIGATIONS* — In this map, the islands of the Caribbean are
too small and numerous to name individually. Captain Hame uses charts but he also relies on sailing directions with course
recommendations and descriptions of what he is likely to see from his ship. Even so, the best sailing directions alone do not
give Hame the confidence to be sure of his landfall. Hame also uses native informants to ascertain his location. This region
features hundreds of islands. Credit: The Rosenbach Museum & Library, Philadelphia, shelf mark A589p

Months and days	Latitude	Course	Leagues	Winds
November 26, 1611	20G 0M	N & by W	34	Gale at W

The Discourse
The eastern coast of Hispaniola bears S & by W from us. Hispaniola has a latitude of 18G 29M and longitude 306G 0M. The wind shifted from a strong E gale to a storm from the W by afternoon.

Almanac
Tuesday, Feast of St. Linus, Pope and Martyr. New moon. Saturn is still southeast at sunset, Jupiter is southeast at sunrise, and Mars, Venus, and Mercury sup with sovereign Sol. An evil day with love's labor's lost.

Englishmen, they were bolder to come near in their canoa [canoe]: we threw them a rope and one came aboard us. We traded with them for some tobacco, pineapples, plantains, pompions [pumpkins] and such things as they had. We gave them knives, whistles, and such toys. Here we kept close by the shore. One of them told us that island was Santa Lucia.[9]

Santa Lucia was close enough. Approaching the Caribbean, Hame followed his rutter, but as he entered the Western Hemisphere, storms assailed his ship. Hame records:

The 21st of November, all the morning, was very foul weather; and a high-grown sea. The storm held as the day before with as much extremity and about noon we struck our foretopmast thus remaining according to the pleasure of the almighty God in the surging and overgrown seas in which dangers the Lord has hitherto preserved us. Our long boat, which we were fain to tow at stern, broke away, and put us to some trouble to recover her again. This we did, and made means to heave her into the ship, though very much bruised, and that I had two men fore hurt, and like to be lost in the heaving of her in.[10]

The long boat is the ship's small boat, used to convey people and cargo through shallows to and from an anchorage, to explore creeks and rivers, to tow a becalmed ship, or function as a lifeboat. Hame cannot afford to lose it. *Guyft*, since the storm, has experienced calm seas and vigorous winds, and

now proceeds north. Hame's record for the 26th of November is above:

The latitude and longitude of Hispaniola come from John Tapp's *The Sea-Mans Kalendar*.[11] Modern longitude is measured east or west of the prime meridian at Greenwich, England, a datum that became the convention long after Tristram Hame's era. Longitude had no internationally agreed datum in the seventeenth century. Tapp's longitude and latitude are accurate within one of the common schemes in use at the time.

Today, November 27, the winds blew from the northeast at daybreak, shifting to north and by east by noon, to northwest and by north by late afternoon, and north-northeast during the evening. From open-ocean navigating to island-hopping, Hame keeps a careful record of dead reckoning positions, trying to distinguish one island from the next. He has taken altitude sights of the sun during the Atlantic crossing, and continues the practice daily. Throughout the voyage, Hame maintains a regimen of navigational self-study:

The better to strengthen my former studies in this business, I seek after journals, plots, discourses, or whatever else might help my understanding. Before this voyage, I set skillful workmen to make me quadrants, staves [cross-staffs], semicircles, etc., as much as concern the fabric [fabricating] of them, not trusting to their mechanic hands to divide [graduate] them, but had them divided by an ingenious practitioner in the mathematics. I likewise

had compass needles made after the most reason-
ablest and truest ways that could be thought on for
our hopeful ship.[12]

As previously discussed, any woodworker could make
a cross-staff, but the incision of one or more graduated scales might have been assigned to a craftsman
of sharper visual skill, such as an engraver. An "ingenious practitioner in the mathematics," however,
might be an artisan with much experience in gradu-
ating instruments for surveying, astronomy, or other
related application.

Hame prepares to take a sequence of solar-altitude
observations with his cross-staff. In tropical waters,
Hame has noticed how the sun reddens and appears
to flatten as it settles on the horizon at sunset. What
we now describe as atmospheric refraction must be
taken into account for modern sextant observations
of the sun's altitude. The refractive behavior of light
was not known in any systematic fashion in 1611.
Hame and his contemporaries, who study the sun's
motion closely, recognize the effects of atmospheric
refraction although they do not employ modern language to describe it. Hame comments: "The 27th, I
observed the sun to rise like an oval, along the horizon. I called three or four to see it, the better to confirm my judgment, and we all agreed, that it was twice
as long as it was broad. We plainly perceived withal,
that by degrees as it gate [rose] up higher, it also
recovered his roundness."[13]

Hame takes several measurements of the sun's
altitude throughout late morning and past noon,
reckoning the sun's meridian passage at 46G. Hame
consults his declination table to obtain today's value
of the sun's distance below the equinoctial. Hame
compute's *Guyft*'s latitude as follows:

1. The sun's altitude at meridian passage was
   46G.
2. For today, the correct relationship for the
   zenith, equinoctial, and the altitude of the
   sun is:
   zenith - equinoctial - sun

3. Today's declination of the sun is 22G 42M
   South. The sun, therefore, is situated
   below the equinoctial by this value.
4. The latitude formula that applies is:
   latitude = zenith distance – declination
   altitude of the sun = 46G
   zenith distance = 90 – 46G = 44G
   latitude = 44G – 22G 42M = 21G 18M
   The distance between the zenith and the
   equinoctial is 21G 18M.

   The latitude of *Guyft* at noon today is 21G
   18M.

While the Atlantic passage proved unevent-
ful except for some stormy weather, surgeon Gerard
Chilson reports to Hame the instances of illness on
the voyage from the Canaries to the West Indies:

> After we passed our own climate and drawing
> within four degrees of the tropic line of Cancer at
> which time divers of our men fell suddenly sick and
> such as had thin and dry bodies were infected with
> hot burning and pestifurous [plague-like] fevers. Of
> this infection we had eight. All of them through
> God's providence letting blood and purging were
> all recovered. Many other men fell sick with great
> pain in their heads, stomachs, backs, shortness of
> breath and heaviness of their whole bodies, which
> sickness I gather came partly by the changing of
> the climate and partly through their own disorder
> of insatiable feeding on fresh fish, much drinking
> cold water and lying in the air on the hatches in
> the night season, but God be thanked after purging
> and letting of blood not one perished.[14]

Chilson's chief medical concern is the condition of
William Norrys, seaman, disabled by a cannon shot
from the French ship that Hame engaged at the Island
of Tercera. Norrys has not recovered from the wound:
Chilson informs Hame that Norrys may be dying.

As earlier discussed, everything in the universe
is made of four elements: earth, air, fire, and water.
Chilson's application of medicines and treatments
recognizes the human body's constituency of complexions, or combinations of elements. Each element

has two qualities. For example, the qualities of fire are heat and dryness. Each complexion is a mix of two predominant qualities taken from the four elements. Norrys' diet and the treatment of his injury are based on an accurate diagnosis of his complexion. Chilson judges Norrys to be of sanguine complexion. Chilson observes that Norrys' body is sanguine because heat and moisture predominate. Chilson knows that he is sanguine because certain signs have preeminence in his body, such as large arteries and veins, thick, reddish hair, a great and full pulse, and perfect digestion. He is given to short anger, abundant sweat and urine, and the urine is red and thick.[15] Norrys' severe injury has thrown his bodily humors off balance. Since Chilson cannot remove the fragments of iron and wooden splinters from Norrys' wound, he is trying other remedies. Chilson notes that Norrys has a heavy head and dim eyes. He feels a pain in his hips and thighs, and he can hardly fetch his breath. His strength will not sustain the letting of blood, and the time for bleeding is past anyway. It is too painful for him to vomit. To restore the humors, then, Chilson must purge his body without bleeding or vomiting. There are two ways left: by potions or pills by the mouth, or by suppositories or clysters [enemas]. Chilson tries a suppository first, one made of honeycomb, rolled into a small shape so that it can be inserted in his fundiment [anus]. He also adds some saltpeter.[16]

Chilson tries this treatment, but Norrys worsens. Gangrene has set in. Norrys begins to lose consciousness for long periods. Chilson holds little hope for recovery. It is time for Norrys to compose a will before he loses his wits entirely. Popular opinion holds that sailors of this era led a very rough existence, owned few possessions, and outside of the informal fraternity of shipmates, did not participate in a larger social world. This image does not bear scrutiny, as many wills survive from Elizabethan and Jacobean seamen that attest not only to the shipboard fraternity, but to complex social relationships ashore. The master gunner, Silvester Heale, takes the will of William Norrys:

In the name of God, Amen. Here I, William Norrys, being in perfect mind and memory make here my last will and testament. First, I bequeath my soul to Almighty God. And my body where it shall please my company. First, I give to John Chilson, surgeon, all my wages which is one mark a month, and he will see to all my debts to be paid. I will that he pay to Robert Adams of Plymouth 40 shillings. More I will that he pay to the Goodwife Hine of Plymouth 6 shillings 8 pence, and he to receive such things as she has of mine which is a coat cloth and a piece of bustian [fustian, or coarse cotton or linen]. More I will that he pay to Mr. Heale 2 shillings for a book and for making of a cassock. Item, I give to Mr. Heale all such debts as are owing to me which is written in bulls [IOUs] that he shall receive of me. Item, I give to Mr. Heale my chest and all such things as I have here in the ship. Item, I will that he give to George Brasye a piece of white cloth and a shirt. Item, I will that he distribute the rest of my shirts where he thinks best which is a half dozen. Item, I will that he give to William Horwood one of my daggers which he wants. Thus I make an end. In witness hereof I set my hands written the 27th of November.[17]

Norrys, then, looks to his shipboard supervisor, Heale, as the executor of his estate, while expressing his gratitude to surgeon Chilson by leaving extant wages to him. Norrys' possessions are not insubstantial: he owns a personal weapon and a versatile tool, a dagger, raw cloth for use in making garments, a chest, and several shirts. Further, Norrys retains allegiances to Robert Adams and Goodwife Hine, people with whom he lodged when ashore, or people to whom he owed money for looking after his affairs.

Seaman Norrys is not likely to survive the day. The Church of England in 1611 teaches the doctrine of predestination, that few people belong to God's elect. The relationship between predestination, or God's master plan, and Providence is close and complex, particularly relative to Hame's beliefs. Neither Providence nor predestination can be understood or rationalized through empirical observation of the world. Within the Reformed church, predestination is a particularly distressful component of religious practice.[18] Some souls are predestined for the ranks of the elect, those truly saved by God for a state of grace. Unless a person is foreordained as a member of the elect, people are powerless to improve their status with God. Whether or not a Christian is destined to be elect cannot be discerned by any evidence, but might be intuited. And if one is not part of the elect, then one is damned. People who feel that God speaks directly to them, to their consciences, place themselves within the elect.[19] Norrys, however, suspects that he is not part of the elect, and he is painfully aware that if he is not part of this select group, then he is damned. He has been praying often to help ensure godly favor.

Aware that he is dying, Norrys asks Heale to read from *The Plaine Mans Path-way to Heaven*, a popular book by Arthur Dent, specifically inventoried in the ship's cargo. This book features a dialogue between the divine, Master Theologus; Philagathus, an honest man; Asunetus, an ignorant man; and Antilegon, a "caviller" or a skeptic. As a good Protestant, Norrys believes in the doctrine of justification by faith alone and in predestination as a member of the elect. Living by these and other doctrines, the Christian aspires to sanctification, a difficult process. The dialogue in *Plaine Mans Path-way* instructs these doctrines. Gunner Heale reads to Norrys what Master Theologus says about death and vanity:

> There is no cause why men should be so given to this world, for they must leave it, when they have done all that they can. As they say, today a man, tomorrow none. And as the Apostle said, We brought nothing into this world, and now shall carry nothing out. We must all die we know not how soon. Why therefore should men set their hearts upon such uncertain and deceivable [deceitful] things? For all things in this world are more light than a feather, more brittle than glass, more fleeting than a shadow, more vanishing than smoke, more inconstant than the wind.
>
> The world is a sea of glass, a pageant of fond delight, a theater of vanity, a labyrinth of error, a gulf of grief, a sty of filthiness, a vale of misery, a river of tears, a cage full of devils, a den of scorpions, a whirlwind of passions, a delectable frenzy, certain sorrow, fickle wealth, long heaviness, short joy.[20]

William Norrys, age 24, dies around dusk. Aided by some passengers, Roger Coopy, the ship's carpenter, and sailors Robert Pyke and Thomas Blunt prepare a simple burial shroud out of canvas and stitch it closed.[21] Hame records: "During past days, our gunner did languish unrecoverably, and grew very weak, desiring, that for the little time he had to live, he might drink sack altogether, which I ordered he should do. The 27th in the morning he died. An honest and a strong-hearted man. He abided in a close-boarded cabin in the gunroom, which was very close indeed."[22] Master Hame summons the ship's company and reads from *The Booke of Common Prayer*:

> I am the resurrection and the life, says the Lord. He that believes in me, yea though he were dead, yet shall he live. And whosoever lives and believes in me, shall not die forever. I know that my Redeemer lives, and that I shall rise out of the earth in the last day, and shall be covered again with my skin, and shall see God in my flesh: yea, and I myself shall behold him, not with other, but with these same eyes. We brought nothing into this world, neither may we carry anything out of this world. The Lord giveth, and the Lord taketh away. Even as it pleases the Lord, so comes things to pass: Blessed be the name of the Lord.[23]

Hame asks Pyke and Blunt to cast the body overboard, and then he continues: "For as much as it has pleased Almighty God of his great mercy, to take unto himself the soul of our dear brother here departed, we therefore commit his body to the ground, earth to earth, ashes to ashes, dust to dust, in sure and certain hope of resurrection to eternal life, through our Lord Jesus Christ, who shall change our vile body, that it may be like to his glorious body, according to the mighty working, whereby he is able to subdue all things to himself."[24] Hame reads a lesson, provided in *The Booke of Common Prayer*, taken from 1 Corinthians 15 about the resurrection of the body. "Therefore, my beloved brethren, be ye steadfast, unmovable, abundant always in the work of the Lord, forasmuch as ye know that your labor is not in vain in the Lord."[25]

Norrys' shipmates reflect on his death; some wonder if his death is God's punishment for attacking the French ship. Or was God punishing Norrys? As an immediate practical concern, Hame considers how Norrys' death will affect the distribution of duties on the ship. Norrys had been a member of a watch crew and until recently, he had managed to perform some of his duties. Although a seaman, Norrys had become a gunner's mate. The loss of Norrys, a gunner's mate, is a blow to the ship's offensive and defensive capabilities.

A Religious Context to Navigation?

Hame's Protestant upbringing gives him a perspective on the world in which his navigational art has a place. First, many theologians promote geometry, which undergirds the construction and use of navigational tools, as God's own method of constructing the universe. Second, Protestants may have interfered less in early scientific matters than Catholics, or perhaps there was more space for development within the Protestant church.[26] Did this Protestant space encourage the application of mathematics generally to identify and extinguish instrumental errors or offer refinements? The theory that late seventeenth-century Protestant ideology (its asceticism) favored nascent practical science is an attractive model, but possibly Reformed theology's main influence was its support for those who viewed progress as facilitated by experimental philosophy. Did technological innovation come to be seen as a Protestant virtue? This question merits further investigation.[27] Third, nautical (and navigational) imagery remains pervasive in a metaphorical sense as illustrating the path to salvation. This imagery kept navigation in

the consciousness of many people not associated with maritime trades. Fourth, and perhaps most important, Reformation ideology was disseminated in the vernacular for popular audiences. This dissemination stimulated non-university learning, from sermons to the how-to texts widely quoted in this book. Hame's Gresham lectures were given by academics, and if these lectures did not exist, then Hame likely would have been ignorant of university knowledge of mathematics.[28] Indeed, as we have seen, the texts most influential to Hame on navigation and cosmology were produced by artisans—Davis the navigator, Bourne the gunner—who exploited or ignored past authorities, but who nevertheless acquired mathematical learning from many sources.

Examining the mutual influence of navigation and religion requires us to abandon the terms "science" and "religion" as polarized categories, so tainted as they are with visions of progress toward modernity.[29] Further, a "triumphalist" saga of the victory of science over religion during the seventeenth century will not do with its replacement of credulity and superstition by the dispassionate rationality of scientific investigation. Historical analysis has moved on from this picture.[30] Hame's worldview is replete with charms, omens, and symbolism, a mix of medieval, pre-Reformation ritual, Protestant dogma, natural philosophy as reflected in the early cosmographical texts used for navigation, all tempered by the unfathomable workings of Providence. These ingredients are all contingent and complex.[31] How did Hame practice or apply the beliefs and knowledge that combine to constitute his worldview? To us, Hame's celestial navigational tools occupy the category of "scientific instruments." "Science," to Hame, carried a meaning different from its modern sense. We now characterize science as the formulation and testing of hypotheses through empirical investigation. For Hame, science is "theoretical knowledge that could be ascertained with certainty, usually by deductive means."[32] Theology, in Hame's era, is the "queen of the sciences."[33] The mathematical refinement of navigation in the late sixteenth century did not constitute a branch of science apart from and ideologically foreign to the Reformed theology.[34] Hame's navigational tools are all touched by religious ideology, from metaphors of the sea to the divine nature of the geometry inherent in the navigational art. To Hame, no conflict exists between his religion and what we classify as his early modern scientific outlook.[35]

Navigation linked to astronomy, a subject promoted by the Lutheran ideologue, Philip Melanchthon, because it afforded an understanding of Providence, an insight into God's construction of the heavens.[36] To Melanchthon, "arithmetic and geometry are the wings of the human mind."[37] Geometry gave instruction on how God organized nature, so geometry represented God's method of constructing and governing the world.[38] The English Reformation took this another step. John Dee's *Mathematicall Praeface* to the first English edition of Euclid attests to the Protestant re-invention of scientific tools as testimonies to man's talent for invention for beneficial purposes.[39] Dee, too, exemplifies the scholar who learned to apply his learning. Dee was a Cambridge student, where Edward Wright later taught, and both men learned to read and study with the object of improving the management of human affairs.[40] Mathematics had come to encompass the very processes in the mind of God at the Creation, a humanistic view put forward by Melanchthon.[41] Man could now use God's tools for improving his estate. Thus Dee defines geometry as "this science of magnitude, his properties, conditions, and appurtenances" but hastens to define its spiritual value: "No man, therefore, can doubt, but toward the attaining of knowledge incomparable, and heavenly wisdom: mathematical speculations . . . are means, aids, and guides."[42]

The Metaphorical Universe

William Barlow, author of *The Navigators Supply* (1597) and *Magneticall Advertisements* (1616), argues

the divinely inspired invention of navigational tools (a view taken up by contemporaries) by asserting that after the creation of nations and the proliferation of languages, God "had ordained the sailing compass" as the means "thereby to join dispersed nations."[43] Barlow, in fact, perceived his vocation as a preacher well matched to a study of navigation and believed that his publications lent "his helping hand for advancing a faculty that so much tends to God's glory in the spreading of the Gospel. Now if this be not against Divinity, doubtless to preserve men from danger, and to direct the wanderer, cannot be against humanity."[44] Hame shares this vision.

Hame's Ptolemaic universe blends with Christian metaphors or salvation and purpose. The separation of the sub- and superlunar spheres in the Ptolemaic universe translated into Christian metaphors in that both the physical and spiritual man occupy an intermediate position in the Chain of Being between "dull" earth—hell—and the empyrean realm of God and the angels—heaven.[45] This cosmography stressed the utility of nature for man's purposes, complementing the new view of navigational tools as beneficent inventions inspired by God. Samuel Purchas, who pushed Protestant ideology more than Hakluyt, elegantly bends oceanic navigation to the theological end of utility through divine guidance: "Now for the virtues called theological, faith, hope, and charity, the sea is a great temple not to contemplate theory, but really to practice them."[46] To Purchas, faith guides man at sea where "no earth is seen, only the heaven," but navigation itself gives hope against tempests "where the life we live is hope," and charity is found in navigation "where one man is not good to another man, but so many nations as so many persons hold commerce and intercourse of amity withal."[47]

Oceans are made of the primordial element of water, the essence of which expressed God's creative power.[48] Until the Reformation, a priest, invoking God's protection for the ark of Noah, blessed merchant ships with holy water to protect them, a practice that Protestants never really shook off.[49] The church applied seafaring imagery to Christian duty, with the church symbolized by a ship, tempestuous seas symbolizing the painful Christian route to the final judgment.[50] In fact, the early church used the emblem of the ship as a metaphor for itself, the bishop as helmsman, an office sometimes depicted with Christ or St. Peter at the whipstaff. No matter the circumstances, God guides the helm of life's ship.[51] More enduring, perhaps, is the incorporation of the ship metaphor in church architecture: the nave, derived from the Latin *navis*, means "ship."[52]

John Davis unifies his own practice of the new mathematical navigation with a biblically inspired view of the English predestination to voyage and discover what God provided for man's use. He sees voyages of discovery as producing two kinds of benefits, spiritual and corporeal, both bound by God's law. In seeking to discover, man is first obligated "to seek the kingdom of God and the righteousness thereof," but, secondly, man is obligated to go forth and multiply "and increase the flock of the faithful."[53] Davis sees the need to propagate the Gospel throughout the world as declared "by the mouth of [God's] prophet Easias 66": "I will come to gather all people and tongues, then shall they come and see my glory."[54] Davis not only assumes that the earth's resources exist for mankind's use and advancement, but he also argues that the English are pre-eminent: "there is no doubt but that we of England are this saved people by the eternal and infallible presence of the Lord, predestinated to be sent unto these Gentiles in the sea."[55] In short, Davis the master mariner not only writes an influential manual that advocates the new mathematical navigation, but he advocates a biblically grounded manifest destiny for England, relying on scripture to justify exploration and colonization. Davis undoubtedly finds all of these views complementary, just as Sir Francis Drake who, during his circumnavigation, held religious services, led sailors in prayer, and read from the psalms and John Foxe's works to enforce a Protestant identity within a theological history of martyrdom, all while sacking Spanish colonies.[56]

Beyond mariners, even landsmen evoke Christian allegory in seafaring. John Flavell's *Navigation Spiritualized* (1663) constructs and teaches a metaphorical seascape to mariners by drawing spiritual parallels between navigation and seamanship: "The truth is, *Divinity* (the doctrine of living to God), is nothing else, but the *art of soul-navigation* revealed from heaven" (italics in the original).[57] The spiritually conscious seaman should refer to the compass "in order to the steering rightly and safely to the *Port of Happiness*, he reduces to four heads, answerable to the four general points of the compass; making *God* our *north*; *Christ* our *east*; *holiness* our *south*; and *death* our *west* points."[58] The compass metaphor evokes a religious convention in that maps and charts denote east on most compass roses by a cross to indicate the way to the Holy Land. Henry Mainwaring, by contrast, constructs a considerably denser allegorical system very similar to the mental images used for memory arts in explicating the "state of a Christian, lively set forth by an allegory of a ship under sail": "My body is the hull; the keel my back; my neck the stem, the sides are my ribs."[59] Mainwaring leads the reader from the naming of body parts to Christian abstractions: "The foredeck is humility; the stern charity," proceeding to, "The law of God is my pilot; faith my captain," and finally to navigational instruments (the compass represents the five senses) and celestial objects (the "lode-star" represents the conscience).[60]

Navigational texts draw similar connections. Mathematician Thomas Hood, writing on the cross-staff and a variant, the Jacob's staff, explicates the name of the latter by referring to Genesis 32:10, "where the Patriarch says, That with his staff he came over Jordan."[61] In describing the celestial sphere in one of his texts, Robert Recorde notes that the Milky Way "might seem to be made by God, which has wrought man the means to lead men unto truth. This way is in the sky itself."[62]

Christian Cosmography

Creating a cartographic, God's-eye view of the world encouraged users of charts to reflect on the spiritual. Waghenaer's *Mariners Mirrour* not only promotes practical piloting information but also encourages "cosmographical meditations," which aid the understanding of the Scriptures.[63] Maps, then, allow their users a God's-eye view, so in addition to their practical applications, maps and their mathematical projections represent Christian authority.[64] In fact, some maps and charts of Hame's era feature mythical realms within the seascape, beyond the Fortunate Isles to the oceanic Sea of Perpetual Gloom to paradise, biblical narratives placed within maps and charts.[65] Reformed thinking believed that artistic expression and cartography should serve God, and a true art, per John Calvin, must portray the real, the sensible, and not the imaginary.[66]

Alongside mathematical projections and models, astrological influences govern Hame's cosmography. The sixteenth-century cosmos relied on judicial astrology to explain and predict events, a practice that inferred human action from celestial movements, with judgment as its end.[67] Because the world had been created for man's utility, it will be destroyed after the Day of Judgment when it is no longer needed, a common perception among Hame's contemporaries.[68] If tempests at sea are wrought by God for a purpose known only to Himself, possibly He leaves discoverable clues to His own mind. Astrology furnished this hidden language of clues by examining celestial movements. Astrology is, however, inimical to Christian dogma because of its pretence to know what theologians claim is unknowable.[69] The value of astrology remains controversial, and at least one author invokes navigational instruments in arguing against it: "To what end has God placed us so far from the stars, if with astrolabes, staves and quadrants we can do all things as if we were nearer?"[70] Despite arguments against it by scholars and theologians, astrology remains a fixed feature of any intellectual endeavor

involving astronomy, particularly navigation. William Bourne's *Regiment for the Sea*, for instance, is partially an astrological almanac.

Post-Reformation theology, then, influenced cartographic advances: the belief that God provided earth's dominions for man's exploitation facilitated the invention of new mathematical models for cartography, but descriptions of sublunar, earthly phenomena were governed by Providence fused with astrology, despite arguments against the latter. Meteorological and celestial phenomena were key features of the seascape, and the imaginary celestial circles used for measurements in the sky were superimposed on maps and charts to help man find his position on the earth's surface. Not surprisingly, constant attention to celestial phenomena to guide an earthly voyage meant a reliance on astrology to reduce risks and minimize misfortune. In a politically adroit 1613 tract to support the colonization of Virginia, Alexander Whitaker, a cleric at Jamestown, wrote that Providence had provided portents proving the divine underpinnings of English efforts. As one of the "plain demonstrations, that have convinced [him] to believe that assuredly God himself is the founder, and favorer of this plantation," he cites the "miraculous deliverance of our worthy governors" (Sir Thomas Gates and Sir George Somers) who reached Virginia a year later after a shipwreck at Bermuda in 1609, an account of which furnished the basis for Shakespeare's *The Tempest*.[71] The two other portents he identified were the discovery that Bermuda was habitable and the timely arrival of Gates and company just as the resident leader at Jamestown had decided to abandon the settlement. As Whitaker observes, "If ever the hand of God appeared in action of man, it was here most evident: for when man had forsaken all this business, God took it in hand; and when men said, now has all the earth cast off the care of this plantation, the hand of heaven has taken hold of it."[72] Whitaker had written at once a defense of the Virginia adventure in the spirit of Hakluyt, an affirmation of English manifest destiny, and a justification of exploration and discovery in providential and auspicious terms. Whitaker exemplifies the language of those who viewed the seascape through the lens of Christian cosmography.

New Learning and New Audiences

The interest and involvement of academicians spurred the rapid development of English navigation. This connection, too, relates to religion as all universities were operated as religious charities. Hame's apprenticeship and the Gresham College lectures he attended acquaint him with university professor Edward Wright's work. Did the Reformation permit an environment which encouraged academicians to lend their expertise to the improvement of artisanal trades such as navigation?

Unlike a modern student, Hame acquires most learning aurally, supplemented by reading and discussion. The utility of Hame's how-to books has increased through improved printing techniques. Although most illustrative material depicting instruments and celestial phenomena appears in woodcuts, the newer copperplate engraving enables more detailed illustrations. Further, diagrams appear more frequently in texts as a form of object teaching.[73] The sermons Hame quotes, however, not only testify to an application of spiritual teaching to the courage, endurance, and purpose of voyaging, but they also represent a familiar didactic method. Hame and his contemporaries heard many sermons. The length, tone, and structure of a sermon conveyed instruction. Additionally, Hame's memory could outmatch a modern student's for volume of information and ready recall, owing to disciplined memorization techniques. This learning method presents another tangent to theology. Pre-Reformation memory systems employed images as emblems of theological concepts. Adepts visualized texts as castles or gardens, say, where each feature functioned as a portal to a segment of text.

Through various techniques, memory virtuosos could summon entire texts, an ability no longer found in western cultures. By the late sixteenth century, however, Protestant intellectuals disparaged memory arts.[74] The Elizabethan Puritan theologian William Perkins found memory arts morally objectionable because the images used not only inflame the passions but also violate God's commandment not to set up idols: "So soon as the mind frames unto itself any form of God (as when he is popishly conceived to be like an old man sitting in heaven in a throne with a scepter in his hand) an idol is set up in the mind. . . . A thing feigned in the mind by imagination is an idol."[75] The Protestant argument holds that an object diverts people's minds from God; idolatry follows closely as a sin against God. In Reformed thinking, things must have practical uses only; things must be demystified.[76] Hame may have heard the admonitions against objects and idolatry, but he does not believe that images and instruments of navigation and cosmography fit this category.

Sermons proliferated during the English Reformation, serving a demand borne of increased literacy plus an appetite for religious introspection leading to self-improvement. Indeed, Hame takes published copies of sermons on his voyage. Sermons not only serve as an index to what religious instruction people receive, but they bear witness to literacy and exemplify how most learning occurred. Hame's contemporaries see sermons as rhetorical compositions that spread Reformed thinking and create a Reformed culture of reasoning and argument.[77] Sermons are quite popular, and extant ones comprise about 15 percent of all surviving published titles for the era.[78] Possibly Hame has heard sermons that emulate the rhetorical technique of the Gresham College lectures for rhetorical structure, length, and complexity.[79] Sermons and Gresham lectures parallel other didactic methods by which Hame learns his art.

A Nautical Sermon

We shall examine in detail an early modern sermon with detailed navigational imagery: John Dyos' *A Sermon Preached at Paules Crosse the 19 of Juli 1579*. Paul's Cross in London was a popular and prestigious place for delivering sermons. Many sermons preached there were published. Hame has read this sermon and carries a copy with his personal effects. The nautical imagery particularly appeals to him. Dyos may have been the Catholic priest who christened William Shakespeare's older brother before 1569. If so, then Dyos evidently chose to conform to the Church of England sometime between 1569 and 1579.[80] Dyos opens his sermon with an Epistle Dedicatory to the Bishop of London that includes a lengthy description of the perfection of God's universe. This description employs much astronomical imagery:

> The wonderful workmanship of the whole world: the great beauty of the celestial bodies; the inviolable order which they keep in their continual & most swift moving; the inestimable benefits which they yield to the inferior parts by their seasonable interchanges; the strange and sometime terrible effects that proceed of their secret influences and operations; the continual intercourses of the days and nights . . . the situation of the huge earth in the middle of the world [universe] without any prop or stay to hold it up . . . the unmeasurable wideness of the main seas, some environing the compass of the whole earth, and some shooting forth into the main land . . . the marvelous coming and going of the tides; the dreadfulness of the waves raised by tempestuous winds.[81]

This description prepares the reader for an interconnected set of sea and sky metaphors.

The sermon's text is John 21:1–14, which recounts when Christ walked by two berthed fishing vessels by the lake of Genezareth. The fishermen were washing their nets, so Christ entered one of the ships (owned by Simon Peter) and gave a sermon to people on the shore. "The ship wherein Christ was, is an image of the Church of Christ militant, the request of Christ and faithful obedience of Peter."[82] Dyos explains how Peter had fished all night with no luck and how, when he recast his nets at Christ's command, he caught enough fish to fill two ships, breaking his net in the process. "When Simon Peter saw this, he fell down at Jesus's knees, saying: Lord go from me, for I am a sinful man."[83] Christ, of course, responded, "Fear not, from henceforth you shall catch men," and Peter, along with James and John, "forsook all and followed him." This summary is repeated several times throughout the sermon at points where Dyos wishes to remind his audience of the scriptural source for the sea and sky metaphors that he develops throughout his exposition.

Dyos' first extended nautical metaphor concerns the ship as an image of the pulpit. The language of Dyos' text compares the ship, which "thrusts out a little" away from and above Christ's auditors, to the pulpit of a preacher, the role Christ assumed when he "taught the people out of the ship."[84] Dyos becomes even more explicit: "because [Christ] had not a pulpit on the land, and the people pressed upon him: he entered into a ship, and taught upon the sea."[85] Unlike those who venture into the sea (which represents the earth, Satan's dominion), Christ's auditors can hear his message because of their sure footing ashore: "Most safe and sure is the standing of the hearers, which standing on the land hear the word of salvation. The greatest part of hearers keep themselves out of peril: for when any sudden storm of persecution arises for the Gospel on the sea of the world: either they hide themselves: or else utterly forsaken the ship, chair, teacher and all."[86] The pulpit, of course, symbolizes of the whole church, as Dyos says: "The ship wherein Christ was, is an image of the Church of Christ militant."[87] Christ's word from this vantage point is inclusive, addressed to all people: "[Christ] teacheth all men out of the ship, of whatsoever age, sex, state or condition they be."[88] In this text, says Dyos, "the ship [is] an image of the true Church."[89] Explaining why the ship is such an "excellently depainted" image of the church militant, Dyos says, "The Church of Christ is that ship where against Satan blows out so many blasts. . . . This ship is like to the Ark of Noah. Even as a ship on the sea when any stormy tempests arise, is terribly shaken: right so nothing in the waste and wide world is more shaken with storms and tempests of all manner evils, than the Church."[90] The storms and tempests that shake the ship of the church are, of course, "Turks, Jews, Anabaptists, Libertines, Sectaries," and "the Romish rabble."[91] In short, says Dyos, "the devil and all his members shake this ship [of the church]: but they shall never be able to drown it . . . because Christ sits at the stern and has the helm in his own hand."[92] Later, Dyos clarifies that the church of which he speaks is not a mere physical structure or a small earthly congregation, but Christ's whole kingdom: "Out[side] of the ark of Noah, that is, out[side] of the Church, which is the body of Christ: no man is saved. That is most certain: but that is not in respect of the unity of the body in itself: but in respect of the unity of the whole body with the head, which is Christ."[93]

The second of Dyos' two extended metaphors is the ocean as an image of the earth (Satan's dominion). Dyos offers his thesis that "the sea is an image of the world."[94] His first point of comparison is that the sea is "very bitter," just as the world's dealings are bitter: pride, covetousness, usury, adultery, fornication, swearing, and many more "horrible and hateful vices, overflow the world."[95] His second point of comparison is that, like the earth, the sea is inconstant, perpetually in motion, "it ebbs and flows."[96] Man must continually accommodate his changing circumstances and has no hope of rest. A third point of similarity is that the sea, like the world, is dangerous: "Dangers of winds, pirates, mermaids, rocks, quicksands, and other dangers. . . . There is that Leviathan whom God has made to play therein. They that sail over the sea tell the perils thereof. . . . They that go down to the sea in ships, and occupy by the great waters: they see the words of the Lord, and his wonders in the deep."[97] Dyos continues to develop this

metaphor point by point: the sea and the earth are alike because they are both tempestuous and full of monsters, the earth's monsters being drunkards, heretics, blasphemers, slanderers, and the like. Just as the sea "casts out her dead to the shore," the earth casts out those "who are dead to the world, and do not the works thereof."[98] Both the sea and the earth are merely temporary homes for men, "no place to make our continual abode," places that people "but speedily pass over."[99] The sea is filled with "devouring fishes" that consume anything slower, weaker, or smaller than they, just as society is filled with "great men, mighty men [who] devour and undo poor men."[100] Dyos concludes: "You see now how the sea is an image of the world. . . . The world is the kingdom and court of Satan . . . no place for godly men, here devouring fishes destroy all."[101]

The ship and the sea are Dyos' most important metaphors, but he also uses celestial bodies, for instance, when he parallels scripture with the sun. The word of God is mankind's only light in the spiritual darkness that overwhelms the earth. Scripture "is compared to the sun, whose office is, by spreading of his radiant and bright beams to expel darkness, and to dispose every thing to bear fruit: right so the office of God's word is, with his bright & shining beams of grace to expel the darkness of heresies & errors, to take away the cold frost of iniquity, and to dispose and frame every man and woman to bring forth the fruits of piety & godliness."[102] Scripture is also like the polestar in its capacity to orient man toward his true destination (referring to Exodus 13:21): "This [the word of God] is that star of the sea, descrying port and country to the sailors on the sea of this world. . . . This word is light. The people that walked in darkness have seen a great light."[103] Another metaphor compares the setting of Venus with the fall of Lucifer. This fall preceded the coming of Christ just as Venus is eclipsed by the rising sun: "This is that Lucifer, the bright morning star, which comes before the sun of righteousness, by whom the light of grace does rise, whom follows the day of glory."[104]

Other important nautical tropes are casting nets and launching boats, both used consistently as metaphors for the godly labor of mankind. Man must work as penalty for his fall, but performs this work with faith and to the glory of God: "every man must labor: Every man must launch. Whether into the deep: what to do to make a draught: not to deceive men, not to seek temporal profit, but to edify, to seek the profit of the church, and glory of God."[105] Man is no exception to the rule that the entire universe must work unceasingly: "The sun labors continually: The stars are doing: The moon never stays."[106] And man's part in the work of the universe is to "launch," to strike out boldly in the name of God.

Other metaphors derived from the sea also make brief appearances, such as a vivid image of Satan as a crab and man as an oyster. God has provided man with protection against evil; like oysters, men are "strongly fenced with two hard shells [faith and scripture] which [Satan] cannot break by strength."[107] When Satan's temptations are subtle, however, they often go unnoticed—and therefore unresisted—by his victim: "the crab presently puts a little stone into the oyster as he gapes: whereby he cannot close or bring together again his shells. Then afterward the crab without danger puts in his claws and eats the meat of the oyster at his pleasure."[108]

Ships, ocean, sun, polestar, Venus, nets, crabs, and oysters—these vivid, concrete, and familiar images are essential to Dyos' successful presentation of abstract concepts to an audience much more comfortable with sea and sky than with theology. While Hame finds these images particularly apposite, Dyos' reliance on nautical metaphors attests to how pervasive they must have been within common discourse.

Conclusion

We have glimpsed some attributes of Hame's religious universe. We have not tried to circumscribe his faith. A good Anglican, he carries a copy of Arthur Dent's *Plaine Mans Path-way*, the Bible (a Geneva version),

and the *Booke of Common Prayer*. Hame's father or grandfather might have observed different seasonal rituals of Christianity with multiple sacraments, including a belief in intercessory prayer and purgatory, and a constellation of images since removed from most churches.[109] Hame observes two sacraments—baptism and the Lord's supper—but otherwise hears (and reads) sermons and participates in various rituals throughout a yearly calendar of holy days. Defining the religious context of Hame's voyage means a mental seascape with its Christian moral order and its representation through Christian imagery. The religious context is best expressed in the metaphorical language of a spiritual voyage, expressions of wonder at and terror of the seascape, anguish at the loss of a crew member, or resignation when hope vanishes during a tempest. This language may express allegory, ritual prayers, and oaths to God for health, safety, and deliverance. The notion of the voyage as a spiritual journey, or instrumental observations of the sun, moon, and stars as a conscious employment of God's natural gifts for man's utility, translates into "a thought experiment."[110] We can equip Hame with his tools and texts, furnish him with a ship and crew, but only with great effort can modern readers *see* with his eyes a world of decay surrounded by concentric shells of celestial perfection, a world in which Hame takes consolation in reliance on God's will, but within a shadow of terror that perhaps he might not be one of God's Elect.

Hearing a sermon aboard *Guyft*, sailors and passengers stand by silently and pensively, contemplating the innumerable afflictions that are visited upon people. The cosmos does not deal in random grief; God has a purpose for each soul aboard *Guyft*, although His purposes are inscrutable. The ocean may appear limitless, and the fate of man may seem ignoble as Norrys' body enters watery oblivion, but each sailor and passenger knows with certainty that their mortal remains will be recalled on Judgment Day. Norrys' death has a meaning; that meaning can be inferred as a sign that Gold does indeed have His eye on a solitary English ship. Impatient to reach Virginia, passengers know that God guides the helm and will reveal their fortunes and travails in good time.

Guyft heads into a tempest. The coming storm will tax the steadfastness of Hame's and his crew's beliefs in Providence, and even their very faith.

And since the sea does some so far divide,
That they may seem another world to be:
Teach us our ships like horses to ride,
That we may meet in one, and all in thee:
And as the [compass] needle does the north respect,
So all in Christ may only thee affect.

Neither is there any other art, wherein God shows his divine power so manifestly, as in [navigation]; permitting unto you certain rules to work by, and increasing them from time to time, growing still onwards toward perfection, as the world does toward his end. . . . That when you have done what you can, according to the skill you already have, or shall do, by any that you may learn hereafter: yet always will he make it manifest, that he alone is the Lord of the Seas, that all storms and tempests do but fulfill his will and pleasure, and that all the waves of the sea are continually at his commandment: finally that it is He, who oftentimes administers many help beyond all expectation, when the art of man utterly fails.

— WILLIAM BARLOW, *The Navigators Supply*, 1597

CHAPTER 9

VIRGINIA

*I wish the mariner to have a great regard unto this, as a principal point in navigation,
and not to sail by a compass of one parish, and a plat [chart] of another: I mean, that
they have a respect, as near as they may, to sail by a compass of that country, where
his plat was made.*

—Robert Norman, *The Newe Attractive*, 1581

*Therefore come life, come death, we must run this hazard.
We were leaped out of the frying pan into the fire.*

—Captain Thomas James, *The Strange and Dangerous Voyage*, 1633

About two weeks have elapsed since *Guyft* arrived in the West Indies. The ship has voyaged north along a sinuous course, following the distribution of the Windward and Leeward Islands. Fair weather has prevailed with easterly winds. Stopping briefly first at Santa Lucia, then voyaging north and northwest to the latitude of Puerto Rico around November 26, Tristram Hame turns southward to visit islands to forage for food, replenish supplies, and reconnoiter for other European ships. Hame encounters no one except people native to the islands. At times, islanders approach, briskly paddling canoes laden with fruits or live animals, eager for trade. Ferdinando Morgan relates:

> We fell with Dominica, and the same evening we sailed between it and Guadalupe. Later we came to an anchor at an island called Santa Cruz [Saint

Croix]. At our first landing on this island, Thomas Davye and Christopher Hills, by eating a small fruit like green apples, were fearfully troubled with a sudden burning in their mouths, and swelling of their tongues so big, that they could not speak. Also the first night of our being on this island, we took five great tortoises, some of them of such bigness, that six of our strongest men were tired with carrying one of them from the seaside to our cabins. In this island we found no watering place, but a standing pond, the water whereof was so evil, that many of our company fell sick with drinking thereof; and as many as did but wash their faces with that water, in the morning before the sun had drawn away the corruption, their faces did so burn and swell, that their eyes were shut up, and could not see in five or six days, or longer.

> The next day of our abode there, Captain Lynnis and some of our men went forth to search the island for fresh water. They went up to the top of a high hill to view the island, but could perceive

44. CUBA, BERMUDA, FLORIDA COAST, FROM RICHARD HAKLUYT'S *THE PRINCIPAL NAVIGATIONS* — *Guyft* voyages northerly along the Windward and Leeward Islands, past Puerto Rico and Hispaniola by the Bahamas and parallel to the Florida coast. From his arrival in the West Indies and by the Bahamian Islands, Captain Hame can see other islands along his western horizon. Note Bermuda at upper right, an important way station for English voyages from the West Indies to the American coast. While Florida is recognizable, the Chesapeake Bay does not appear. Credit: The Rosenbach Museum & Library, Philadelphia, shelf mark A589p

no sign of any men, or beasts, nor any goodness, but parrots and trees of guaiacum [a tropical fruit-bearing tree with purple flowers, known for its hardwood]. Returning back to our cabins another way, they found certain potsherds of savage making, made of the earth of that island, whereupon it was judged, that this island was inhabited by savages.[1]

Hame does not record these circumstances. His own account relates:

We weighed anchor and sailed NW and by N, and that night passed by Saint Christopher and another little island. We went [onto the island] and we sought for fresh water, and found none [but] there we got a good store of fine fresh fish, and much more, enough to have laden our boat we should have gotten, if at every draught we had not had in the net a tortoise, which still broke through and so carried away the fish with them. We weighed [anchor] and went through between the two islands into the main ocean, toward our long desired country Virginia.[2]

Hame now hastens to Virginia. He expects to arrive before winter begins, but too late for autumn planting. His crew and the colonists will live out of the ship's store and consume any fresh food they can obtain from the islands. Hame is at all times aware of navigational clues, and in the evening, on this clear night, he looks skyward frequently. He marvels at the changing aspect of the sky due to his travel. The polestar is much lower in the sky than when seen from Bristol. He recognizes many familiar constellations, and stares in wonder at the celestial canopy. He writes: "There appeared in the beginning of the night, more stars in the firmament, than ever I had before seen by two thirds. I could see the Cloud in Cancer full of small stars [Beehive star cluster], and all the Via Lactea [Milky Way], nothing but small stars, and amongst the Pleiades, a great many small stars. About ten a-clock, the moon did rise.[3] Hame returns to his cabin and writes his log.

Months and days	Latitude	Course	Leagues	Winds
December 1, 1611	31G 12M	N & by W	24	E

The Discourse
E tip of Hispaniola has latitude 18G 29M and bears S & by E

Almanac
Sunday. Saturn is due south at sun setting, Jupiter is southwest at sun rising, Mars and Mercury are in private parley before the sunrise, Venus is a spot in the Sun's garment. An evil day.

Guyft embarks on the final leg of her voyage and Hame does not expect to see land, except for some very small islands, until reaching the Chesapeake Bay. Throughout the day, *Guyft* does not come into soundings. Hame plans to steer clear of the Florida coast, avoiding Spanish shipping, to reach latitude 36G North. The ship's heading at daybreak was north by west. Hame will try to maintain a constant north by west heading, so he considers how many leagues he will traverse before entering the Chesapeake Bay. In 1611, methods do not exist for estimating longitude mechanically, but Hame can employ a tedious arithmetical method to determine it. Based on this method, Hame can reckon how many leagues remain ahead to reach the Chesapeake Bay. Hame will sail through the Channel of Bahama heading north by west. A rutter he has consulted warns: "Go on the south side of Bermuda, and go with great care, because many have been lost here about this island because of their negligence."[4]

Before undertaking this voyage, Hame had read a log kept by Samuel Argall on a voyage to Virginia in 1610, which depicts conditions that may lie ahead. From Samuel Argall's log:

> The 17th and 18th days [of July] were very wet and stormy, and the winds shifting all points of the compass. The 19th day, about four of the clock in the morning it began to clear up, and then we had a very stiff gale between E and NE. From the 17th at noon to the 19th at noon, I had sailed 55 leagues NNW, and then I found the ship to be 36 degrees 30 minutes. From the 19th at noon to the 20th at noon, 35 leagues NW, and then I was in 37 degrees 52 minutes. The weather now was fairer and the wind all easterly. From the 20th at noon to the 21st at noon, we sailed 20 leagues N by W, the wind between E and SE, and the weather very fair. At the sun setting I observed and found 13 degrees and a half of westerly variation, and until midnight we had a reasonable fresh gale of wind all southerly, and then it fell calm and rained.[5]

For comparative purposes, the modern latitude and longitude of Norfolk, Virginia, near the entrance to the Chesapeake Bay, is 36° 54' N 76° 18' W. Note that Argall does not record any longitude measurement, only latitude based on solar observations and dead-reckoning measurements of distance traversed. In 1611, no *practical* way to measure longitude at sea exists. About 150 years later, the development of the ship's chronometer, the publication of ephemerides with tabulated data of key astronomical phenomena, and the invention of the marine octant and sextant enabled longitude determination. Hame needs to estimate the distance remaining for his ship to voyage to Virginia, and the time required for the journey. To obtain a reliable estimate, Hame employs published longitudes to calculate, through geometry, the distance remaining.

Determining Longitude

The longitude system familiar to Hame is not the one we use today, which is measured from the Prime Meridian in Greenwich, England. Hame employs a system of longitude taken from Tapp's *Sea-Mans Kalendar*. In Tapp's work, Hame has obtained the longitude and latitude of Hispaniola from a listing of longitudes and latitudes for places throughout the world. Tapp defines longitude as "the distance of the meridian of any place, from the meridian which passes over the Isles of Azores, where the beginning of longitude is said to be."[6] Tapp reckons the zero-degree meridian to pass over St. Michael, an island in the Azores, where zero variation was believed to obtain, and in this system longitude is measured eastward.

In trying to estimate his distance to Virginia by employing longitudes in a calculation, Hame recalls the advice given him by his tutor, John Dee:

> Now some mariners are very inquisitive to have a way to get the longitude, but that is too tedious. You may get the latitude with your instruments, but the longitude you must bring from another place, which you can do with a globe or else a map or card [chart], and then you must measure from the meridian of the Canary Islands, otherwise called

the Fortunate Islands. Seamen should not be of the opinion that they might get longitude with instruments. Let no seamen therefore trouble themselves with any particular rule for getting longitude, but let them keep a perfect account and reckoning of the way of their ship, considering always the things that may be against them such as tides, currents, winds, or such like.[7]

Dee expresses a difference of opinion in the reckoning of longitude: Hame and Tapp measure longitude from a datum in the Azores, whereas Dee proposes the Canary Islands. By 1611, the Prime Meridian has migrated. Claudius Ptolemy had placed Ferro in the Canary Islands as the Prime Meridian 1,500 years earlier, as the western rim of the world known at the time to people in the Near East and Europe. By Hame's era, Spanish and Portuguese competition had caused the meridian to go on a progress among the Canaries, Azores, and Cape Verde Islands.[8] The congruence of a geographic prime meridian with a magnetic one was never the determining factor: the selection of a prime meridian was mainly political. Dee also advises that instruments will not yield longitude, but that mariners should rely on dead-reckoning techniques.

Based on Hame's account of the distance *Guyft* has traversed and in what direction, he computes his longitude as of noon today. The last position for which Hame has both latitude and longitude is the easternmost part of Hispaniola, 18G 29M N latitude, 307G longitude, as taken from the list in Tapp. Hame computes his latitude today as 25G 11M N. What is the difference in degrees between the two latitudes? Subtraction gives 6G 42M. Hame knows that he is at a different longitude than Hispaniola because he has been sailing north by west, just one point to the west of true north. *Guyft* has not voyaged far from Hispaniola, and as she has been sailing close to true north, the change in longitude will be slight.

Hame has two methods of reckoning his longitude. The first method employs plane geometry. Some of Hame's contemporaries apply plane geometry to projecting courses on the curved surface of the earth. Mathematicians and other mariners criticize this geometric method, but nautical trigonometry and spherical geometry in 1611 require tedious arithmetical calculations. Simplified methods of calculation, such as involving logarithms, do not yet exist. Hame constructs the following diagram:

1. On a piece of paper, mark point A near the center top and draw a vertical line through it.
2. Towards the bottom of the paper, mark point B on the line. B represents Hispaniola. A represents a point north of Hispaniola on its meridian (the same longitude).
3. Now draw a point C, *Guyft*'s present position, to the left of point A, horizontal to point A, and connect the points. The resulting figure is a right triangle. The angle at A, between line AC and line AB, should be a 90-degree angle. This is commonly called the *sailing triangle*. To alter a ship's course over degrees of latitude and estimate the change of longitude is called *departure*.
4. By applying the Pythagorean Theorem, Hame knows that the square of the hypotenuse (line BC) is the sum of the squares of the other two sides, lines AC and AB. (The hypotenuse is the line opposite the 90-degree angle.) Line BC represents the ship's course, assuming a constant N by W bearing. Hame computes this formula to find the length of line AC, the ship's distance due W of meridian AB.
Pythagorean Theorem: $x^2 + y^2 = z^2$ (hypotenuse of a right triangle)
or: $AB^2 + AC^2 = BC^2$

To solve the ship's departure using the Pythagorean Theorem, Hame needs more information, specifically, the length of sides AB and BC. Hame wants to solve the length of side AC.[9]

Hame now has a method to compute longitude, but he needs to supply numbers for two sides of the

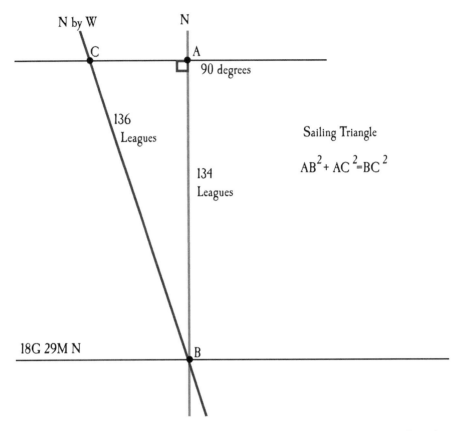

N by W   N

C   A

□   90 degrees

136
Leagues

Sailing Triangle

$AB^2 + AC^2 = BC^2$

134
Leagues

18G 29M N   B

45. CALCULATING DEPARTURE ⤙ Captain Hame's departure diagram relies on the geometry of a right triangle to determine distance yet to cover. This use of triangles works best over small regions near the equator. Refer to the text for a detailed discussion. Credit: Evi Numen

sailing triangle to compute his third, the ship's course, line BC. Fortunately, Hame's navigational texts contain abbreviated rules and shortcuts to save laborious calculations. In *A Regiment of the Sea*, William Bourne provides another paper instrument, the *Rule to Raise or Lay a Degree of Latitude*. This diagram instructs Hame how many leagues he will have to sail along each compass point in order to alter his latitude by one degree.[10] Note the upper half of the circle enclosing the compass rose (see Illustration 46). The left-hand quarter of the circle shows the number of English leagues Hame must sail in the given directions to alter his course one degree of latitude. The right-hand quarter gives Spanish leagues. In 1611, there is no consensus on the length of a nautical mile, and therefore on the length of a league

(three nautical miles). By about 1500, Iberian sailors had evolved the rule to raise or lay a degree of latitude, and thereafter latitude scales became integrated into portolan charts. Ironically, and this paradox was recognized almost immediately, while a latitude scale had obvious application to wayfinding, mariners now had to reconcile estimated distances by compass and dead reckoning with those gauged by latitude calculations, set down on a plane chart representing the curved surface of the earth.[11] The Mercator chart projection resolved the paradox in some respects, but Hame opts for employing multiple methods of wayfinding and comparing the results.

Hame has been sailing north by west. How many English leagues does he sail in this direction to alter his latitude by one degree? According to Bourne's diagram (Illustration 46), to raise a degree of latitude by sailing due north, one must voyage 20 leagues, and to raise a degree by sailing north by west, 20⅓ leagues. With this information, Hame can solve the sailing triangle.

Hame knows that he has voyaged 6G 42M since leaving Hispaniola. Per the Bourne diagram, if Hame had sailed due north, *Guyft* would have traversed 134 leagues (20 leagues x 6G 42M). By traveling north by west, however, *Guyft* has traversed 136 leagues (20⅓ leagues x 6G 42M). Hame now has two sides of the sailing triangle. To solve for the third side:

$$AB^2 + AC^2 = BC^2 \text{ or } (134)^2 + AC^2 = (136)^2$$

(For Hame, this calculation will take time. Primarily, he relies on computational tables. Readers should use a pocket calculator.)

The calculation proceeds thus:

$$AC^2 = (136)^2 - (134)^2$$
$$AC^2 = 18496 - 17956$$
$$AC^2 = 540$$
$$AC = \sqrt{540} \text{ (square root of 540)} = 23 \text{ leagues}$$
(rounded off)

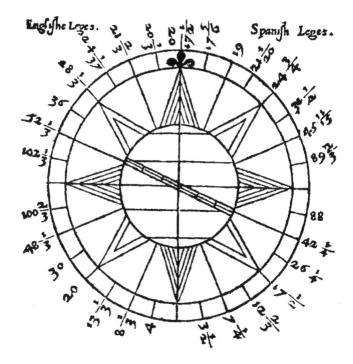

46. DEPARTURE DIAGRAM — The illustration, from William Bourne, A *Regiment for the Sea,* 1574, gives the rule to raise or lower a degree of latitude. Hame uses several paper graphical templates to reduce the need for calculation. This diagram shows how many leagues *Guyft* must sail in given directions to alter her position by a degree of latitude. Credit: William Bourne, A Regiment for the Sea, 1574. Reprint, introduction by E. G. R. Taylor (Cambridge: Cambridge University Press, 1963), 233. Reproduced by kind permission of the Syndics of Cambridge University Library, shelf mark 694:01.c.4.121

According to this calculation, *Guyft*'s present position is 23 leagues west of the meridian of the eastern tip of Hispaniola, or approximately 69 miles. At the equator, 60 miles of latitude separate each degree of longitude. Hame therefore assumes that his longitude is 1 degree west of that of Hispaniola, or 306G.

Hame has another, easier, way to arrive at his longitude because someone else has done the arithmetic. Examine the numbers on the bottom semicircle of Bourne's compass rose. These numbers represent the number of leagues the ship has departed from the meridian once the latitude has been altered by one degree. Directly opposite 20 1/3 leagues at the north by west point in the compass in the upper half-circle is 3½ leagues on the lower half-circle. By sailing far enough in a north by west direction to raise latitude by one degree, Hame is now 3½ leagues west of his original meridian. By this method, Hame computes the number of *leagues* he is from the meridian of Hispaniola. Hame multiplies 3½ by 6G 42M to obtain 23 leagues, rounded off, or about 69 miles. Bourne's compass rose gives an identical answer to the Pythagorean computation.

Distance to Virginia

Hame now estimates how many leagues he must sail to reach the Chesapeake Bay. According to Tapp's *Kalendar*, Virginia has latitude 36G 0M N, longitude 302G 10M. Hame now has the information he needs to compute his distance to Virginia. Hame employs Tapp's method for finding the distance between any two places, given the latitude and longitude of both.

1. Compute the latitude and longitude differences between *Guyft*'s present position and Virginia. (*Answer: a difference of 11G in latitude, rounded off, and 3G 50M in longitude*)
2. Recall that one degree of latitude equals sixty miles. Multiply the difference in latitude by 60. (*Answer: 11G x 60 = 660*)

3. The longitude computation is more tedious. Examine William Bourne's longitude protractor (Illustration 47). Remember that the number of miles separating meridians of longitude varies depending on the latitude because meridians all converge at the poles. At the equator, sixty miles separate each meridian of longitude. Hame needs to determine the number of miles between meridians of longitude at his present position and that of Virginia. The protractor shown in the Illustration 47 will enable Hame to determine these values. To mimic Hame's use of this template, tape the end of a white thread or string to the corner of the protractor marked 90. The semidiameter shows miles. The semicircle gives degrees of latitude. Take the string and gently pull it taut and swing it to the semicircle. Lay the string over *Guyft*'s present latitude, 25G 11M. (This will be approximate.) With a pencil, mark the thread where it crosses the protractor. Swing the thread over to the semidiameter and read the number of miles that "answer unto a degree in longitude." Repeat this process with the latitude of Virginia.

Using Bourne's protractor, Hame obtains fifty-four miles between meridians at his present position, and forty-eight for the latitude of Virginia. Resume the calculation.

4. Multiply the difference in longitude, obtained in step one (3G 50M) by 54, and then by 48. (*Answer: 207 and 184, respectively, rounded off to the nearest mile*)
5. Add the two figures obtained in step four. (*Answer: 207 + 184 = 391*). Divide the answer by two to obtain an average. (*Answer: 196*)
6. Multiply the value obtained in step two by itself. (*Answer: 660 x 660 = 435,600*). Multiply the average obtained in step five by itself. (*Answer: 196 x 196 = 38,416*)

7. Add the two values obtained in step six together. (*Answer: 435,600 + 38,416 = 474,016*) Compute the square root of the result. The result is the number of miles Hame must voyage to reach Virginia. (*Answer: 688 miles or 229 leagues*)

Note that in steps six and seven we inflated our results to obtain very large numbers. Minute differences in quantities show up more conspicuously in large numbers, and Hame can turn to a published

square-root table to look up the most accurate value based on the larger figures. Hame reflects that his methods of ascertaining latitude, variation, and determining his course to Virginia were criticized by mathematicians in the sixteenth century, even as mariners relied on them. Leonard and Thomas Digges observe:

> The rules [mariners] have to know how many leagues they shall run upon every point to raise one degree in latitude, are false. For they search that [great circle] as though it were the hypotenuse to a right angled triangle whose sides are circles of

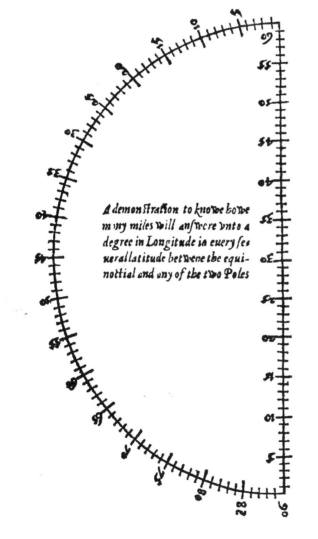

47. LONGITUDE DIAGRAM — With a string or thread, Captain Hame uses this diagram to determine his longitude. Tape one end of a thread or string to the corner of the protractor marked 90. The semidiameter shows miles and the semicircle gives degrees of latitude. Take the string and gently pull it taut and swing it to the semicircle. Place the string over *Guyft*'s present latitude, 25G 11M. With a pencil, mark the thread where it crosses the protractor. Swing the thread over to the semidiameter and read the number of miles that "answer unto a degree in longitude." Repeat this process with the latitude of Virginia. See text for the application of this information. Credit: William Bourne, *A Regiment for the Sea*, 1574. Reprint, introduction by E. G. R. Taylor (Cambridge: Cambridge University Press, 1963), 241. Reproduced by kind permission of the Syndics of Cambridge University Library, shelf mark 694:01.c.4.121

contrary nature, the one a parallel [of latitude], the other a great circle, and therefore without all sense they seek by proportion of right lines to deliver their [measurement]. But besides [this error] they have one great imperfection, and that is the want of exact rules to know the longitude, without which they can neither truly give the place of any coast, harbor, road or town, nor yet in sailing discern how the place they fall unto bears from them.[12]

Father and son Digges criticize the very method that Hame has used. Their key criticism is that the right-angled triangle method mixes unlike quantities, that is, superimposing a triangle from plane geometry onto a curved surface of the earth, with a ship's track that in actuality is a curved line hugging the globe, a great circle. Hame has heard the debates about this inaccuracy, but he also knows that his geometrical method works best near the equator. Far to the north, the errors engendered by his methods would be unacceptable.

A Tempest

Tuesday, December 3. Days have passed since Hame reckoned his longitude near Hispaniola and estimated his distance to Virginia. The weather has turned much cooler and a storm looms in the distance. Hame records:

> Our course when we came about the height [latitude] of between 26 and 27 degrees, we declined to the northward and found the wind to this course friendly. We had followed this course so long, as now we were within seven or eight days at the most, by my reckoning of making Cape Henry upon the coast of Virginia. When on the morning of the third (preparing for no less all the black night before) the clouds gathering thick upon us, and the winds singing, and whistling most unusually, which made us cast off our pinnace towing the same until then astern, a dreadful storm and hideous began to blow from out the NE, which swelling, and roaring as it were by fits, some hours with more violence than others, at length did beat all light from heaven; which like an hell of darkness

turned black upon us, so much the more fuller of horror, as in such cases horror and fear use to overrun the troubled, and overmastered senses of all, which the ears lay so sensible to the terrible cries and murmurs of the winds, and distraction of our company, as who was most armed, and best prepared, was not a little shaken.[13]

At daybreak on December 4, Wednesday, the wind blew from the east, and as the wind increased, it shifted to east by north, then east northeast, and then northeast, as Hame has reported. Into the evening, the wind abruptly shifted to the south, and by midnight had returned northeast by north. Past midnight, the winds have strengthened, the sky has remained dark as the wind becomes a gale. For a short while, before gale winds came up, Hame and his crew see a brown pelican, a familiar sight along the Atlantic coast near the Carolinas, and a sure sign of land, but the bird disappears as the weather worsens.[14]

Hame experiences conditions still common within the Caribbean today during late autumn. Data from British Admiralty publications and charts from the U.S. Defense Mapping Agency show that, in late November and early December, the mean wind direction at *Guyft*'s location today is northeast by east, and at the Chesapeake Bay it is northwest by west. September and October are the high-risk months for severe tropical storms, tapering off in November. Tropical storms may form into hurricanes at no fixed longitude, but may appear as far west as the Caribbean and as far east as the Cape Verde Islands, and within latitude 7° N to 15° N.[15]

Hame and his crew see lightning ahead and hear faint thunder. In 1611, what are the causes of thunder and lightning? Leonard and Thomas Digges explain: "Thunder is the quenching of fire in a cloud. Thunder is an exhalation, hot and dry, mixed with moisture carried up into the middle region, there thickened and wrapped into a cloud. When the hot matter couples with moisture, enclosed within the cloud the heat increases and breaks out of the sides of the cloud with a thundering noise. Lightning is the

48. CHESAPEAKE BAY AND JAMES RIVER, FROM CAPTAIN JOHN SMITH'S MAP OF VIRGINIA, 1612 ⟶ Captain John Smith's map of Virginia and the Chesapeake Bay shows the route of *Guyft* upriver to Jamestown, by the time of Hame's visit only four years old and a precarious place for establishing plantations. Smith meticulously drafted this chart after exploring each shown waterway in a shallow-draught vessel called a shallop. Credit: The Rosenbach Museum & Library, Philadelphia, shelf mark A612m

fire being dispersed."[16] As they experience these conditions, however, Hame and his crew are not disin-
terested scientific observers of the weather. As they
understand what they are experiencing, God is clearly
meddling with the crew's safety for his own inscrutable purposes. Even as the mariners attend to their
jobs to ensure their ship's safety, they wonder about
the meaning of the coming tempest: the natural, the
unnatural, the supernatural all blend into moral theater. Providence is at work.[17]

Tension and terror possess the ship; the crew are
all salt-sprayed, strained muscle as they struggle to
control the ship's sinews, the running rigging. The
passengers help where they can, or huddle out of the
way. Ferdinando Morgan stays out of the way and, to
stay calm, writes:

> For surely as death comes not so sudden nor appar-
> ent, so he comes not so elvish [spitefully] and pain-
> ful as at sea. For indeed death is accompanied at no
> time, nor place with circumstances every way so
> incapable of particularities of goodness and inward
> comforts, as at sea. For it is most true, there arises
> commonly no such unmerciful tempest, but that it
> works upon the whole frame of the body, and most
> loathsomely affects all the powers thereof: and the
> manner of sickness it lays upon the body, being so
> insufferable, gives not the mind any free and quiet
> time, to use her judgment and empire.
>
> Since yesterday, the storm passed in a rest-
> less tumult, had blown so exceedingly, as we could
> not apprehend in our imaginations any possibil-
> ity of greater violence, yet did we still find it, not
> only more terrible, but more constant, fury added
> to fury, and one storm urging a second more outra-
> geous than the former. Prayers might well be in the
> heart and lips, but drowned in the outcries of the
> officers. Nothing heard that could give comfort,
> nothing seen that might encourage hope.
>
> Our sails wound up lay without their use, and if
> at any time we bore but a hollock [scrap of sail], or
> half forecourse, to guide her before the sea, six and
> sometimes eight men were not enough to hold the
> whipstaff in the steerage, and the tiller below in the
> gunner room, by which be imagined the strength
> of the storm: in which the sea swelled above the
> clouds, and gave battle unto heaven. Winds and

seas were as mad, as fury and rage could make them.
All that we had ever suffered gathered together,
might not hold comparison with this: there was not
a moment in which the sudden splitting, or instant
over-setting of the ship was not expected.[18]

> Howbeit this was not all: it pleased God to
> bring a greater affliction yet upon us; for in the
> beginning of the storm we had received likewise a
> mighty leak. And the ship in every joint almost,
> having spewed out her oakum, before we were
> aware was grown five foot suddenly deep with
> water above her ballast, and we almost drowned
> within, whilst we sat looking when to perish from
> above. So as joining in the public safety, there
> might be seen master, boatswain, carpenter and
> who not, with candles in their hands, creeping
> along the ribs viewing the sides, searching every
> corner, and listening in every place, if they could
> hear the water run. Many a weeping leak was this
> way found and hastily stopped, and at length one
> [leak] in the gunner room made up [was plugged]
> with I know not how many pieces of beef. But all
> to no purpose, the waters still increasing.[19]

Captain Hame, during a brief slackening of wind,
takes the time to gather passengers and some of the
crew together. He comforts them as he can:

> My faithful companions, be not dismayed for any
> of these disasters, but let us put our whole trust
> in God. It is He that giveth, and He that taketh
> away. He throws down with one hand, and raises
> up with another. His will be done. If it be our for-
> tunes to end our days here, we are as near heaven,
> as in England, and we are much bound to God
> Almighty for giving us so large a time of repen-
> tence, who as it were daily calls upon us, to prepare
> ourselves for a better life in heaven. He does not in
> the meantime deny, but that we may use all honest
> means to save and prolong our natural lives withal.
> Yet there is nothing too hard for courageous minds,
> which hitherto you have shown, and I doubt not
> will still do, to the uttermost.[20]

Despite his words, Hame worries that his ship
has taken on too much water. The crew has applied
themselves to the pumps, but this work has been
insufficient. Hame records:

Upon the next morning, 5th December, I caused the whole company to be equally divided into three parts, and opening the ship in three places (under the forecastle, in the waist, and hard by the bittacle) appointed each man where to attend, and thereunto every man came duly upon his watch, took the bucket, or pump for one hour, and rested another. Then men might be seen to labor for life, and the better sort, even our gentlemen, not refusing their turn, to spell each other, to give example to the others. The common sort stripped naked, as men in galleys, the easier both to hold out, and to shrink from under the salt water, which continually leapt in among them, kept their eyes waking, and their thoughts and hands working, with tired bodies and wasted spirits, three days and four nights destitute of outward comfort, and desperate of any deliverance.

Once, so huge a sea broke upon the poop and quarterdeck, as it covered our ship from stern to stem, like a garment or vast cloud, it filled her brim full for awhile within. This source of water was so violent, as it rushed and carried the helmsman from the helm, and wrested the whipstaff out of his hand, which flew from side to side, that when he would have ceased the same again, it so tossed him from starboard to larboard, as it was God's mercy it had not split him.[21]

Morgan continues his narrative:

During all this time of privation, the heavens looked so black upon us, that it was not possible the elevation [altitude] of the pole might be observed: not a star by night, not sunbeam by day was to be seen. Only upon the Thursday night, 5th December, the captain being upon watch, had an apparition of a little round light, like a faint star, trembling, and streaming along with a sparkling blaze, half the height upon the main mast, and shooting sometimes from shroud to shroud, and for three or four hours it kept with us, running sometimes along the main yard to the very end, and then returning. The superstitious seamen make many constructions of this sea fire, which nevertheless is usual in storms. The Italians call it *Corpo sancto*, the Spaniards call it Saint Elmo.[22]

St. Elmo's Fire is an atmospheric discharge that, under some conditions, imparts a luminous glow to the masts and yards of a ship. The phenomenon has been described since antiquity, and has been known by many names which reflect interpretations of its providential meaning. The Italians' epithet of *Corpo sancto* derives from the folklore that the phenomenon sprung from Christ's body. To Hame and his crew, however, St. Elmo's Fire betokens the arrival of fair weather, therefore a good omen.[23]

Morgan continues the story:

We much unrigged the ship and threw overboard much luggage and staved many a butt of beer, hogsheads of oil, cider, wine, and heaved away all the ordnance on the starboard side, and had now purposed to cut down the main mast, the more to lighten her. And now the men so weary, having travailed now from Tuesday till Friday morning, day and night, without either sleep or food, for the leakage taking up all the hold, we could neither come by beef nor fresh water. From Tuesday noon till Friday noon, we bailed and pumped two thousand tons of water, and yet do what we could, when our ship held least in her, she bore ten foot deep. It being now Friday, 6th December, the fourth morning of the tempest, there had been a general determination to have shut up the hatches, and commending our sinful souls to God, committed the ship to the mercy of the sea: surely, that night we must have done it, and that night we then perished.

But we see the goodness and sweet introduction of better hope, by our merciful God given unto us. Captain Hame, when no man dreamed of such happiness, had discovered and cried, Land. Indeed the morning now three quarters spent, had won a little clearness from the days before, and it being better surveyed, the very trees were seen to move with the wind upon the shore side, whereupon our captain commanded the helmsman to bear up, the boatswain sounding at the first, found it 13 fathom and presently heaving his lead the third time, had ground at 4 fathom, and by this, we had got her within a mile under the southeast point of the land where we had somewhat smooth water. We were

forced to run the ship near shore, as near the land
as we could, and by the mercy of God unto us,
making out our boat, we had brought all our men
and women safe unto the island.[24]

And what island? Captain Hame details a cautious
approach:

> 6th December in the morning, it began to blow
> hard at SE, which was partly off the shore; and the
> ship began to drive, it being soft oozy ground. We
> came to sail under two courses. While the most
> were busy in heaving out of topsails, some, that
> should have had special care of the ship, almost
> ran her ashore upon some rocks, out of mere care-
> lessness. After I had controlled a little passion in
> myself, I ordered what should be done to get past
> these rocks and stones. Whereupon we struck all
> our sails amain, and furled them up close, and so
> put out an anchor. Then stood we to the capstan,
> but the cable broke, and we lost our anchor. Out,
> with all speed, therefore, we put another. We could
> not now perceive whether the ship did still leak or
> no, and that by reason we were employed in pump-
> ing out the water, which we had bilged in hold.[25]
>
> We found it to be the dangerous and dreaded
> islands of Bermuda. Because they be so terrible to
> all that ever touched on them, and such tempests,
> thunders, and other fearful objects are seen and
> heard about them, that they be called the Devil's
> Islands, and are feared and avoided of all sea travel-
> ers. Yet it pleased our merciful God to make even
> this hideous and hated place both the place of our
> safety and means of our deliverance. Indeed we find
> these islands now by experience to be as habitable
> and commodious as most countries of the same cli-
> mate and situation.[26]

The Bermuda Islands provide a respite, a haven
from the travails of the previous days. Uninhabited,
the islands had acquired an infernal reputation, as
Hame says, but for *Guyft*, as for the voyage of *Sea
Venture* to Virginia in 1609, they provide sustenance
and shelter. The latter ship crashed onto rocks and
sank during a storm, although all passengers made
it to the islands in safety, and the expedition lead-
ers, bound to relieve the Jamestown colony, directed

the construction of two small ships, named *Patience*
and *Deliverance*, to take the survivors to their destination a year later, long after *Sea Venture*'s companion
ships had reached Virginia.[27] Hame, however, has not
heard of *Sea Venture*'s travails.

Morgan has occasionally read to the crew and
passengers from the Bible and homiletic publications
including sermons. Following the treacherous circumstances of the previous days, however, he has also
been moved to write a poem to collect his thoughts
about the experience:

In commendation of the painful seamen

Who so in surging seas, his season will consume,
And means thereof to make his only trade to live:
That man must surely know the shifting sun
and moon,
For trying of his tides, how they do take and give.

So must he duly seek the ecliptic course of sun,
How he from west to east his proper course
do keep:
His labor then (God knows) as yet is but begun,
For he must watch and ward, and shake off slug-
gish sleep.

And have a careful eye, to hand that is at helm,
For many one there is, that false his course will ply:
And swelling seas likewise, the ship may
overwhelm,
Or set her on the shore, without the pilot's eye.

When Boreas is abroad, and blustering blasts do
blow,
In season must he seek to short in lofty sail:
For that, if not in time he very well do know,
That all too late indeed, no labor will prevail.

But when the raging storms do swing the ship
on high,
Oft times (against his will) he spoons [running
before a gale] before the seas:
Else in goes all the sails, and takes her from her try,
In haste to drive or hull, till God the same appease.

Thus when he all the night, with weary toil
has tried,

And sees the swelling seas have set him from
his way:
Then with a little slack of calm he has espied,
With joyful heart to take the height he do assay.

His astrolabe then he setteth for the sun,
Or cross-staff for the star called the Ballastile
[polestar]:
And thus with help of them and declination
How land do bear of him, he knows within a while.

Then by his compass straight he duly sets
his course,
And thus he brings the ship in safety to her port:
Whereof his hazards past he makes a great
discourse,
And each man (by dessert) do give him
good report.

If pilot's painful toil be lifted then aloft,
For using of his art according to his kind:
What fame is due to them that first this art
outsought,
And first instructions gave to them that were
but blind?[28]

The islands have a reputation for "tempests, great
strokes of thunder, lightning and rain in the extremity of violence," and in December, hailstorms are possible.[29] The Bermudan soil appears dry, sandy, and
dark red, and inhospitable to fresh fruits and vegeta-
bles familiar to the English. Tall cedar and palm trees
form a dense covering within which Captain Lynnis
discovers a ripe and luscious black berry as big as a
damson, a supply of which some of his colonists carry
back to the ship. Hogs are abundant, and Captain
Lynnis and some colonists armed with muskets shoot
a few, the roasted flesh of which buoy the spirits of
passengers and crew.[30]

To Virginia

By Sunday, December 8, the ship, its water replen-
ished, some fresh fruit and meat acquired, minor
repairs undertaken, and the weather fair, prepares to
depart for Virginia. Hame had considered a longer

delay in order to bream (clean) the hull with a lime
compound, but after consultation with Captain
Lynnis, he decides to make for Virginia and under-
take repairs upon his arrival.

Hame continues his narration:

From this time we only awaited a favorable wind
to carry us forth, and later set sail an easy gale, the
wind at south. The wind served us easily all day
the 8th and the next when to the no little joy of
us all, we got clear of the islands. After holding
a northerly course, for five days we had the wind
sometimes fair, and sometimes scarce and contrary.
On Friday, the 13th December, we saw change of
water and had much rubbish swim by our ship side,
whereby we knew we were not far from land. At
about midnight we sounded, with the dipsie lead
and found 37 fathom. The 14th in the morning we
sounded, and had 19 and a half fathom, stony, and
sandy ground. The 14th about midnight, we had a
marvelous sweet smell from the shore, strong and
pleasant, which did not a little glad us.[31]

Sunday, the 15th in the morning, about eight of
the clock we saw land in the height of 40 degrees
and odd minutes, very fine low land, appearing far
off to be full of tall trees, and a fine sandy shore; we
saw no harbor, and therefore coasted along to seek
one to the NW, the wind being at W.

Monday, the 16th the wind being about the
NE we beat hard to fetch an headland, where we
thought we saw an harbor: but when we came
up with it, we perceived it was none, and all our
labor lost. And therefore the wind being now
more full in our teeth at the NE, we considered it
were better to put room, so that if the wind should
stand, then we should fetch the Bay of Chesepian
[Chesapeake], to seek out the people for Sir Walter
Raleigh left near those parts in the year 1587. If
not, perhaps we might find some road or harbor
in the way to take in some fresh water, for now we
had none aboard.

To the English, the American coastline from the
Carolinas to present New England is Virginia; the
Raleigh settlement was as much Virginia as the object
of *Guyft*'s voyage, the James River in present-day
Virginia. Hame, his crew and passengers, long for

49. GUYFT COASTING UP THE JAMES RIVER — *Guyft* voyages
up the James River to Jamestown. To Captain Hame and his
crew, Virginia appeared a "desert," seventeenth-century vernacular for a wild place. This image conveys the loneliness
and isolation experienced by many Europeans in Virginia in
1611. Credit: Ann Berry

landfall, but Hame will not risk it until the weather
conditions become favorable. Hame fears a lee shore,
that is, he fears finding his ship between shore and
the wind. A fierce wind could force his ship aground
with consequent loss of ship and life.

> On Tuesday at night and about 11 a clock one
> went up in the main top and descried land, which
> was no small joy to the whole company. Thus we
> came near the mouth of the Bay: but the wind
> blew so sore, and the sea was so high, that we durst
> not put in that night into the sea, and so continued
> next day.
>
> On Wednesday at night the wind came fair
> again, and we bare again for it all night, and the
> wind presently turned again. Thursday, consider-
> ing our extremity for water and wood, victuals and
> beer likewise consuming very fast, we desired land.
> We being not far from the shore, which appeared
> unto us exceeding pleasant and full of goodly trees,
> and with some show of the entrance of a river. We
> had the wind at SW, and we bore up at the W and
> by N and in the morning we sounded and had land

at 11 fathom of water and this night we came to
an anchor in Chesapeake Bay. Captain Lynnis and
some men went on shore in the boat from the ship,
which lay above a mile from the land, and with
their weapons marched up into the country.[32]

After briefly reconnoitering, Lynnis and his armed
men return to the ship. Under *Guyft*'s topsails, Hame
gently coasts up the James River to seek Jamestown,
where the law requires him to put in and present a
certificate of arrival to the governor. The passengers stand by the gunwales, peering into the impenetrable wall of green along the shore. For the most
part, Hame sees no one, although a canoe or two
make brief appearances close to the shore. Finally,
Jamestown comes into sight, at first evident by the
smoke from chimneys and firepits, the shoreline trees
giving way to cleared land. As the ship closes with
the settlement, Hame gives order to discharge one of
the swivel guns to alert the Jamestown guard of the
ship's approach. Jamestown presents, to some passengers, a pitiful sight, a pentagonal fort isolated in the
desert (a 17th-century synonym for wilderness) of
Virginia. To others, Jamestown gives reassurance that
a life is possible here.

The certificate of arrival reads:

*To the Treasurer Counsel and Company of
Adventurers and Planters of the City of London for
the first Colony in Virginia*

This is to certify that in the good ship of Bristol
called *Guyft* this present 20th day of December
1611, arrived in this port of James City for plantation here in Virginia at the charges of Peter
Fayrewether, and Thomas Gould, and Josias Quick
Esquires under the conduct of Capt. James Lynnis,
these 22 persons all in safety and perfect health
whose names ensue.

[Names are listed.]
This certificate I affirm to be true.

   Sir Thomas Gates, Lieutenant-Governor
   Charles City, December 20th, 1611[33]

Guyft slips its mooring off Jamestown Island and
proceeds upriver to the plantation to be worked by

50. Entrance to the James Fort *Guyft*'s crew and passengers enter the fortification's riverside port, shown here. The cannon reminds passengers —settlers—that they are the lone English in the New World and must fend for themselves. Captain Hame's work is almost done. Credit: Author's collection

the indentured passengers led by Captain Lynnis. Upon their safe arrival on a cold, dry, December Sunday, days before Christmas, Hame reads from a sermon, evoking images of the recent ordeal:

There was a thick darkness upon all the land of Egypt: but all the children of Israel had light where they dwelled. Where the word of God is, there is light: where the same is not, there is darkness. This is that Lucifer the bright morning star, which comes before the sun of righteousness, by whom the light of grace do rise, whom follows the day of glory.[34] This is that star of the sea, descrying port and country to the sailors on the sea of this world. This is that star, which led the wise and faithful men from a far country to Christ.[35]

The sea is inconstant, it ebbs and flows: the world is inconstant, it changes every day. The sea is full of dangers: dangers of winds, pirates, mermaids, rocks, quicksands. The sea is tempestuous: the world is tempestuous. The sea is full of monsters: the world is full of monsters, the world is full of monstrous men. You see now how the sea is an image of the world: you see the sea, you see the world.[36]

Christ taught out of the ship; He performed his office, to the which he was sent of his father into this world: and because he had not a pulpit on the land, and the people pressed upon him, he entered into a ship, and taught upon the sea. By his example he teaches us to do the duties of our vocations faithfully.[37]

At Jamestown, the cape merchant supplements the colonists' supplies with additional clothing, tools, and food from the common store. Passengers and crew unload cargo and supplies, and the colonists immediately set to work building their new lodgings. Captain Lynnis and his company depart, and exchange good-byes with the crew.

Hame has completed his task and will prepare to return to England once the ship has been repaired, supplies taken on board, and the ship laden with Virginia commodities, primarily timber, for the return journey, the famous Virginia tobacco a phenomenon of a few years hence.

Conclusion

Hame's navigational tools and methods occupy a space within his larger experience, skills, and abilities at seamanship. Hundreds of other ships and ships' masters will accomplish similar voyages to the Americas. Over time, the methods and technology of navigation will change, but whether the voyage occurs in 1688, 1759, or 1872, Tristram Hame's counterparts will require the same combination of personal and professional characteristics of competence, leadership, respect for sea and wind, skill in navigation and seamanship, and particularly a perspective for the seascape, which this book has labored to circumscribe.

Readers may seek copies of Hakluyt or Purchas to acquaint themselves with early exploration narratives, or may wish to visit with John Davis, John Smith, William Bourne, or the others whose words have been abundantly quoted. Readers will find that an Elizabethan exploration narrative informs many tales, the search for a distant, hidden land, rich in precious treasures, reached following many trials and obstacles. The explorer who achieves the discovery must be plucky, courageous, and persevering. Readers may be delighted to find that some navigational and mathematical texts also harness the exploration motif, in this case the seeker after knowledge who achieves understanding following a challenging search through arguments and demonstrations.[38] The mathematics and geometry found within Hame's how-to books should not daunt the reader: he or she may appreciate the culture of practical mathematics shared by Hame and his contemporaries with its predilection to seek solutions to problems through shared methods involving numbers and measures.[39]

This book has conveyed the experience of a ship's master, crew, and passengers for a single voyage to North America in 1611; we now remove this voyage from the microscope of historical study and allow the voyage to merge with hundreds of others, spanning centuries, which conveyed Europeans to North America and elsewhere, where peoples "weave each other into their worlds."[40] *Guyft*'s voyage thus dissolves into larger ambitions of empire, mercantile exchange, competition, war, the expansion of populations, changes in technology and knowledge about the world, and volatile encounters with distant races and cultures. At a distance of four centuries, we can piece together the maritime circumstances that led to a European-dominated, largely English-speaking North American continent. We can muster empathy and sympathy for the anguish of the European threat to and displacement of the native peoples of the Americas. Against all of these circumstances, however, Hame, his crew, and his prototype, Tobias Felgate, deserve our respect.

I have set down whatsoever I could find by exact trial, and perfect experiments, founding my arguments only upon experience, reason, and demonstration, which are the grounds of arts.

—Robert Norman, *The Newe Attractive*, 1581

And here I leave to trouble thee any further for this time. If these my labors may profit my country, then have I my desire. And thus I bid thee most heartily farewell.

—William Bourne, *A Regiment for the Sea*, 1574

Notes

Chapter 1. Introduction: The Haven-Finding Art

1. Paraphrased from Cole Porter, "Let's Do It (Let's Fall in Love)," *Cole Porter Songbook*, disk 2 (Paris, 1928).

2. Talbot H. Waterman, *Animal Navigation* (New York: Scientific American Books, Inc., 1989), 15, 99, 111.

3. Ibid., 71.

4. M. H. Abrams, general ed., *The Norton Anthology of English Literature*, 4th ed. (New York: W. W. Norton & Co., 1979), 1:111.

5. Seán McGrail, *Ancient Boats in North-West Europe: The Archaeology of Water Transport to AD 1500* (London: Longman, 1998), 303.

6. Barry Cunliffe, *Facing the Ocean: The Atlantic and its Peoples 8000 BC–AD 1500* (Oxford: Oxford University Press, 2001), 79.

7. John Davis, *The Seamans Secrets* (1607), reprinted in *The Voyages and Works of John Davis the Navigator*, ed. Albert Hastings Markham (London: Hakluyt Society, 1880), 238. Readers interested in consulting broad perspectives on key themes germane to this book, written by leading scholars, should examine John B. Hattendorf, ed. in chief, *The Oxford Encyclopedia of Maritime History*, 4 vols. (New York: Oxford University Press, 2007).

8. Samuel Purchas, "The commendations of Navigation, as an Art worthy the care of the most Worthy," in Purchas, ed., *Hakluytus Posthumus or Purchas His Pilgrimes* (1625; reprint, Glasgow: James MacLehose and Sons, 1905–7), 1:45–7.

9. John Dee, *The Mathematicall Praeface to the Elements of Geometrie of Euclid of Megara* (1570; reprint, introduction by Allen Debus, New York: Neale Watson Academic Publications, Inc., 1975), fols. diiiiv, Air.

10. McGrail, *Ancient Boats*, 275.

11. Martín Cortés, *Arte of Navigation* (1561; reprint, intro. by David W. Waters, Delmar, N.Y.: Scholars' Facsimiles & Reprints, 1992), 11.

12. Ibid., fol. iiiv.

13. Waterman, *Animal Navigation*, 71.

14. Richard Polter, *Pathway to Perfect Sayling* (London, 1605), fol. A2r.

15. McGrail, *Ancient Boats*, 277.

16. Aaron Gurevich, *Historical Anthropology of the Middle Ages* (Chicago: University of Chicago Press, 1992), 4; G. E. R. Lloyd, *Demystifying Mentalities* (Cambridge: Cambridge University Press, 1990), 137.

17. Douglas M. Knudson, Ted T. Cable, and Larry Beck, *Interpretation of Cultural and Natural Resources* (State College, Pa.: Venture Publishing, Inc., 1995), 338–9.

18. The American National Association for Interpretation finds professional interpreters evenly distributed among various kinds of sites and museums in North America. See Knudson et al., *Interpretation of Cultural and Natural Resources*, 26.

19. William T. Alderson and Shirley Payne Low, *Interpretation of Historic Sites* (Nashville, Tenn.: American Association for State and Local History, 1976), 24.

20. John Coles, *Archaeology by Experiment* (New York: Charles Scribner's Sons, 1973), 15.

21. Patty Jo Watson, Steven A. LeBlanc, and Charles L. Redman, *Explanation in Archeology: An Explicitly Scientific Approach* (New York: Columbia University Press, 1971), 65.

22. Alan Morton, "Tomorrow's Yesterdays: Science Museums and the Future," in Robert Lumley, ed., *The Museum Time-Machine* (London: Methuen, 1988), 128–43.

23. Watson et al., *Explanation in Archeology*.

24. Jules David Prown, "Mind in Matter: An Introduction to Material Culture Theory and Method," *Winterthur Portfolio* 17, no. 1 (1982): 1–19.

25. Raphael Samuel, *Theatres of Memory*, vol. 1: *Past and Present in Contemporary Culture* (New York:

Verso, 1994), 15; Allan Chapman, *Dividing the Circle: The Development of Critical Angular Measurement in Astronomy 1500–1850* (New York: Ellis Horwood, 1990), 15; Jim Bennett, "Can Science Museums Take History Seriously?," in Sharon Macdonald, ed., *The Politics of Display: Museums, Science, Culture* (New York: Routledge, 1998), 173–82.

26. Deborah Jean Warner, "What Is a Scientific Instrument, When Did It Become One, and Why?," *British Journal for the History of Science* 23 (1990): 84-6.

27. John B. Hattendorf, "Introduction, the Study of Maritime History," in Hattendorf, ed., *Maritime History*, vol. 1: *The Age of Discovery* (Malabar, Fla.: Krieger Publishing Co., 1996), xiii; Frank Broeze, editor's introduction, in Broeze, ed., *Maritime History at the Crossroads: A Critical Review of Recent Historiography*, Research in Maritime History No. 9 (St. John's, Newfoundland: International Maritime Economic History Association, 1995), xv.

28. Hattendorf, "Introduction," in *Maritime History*, vol. 1, xiii.

29. Richard W. Unger, "Politics, Religion and the Economy of Renaissance Europe," in *Maritime History*, vol. 1, 4; Richard W. Unger, "Theoretical and Practical Origins of Methods of Navigation," in *Maritime History*, vol. 1, 21; David M. Williams, "The Progress of Maritime History," *Journal of Transport History* 14, no. 2 (1993): 126–41; Malcolm Tull, "Maritime History in Australia," in *Maritime History at the Crossroads*, 3.

30. Peter Burke, "Overture: The New History, its Past and its Future," in Peter Burke, ed., *New Perspectives on Historical Writing* (Cambridge: Cambridge University Press, 1991), 3.

31. Frank Broeze, "Maritime Museums: An Historian's Reflections on Their Purposes, Objectives, and Methods," in L. M. Akveld, ed., *VIth International Congress of Maritime Museums Proceedings* (Rotterdam, 1987), 36–7; David B. Quinn, *England and the Discovery of America* (New York: Alfred A. Knopf, 1974), xviii.

32. Paul Butel, *The Atlantic*, trans. Iain Hamilton Grant (New York: Routledge, 1999), 6.

33. David Armitage, "Three Concepts of Atlantic History," in Armitage and J. Braddick, eds., *The British Atlantic World, 1500–1800* (New York: Palgrave Macmillan, 2002), 11–30.

34. Butel, *Atlantic*, 2.

35. Philip de Souza, *Seafaring and Civilization: Maritime Perspectives on World History* (London: Profile Books, 2001), 200.

36. Philip E. Steinberg, *The Social Construction of the Ocean* (Cambridge: Cambridge University Press, 2001), 75.

37. Cunliffe, *Facing the Ocean*, 34.

38. Broeze, "Maritime Museums."

39. David Lambert, Luciana Martins, and Miles Ogborn, "Currents, Visions and Voyages: Historical Geographies of the Sea," *Journal of Historical Geography* 32 (2006): 482.

40. National Maritime Museum, *Souvenir Guide* (London: n.p., 1999).

41. Quoted in Allan Sekula, *Fish Story* (Rotterdam: Richter Verlag, 1995), 44.

42. Cunliffe, *Facing the Ocean*, 554.

43. Peter Neill, "Maritime Museums in Maritime Settings," in *VIIth International Congress of Maritime Museums Proceedings* (Stockholm, 1990), 219–28.

44. Cunliffe, *Facing the Ocean*, 554.

45. Christer Westerdahl, "The Maritime Cultural Landscape," *International Journal of Nautical Archaeology* 21, no. 2 (1992): 5–14; Lambert et al., "Currents, Visions and Voyages," 479–93.

46. Westdahl, "The Maritime Cultural Landscape," 5–14.

47. Francois Bellec, "The Sea-Venture Museum," in *VIth International Congress*, 33.

48. Evan M. Zeusse, "Ritual," in Mircea Eliade, ed., *The Encyclopedia of Religion* (New York: Gacl, 1987), 12:406.

49. Martin Banham, ed., *The Cambridge Guide to World Theatre* (Cambridge: Cambridge University Press, 1983), 286.

50. Greg Dening, *Mr. Bligh's Bad Language* (Cambridge: Cambridge University Press, 1992), 57.

51. Captain John Smith, *A Sea Grammar* (1627), in Philip L. Barbour, ed., *The Complete Works of Captain John Smith* (Chapel Hill: University of North Carolina Press, 1986), 3:85. See also Dean King, *A Sea of Words*, 3rd ed. (New York: Owl Books, 2000). Written to complement Patrick O'Brian's novels, King's lexicon is an encyclopedia of obsolete maritime arcana. Although the work addresses eighteenth-century naval matters, much of the lexicon applies to 1611.

52. Jonathan Raban, *The Oxford Book of the Sea* (New York: Oxford University Press, 1992), 7.

53. William Sayers, "Some International Nautical Etymologies," *Mariner's Mirror* 88, no. 4 (November 2002), 408.

54. Purchas, *Hakluytus Posthumus*, 1:46–7.

55. Donald Wharton, "The Colonial Era," in Haskell Springer, ed., *America and the Sea: A Literary History* (Athens: University of Georgia Press, 1995), 34.

56. Eric Gethyn-Jones, *George Thorpe and the Berkeley Company: A Gloucestershire Enterprise in Virginia* (Gloucester: Sutton, 1982), 254ff.

57. The voyage narrative derives from the accounts of the five Roanoke voyages as related in Richard Hakluyt, *The Principal Navigations Voyages Traffiques & Discoveries of the English Nation*, vol. 8 (1600; reprint, Glasgow: James MacLehose and Sons, 1903); the voyage of Captain Bartholomew Gilbert to Virginia in 1603, detailed in Purchas, *Hakluytus Posthumus*, vol. 18; the voyage of Captain Samuel Argal to Virginia in 1610, in Purchas, *Hakluytus Posthumus*, vol. 19; and "A True Repertory of the Wracke, and Redemption of Sir Thomas Gates Knight . . . ," July 15, 1610, by William Strachey, in Purchas, *Hakluytus Posthumus*, vol. 19; Ferdinando Yates' account of the voyage of the *Margaret* to Virginia from September–November 1619 as it appears in the Smyth of Nibley Papers, 13, reprinted in the *Bulletin of the New York Public Library* I, no. 3 (1897), 68–72. Richard Hakluyt's spirit permeates this book: the voyage accounts, the navigational texts, and even the sermons of Tristram Hame's era were read, assimilated, published, discussed, and promulgated by Hakluyt. Of Hame's contemporaries, Hakluyt was omniscient on matters of maritime exploration. For an invigorating account of his life, times, and labors, see Peter C. Mancall, *Hakluyt's Promise: An Elizabethan's Obsession for an English America* (New Haven, Conn.: Yale University Press, 2007).

Chapter 2. "Sea Chariots and Horses of England":
Guyft, **Her Master, and the American Enterprise**

1. Kenneth R. Andrews, *Trade, Plunder and Settlement: Maritime Enterprise and the Genesis of the British Empire, 1480–1630* (Cambridge: Cambridge University Press, 1984), 30.

2. John C. Appleby, "Abraham Jennings of Plymouth: The Commercial Career of a 'Western Trader,' c. 1602–49," *Southern History* 16 (1996): 24–42.

3. Andrews, *Trade, Plunder and Settlement*, 314; Kenneth R. Andrews, "Christopher Newport of Limehouse, Mariner," *William and Mary Quarterly*, 3rd ser., XI (1954), 40; David B. Quinn, "Christopher Newport in 1590," *North Carolina Historical Review* XXIX, no. 3 (1953); 305–16.

4. David B. Quinn, *England and the Discovery of America, 1481–1620* (New York: Alfred A. Knopf, 1974), 209.

5. Andrews, "Christopher Newport," 33.

6. Alison Grant, "Devon Shipping, Trade, and Ports, 1600–1689," in Michael Duffy et al., eds., *The New Maritime History of Devon*, vol. I: *From Early Times to the Late Eighteenth Century* (London: Conway Maritime Press, 1992), 135.

7. Quoted from the "Preface to the Reader," in William Bourne, *A Regiment for the Sea*, ed. E. G. R. Taylor (1574; reprint, Cambridge: Cambridge University Press, 1963), 293–5; Kenneth R. Andrews, "The Elizabethan Seaman," *Mariner's Mirror* 68, no. 3 (1982): 259.

8. John Smith, *A Sea Grammar* (1627), in Philip L. Barbour, ed., *The Complete Works of Captain John Smith*, (Chapel Hill: University of North Carolina Press, 1986), 3:34.

9. G. V. Scammell, *Ships, Oceans and Empire: Studies in European Maritime and Colonial History, 1400–1750* (Aldershot, Hampshire: Variorum, 1995), 145; Scammell, "Manning the English Merchant Service in the Sixteenth Century," *Mariner's Mirror* 56, no. 2 (1970): 144–7; Fernand Braudel, *Civilization and Capitalism, 15th–18th Century: The Wheels of Commerce*, trans. Siân Reynolds, vol. 2 (New York: Harper & Row, 1979), 361–3.

10. John Dee, *The Mathematicall Praeface to the Elements of Geometrie of Euclid of Megara*, introduction by Allen G. Debus (1570; reprint, New York: Neale Watson Academic Publications, Inc., 1975), fols. diiiiv, Air.

11. Richard Hakluyt, "The examination of the Masters and Pilots which sail in the Fleetes of Spaine to the West Indies," in Hakluyt, ed., *The Principal Navigations Voyages Traffiques & Discoveries of the English Nation* (1600; reprint, Glasgow: James MacLehose and Sons, 1904), 11:453.

12. Ibid., 454.

13. Ibid., 455.

14. Alison Sandman, "Educating Pilots: Licensing Exams, Cosmography Classes, and the *Universidad de Mareantes* in 16th Century Spain," *Fernando Oliveira and his Era. Humanism and the Art of Navigation in Renaissance Europe. Proceedings of the IX International Reunion for the History of Nautical Science and Hydrography*, September 19–24, 1998 (Cascais, Portugal: Patrimónia), 99–110.

15. Richard W. Unger, "Theoretical and Practical Origins of Methods of Navigation," in John B. Hattendorf, ed., *Maritime History*, vol. 1: *The Age of Discovery* (Malabar, Fla.: Krieger Publishing Co., 1996), 33; J. H. Parry, *The Age of Reconaissance* (New York: The World Publishing Company, 1963), 1, 66–7.

16. Peter Dear, *Revolutionizing the Sciences: European Knowledge and Its Ambitions, 1500–1700* (Princeton, N.J.: Princeton University Press, 2001); Hester Higton, "Does Using an Instrument Make You Mathematical? Mathematical Practitioners of the 17th Century," *Endeavour* 25, no. 1 (2001): 18–22.

17. Paula Findlen, *Possessing Nature: Museums, Collecting, and Scientific Culture in Early Modern Italy* (Berkeley: University of California Press, 1994), 10.

18. Hester K. Higton, *Elias Allen and the Role of Instruments in Shaping the Mathematical Culture of Seventeenth-Century England*, Ph.D. diss., Cambridge University, 1996, ii.

19. Dee, *The Mathematicall Praeface.*

20. I. R. Adamson, "The Administration of Gresham College and its Fluctuating Fortunes as a Scientific Institution in the Seventeenth Century," *History of Education* 9, no. 1 (1980): 13–25.

21. Lesley B. Cormack, *Charting an Empire: Geography at the English Universities, 1580–1620* (Chicago: University of Chicago Press, 1997), 204–5; J. A. Bennett, "The Challenge of Practical Mathematics," in Stephen Pumfrey, Paolo L. Rossi, and Maurice Slawinski, eds., *Science, Culture and Popular Belief in Renaissance Europe* (Manchester: Manchester University Press, 1991), 188.

22. John Ward, *The Lives of the Professors of Gresham College* (London, 1740; reprint, New York: Johnson Reprint Corporation, 1967), iii.

23. Ibid., vi.

24. Ibid., viii.

25. Higton, *Elias Allen*, 19; Cormack, *Charting an Empire*, 204.

26. Adamson, "The Administration of Gresham College," 19; Cormack, *Charting an Empire*, 83.

27. Higton, *Elias Allen*, 28.

28. Ibid., 279.

29. Readers interested in exploring Dutch and Iberian contributions to navigation might begin with C. R. Boxer's two foundational works, *The Dutch Seaborne Empire 1600–1800* (London: Hutchinson, 1965), and *The Portuguese Seaborne Empire 1415–1825* (New York: Alfred A. Knopf, 1969) for overview. Readers interested in recent scholarship on Iberian navigational learning, technology, and theory should consult Ursula Lamb, ed., *Cosmographers and Pilots of the Spanish Maritime Empire* (Aldershot: Variorum, 1995), and W. G. I. Randles, ed., *Geography, Cartography and Nautical Science in the Renaissance* (Burlington, Vt.: Ashgate, 2000).

30. I am indebted to Felgate descendent Don Felgate, Middlesex, England, for the genealogical information on Tobias Felgate. His research has yielded no baptism record for Tobias, but Tobias's siblings were baptized in Stonham Aspal. His parents lived in Pettaugh at some time, so Tobias may have been born there (Don Felgate, correspondence, November 24, 2003). A legal document of 1627 refers to Tobias as 40 years of age, hence a possible birth year of 1587 (R.O. C.24/531/55).

31. Don Felgate, correspondence, September 25, 2000.

32. Interrogatories and Depositions of Witnesses in the case of *Bargrave vs Smyth, Wolstenholme, Johnson, Canninge and Easington*, Tobias Felgate deposition, 27 July 1620, R.O. C24/473 Pt.

33. Smyth of Nibley Papers, 13, reprinted in the *Bulletin of the New York Public Library* I, no. 3 (1897): 68–72.

34. Susan Myra Kingsbury, ed., *The Records of the Virginia Company of London* (Washington, D.C.: U.S. Government Printing Office, 1906), 3:213.

35. Ibid., 2:386.

36. Ibid., 3:388.

37. *Virginia Historical Magazine* XXXI, no. 4 (October 1923): 293.

38. Ibid., XXVI, no. 4 (October 1918): 350.

39. *Virginia Historical Magazine* 2 (1895): 182.

40. Warrants for issuing Letters of Marque or Commissions for taking Pirates for April 14, 1626, July 26, 1627, and July 1, 1628, for the *James* (first two) and *The William and John* (third), all listed as owned by Tobias Felgate, and on which he served as master. Information provided by Don Felgate, correspondence, December 9, 2003.

41. Kingsbury, *Records of the Virginia Company*, 2:17.

42. Ibid., 90, 75, respectively.

43. *Virginia Historical Magazine* 4, no. 3 (January 1897): 307. This transaction is recorded in PRO 2/33 (1615).

44. R.O. C3/416/88.

45. *William and Mary Quarterly* XV, no. 1 (1st series) (July 1906): 36.

46. *Virginia Historical Magazine* 14, no. 2 (October 1906): 191. Land patents for John, William, Robert, and Tobias Felgate can be found in *Cavaliers and Pioneers*, ed. Nell Marion Nugent (Richmond: Library of Virginia, 1992), 1:14, 15, 36, 70, 98, 121, 123.

47. *Virginia Historical Magazine* VIII, no. 2 (October 1900): 153.

48. Virginia M. Meyer and John Frederick Dorman, eds., *Adventurers of Purse and Person, Virginia 1607–1624/5* (Richmond, Va.: Genealogical Publishing Co., 1987), 198.

49. Ibid., 448; *Virginia Historical Magazine* XXIX, no. 3 (July 1921): 297.

50. *William and Mary Quarterly* V, no. 2 (1st series) (October 1896): 80.

51. Ibid., 24, no. 1 (1st series) (July 1915): 41.

52. Ibid.

53. Ibid., XXII, no. 2 (1st series) (October 1913): 76; *Virginia Historical Magazine* 2 (1895): 181; *William and Mary Quarterly* 4, no. 3 (2nd series) (July 1924): 161.

54. Brian Lavery, *The Colonial Merchantman* Susan Constant *1605* (Annapolis, Md.: Naval Institute Press, 1988), 10.

55. Ibid.; Allan J. Wingood, "*Sea Venture* Second Interim Report—Part 2: The Artifacts," *International Journal of Nautical Archaeology and Underwater Exploration* 15, no. 2 (1986): 149–59; Wingood, "*Sea Venture*: An Interim Report on an Early 17th Century Shipwreck Lost in 1609," *International Journal of Nautical Archaeology and Underwater Exploration* 11, no. 4 (1982): 333–47.

56. Andrews, *Trade, Plunder and Settlement*; Richard W. Unger, *The Ship in the Medieval Economy 600–1600* (London: Croom Helm, 1980), 262–9; W. Sears Nickerson, *Land Ho!—1620: A Seaman's Story of the* Mayflower, *Her Construction, Her Navigation, and Her First Landfall* (East Lansing: Michigan State University Press, 1997).

57. Carla Rahn Phillips, "The Galleon," in Richard W. Unger, ed., *Cogs, Caravels and Galleons: The Sailing Ship 1000–1650* (London: Conway Maritime Press, 1994), 101; Ian Friel, "The Three-Masted Ship and Atlantic Voyages," in Joyce Youings, ed., *Privateering and Colonisation in the Reign of Elizabeth I*, Exeter Studies in History No. 10 (Exeter: University of Exeter Press, 1985), 29.

58. Friel, "Three-Masted Ship," 29.

59. David W. Waters, *The Art of Navigation in England in Elizabethan and Early Stuart Times* (New Haven, Conn.: Yale University Press, 1958), Appendix 27.

60. Warwick Charlton, *The Second* Mayflower *Adventure* (Boston, Mass.: Little, Brown, 1957); Friel, "The Three-Masted Ship," 21–37; Peter Allington, "The Principles of Shiphandling," in *New Maritime History of Devon*, 45–50.

61. Scammell, *Ships, Oceans and Empire*, 362–70.

62. Ibid., 364.

63. *Griffith & H. Rastall vs. Lennarts & H. Beale*, June 1627, R.O. C24/531/55.

64. Ibid.; High Court of Admiralty 1, 14 June 1624.

65. Joyce Youings and Peter W. Cornford, "Seafaring and Maritime Trade in Sixteenth-Century Devon," in *New Maritime History of Devon*, 105.

66. Ibid., 103.

67. Joyce Youings, *Ralegh's Country, The South West of England in the Reign of Queen Elizabeth I* (Raleigh: North Carolina Division of Archives, 1986), 13.

68. Todd Gray, *Early-Stuart Mariners and Shipping: The Maritime Surveys of Devon and Cornwall, 1619–35*, New Series, vol. 33 (Exeter: Devon & Cornwall Record Society, 1990) xv.

69. Scammell, *Ships, Oceans and Empire*, 149; Scammell, "Manning the English Merchant Service," 138.

70. Quinn, *England and the Discovery of America*, 223.

71. E. H. Hair and J. D. Alsop, *English Seamen and Traders in Guinea 1553–1565: The New Evidence of Their Wills* (Lewiston, N.Y.: Edwin Mellen Press, Ltd., 1992), 2.

72. Ibid., 135; Scammell, *Ships, Oceans and Empire*, 136.

73. Scammell, *Ships, Oceans and Empire*, 141-2; Scammell, "Manning the English Merchant Service," 140–3.

74. N. A. M. Rodger, *The Safeguard of the Sea: A Naval History of Britain* (New York: W. W. Norton & Company, 1998), 199–200.

75. Cheryl A. Fury, "Training and Education in the Elizabethan Maritime Community," *Mariner's Mirror* 85, no. 2 (1999): 147. For further insight into the skills of mariners, see Henry Mainwaring's *Sea-mans Dictionary* (London, 1644), our earliest source in English of definitions of nautical terms, which illuminates the sailor's lexicon, and Smith's *Sea Grammar*, which not only gives advice on many practical matters ranging from victualling to gunnery, but also explicates twenty-two functions of the ship's company within the context of a working ship, an ethnographic account of shipboard culture. See L. Barbour, "Captain John Smith's Sea Grammar and its Debt to Sir Henry Mainwaring's 'Seaman's Dictionary,'" *Mariner's Mirror* 58, no. 1 (1972): 93.

76. Fury, "Training and Education," 148.

77. Cheryl Fury, "Elizabethan Seamen: Their Lives Ashore," *International Journal of Maritime History* X, no. 1 (June 1998): 33; also Fury, *Tides in the Affairs of Men: The Social History of Elizabethan Seamen, 1580–1603* (Westport, Conn.: Praeger, 2002), 197ff.

78. Scammell, *Ships, Oceans and Empire*, 145; Scammell, "Manning the English Merchant Service," 140–3; Peter Pope, "The Practice of Portage in the Early Modern North Atlantic: Introduction to an Issue in Maritime Historical Anthropology," *Journal of the Canadian Historical Association* 6, new series (1995): 39; Braudel, *Civilization and Capitalism*, 2:361–3; Fury, *Tides in the Affairs of Men*, 85ff.

79. Hakluyt, *Principal Navigations*, 7:322–9.

80. Andrews, *Trade, Plunder and Settlement*, 226; David B. Quinn and A. N. Ryan, *England's Sea Empire, 1550–1642* (London: George Allen & Unwin, 1983), 39–40.

81. Cormack, *Charting an Empire*, 83; Amir R. Alexander, *Geometrical Landscapes: The Voyages of Discovery and the Transformation of Mathematical Practice* (Stanford, Calif.: Stanford University Press, 2002), 71.

82. Andrews, *Trade, Plunder and Settlement*, 147; J. H. Parry, "Introduction: The English in the New World," in K. R. Andrews, N. Canny, and E. H. Hair, eds., *The Westward Enterprise: English Activities in Ireland, the Atlantic, and America 1480–1650* (Liverpool: Liverpool University Press, 1978), 2.

83. Andrews, *Trade, Plunder and Settlement*, 4–5; Andrews, "English in the Caribbean 1560–1620," in Andrews et al., *Westward Enterprise*, 103–23; Andrews, "Elizabethan Privateering," in *Privateering and Colonisation in the Reign of Elizabeth I*, 1–20.

84. Andrews, "English in the Caribbean," 123.

85. Andrews, "Elizabethan Privateering," 15.

86. E. G. R. Taylor, *Late Tudor and Early Stuart Geography 1583–1650* (London: Methuen & Co., Ltd., 1934), 1, 15.

87. Mary C. Fuller, *Voyages in Print: English Travel to America, 1576–1624* (Cambridge: Cambridge University Press, 1995), 2.

88. Scammell, G. V., *The World Encompassed: The First Maritime Empires c. 800–1650*, Los Angeles: University of California Press, 1981; Keith Thomas, *Religion and the Decline of Magic* (New York: Charles Scribner's Sons, 1971), 91.

89. Peter C. Mancall, *Hakluyt's Promise: An Elizabethan's Obsession for an English America* (New Haven, Conn.: Yale University Press, 2007), 363ff.

90. Robert Gray, *A Good Speed to Virginia* (1609; reprint, New York: Walter J. Johnson, 1970), fol. B3r.

91. Ibid.

92. Andrews, *Trade, Plunder and Settlement*, 34–6; Boies Penrose, *Travel and Discovery in the Renaissance* (Cambridge, Mass.: Harvard University Press, 1952), 268; Quinn, *England and the Discovery of America*, 289; described in Mancall, *Hakluyt's Promise*.

93. Rodger, *Safeguard of the Sea*, 311.

94. Fuller, *Voyages in Print*, 144; Mancall, *Hakluyt's Promise*, 264ff.

95. Braudel, *Civilization and Capitalism*, 3:365.

96. Parry, *Age of Reconaissance*, 216; Quinn, *England and the Discovery of America*, 483; Fernand Braudel, *Civilization and Capitalism, 15th–18th Century: The Structures of Everyday Life: The Limits of the Possible*, trans. Siân Reynolds, vol. 1 (New York: Harper & Row, 1981), 124.

97. Robert Brenner, *Merchants and Revolution, Commercial Change, Political Conflict, and London's Overseas Traders, 1550–1653* (Princeton, N.J.: Princeton University Press, 1993), 99.

98. Patrick McGrath, "Bristol and America 1480–1631," in *Westward Enterprise*, 93–7.

99. Wolfgang Reinhard, "The Seaborne Empires," in Thomas A. Brady, Heiko A. Oberman, and James D. Tracy, eds., *Handbook of European History 1400–1600: Late Middle Ages, Renaissance and Reformation* (New York: E. J. Brill, 1994), 1:657; Braudel, *Civilization and Capitalism*, 3:354–5.

100. Andrews, *Trade, Plunder and Settlement*, 68; see Carole Shammas, "English Commercial Development and American Colonization 1560–1620," in *Westward Enterprise*, 167.

101. John Dee, *General and Rare Memorials pertayning to the Perfect Arte of Navigation* (1577; reprint, New York: Da Capo Press, 1968), 2–4; Andrews, *Trade, Plunder and Settlement*, 67–8; E. G. R. Taylor, *Tudor Geography 1485–1583* (London: Methuen & Co., Ltd., 1930), 96–7; Taylor, "Instructions to a Colonial Surveyor in 1582," *Mariner's Mirror* 37, no. 1 (1951): 54; Taylor, *Mathematical Practitioners of Tudor & Stuart England* (Cambridge: Cambridge University Press, 1954), 18–21; Charles H. Cotter, *A History of Nautical Astronomy* (New York: American Elsevier Publishing Company, Inc., 1968), 44; Penrose, *Travel and Discovery*, 314–17.

102. Andrews, *Trade, Plunder and Settlement*, 359.

103. Richard W. Unger, "Politics, Religion and the Economy of Renaissance Europe," in *Maritime History*, 1:19.

104. David M. Loades, "England under the Tudors," in *Handbook of European History*, 1:423.

105. Ibid., 417.

106. Donald Woodward, "Ships, Masters and Shipowners of the Wirral 1550–1650," *Mariner's Mirror* 63, no. 3 (1977): 233–47.

107. R.O. C3/416/88.

108. Braudel, *Civilization and Capitalism*, 2:362–3.

109. Unger, *Ship in the Medieval Economy*, 275.

110. Andrews, *Trade, Plunder and Settlement*, 362.

111. Braudel, *Civilization and Capitalism*, 2:439–42.

112. Brenner, *Merchants and Revolution*, 92.

113. Andrews, *Trade, Plunder and Settlement*, 195.

114. Wesley F. Craven, ed., *Early Accounts of Life in Colonial Virginia 1609–1613* (Delmar, N.Y.: Scholars' Facsimiles & Reprints, 1976), iii.

115. Brenner, *Merchants and Revolution*, 97–8.

116. Unger, "Theoretical and Practical Origins," 33.

117. Unger, *The Ship in the Medieval Economy*, 215–16.

118. David Waters, "Columbus's Portuguese Inheritance," *Mariner's Mirror* 78, no. 4 (1992): 393; Waters, *Science and the Techniques of Navigation in the Renaissance* (Greenwich, UK: National Maritime Museum, 1980), 9.

119. Ben C. McCary, *John Smith's Map of Virginia* (Charlottesville: University of Virginia Press, 1981).

120. Andrews, *Trade, Plunder and Settlement*, 211; Parry, *Age of Reconaissance*, 212. For Ralegh's patent given in full, see Hakluyt, *Principal Navigations*, 8:290–2.

121. Quinn, *England and the Discovery of America*, 218. The five Roanoke voyages are recounted in Hakluyt, *Principal Navigations*, 8:297–422.

122. Peter Quartermaine, *Port Architecture: Constructing the Littoral* (Chichester, West Sussex: John Wiley & Sons, 1999), 29.

123. Ibid., 102.

124. Samuel Eliot Morison, *The European Discovery of America, The Northern Voyages A.D. 500–1600* (Oxford: Oxford University Press, 1971), 161–6.

125. Allan Scott, *St Mary Redcliffe Bristol* (Stanningley, Leeds: n.p., 1986), 7.

126. "The Account of A.B. for Furnishing the Ship *Supply*, September 1620," in *Records of the Virginia Company*, 3:388.

127. Ibid.; Jean Vanes, *The Port of Bristol in the Sixteenth Century*, Local History Pamphlets No. 39 (Bristol, UK: Bristol Branch of the Historical Association, 1977), 20.

128. David H. Sacks, *The Widening Gate: Bristol and the Atlantic Economy, 1450–1700* (Los Angeles: University of California Press, 1991), 52–3.

129. See Braudel, *Civilization and Capitalism*, 3:153.

130. Rodger, *Safeguard of the Sea*, 295.

131. Quinn, *England and the Discovery of America*, 285; Parry, *Age of Reconaissance*, 213; Parry, "English in the New World," 2.

132. Shammas, "English Commercial Development," 165.

133. Ibid., 153; Rodger, *Safeguard of the Sea*, 296.

134. Quinn and Ryan, *England's Sea Empire*, 45.

Chapter 3. "Break Ground or Weigh Anchor": Getting Under Way to Virginia

1. John Smith, "A Letter to Mr. Berkeley, June 1, 1620," in Susan Myra Kingsbury, ed., *The Records of the Virginia Company of London* (Washington, D.C.: U.S. Government Printing Office, 1906), 3:292.

2. "The Account of A.B. for Furnishing the Ship *Supply*, September 1620," *Records of the Virginia Company*, 3:388.

3. David H. Sacks, *The Widening Gate: Bristol and the Atlantic Economy, 1450–1700* (Los Angeles: University of California Press, 1991), 14.

4. Ibid., 15.

5. Adapted from the "Virginia Papers, 1616–19," *Bulletin of the New York Public Library* III, no. 4 (1899): 165–7.

6. Jean Vanes, *The Port of Bristol in the Sixteenth Century*, Local History Pamphlets No. 39 (Bristol, UK: Bristol Branch of the Historical Association, 1977), 1.

7. Henry Mainwaring, *The Sea-mans Dictionary* (London, 1644), 85.

8. Ibid.

9. The names of the crew and passengers are fictitious. To construct names (and their locales of origin) appropriate to 1611, I based the names on those listed in *Records of the Virginia Company*, 3; "Virginia Papers," *Bulletin of the New York Public Library* III, no. 5 (1899): 210–12; Todd Gray, *Early-Stuart Mariners and Shipping: The Maritime Surveys of Devon and Cornwall, 1619–35*, New Series, vol. 33 (Exeter: Devon & Cornwall Record Society, 1990); Virginia M. Meyer, John Frederick Dorman, eds., *Adventurers of Purse and Person, Virginia 1607–1624/5* (Richmond: Order of First Families of Virginia, 1987).

10. Robert Brenner, *Merchants and Revolution: Commercial Change, Political Conflict, and London's Overseas Traders, 1550–1653* (Princeton, N.J.: Princeton University Press, 1993), 93–4.

11. Samuel Eliot Morison, *The European Discovery of America, The Northern Voyages A.D. 500–1600* (Oxford: Oxford University Press, 1971), 165.

12. Vanes, *Port of Bristol*, 6–9.

13. "The Relation of Captaine Gosnols Voyage to the North part of Virginia, begunne the sixe and twentieth of March, Anno 42. Elizabethae Reginae 1602. and delivered by Gabriel Archer, a Gentleman in the said Voyage," in Samuel Purchas, *Hakluytus Posthumus or Purchas His Pilgrimes* (1625; reprint, Glasgow: James MacLehose and Sons, 1905–7), 18:302ff.

14. Brian Lavery, *The Colonial Merchantman Susan Constant 1605* (Annapolis, Md.: Naval Institute Press, 1988), 24–5.

15. Pablo E. Pérez-Mallaína, *Spain's Men of the Sea: Daily Life on the Indies Fleets in the Sixteenth Century*, trans. Carla Rahn Phillips (Baltimore, Md.: Johns Hopkins University Press, 1998), 44, 79, 114.

16. Vanes, *Port of Bristol*, 4.

17. Cal. Pat. 1560–1563, 478, quoted in Vanes, *Port of Bristol*, 5.

18. Taken from Captain Edward Fenton's voyage to Labrador, Newfoundland, and Baffin Island, in E. G. R. Taylor, ed., *The Troublesome Voyage of Captain Edward Fenton 1582–1583* (Cambridge: Cambridge University Press, 1959), 49.

19. From the cost of furnishing the *Margaret*, which voyaged from Bristol to Virginia, in Virginia Papers, 1619, *Bulletin of the New York Public Library* III, no. 5 (1899): 213–19.

20. David W. Waters, *The Art of Navigation in England in Elizabethan and Early Stuart Times* (New Haven, Conn.: Yale University Press, 1958), 171–3.

21. Lucas Jansz. Waghenaer, *The Mariners Mirrour* (1588; reprint, introduction by R. A. Skelton, Amsterdam: Theatrum Orbis Terrarum, 1966), fol. A2r.

22. John Dee, *General and Rare Memorials pertayning to the Perfect Arte of Navigation* (1577; reprint, New York: Da Capo Press, 1968), 3. The bill for charts and nautical instruments for Martin Frobisher's first voyage in search of the Northwest Passage in 1576 and the list in Captain John Smith's 1627 work, *A Sea Grammar* (see full cite in note 27) furnish the list for the *Guyft*. These two sources have been chosen because they bracket the voyage of the *Guyft*, and reflect fast-evolving practice.

23. A. N. Ryan, "A New Passage to Cataia": The Northwest Passage in Early Modern English History," in. John B. Hattendorf, ed., *Maritime History*, vol. 1: *The Age of Discovery* (Malabar, Fla.: Krieger Publishing Co., 1996), 303; Richard Hakluyt, *The Principal Navigations Voyages Traffiques & Discoveries of the English Nation* (1600; reprint, Glasgow: James MacLehose and Sons, 1903), 7:204ff.

24. Waters, *Art of Navigation*, 530–2.

25. Ibid., 244.

26. A. N. Ryan, introduction, in John Davis, *The Seamans Secrets* (1633; reprint, Delmar, N.Y.: Scholar's Facsimiles & Reprints, 1992), 12; Kenneth R. Andrews, *Trade, Plunder and Settlement: Maritime Enterprise and the Genesis of the British Empire* (Cambridge: Cambridge University Press, 1984), 66.

27. Philip L. Barbour, "Captain John Smith's Sea Grammar and its Debt to Sir Henry Mainwaring's 'Seaman's Dictionary,'" *Mariner's Mirror* 58, no. 1 (1972): 93; John Smith, *A Sea Grammar* (1627), in Philip L. Barbour, ed., *The Complete Works of Captain John Smith*, (Chapel Hill: University of North Carolina Press, 1986), 3:41ff.

28. Smith, *Sea Grammar*, 111–12.

29. Waters, *Art of Navigation*, 219–20; E. G. R. Taylor, *The Mathematical Practitioners of Tudor & Stuart England* (Cambridge: Cambridge University Press, 1954), 181; E. G. R. Taylor, *The Haven-Finding Art: A History of Navigation from Odysseus to Captain Cook* (London: Hollis & Carter, 1971), 223–5; Amir R. Alexander, *Geometrical Landscapes: The Voyages of Discovery and the Transformation of Mathematical Practice* (Stanford, Calif.: Stanford University Press, 2002), 139.

30. Waters, *Art of Navigation*, 239; Taylor, *Mathematical Practitioners*, 193, 352.

31. Waters, *Art of Navigation*, 105.

32. Ibid., 243; Taylor, *Mathematical Practitioners*, 176.

33. Waters, *Art of Navigation*, 201, and information on Bourne on 130–43; Taylor, *Mathematical Practitioners*, 178, 332; A. J. Turner, *Early Scientific Instruments, Europe 1400–1800* (London: Sotheby's Publications, 1987), 67–8.

34. Waters, *Art of Navigation*, 153; Taylor, *Mathematical Practitioners*, 37–8, 173, 325; Stephen Pumfrey, *Latitude and the Magnetic Earth: The True Story of Queen Elizabeth's Most Distinguished Man of Science* (New York: MJF Books, 2002), 75; A. R. T. Jonkers, *Earth's Magnetism in the Age of Sail* (Baltimore, Md.: Johns Hopkins University Press, 2003), 62.

35. Waters, *Art of Navigation*, 156; Taylor, *Mathematical Practitioners*, 38, 173, 325; Pumfrey, *Latitude and the Magnetic Earth*, 73; Lesley B. Cormack, *Charting an Empire: Geography at the English Universities, 1580–1620* (Chicago: University of Chicago Press, 1997), 94–5; J. A. Bennett, "The Challenge of Practical Mathematics," in Stephen Pumfrey, Paolo L. Rossi, and Maurice Slawinski, eds., *Science, Culture and Popular Belief in Renaissance Europe* (Manchester: Manchester University Press, 1991), 187.

36. Stephen Gaukroger, *The Emergence of a Scientific Culture: Science and the Shaping of Modernity, 1210–1685* (Oxford: Oxford University Press, 2006), 223.

37. Cormack, *Charting an Empire*, 28–9, 92–5; Bennett, "Challenge of Practical Mathematics," 181, 185.

38. Smith, *Sea Grammar*, 112. Compare Smith's list with the tools carried by the reconstructed ship, *Mayflower II*: a compass, cross-staff, astrolabe, glass, log and line, parallel rules, dividers, and a spyglass. See W. Sears Nickerson, *Land Ho!—1620: A Seaman's Story of the Mayflower, Her Construction, Her Navigation, and Her First Landfall* (East Lansing: Michigan State University Press, 1997), 30.

39. Waters, *Art of Navigation*, 216–8; Taylor, *Mathematical Practitioners*, 176.

40. Waters, *Art of Navigation*, 212; Taylor, *Mathematical Practitioners*, 173; Alexander, *Geometrical Landscapes*, 88; Bennett, "Challenge of Practical Mathematics," 187.

41. Martín Cortés, *Arte of Navigation* (1561; reprint, Delmar, N.Y.: Scholars' Facsimiles & Reprints, 1992), fol. iiiv.

42. Vanes, *Port of Bristol*, 2.

43. Gloria Clifton, *Directory of British Scientific Instrument Makers 1550–1851* (London: Zwemmer, 1995), xii–xv.

44. Mainwaring, *Sea-mans Dictionary*, 114.

45. Waters, *Art of Navigation*, 580–1; Peter Earle, *Sailors, English Merchant Seamen 1650–1775* (London: Methuen, 1998), 71.

46. Most of the crew and passengers listed were on board the *Margaret*, which sailed from Bristol to Virginia in 1619. Derived from *Records of the Virginia Company*, 3:213.

47. *Bulletin of the New York Public Library* III, no. 4 (1899): 161–2.

48. Joyce Youings, *Sixteenth-Century England* (London: Penguin, 1984), 36.

49. Peter Rolt, "Today's Bristol Channel Pilots," *Maritime Life and Traditions*, no. 19 (Summer 2003): 3.

50. Ibid., 4.

51. Vanes, *Port of Bristol*, 3.

52. Ibid., 3–5.

53. Morison, *European Discovery of America*, 161; Peter Cumberlidge, *Bristol Channel and Severn Pilot* (London: Adlard Coles Nautical, 1988), 13, 83.

54. Cumberlidge, *Bristol Channel*, 15.

55. E. Allde, *The Safeguard of Saylers, or great Rutter*, trans. Robert Norman (London, 1605), fol. 37v.

56. Vanes, *Port of Bristol*, 2.

57. Seán McGrail, *Ancient Boats in North-West Europe: The Archaeology of Water Transport to AD 1500* (London: Longman, 1998), 264.

58. J. McDermott and D. W. Waters, "Cathay and the Way Thither: The Navigation of the Frobisher Voyages," in Thomas H. B. Symons, ed., *Meta Incognita: A Discourse of Discovery, Martin Frobisher's Arctic Expeditions, 1576–1578*, Mercury Series Directorate Paper 10 (Hull, Quebec: Canadian Museum of Civilization, 1999), 2:365.

59. McGrail, *Ancient Boats in North-West Europe*, 262.

60. Taylor, *Troublesome Voyage*, 67, 73.

61. Ibid.

62. A .J. R. Russell-Wood, *The Portuguese Empire 1415–1808: A World on the Move* (Baltimore, Md.: Johns Hopkins University Press, 1998), 52.

63. Mainwaring, *Sea-mans Dictionary*, 23.

64. Barry Cunliffe, *Facing the Ocean: The Atlantic and its Peoples 8000 BC–AD 1500* (Oxford: Oxford University Press, 2001), 565.

Chapter 4. October 8, the Azores

1. Robert C. Ritchie, "Piracy," in John B. Hattendorf, ed. in chief, *The Oxford Encyclopedia of Maritime History* (Oxford: Oxford University Press, 2007), 3:296–300; David J. Starkey, "Privateering," ibid., 3:381–4; N. A. M. Rodger, *The Safeguard of the Sea: A Naval History of Britain* (New York: W. W. Norton & Company, 1998), 199–200, 242–96. The European merchant world of 1611 is circumscribed in David Loades, *England's Maritime Empire: Seapower, Commerce and Policy, 1490–1690* (London: Longman, 2000), 138–40.

2. The almanacs used for the ship's log are Arthur Hopton, *An almanack and prognostication serving Shrewsbury* (London, 1611), and Thomas Bretnor, *A new Almanacke and Prognostication* (London, 1611).

3. D. W. Waters, *The Art of Navigation in England in Elizabethan and Early Stuart Times* (New Haven, Conn.: Yale University Press, 1958), 282.

4. John Davis, *The Seamans Secrets* (1607), reprinted in Albert Hastings Markham, ed., *The Voyages and Works of John Davis the Navigator* (London: Hakluyt Society, 1880), 281.

5. William Barlow, *The Navigators Supply* (1597; reprint, New York: Da Capo Press, 1972), fol. h1v.

6. John Smith, *A Sea Grammar* (London, 1627), reprinted in Philip L. Barbour, ed., *The Complete Works of Captain John Smith* (Chapel Hill: University of North Carolina Press, 1986), 3:43.

7. William Bourne, *A Regiment for the Sea* (London, 1574), reprinted in E. G. R. Taylor, ed., (Cambridge: Cambridge University Press, 1963), 58.

8. J. A. Bennett, *The Divided Circle: A History of Instruments for Astronomy, Navigation and Surveying* (Oxford: Phaidon-Christie's Limited, 1987), 28.

9. Smith, *Sea Grammar*, 44.

10. Lucas Jansz. Waghenaer, *The Mariners Mirrour* (1588, reprint, intro. R. A. Skelton, Amsterdam: Theatrum Orbis Terrarum, 1966), fol. A2r.

11. Bourne, *Regiment for the Sea*, 237–8.

12. A good summary of the procedure and its difficulties can be found at Frank Scott, "Speed, Navigational Accuracy and the 'Ship Log,'" *Mariners Mirror* 92, no. 4 (November 2006): 477–81.

13. Ibid., 238.

14. Henry Mainwaring, *The Sea-mans Dictionary* (London, 1644), 110.

15. Edward Wright, *Certaine Errors in Navigation; The Voyage of . . . George Earle of Cumberl. to the Azores* (1599; reprint, Norwood, N.J.: Walter J. Johnson, Inc., 1974), fol. ¶¶4r.

16. From "The description of the Ilands of Açores, or the Flemish Ilands, taken out of Linschoten, with certaine occurrents, and English acts," in Samuel Purchas, *Hakluytus Posthumus or Purchas His Pilgrimes* (1625; reprint, Glasgow: James MacLehose and Sons, 1905–7), 18:360–70; and "Here follow the latitudes of the headlandes, Capes, and Islands, as well of Madera, The Canaries, and the West Indies, as of the Azores and the

Isles of Cabo Verde," in Richard Hakluyt, *The Principal Navigations Voyages Traffiques & Discoveries of the English Nation* (1600; reprint, Glasgow: James MacLehose and Sons, 1904), 10:334.

17. Rodger, *Safeguard of the Sea*, 308.

18. From "Of certaine notable and memorable accidents that happened during my continuance in Tercera in which are related many English fleetes, Sea-fights and Prizes," in *Hakluytus Posthumus*, 18:379–80; and Wright, *The Voyage of . . . George Earle of Cumberland*, 2–3.

19. Joan Druett, *Rough Medicine: Surgeons at Sea in the Age of Sail* (New York: Routledge, 2000), 10ff; A. W. Sloan, *English Medicine in the Seventeenth Century* (Bishop Auckland, Durham, South Africa: Academic Press, 1996), 107.

20. Ibid.

21. Sloan, *English Medicine*, 110.

22. James Watt, "The Medical Climate of Frobisher's England: Maritime Influences," in Thomas H. B. Symons, ed., *Meta Incognita: A Discourse of Discovery, Martin Frobisher's Arctic Expeditions, 1576–1578* (Hull, Quebec: Canadian Museum of Civilization, 1999), 1:265.

23. Ibid., 266.

24. Druett, *Rough Medicine*, 11; Sloan, *English Medicine*, 109–11; John Woodall, *The Surgions Mate*, introduction by John Kirkup (1617; reprint, Bath, England: Kingsmead, 1978), xi–xxiv.

25. Ibid.

26. Ibid., 12.

27. Ibid., 128.

28. Ibid., 140.

29. Ibid., 141.

30. Watt, "Medical Climate," 266–7.

31. Adapted from "Of certaine notable and memorable accidents . . . ," in *Hakluytus Posthumus*, 18:379–80.

32. From Ferdinando Yates' account of the voyage of the *Margaret* to Virginia from September–November 1619, as it appears in the Smyth of Nibley Papers, 13, reprinted in *Bulletin of the New York Public Library* I, no. 3 (1897): 68–72.

33. Wright, *Voyage of . . . George Earle of Cumberland*, 8–10.

34. E. G. R. Taylor, ed., *The Troublesome Voyage of Captain Edward Fenton 1582–1583* (Cambridge: Cambridge University Press, 1959), 133.

35. G. V. Scammell, "European Seamanship in the Great Age of Discovery," in Scammell, ed., *Ships, Oceans and Empire: Studies in European Maritime and Colonial*

History, 1400–1750 (Aldershot, Hampshire: Variorum, 1995), 369.

36. Ibid., 370.

37. Stephen Greenblatt, *Marvelous Possessions: The Wonder of the New World* (Chicago: University of Chicago Press, 1991), 9.

38. Ricardo Padrón, *Cartography, Literature, and Empire in Early Modern Spain* (Chicago: University of Chicago Press, 2004), 12.

39. Michael Jacobs, *The Painted Voyage: Art, Travel and Exploration 1564–1875* (London: British Museum Press, 1995), 104.

40. Anthony Turner, *Early Scientific Instruments, Europe 1400–1800* (London: Sotheby's Publications, 1987), 22.

41. William Cuningham, *The Cosmographical Glasse* (1559; reprint, New York: Da Capo Press, 1968), fol. 114.

42. O. B. Hardison, comments, in John U. Nef, "The Interplay of Literature, Art, and Science in the Time of Copernicus," in Owen Gingerich, ed., *The Nature of Scientific Discovery* (Washington, D.C.: Smithsonian Institution Press, 1975), 469.

43. C. John Sommerville, *The Secularization of Early Modern England: From Religious Culture to Religious Faith* (Oxford: Oxford University Press, 1992), 25–6. Alpers notes the popularization of maps in their multiple perspectives of rendering "visible the invisible." See Svetlana Alpers, *The Art of Describing. Dutch Art in the Seventeenth Century* (Chicago: University of Chicago Press, 1983), 133.

44. Lesley B. Cormack, *Charting an Empire: Geography at the English Universities, 1580–1620* (Chicago: University of Chicago Press, 1997), 11; Wayne K. D. Davies, *Writing Geographical Exploration: James and the Northwest Passage 1631–33* (Calgary, Alberta, Canada: University of Calgary Press, 2003), 125.

45. William Bourne, *The Treasure for Travelers* (1578; reprint, Norwood, N.J.: Walter J. Johnson, Inc., 1979), fol. **iiiv.

46. William Barlow, *The Navigators Supply* (1597; reprint, New York: Da Capo Press, 1972), fol. h1v.

47. Samuel Y. Edgerton Jr., "From Mental Matrix to *mappamundi* to Christian Empire: The Heritage of Ptolemaic Cartography in the Renaissance," in David Woodward, ed., *Art and Cartography: Six Historical Essays* (Chicago: University of Chicago Press, 1987), 46. For a discussion of how the map grid gradually displaced the natural and theological boundaries of time and space, see Alfred W. Crosby, *The Measure of Reality: Quantification and Western Society* (Cambridge: Cambridge University Press, 1997).

48. E. G. R. Taylor, *The Haven-Finding Art: A History of Navigation from Odysseus to Captain Cook* (London: Hollis & Carter, 1971), 225; J. H. Parry, *The Age of Reconaissance* (New York: The World Publishing Company, 1963), 113.

49. Davis, *Seamans Secrets*, 315.

50. Davis, *Seamans Secrets*, 239–40. See also Barlow, *Navigators Supply*, fols. k3r–4r.

51. David Waters, "The Iberian Bases of the English Art of Navigation in the Sixteenth Century," *XXXVII Secção de Coimbra*, Agrupamento de Estudos de Cartografia Antiga (Coimbra, 1970), 12.

52. Davis, *Seamans Secrets*, 274–5.

53. Francis Marbury, *A Sermon Preached at Paules Crosse the 13. of June, 1602* (London, 1602), fol. C2r–v.

54. Ibid., fols. D3–4r–v.

Chapter 5. "Beholding the Diversity of Days and Nights": The Universe of 1611

1. Keith Oatley, "Mental Maps for Navigation," *New Scientist* 64, no. 928 (December 19, 1974): 863–6.

2. Stuart Clark, *Thinking with Demons: The Idea of Witchcraft in Early Modern Europe* (Oxford: Oxford University Press, 1997), 286.

3. Keith Thomas, *Man and the Natural World: Changing Attitudes in England, 1500–1800* (Oxford: Oxford University Press, 1983), 17; see also Allen G. Debus, introduction, in John Dee, *The Mathematicall Praeface to the Elements of Geometrie of Euclid of Megara* (1570; reprint, New York: Neale Watson Academic Publications, Inc., 1975), 17. For a discussion of religious belief in the context of early modern science, see John Hedley Brooke, *Science and Religion: Some Historical Perspectives* (Cambridge: Cambridge University Press, 1991), 37. For a prototypical description of the sublunar realm by a Tudor writer, see William Cuningham, *The Cosmographical Glasse* (1559; reprint, New York: Da Capo Press, 1968), fol. 42.

4. Samuel Purchas, *Hakluytus Posthumus or Purchas His Pilgrimes* (1625; reprint, Glasgow: James MacLehose and Sons, 1905–7), 19:228.

5. Robert Recorde, *The Castle of Knowledge* (1556, reprint, Norwood, N.J.: Walter J. Johnson, Inc., 1975), fol. a–iiiiv.

6. Thomas, *Man and the Natural World*, 35.

7. William Barlow, *The Navigators Supply* (1597; reprint, New York: Da Capo Press, 1972), fol. b2r.

8. John C. Sommerville, *The Secularization of Early Modern England: From Religious Culture to Religious Faith* (Oxford: Oxford University Press, 1992), 43; Peter Dear, *Revolutionizing the Sciences: European Knowledge and Its Ambitions, 1500–1700* (Princeton, N.J.: Princeton University Press, 2001), 50ff.

9. Thomas L. Hankins and Robert J. Silverman, *Instruments and the Imagination* (Princeton, N.J.: Princeton University Press, 1995), 8; Marie Boas Hall, *The Scientific Renaissance 1450–1630* (1962; reprint, New York: Dover, 1994), 51; Thomas, *Man and the Natural World*, 64.

10. Paula Findlen, *Possessing Nature: Museums, Collecting, and Scientific Culture in Early Modern Italy* (Berkeley: University of California Press, 1994), 55.

11. Keith Thomas, *Religion and the Decline of Magic* (New York: Charles Scribner's Sons, 1971), 5.

12. Barlow, *Navigators Supply*, fol. I2v.

13. Alexandra Walsham, *Providence in Early Modern England* (Oxford: Oxford University Press, 2001), 169ff.

14. Ibid., 9–10.

15. Purchas, *Hakluytus Posthumus*, 1:56.

16. Ibid., 45.

17. Barlow, *Navigators Supply*, fol. A4v.

18. Margaret Deacon, *Scientists and the Sea 1650–1900: A Study of Marine Science* (Brookfield, Vt.: Ashgate, 1997); Harold L. Burstyn, "Theories of Winds and Ocean Currents from the Discoveries to the End of the Seventeenth Century," *Terrae Incognitae* 3 (1971): 7–31.

19. John Flavel, *Navigation Spiritualized* (London, 1663), 17.

20. Philip E. Steinberg, *The Social Construction of the Ocean* (Cambridge: Cambridge University Press, 2001), 70.

21. Ibid., 105.

22. Hankins and Silverman, *Instruments and the Imagination*, 10, 37.

23. Frank Lestringant, *Mapping the Renaissance World: The Geographical Imagination in the Age of Discovery* (Los Angeles: University of California Press, 1994), 14.

24. Dee, *Mathematicall Praeface*, fols. diiiiv, Air.

25. Alison Sandman, "Sea Charts, Navigation, and Territorial Claims in Sixteenth-Century Spain," in Pamela H. Smith and Paula Findlen, eds., *Merchants & Marvels: Commerce, Science, and Art in Early Modern Europe* (New York: Routledge, 2002), 83.

26. Scott Atran, *Cognitive Foundations of Natural History* (Cambridge: Cambridge University Press, 1990), 4.

27. Jim Bennett, "Knowing and Doing in the Sixteenth Century: What Were Instruments For?" *British Journal for the History of Science* 36, no. 2 (June 2003): 135, 143.

28. David C. Lindberg, *The Beginnings of Western Science: The European Scientific Tradition in Philosophical, Religious, and Institutional Context, 600 B.C. to A.D. 1450* (Chicago: University of Chicago Press, 1992), 290.

29. Recorde, *Castle of Knowledge*, 12.

30. Deacon, *Scientists and the Sea*, 5–6, 48; Burstyn, "Theories of Winds and Ocean Currents," 8–13.

31. William Bourne, *The Treasure for Traveilers* (1578; reprint, Norwood, N.J.: Walter J. Johnson, Inc., 1979), fol. Bbbbb.iiv.

32. John Davis, *The Seamans Secrets* (1607), in Albert Hastings Markham, ed., *The Voyages and Works of John Davis the Navigator* (London: Hakluyt Society, 1880), 244.

33. Ibid.

34. Atran, *Cognitive Foundations*, 253.

35. Richard Hakluyt, *A Discourse on Western Planting* (London, 1584), in Leonard Woods, ed., *Documentary History of the State of Maine* (Portland, Maine: Bailey and Noyes, 1877), 2:34.

36. Richard Hakluyt, *The Principal Navigations Voyages Traffiques & Discoveries of the English Nation* (1600; reprint, Glasgow: James MacLehose and Sons, 1903), 1:lxxx. For a discussion of climates and zones of habitability, see ibid., 7:252–73.

37. Boies Penrose, *Travel and Discovery in the Renaissance* (Cambridge, Mass.: Harvard University Press, 1952), 142. For a description of climate zones and their effects on human habitability, see Hakluyt, *Principal Navigations*, 7:252–73.

38. E. G. R. Taylor, *Tudor Geography 1485–1583* (London: Methuen & Co., Ltd., 1930), 83; Martín Cortés, *Arte of Navigation* (1561; reprint, introduction by David W. Waters, Delmar, N.Y.: Scholars' Facsimiles & Reprints, 1992), fols. xviv–xxir; Cuningham, *Cosmographical Glasse*, fols. 63–79; Thomas Blundeville, *His Exercises Containing Six Treatises* (1594; reprint, New York: Da Capo Press, 1971), fols. 154v–156r, 192ff.

39. Deacon, *Scientists and the Sea*; Burstyn, "Theories of Winds and Ocean Currents," 7–31.

40. Ann Geneva, *Astrology and the Seventeenth Century Mind: William Lilly and the Language of the Stars* (Manchester: Manchester University Press, 1995), 123.

41. Alfred W. Crosby, *The Measure of Reality: Quantification and Western Society* (Cambridge: Cambridge University Press, 1997), 38.

42. Cuningham, *Cosmographical Glasse*, fol. 74.

43. Ibid., fol. 73; also explicated in Blundeville, *His Exercises*, fol. 193r–v.

44. David B. Quinn and A. N. Ryan, *England's Sea Empire, 1550–1642* (London: George Allen & Unwin, 1983), 80. This proposition is argued in Hakluyt, *Discourse on Western Planting*, 19–22.

45. E. G. R. Taylor, *Late Tudor and Early Stuart Geography 1583–1650* (London: Methuen & Co., Ltd., 1934), 38.

46. Cortés, *Arte of Navigation*, fol. xviv.

47. Hakluyt, *Principal Navigations*, 7: 252.

48. Ibid., 7:273.

49. Blundeville, *His Exercises*, fol. 192r–v.

50. Stephen Pumfrey, *Latitude and the Magnetic Earth: The True Story of Queen Elizabeth's Most Distinguished Man of Science* (New York: MJF Books, 2002), 6.

51. William Gilbert, *De Magnete*, trans. Fleury Mottelay (1600; reprint, New York: Dover, 1958), 127.

52. William H. Sherman, *John Dee: The Politics of Reading and Writing in the English Renaissance* (Amherst: University of Massachusetts Press, 1995), 45; see also Ken MacMillan and Jennifer Abeles, eds., *John Dee: The Limits of the British Empire* (Westport, Conn.: Praeger, 2004). Readers should know that a veritable Dee industry exists. Recent Dee scholarship is best represented by Sherman and S. Clucas (see note 59).

53. Lesley B. Cormack, *Charting an Empire: Geography at the English Universities, 1580–1620* (Chicago: University of Chicago Press, 1997), 82.

54. Dee's influence on navigation has been described in David W. Waters, *The Art of Navigation in England in Elizabethan and Early Stuart Times* (New Haven, Conn.: Yale University Press, 1958), 131, 525; Kenneth R. Andrews, *Trade, Plunder and Settlement: Maritime Enterprise and the Genesis of the British Empire, 1480–1630* (Cambridge: Cambridge University Press, 1984), 30, 169–71; Charles H. Cotter, *A History of Nautical Astronomy* (New York: American Elsevier Publishing Company, Inc., 1968), 44; Taylor, *Tudor Geography*, 103; Hall, *Scientific Renaissance*, 184.

55. E. G. R. Taylor, "John Dee and the Nautical Triangle, 1575," *Journal of the Institute of Navigation* 8, no. 4 (1955): 319; Taylor, *Tudor Geography*, 95; Andrews, *Trade, Plunder and Settlement*, 68; Waters, *Art of Navigation*, 94. Davis acknowledges Dee's contributions for "exquisite execution of Artes Mathematicke" in *Seamans Secrets*, 231. Dee himself describes his work with Richard Chancellor and the Borough brothers in *General and Rare Memorials pertayning to the Perfect Arte of Navigation* (1577; reprint, New York: Da Capo Press, 1968), fol. εiiir.

56. Taylor, *Tudor Geography*, 95; Hall, *Scientific Renaissance*, 206; Anthony Turner, *Early Scientific Instruments, Europe 1400–1800* (London: Sotheby's Publications, 1987), 64.

57. Taylor, "John Dee," 321; Waters, *Art of Navigation*, 211.

58. Taylor, "John Dee," 321; for a description of the paradoxal compass, see Sherman, *John Dee*, 154.

59. Robert Baldwin, "John Dee's Interest in the Application of Nautical Science, Mathematics and Law to English Naval Affairs," in S. Clucas, ed., *John Dee: Interdisciplinary Studies in English Renaissance Thought* (Dordecht, the Netherlands: Springer Verlag, 2006), 101.

60. Richard I. Ruggles, "The Cartographic Lure of the Northwest Passage: Its Real and Imaginary Geography," in Thomas H. B. Symons, ed., *Meta Incognita: A Discourse of Discovery, Martin Frobisher's Arctic Expeditions, 1576–1578*, Mercury Series Directorate Paper 10 (Hull, Quebec: Canadian Museum of Civilization, 1999), 1:180–1.

61. Debus, introduction, in Dee, *Mathematicall Praeface*, 9.

62. Dee, *Mathematicall Praeface*, n.p.

63. Ibid., fol. biiv.

64. Ibid., fol. aiiir.

65. Ibid., fols. ir, iiiiv.

66. Sherman, *John Dee*, 15; Baldwin, "John Dee's Interest," 103–5; related discussions in Debus, introduction, in Dee, *Mathematicall Praeface*, 25; Taylor, *Tudor Geography*, 76; E. G. R. Taylor, *The Mathematical Practitioners of Tudor and Stuart England* (Cambridge: Cambridge University Press, 1954), 21; Waters, *Art of Navigation*, 145–6; Taylor, "John Dee," 319–20.

67. Dee, *Mathematicall Praeface*, fol. diiiiv.

68. Adapted from Ursula Lamb, ed. and trans., *A Navigator's Universe: The* Libro de Cosmographía *of 1538 by Pedro de Medina* (Chicago: University of Chicago Press, 1972), 165.

69. Adapted from Cortés, *Arte of Navigation*, fols. viir–viiir.

70. Ibid.

71. Most of this discussion derives from Sir Thomas Elyot, a diplomat with medical training who published a treatise on health, *The Castell of Helthe*, ed. Samuel A. Tannenbaum (1541; reprint, New York: Scholars' Facsimiles & Reprints, 1937), fol. Biv.

72. Ibid.

73. Ibid.

74. Elyot, *Castell of Helthe*, fols. Ciiiir–Div. To simplify the discussion, I have omitted the distinction between natural and unnatural humours.

75. Elyot, *Castell of Helthe*, fols. Diiir–v.

76. Ibid.

77. Sir James Watt, "The Medical Climate of Frobisher's England: Maritime Influences," in *Meta Incognita*, 1:260.

78. Dear, *Revolutionizing the Sciences*, 50.

79. Adapted from Lamb, *A Navigator's Universe*, 202–3.

80. Ibid., 168–9.

81. Pumfrey, *Latitude and the Magnetic Earth*, 36.

82. Adapted from Cortés, *Arte of Navigation*, fol. xiiiir–v.

83. Ibid., fol. xiir.

84. Adapted from Cortés, *Arte of Navigation*, fols. xiiv–xiiir; Lamb, *A Navigator's Universe*, 174–5.

85. Adapted from Cortés, *Arte of Navigation*, fol. xiiiiv; John Davis, *The Seamans Secrets* (1633; reprint, introduction by David W. Waters, Delmar, N.Y.: Scholar's Facsimiles & Reprints, 1992), second book, fols. B1r–v.

86. Davis, *Seamans Secrets*, first book, fol. D2r.

87. Ibid., first book, fol. H3v.

88. Ibid.

89. Ibid.

90. Cortés, *Arte of Navigation*, fols. lxxiiiiv–lxxvr.

91. Ibid.

92. Lamb, introduction, *A Navigator's Universe*, 30.

Chapter 6. October 27, Madeira

1. Edward Wright, *Certaine Errors in Navigation; The Voyage of . . . George Earle of Cumberland to the Azores* (1599; reprint, Norwood, N.J.: Walter J. Johnson, Inc., 1974), 22–4.

2. Captain Thomas James, *The Strange and Dangerous Voyage* (1633; reprint, New York: Da Capo Press, 1968), 103.

3. Ibid., 29.

4. E. G. R. Taylor, ed., *The Troublesome Voyage of Captain Edward Fenton 1582–1583* (Cambridge: Cambridge University Press, 1959), 139–40, 167–8.

5. Paul Butel, *The Atlantic*, trans. Iain Hamilton Grant (New York: Routledge, 1999), 39.

6. Ibid., 37–8.

7. Richard Hakluyt, "A description of the Canarie Islands, with their strange fruits and commodities," in Hakluyt, ed., *The Principal Navigations Voyages Traffiques & Discoveries of the English Nation* (1600; reprint, Glasgow: James MacLehose and Sons, 1904), 6: 134–5.

8. Taylor, *Troublesome Voyage*, 124.

9. James, *Strange and Dangerous Voyage*, 25.

10. From Ferdinando Yates' account of the voyage of the *Margaret* to Virginia from September–November 1619 as it appears in the Smyth of Nibley Papers, 13, reprinted in the *Bulletin of the New York Public Library* I, no. 3 (1897): 68–72.

11. Harold Gatty, *The Raft Book: Lore of the Sea and Sky* (New York: George Grady Press, 1943), 55. Gatty's book, republished later as *Finding Your Way without Map or*

Compass, appeared in a box with accompanying charts, sky maps, and tables to enable downed World War II pilots to navigate in small inflatable rafts without instruments.

12. Gatty, *Raft Book*, 56–7.

13. Martín Cortés, *Arte of Navigation* (1561; reprint, introduction by David W. Waters, Delmar, N.Y.: Scholars' Facsimiles & Reprints, 1992), fol. lviv.

14. Stephen Pumfrey, *Latitude and the Magnetic Earth: The True Story of Queen Elizabeth's Most Distinguished Man of Science* (New York: MJF Books, 2002), 62–3.

15. Ibid., fol. lxiiiir.

16. Henry Mainwaring, *The Sea-mans Dictionary* (London, 1644), 27; Frederick C. Lane, "The Economic Meaning of the Invention of the Compass," *The American Historical Review* LXVIII, no. 3 (1963): 610.

17. David W. Waters, "Columbus's Portuguese Inheritance," *Mariner's Mirror* 78, no. 4 (1992): 397; A. R. T. Jonkers, *Earth's Magnetism in the Age of Sail* (Baltimore, Md.: Johns Hopkins University Press, 2003), 49.

18. Ernst Crone, E. J. Dijksterhuis, M. G. J. Minnaert, and A. Pannekoek, eds., *The Principal Works of Simon Stevin*, vol. III (Amsterdam: C. V. Swets & Zeitlinger, 1961); Karel A. Davids, "Finding Longitude at Sea by Magnetic Declination on Dutch East Indiamen, 1596–1795," *The American Neptune* 50 (1996): 281–90.

19. Waters, "Columbus's Portuguese Inheritance," 399.

20. William Borough, *A Discourse of the Variation of the Cumpas* (1581; reprint, Norwood, N.J.: Walter J. Johnson, Inc., 1974), fol. Bir. See also Wright, *Certaine Errors*, fols. M1v–M2r.

21. Mainwaring, *Sea-mans Dictionary*, 28.

22. William Barlow, *Magneticall Advertisements* (1616; reprint, New York: Da Capo Press, 1968), 49; Borough, *Discourse of the Variation*, fol. Bir. An almost identical description but with more attention to spherical geometry appears in Wright, *Certaine Errors*, 100–3. Borough states that the magnetical meridian is another great circle around the globe with its own "Pole of Magnes" (fol. Bir). Also, Cortés, *Arte of Navigation*, fols. lxv–lxvi.

23. Jonkers, *Earth's Magnetism*, 15–20; Pumfrey, *Latitude and the Magnetic Earth*, 36–9.

24. Jonkers, *Earth's Magnetism*, 32; Pumfrey, *Latitude and the Magnetic Earth*, 38.

25. Jonkers, *Earth's Magnetism*, 63.

26. J. A. Bennett, *The Divided Circle: A History of Instruments for Astronomy, Navigation and Surveying* (Oxford: Phaidon-Christie's Limited, 1987), 52. An example of this device is described and recommended in Wright, *Certaine Errors*, fols. M3r–v.

27. Borough, *Discourse of the Variation*, fol. Biv.

28. This method became widespread: Prince Maurice of Nassau recommended its practice to Dutch ships, promoted by his cosmographer Simon Stevin, in Stevin, *The Haven-Finding Art* (1599; reprint, New York: Da Capo Press, 1968), 21–4. Stevin was a Dutch mathematician and engineer. Edward Wright, the mathematician, translated his book from Dutch.

29. W. E. May, *A History of Marine Navigation* (New York: W. W. Norton & Company, 1973), 12–13.

30. Robert Norman, *The Newe Attractive* (1581; reprint, Norwood, N.J.: Walter J. Johnson, Inc., 1974); Borough, *Discourse of the Variation*.

31. D. W. Waters, *The Art of Navigation, in England in Elizabethan and Early Stuart Times* (New Haven, Conn.: Yale University Press, 1958), 153–60; Bennett, *Divided Circle*, 53.

32. Jonkers, *Earth's Magnetism*, 51.

33. Discussed in Bennett, *Divided Circle*, 54, and Anthony Turner, *Early Scientific Instruments, Europe 1400–1800* (London: Sotheby's Publications, 1987), 70. Sixteenth-century examples can be found in William Bourne, *A Regiment for the Sea* (1574; reprint, E. G. R. Taylor, ed. and introduction, Cambridge: Cambridge University Press, 1963), 273, and Stevin, *Haven-Finding Art*, 3–4.

34. Edmond R. Kiely, *Surveying Instruments: Their History and Classroom Use* (New York: Bureau of Publications, Teachers College, Columbia University, 1947), 213; D. W. Waters, *Science and the Techniques of Navigation in the Renaissance*, Maritime Monographs and Reports, No. 19 (Greenwich: National Maritime Museum, 1980), 5.

35. Norman, *Newe Attractive*, 25; Pumfrey, *Latitude and the Magnetic Earth*, 75.

36. Jonkers, *Earth's Magnetism*, 43.

37. Bourne, *Regiment for the Sea*, 277.

38. Norman, *Newe Attractive*, 24.

39. Borough, *Discourse of the Variation*, fol. Biiir; Pumfrey, *Latitude and the Magnetic Earth*, 73.

40. Thomas Blundeville, *His Exercises Containing Six Treatises* (1594; reprint, New York: Da Capo Press, 1971), fol. 323r; Waters, *Art of Navigation*, 212–15.

41. Waters, *Art of Navigation*, 239; Borough, *Discourse of the Variation*, fols. Divv–Eiv.

42. Norman, *Newe Attractive*, 14.

43. Waters, *Art of Navigation*, 219; assessed in Jim Bennett, "Knowing and Doing in the Sixteenth Century: What Were Instruments For?," *British Journal for the History of Science* 36, no. 2 (June 2003): 144ff; Jonkers, *Earth's Magnetism*, 58–9; Lesley B. Cormack, *Charting an*

Empire: Geography at the English Universities, 1580–1620 (Chicago: University of Chicago Press, 1997), 97.

44. Wright, *Certaine Errors*, fol. A3v.

45. Ibid., fol. A4r.

46. Ibid.

47. Ibid., fols. N2r–N3r.

48. Ibid., fol. N1v.

49. Cormack, *Charting an Empire*, 97.

50. Stevin, *Haven-Finding Art*, 2.

51. Ibid., 3–4.

52. William Barlow, *Navigators Supply* (1597; reprint, New York: Da Capo Press, 1972), fols. a3r–a4r. For an assessment of Barlow's achievements, consult Waters, *Art of Navigation*, 217–19.

53. John Davis, *The Seamans Secrets* (1607), in Albert Hastings Markham, ed., *The Voyages and Works of John Davis the Navigator* (London: Hakluyt Society, 1880), 244.

54. Ibid., 242.

55. Ibid., 244.

56. Davis, *Seamans Secrets*, 247.

57. Ibid.

58. Ibid., 247–9.

59. Almanacs first appeared in England in 1503 as a translation of the French *Kalendayr of Shyppars* or *Calendar of Shepherds*, and from 1539 almanacs began to show both almanac and calendrical information. See Waters, *Art of Navigation*, 17ff.

60. Lucas Jansze Waghenaer, *Mariners Mirrour* (1588; reprint, introduction by R. A. Skelton, Amsterdam: Theatrum Orbis Terrarum, 1966), fol. C.1.v.

61. Bourne, *Regiment for the Sea*, 63.

62. Charles O. Frake, "Cognitive Maps of Time and Tide among Medieval Seafarers," *Man* 20 (1985): 262. For a further exploration of early modern tidal prediction with illustrations of sixteenth-century tidal charts or tables, see Derek Howse, "Some Early Tidal Diagrams," *Mariner's Mirror* 79, no. 1 (1993): 27–43.

63. Butel, *The Atlantic*, 36.

64. Taylor, *Troublesome Voyage*, 89–90.

65. Butel, *The Atlantic*, 65.

66. Ibid.

67. Ibid., 53.

68. Richard Hakluyt, "A ruttier for the West Indies," in *Principal Navigations*, 282.

69. James, *Strange and Dangerous Voyage*, 87.

70. Gerard Chilson is based on John Singer, a surgeon sent to Virginia in 1619 on board the *Margaret* [Virginia Papers, 1619, *Bulletin of the New York Public Library* III, no. 5 (1899): 212]. Singer, who accompanied 35 settlers to found a new settlement along the James River, came with 50 shillings to furnish his medicinal chest, and was to be paid a monthly salary of 30 shillings; Taylor, *Troublesome Voyage*, 139–40, 167–8.

71. David Potterton, ed., *Culpeper's Color Herbal* (New York: Sterling Publishing Company, 1983), 196, 30, 159, respectively.

72. The description of the bullet wound comes from Richard Wiseman, *Of Wounds, of Gun-Shot Wounds, of Fractures and Luxations* (1676; reprint, introduction by John Kirkup, Bath, England: Kingsmead, 1977), 409–12. Kirkup furnishes the definitions of the medical terms.

73. Daniel Price, *Sauls Prohibition Staide. Or the Apprehension, and Examination of Saule* (London, 1609), fol. D3v. Sermon delivered at Pauls Crosse, Rogation Sunday, May 28, 1609. Subtitled "And the Inditement of all that persecute Christ, with a reproofe of those that traduce the Honourable Plantation of Virginia." Price was chaplain in ordinary to the Prince of Wales.

74. Ibid., fol. F2r.

75. Ibid., fol. F2v.

76. Ibid., fol. F3r.

77. Gatty, *Raft Book*, 149.

78. Ibid., 146.

79. Ibid., 15.

80. John B. Hattendorf, "Atlantic Ocean," in Hattendorf, ed. in chief, *The Oxford Encyclopedia of Maritime History* (Oxford: Oxford University Press, 2007), 1:195–202.

Chapter 7. "He Setteth for the Sun": Finding Latitude

1. William Bourne, *A Regiment for the Sea* (1574; reprint, E. G. R. Taylor, ed. and introduction, Cambridge: Cambridge University Press, 1963), 209.

2. Allan Chapman, *Dividing the Circle, the Development of Critical Angular Measurement in Astronomy 1500–1850* (New York: Ellis Horwood, 1990), 25; David W. Waters, *The Art of Navigation in England in Elizabethan and Early Stuart Times* (New Haven, Conn.: Yale University Press, 1958), 53, 170–1.

3. John Davis, *The Seamans Secrets* (1607), in Albert Hastings Markham, ed., *The Voyages and Works of John Davis the Navigator* (London: Hakluyt Society, 1880), 335.

4. David Waters, "The Iberian Bases of the English Art of Navigation in the Sixteenth Century," in *XXXVII Secção de Coimbra, Agrupamento de Estudos de Cartografia Antiga* (Coimbra, 1970), 5.

5. The idea of using mathematical skill as "empire broker-age" is explored in Eric H. Ash, *Power, Knowledge, and Expertise in Elizabethan England* (Baltimore, Md.: Johns Hopkins University Press, 2004).

6. Martín Cortés, *Arte of Navigation* (1561; reprint, intro-duction by David W. Waters, Delmar, N.Y.: Scholars' Facsimiles & Reprints, 1992), fols. iiv–iiir.

7. John Tapp, *The Sea-Mans Kalendar* (London, 1631), fol. A2v.

8. Ken Arnold, "Presenting Science as Product or as Process: Museums and the Making of Science," in Susan Pearce, ed., *Exploring Science in Museums* (London: Athlone Press, 1996), 64.

9. W. F. J. Mörzer Bruyns, *The Cross-Staff* (Zutphen, the Netherlands: Walburg Pers, 1994), 14.

10. Charles H. Cotter, *A History of the Navigator's Sextant* (Glasgow: Brown, Son & Ferguson, Ltd., 1983), 65.

11. Waters, *Art of Navigation*, 53; S. Q. Fatimi, "History of the Development of the *kamal*," in Himanshu Prabha Ray, Jean-François Salles, eds., *Tradition and Archaeology: Early Maritime Contacts in the Indian Ocean* (New Delhi: Manohar, 1996), 283–92.

12. Cotter, *History of the Navigator's Sextant*, 65; Anthony Turner, *Early Scientific Instruments, Europe 1400–1800* (London: Sotheby's Publications, 1987), 66; Mörzer Bruyns, *Cross-Staff*, 24. The *kamal* has excited new scholarship in recent years. See Fatimi, "History of the development of the *kamal*," in *Tradition and Archaeology*, 283–92; José Manuel Malhão Pereira, *The Stellar Compass and the Kamal* (Lisbon: Academia de Marinha, 2003).

13. David W. Waters, "Columbus's Portuguese Inheritance," *Mariner's Mirror* 78, no. 4 (1992): 393; Luís de Albuquerque, *Astronomical Navigation* (Lisbon: National Board for the Celebration of the Portuguese Discoveries, 1988), 13.

14. W. G. L. Randles, "The Emergence of Nautical Astronomy in Portugal in the XVth Century," *Journal of Navigation* 51 (January 1998): 48.

15. This point about linearity in instrument design is well articulated in Jim Bennett, "Catadioptrics and Commerce in Eighteenth-Century London," *History of Science* xliv (2006): 247–78.

16. John J. Roche, "The Radius Astronomicus in England," *Annals of Science* 38 (1981): 3. For a similar argument that technological change never occurs in a linear fash-ion, see Fernand Braudel, *Civilization and Capitalism, 15th–18th Century: The Structures of Everyday Life: The Limits of the Possible*, trans. Siân Reynolds, vol. 1 (New York: Harper & Row, 1981), 334–5.

17. Mörzer Bruyns, *Cross-Staff*, 15–16.

18. Roche, "The Radius Astronomicus," 18. See also Edmond R. Kiely, *Surveying Instruments: Their History and Classroom Use* (New York: Bureau of Publications, Teachers College, Columbia University, 1947), 194–9; Turner, *Early Scientific Instruments*, 64–5; Mörzer Bruyns, *Cross-Staff*, 21–4.

19. Waters, *Art of Navigation*, 58.

20. Roche, "The Radius Astronomicus," 22; Cotter, *History of the Navigator's Sextant*, 83.

21. Cortés, *Arte of Navigation*, fol. lxxiiv; Roche, "The Radius Astronomicus," 19.

22. Waters, *Art of Navigation*, 220.

23. Edward Wright, *Certaine Errors in Navigation; The Voyage of . . . George Earle of Cumberland to the Azores* (1599; reprint, Norwood, N.J.: Walter J. Johnson, Inc., 1974), fol. 3v.

24. Waters, *Art of Navigation*, 584ff; John W. Shirley, ed., *Thomas Harriot, Renaissance Scientist* (Oxford: Oxford University Press, 1974). Harriot scholarship has moved on, but a relevant essay on Harriot and navigation is John J. Roche, "Harriot's 'Regiment of the Sun' and its Background in Sixteenth-Century Navigation," *British Journal for the History of Science* XIV, part 3, no. 48 (November 1981): 245–62; see also Amir R. Alexander, *Geometrical Landscapes: The Voyages of Discovery and the Transformation of Mathematical Practice* (Stanford, Calif.: Stanford University Press, 2002), 98–100.

25. Waters, *Art of Navigation*, 46ff.

26. Randles, "Nautical Astronomy in Portugal," 49.

27. Waters, *Art of Navigation*, 57.

28. Jim Bennett, "Knowing and Doing in the Sixteenth Century: What Were Instruments For?," *British Journal for the History of Science* 36, no. 2 (June 2003): 133; Stephen Johnston, "Reading Rules: Artefactual Evidence for Mathematics and Craft in Early-Modern England," in Liba Taub and Frances Willmoth, eds., *The Whipple Museum of the History of Science: Instruments and Interpretations, to Celebrate the Sixtieth Anniversary of R. S. Whipple's Gift to the University of Cambridge* (Cambridge: Cambridge University Press, 2006), 242.

29. Gloria Clifton, *Directory of British Scientific Instrument Makers 1550–1851* (London: Zwemmer, 1995), xii; for a full treatment of the methods, learning, and culture of instrument makers, see Gerard L'E. Turner, *Elizabethan Instrument Makers* (Oxford: Oxford University Press, 2000).

30. Mörzer Bruyns, *Cross-Staff*, 32.

31. Cotter, *History of the Navigator's Sextant*, 25.

32. Bennett, "Knowing and Doing," 140.

33. Ibid., 141; see the analysis of a craftsman's tool in Johnston, "Reading Rules"; J. A. Bennett, "The Challenge of Practical Mathematics,"in Stephen Pumfrey, Paolo L. Rossi, and Maurice Slawinski, eds., *Science, Culture and Popular Belief in Renaissance Europe* (Manchester: Manchester University Press, 1991), 176–90.

34. Pamela H. Smith, "Art, Science, and Visual Culture in Early Modern Europe," *Isis* 97, no. 1 (March 2006): 83–100.

35. Robert B. Gordon, "Sixteenth-Century Metalworking Technology Used in the Manufacture of Two German Astrolabes," *Annals of Science* 44 (1987): 71–84; Allan Chapman, "A Study of the Accuracy of the Scale Graduations on a Group of European Astrolabes," *Annals of Science* 40 (1983): 473–88.

36. Eugene S. Ferguson, "The Mind's Eye: Nonverbal Thought in Technology," *Science* 197, no. 4306 (August 26, 1977): 827–36.

37. E. G. R. Taylor, *The Mathematical Practitioners of Tudor & Stuart England* (Cambridge: Cambridge University Press, 1954), 28. See also William Borough, *A Discourse of the Variation of the Cumpas* (1581; reprint, Norwood, N.J.: Walter J. Johnson, Inc., 1974), fols. iiv–iiir.

38. Taylor, *Mathematical Practitioners*, 28.

39. J. A. Bennett, *The Divided Circle: A History of Instruments for Astronomy, Navigation and Surveying* (Oxford: Phaidon-Christie's Limited, 1987), 20.

40. "Technology and Invention in the Middle Ages," in Lynn White, ed., *Medieval Religion and Technology* (Los Angeles: University of California Press, 1978), 1–22; Peter Dear, *Revolutionizing the Sciences: European Knowledge and Its Ambitions, 1500–1700* (Princeton, N.J.: Princeton University Press, 2001), 37, 53; Hester Higton, "Does Using an Instrument Make You Mathematical? Mathematical Practitioners of the 17th Century," *Endeavour* 25, no. 1 (2001): 18–22.

41. Borough, *A Discourse*, fol. iiir.

42. Davis, *Seamans Secrets* (1607), 274.

43. Waters, "Columbus's Portuguese Inheritance," 395; Bourne, *Regiment for the Sea*, 87–8; Albuquerque, *Astronomical Navigation*, 52; Simon Stevin, *The Haven-Finding Art* (1599; reprint, New York: Da Capo Press, 1968), fol. B4r.

44. Waters, "Columbus's Portuguese Inheritance," 396; Albuquerque, *Astronomical Navigation*, 24; Cortés, *Arte of Navigation*, fols. xlvr–xlviir.

45. Albuquerque, *Astronomical Navigation*, 20–1.

46. Ibid., 14.

47. David Waters, *Science and the Techniques of Navigation in the Renaissance*, Maritime Monographs and Reports, No. 19 (Greenwich: National Maritime Museum, 1980), 25; Bourne, *Regiment for the Sea*, 231; Cortés, *Arte of Navigation*, fol. lxxixv; Tapp, *Sea-Mans Kalendar*, 99; Davis, *Seamans Secrets* (1607), 256.

48. John Davis, *The Seamans Secrets* (1633; reprint, intro. by A. N. Ryan, Delmar, N.Y.: Scholar's Facsimiles & Reprints, 1992), fol. D2r.

49. Davis, *Seamans Secrets* (1607), 259; in the 1633 edition, discussed at fols. D2v–D3r.

50. Bourne, *Regiment for the Sea*, 208.

51. Thomas Blundeville, *His Exercises Containing Six Treatises* (1594; reprint, New York: Da Capo Press, 1971), fol. 312v.

52. Gerald Forty, "Sources of Latitude Error in English Sixteenth Century Navigation," *The Journal of Navigation* 36 (1983): 401. Systematic observations with a replica astrolabe, cross-staff, and quadrant have been undertaken recently by Captain José Manuel Malhão Pereira of the Portuguese Navy: "Experiências com Instrumentos de Navegação de Época dos Descobrimentos," *Mare Liberum* 7 (1994): 165–92.

53. Forty, "Sources of Latitude Error," 402.

54. Wright, *Certaine Errors*, fols. A4v, N3v.

55. Bourne, *A Regiment*, 207–9.

56. Cotter, *History of the Navigator's Sextant*, 77; Davis, *Seamans Secrets* (1607), 263; Waters, *Art of Navigation*, 222.

57. Cotter, *History of the Navigator's Sextant*, 75; Cotter, *A History of Nautical Astronomy* (New York: Elsevier Publishing Company, Inc., 1968), 109; Waters, *Art of Navigation*, 585; W. E. May, *A History of Marine Navigation* (New York: W. W. Norton & Company, 1973), 12–13.

58. Turner, *Early Scientific Instruments*, 67; Bourne, *Regiment for the Sea*, 209; Waters, *Art of Navigation*, 135.

59. Bourne, *Regiment for the Sea*, 209; see also Blundeville, *His Exercises*, fol. 319r.

60. Cotter, *History of the Navigator's Sextant*, 64.

61. Ibid., 73; Ad. Meskens, "Michiel Coignet's Nautical Instruction," *Mariner's Mirror* 78, no. 3 (1992): 265; Blundeville, *His Exercises*, fol. 314r.

62. Mörzer Bruyns, *Cross-Staff*, 34.

63. Ibid., 28

64. Waters, "Columbus's Portuguese Inheritance," 395; see also Cotter, *History of the Navigator's Sextant*.

65. Alan Neale Stimson and Christopher St. J. Hume Daniel, *The Cross Staff, Historical Development and Modern Use* (London: Harriet Wynter, 1977), 15–16; see also Pereira, "Experiências com Instrumentos."

66. Borough, *A Discourse*, fol. Divv; Davis, *Seamans Secrets* (1607), 260; Blundeville, *His Exercises*, fol. 319r; Stimson and Daniel, *Cross Staff.*

67. Stimson and Daniel, *Cross Staff*, 16–21.

68. Blundeville, *His Exercises*, fol. 312v; Cotter, *History of the Navigator's Sextant*, 89–95.

69. Turner, *Early Scientific Instruments*, 68.

70. Cotter, *History of the Navigator's Sextant*, 26; Kiely, *Surveying Instruments*, 178.

71. Allan Sekula, *Fish Story* (Rotterdam: Richter Verlag, 1995), 108.

72. Scott Atran, *Cognitive Foundations of Natural History* (Cambridge: Cambridge University Press, 1990), 4.

Chapter 8. November 27, New Spain

1. Harold Gatty, *The Raft Book: Lore of the Sea and Sky* (New York: George Grady Press, 1943), 39, 42–3.

2. Ibid., 44–5.

3. Ibid., 62.

4. Paul Butel, *The Atlantic*, trans. Iain Hamilton Grant (New York: Routledge, 1999), 66.

5. Ibid., 91.

6. Richard Hakluyt, "A principal ruttier conteining most particular directions to sail from S. Lucar in Andaluzia by the Isles of the Canaries. . . . ," in Hakluyt, ed., *The Principal Navigations Voyages Traffiques & Discoveries of the English Nation* (1600; reprint, Glasgow: James MacLehose and Sons, 1904), 10:307–9.

7. Gatty, *Raft Book*, 10, 12, 146, 148.

8. Ibid., 143.

9. From "A Relation of the Voyage made to Virginia, in the Elizabeth of London, a Barke of fiftie tunnes by Captaine Bartholomew Gilbert, in the yeere 1603. Written by Master Thomas Canner a Gentleman of Bernards Inne his companion in the same Voyage," in Samuel Purchas, *Hakluytus Posthumus or Purchas His Pilgrimes* (1625; reprint, Glasgow: James MacLehose and Sons, 1905–7), 18:330–1.

10. Captain Thomas James, *The Strange and Dangerous Voyage* (1633; reprint, New York: Da Capo Press, 1968), 7; Ferdinando Yates' account of the voyage of the *Margaret* to Virginia from September–November 1619 as it appears in the Smyth of Nibley Papers, 13, reprinted in *Bulletin of the New York Public Library* I, no. 3 (1897): 68–72.

11. John Tapp, *The Sea-Mans Kalendar* (London, 1631), fol. L4r.

12. James, *Strange and Dangerous Voyage*, 4.

13. Ibid., 61–2.

14. From E. G. R. Taylor, ed., *The Troublesome Voyage of Captain Edward Fenton 1582–1583* (Cambridge: Cambridge University Press, 1959), 273–4. For general information on shipboard medical treatment, see Cheryl A. Fury, *The Tides in the Affairs of Men: The Social History of Elizabethan Seamen, 1580–1603* (Westport, Conn.: Praeger, 2002), 166–73.

15. Chilson's assessment of Norrys' complexion and his remedy to restore humoral balance derive from a popular medical treatise of the sixteenth century, Sir Thomas Elyot's *The Castel of Helthe* (1539, reprint, Samuel A. Tannenbaum, ed., New York: Scholars' Facsimiles & Reprints, 1937). The discussion of complexions is found at fol. iia, and that of the suppository remedy and purgations on fol. lvia, b. For a concise explanation of humoral theory, see Nancy G. Siraisi, *Medieval and Early Renaissance Medicine: An Introduction to Knowledge and Practice* (Chicago: University of Chicago Press, 1990), 101–41.

16. Elyot, *The Castel of Helthe*, fol. lvia, b.

17. William Norrys is based on Thomas Barker, a member of the crew of *The Primrose* that sailed to Guinea in 1553–4, and died on June 15, 1554, of unknown causes. Silvester Heale is based on Thomas Swallow, the master gunner on at least one voyage of *The Primrose* who served as executor of several seamen's wills. The will included here is derived from Barker's own will, probated August 24, 1554. See E. H. Hair and J. D. Alsop, *English Seamen and Traders in Guinea 1553–1565* (Lewiston, N.Y.: Edwin Mellen Press, Ltd., 1992), 163–4, for the text of Barker's will and a description of how mariners' wills were probated. For a related discussion, see Fury, *Tides in the Affairs of Men*, 97–9.

18. Many sources describe the spiritual experience of understanding predestination and the trajectory of mankind's sin and damnation. See Charles Lloyd Cohen, *God's Caress: The Psychology of Puritan Religious Experience* (New York: Oxford University Press, 1986), 62–3, 86–7, 116–7; Alexandra Walsham, *Providence in Early Modern England* (Oxford: Oxford University Press, 1999), 15–7.

19. See Paul S. Seaver, *Wallington's World: A Puritan Artisan in Seventeenth-Century London* (London: Edwin Mellen Press, Ltd., 1985), especially 17–20, and Christopher Hill, *The World Turned Upside Down* (New York: Penguin, 1972), 122ff.

20. Arthur Dent, *The Plaine Mans Path-way to Heaven* (1601; reprint, Norwood, N.J.: Walter J. Johnson, Inc.,1974), 84–6, 97. A discussion of predestination begins at p. 313.

21. Pyke and Blunt are based on Morrice Adams and William Eliott, respectively, whose names appear in the Duke of

Buckingham's survey of mariners and ships, 1619 [Todd Gray, ed., *Early-Stuart Mariners and Shipping: The Maritime Surveys of Devon and Cornwall, 1619–35*, New Series, vol. 33 (Exeter: Devon & Cornwall Record Society, 1990), 19, 46]. Eliott is listed as a mariner from Dartmouth, age 36, and Adams as a sailor from Topsham, age 22. Samuel Coopy, the prototype for Roger Coopy, was on board the *Margaret* to Virginia in 1619, under Toby Felgate.

22. James, *Strange and Dangerous Voyage*, 46–7.

23. Derived from "The order for the buriall of the dead," *The Booke of Common Prayer* (London, 1604), fol. T4r. The 1604 edition of this work was the first update since 1559. The 1559 version was the third edition and the first published under Elizabeth I. The burial order read by Hame derives from John 11, Job 19, 1 Tim. 6, and Job 1.

24. Ibid.

25. 1 Corinthians 15:58, as quoted in the *Booke of Common Prayer*. The same wording for this verse appears in the so-called Geneva Bible (London, 1559).

26. Peter Dear, "The Church and the New Philosophy," in Stephen Pumfrey, Paolo L. Rossi, and Maurice Slawinski, eds., *Science, Culture and Popular Belief in Renaissance Europe* (Manchester: Manchester University Press, 1991), 136–7.

27. John Hedley Brooke, *Science and Religion: Some Historical Perspectives* (Cambridge: Cambridge University Press, 1991), 110; Robert K. Merton, *Science, Technology & Society in Seventeenth-Century England* (New York: Howard Fertig, 2001). The so-called "Merton Thesis" advanced by this book examines the relationship between Puritan ideology and early modern science in the seventeenth century. There is an industry in Merton scholarship. For representative essays, see I. Bernard Cohen, ed., *Puritanism and the Rise of Modern Science: The Merton Thesis* (New Brunswick: Rutgers University Press, 1990).

28. Andrew Cunningham, "Protestant Anatomy," in Jürgen Helm and Annette Winkelmann, eds., *Religious Confessions and the Sciences in the Sixteenth Century* (Leiden: Brill Academic Publishers, 2001), 46–7; Lesley B. Cormack, *Charting an Empire: Geography at the English Universities, 1580–1620* (Chicago: University of Chicago Press, 1997), 28–9.

29. John Hedley Brooke, "Religious Belief and the Content of the Sciences," in John Hedley Brooke, Margaret J. Osler, and Jitse M. van der Meer, eds., *Science in Theistic Contexts: Cognitive Dimensions*, special issue of *Osiris*, 2nd ser., 16 (2001): 3.

30. Stuart Clark, *Thinking with Demons: The Idea of Witchcraft in Early Modern Europe* (Oxford: Oxford University Press, 1997), 180.

31. Ibid., 157; Paolo L. Rossi, "Science, Culture and the Dissemination of Learning," in *Science, Culture and Popular Belief in Renaissance Europe*, 157.

32. Pamela H. Smith, "Art, Science, and Visual Culture in Early Modern Europe," *Isis* 97, no. 1 (March 2006): 84.

33. Brooke, *Science and Religion*, 7.

34. Sachiko Kusukawa, *The Transformation of Natural Philosophy: The Case of Philip Melanchthon* (Cambridge: Cambridge University Press, 1995), 8.

35. Alastair Fowler, *Time's Purpled Masquers: Stars and the Afterlife in Renaissance English Literature* (Oxford: Oxford University Press, 1996), 32. See also Brooke, *Science and Religion*, 18–23.

36. Kusukawa, *Transformation of Natural Philosophy*, 129, 134.

37. Ibid., 138.

38. Paul Richard Blum, "The Jesuits and the Janus-Faced History of Natural Sciences," in *Religious Confessions and the Sciences*, 23.

39. David W. Waters, *The Art of Navigation in England in Elizabethan and Early Stuart Times* (New Haven, Conn.: Yale University Press, 1958), 131; E. G. R. Taylor, *The Mathematical Practitioners of Tudor & Stuart England* (Cambridge: Cambridge University Press, 1954), 39; Marie Boas Hall, *The Scientific Renaissance 1450–1630* (1962; reprint, New York: Dover, 1994), 184; A. N. Ryan, introduction, in John Davis, *Seamans Secrets* (1633; reprint, New York: Scholar's Facsimiles & Reprints, 1992), 13.

40. William H. Sherman, *John Dee: The Politics of Reading and Writing in the English Renaissance* (Amherst: University of Massachusetts Press, 1995), 60–2; Cormack, *Charting an Empire*, 82.

41. Allen G. Debus, introduction, in John Dee, *The Mathematicall Praeface to the Elements of Geometrie of Euclid of Megara* (1570; reprint, New York: Neale Watson Academic Publications, Inc., 1975), 9.

42. Dee, *Mathematicall Praeface*, fols. aiir, aiiir.

43. William Barlow, *The Navigators Supply* (1597; reprint, New York: Da Capo Press, 1972), fol. B2r.

44. Ibid.

45. Thomas S. Kuhn, *The Copernican Revolution: Planetary Astronomy in the Development of Western Thought* (Cambridge, Mass.: Harvard University Press, 1976), 113.

46. Purchas, *Hakluytus Posthumus*, 1:56.

47. Ibid.

48. Catholic University of America, ed., *New Catholic Encyclopedia* (New York: McGraw Hill, 1967), 13:861.

49. Charles G. Herbermann et al., eds., *The Catholic Encyclopedia* (New York: The Encyclopedia Press, 1914), 2:273–4.

50. Catholic University, *New Catholic Encyclopedia*, 13:867.

51. Keith Thomas, *Religion and the Decline of Magic* (New York: Charles Scribner's Sons, 1971), 79. See also Christopher Marsh, *Popular Religion in Sixteenth-Century England* (New York: St. Martin's Press, 1998), 151.

52. Herberman et al., *Catholic Encyclopedia*, 14:375.

53. John Davis, *The Worldes Hydrographical Discription* (1595), in Albert Hastings Markham, ed., *The Voyages and Works of John Davis the Navigator* (London: Hakluyt Society, 1880), 224–6.

54. Ibid.

55. Ibid.

56. Irvonwy Morgan, *The Godly Preachers of the Elizabethan Church* (London: Epworth, 1965), 14; Kenneth R. Andrews, *Trade, Plunder and Settlement: Maritime Enterprise and the Genesis of the British Empire, 1480–1630* (Cambridge: Cambridge University Press, 1984), 147.

57. John Flavel, *Navigation Spiritualized* (London, 1663), 12.

58. Ibid., 13.

59. Henry Mainwaring, *The Sea-mans Dictionary* (London, 1644), fol. A3r.

60. Ibid.

61. Thomas Hood, *The use of the two Mathematicall instruments, the crosse Staffe . . . And the Jacobs Staff. . . .* (1596; reprint, New York: Da Capo Press Inc., 1972), fol. Ciiv.

62. Robert Recorde, *The Castle of Knowledge* (1556; reprint, Norwood, N.J.: Walter J. Johnson, Inc., 1975), 105–6.

63. Frank Lestringnant, *Mapping the Renaissance World: The Geographical Imagination in the Age of Discovery*, trans. David Fausett (Los Angeles: University of California Press, 1994), 6.

64. Ibid., 19; Samuel Y. Edgerton Jr., "From Mental Matrix to *Mappamundi* to Christian Empire: The Heritage of Ptolemaic Cartography in the Renaissance," in David Woodward, ed., *Art and Cartography: Six Historical Essays* (Chicago: University of Chicago Press, 1987), 11.

65. Butel, *The Atlantic*, 296.

66. Daniel W. Hardy, "Calvinism and the Visual Arts: A Theological Introduction," in Paul Corby Finney, ed., *Seeing Beyond the Word: Visual Arts and the Calvinist Tradition* (Grand Rapids, Mich.: William B. Eerdmans Publishing Company, 1999), 7–15.

67. Ann Geneva, *Astrology and the Seventeenth Century Mind: William Lilly and the Language of the Stars* (Manchester: Manchester University Press, 1995), 9. In recent years, astrology has seen much scholarly attention. For some relevant views, see Lauren Kassell, *Medicine and Magic in Elizabethan London* (Oxford: Clarendon Press, 2004); Richard Dunn, "The True Place of Astrology among the Mathematical Arts of Late Tudor England," *Annals of Science* 51 (1994): 151–63.

68. Keith Thomas, *Man and the Natural World: Changing Attitudes in England, 1500–1800* (Oxford: Oxford University Press, 1983), 18.

69. Thomas, *Religion and the Decline of Magic*, 358.

70. J. Chamber, *A Treatise against Judicial Astrologie* (London, 1601), 102, quoted in Thomas, *Religion and the Decline of Magic*, 359.

71. Alexander Whitaker, *Good Newes from Virginia* (1613), in Wesley F. Craven, ed., *Early Accounts of Life in Colonial Virginia 1609–1613* (Delmar, N.Y.: Scholars' Facsimiles & Reprints, 1976), fol. A4v.

72. Ibid., fol. B2r.

73. Eugene S. Ferguson, "The Mind's Eye: Nonverbal Thought in Technology," *Science* 197, no. 4306 (August 26, 1977), 831–2.

74. Frances Yates, *The Art of Memory* (London: Pimlico, 1992), 166–7, 176–7.

75. Quoted in ibid., 270. I am indebted to Kathleen R. D. Sands for calling my attention to Perkins. See Sands, "Word and Sign in Elizabethan Conflicts with the Devil," *Albion* 31, no. 2 (2000): 238–56.

76. Barbara Maria Stafford, "Revealing Technologies/Magical Domains," in Barbara Maria Stafford and Frances Terpak, eds., *Devices of Wonder: From the World in a Box to Images on a Screen* (Los Angeles: Getty Publications, 2001), 48–9.

77. Mary Morrisey, "Interdisciplinarity and the Study of Early Modern Sermons," *The Historical Journal* 42, no. 4 (1999): 1112.

78. Ibid., 1113.

79. Ibid., 1117; G. Stanwood, "Critical Directions in the Study of Early Modern Sermons," in Claude J. Summers and Ted-Larry Pebworth, eds., *Fault Lines and Controversies in the Study of Seventeenth-Century English Literature* (Columbia: University of Missouri Press, 2002), 140–55.

80. Dennis Taylor, *Shakespeare and Religion and Reformation and Post-Reformation England: A Chronology, with Special Emphasis on Shakespeare's Catholic and Protestant Contexts* (August 21, 2002), http://www2bc.edu/~taylor/shakes.html.

81. John Dyos, *A Sermon Preached at Paules Crosse the 19 of Juli 1579* (London, 1579), fols. A.ii–A.iii.

82. Ibid., fol. Biiv.

83. Ibid., 2r.

84. Ibid., 28v.

85. Ibid., 34r.

86. Ibid., 36r.

87. Ibid., fol. Biiv.

88. Ibid., 28v.

89. Ibid., 29v.

90. Ibid., 36v.

91. Ibid.

92. Ibid.

93. Ibid., 41r.

94. Ibid., 29r.

95. Ibid., 29v.

96. Ibid., 30r.

97. Ibid.

98. Ibid., 31v.

99. Ibid., 32r.

100. Ibid., 33r.

101. Ibid., 33v.

102. Ibid., 12v.

103. Ibid., 14v.

104. Ibid., 14r.

105. Ibid., 55v.

106. Ibid., 52r.

107. Ibid., 53v.

108. Ibid., 54r.

109. Eamon Duffy, *The Stripping of the Altars: Traditional Religion in England 1400–1580* (New Haven, Conn.: Yale University Press, 1992). Literature on the experience of the religious in early modern England is a growth industry. Duffy is a good place to start.

110. Edward Muir, *Ritual in Early Modern Europe* (Cambridge: Cambridge University Press, 1997), 9.

Chapter 9. Virginia

1. Richard Hakluyt, "The fourth voyage made to Virginia with three ships, in the yere 1587. Wherein was transported the second Colonie," in Hakluyt, ed., *The Principal Navigations Voyages Traffiques & Discoveries of the English Nation* (1600; reprint, Glasgow: James MacLehose and Sons, 1904), 8:387–8.

2. "A Relation of the Voyage made to Virginia, in the Elizabeth of London, a Barke of fiftie tunnes by Captaine Bartholomew Gilbert, in the yeere 1603. Written by

Master Thomas Canner a Gentleman of Bernards Inne his companion in the same Voyage," in Samuel Purchas, ed., *Hakluytus Posthumus or Purchas His Pilgrimes* (1625; reprint, Glasgow: James MacLehose and Sons, 1905–7), 18:332–33.

3. Captain Thomas James, *The Strange and Dangerous Voyage* (1633; reprint, New York: Da Capo Press, 1968), 62.

4. The rutter is taken from Richard Hakluyt, "An excellent ruttier for the Ilands of the West Indies, and for Tierra firma, and Nueva Espanna," *Principal Navigations*, 10:300.

5. Argall's log is taken from "The voyage of Captaine Samuel Argal, from James Towne in Virginia, to seeke the Ile of Bermuda, and missing the same, his putting over toward Sagahadoc and Cape Cod, and so backe againe to James Towne, begun the nineteenth of June, 1610," *Hakluytus Posthumus*, 19:73–7.

6. John Tapp, *The Sea-Mans Kalendar* (London, 1631), 8. Although this edition is twenty years later than Hame's voyage, the first edition appeared in 1601.

7. Hame's statement derives from William Bourne, *A Regiment for the Sea* (1574; reprint, E. G. R. Taylor, ed. and introduction, Cambridge: Cambridge University Press, 1963), 238–40. The latitude and longitude of Hispaniola in Hame's log entry comes from the list in Tapp, *Sea-Mans Kalendar*.

8. Willem F. J. Mörzer Bruyns, "Prime Meridians," in John B. Hattendorf, ed. in chief, *The Oxford Encyclopedia of Maritime History* (Oxford: Oxford University Press, 2007), 3:369–70.

9. A discussion and illustration of the use of plane geometry for course measurement appears in E. G. R. Taylor, *The Haven-Finding Art: A History of Navigation from Odysseus to Captain Cook* (London: Hollis & Carter, 1971), 239ff. A lengthy discussion of the sailing triangle and the various means for measuring distance and departure involving plane and spherical geometry and trigonometry is found in David W. Waters, *The Art of Navigation in England in Elizabethan and Early Stuart Times* (New Haven, Conn.: Yale University Press, 1958), 349ff.

10. Tables giving the rule to raise or lay a degree of latitude occur in many contemporary texts. For comparative examples, consult Martín Cortés, *Arte of Navigation* (1561; reprint, introduction by David W. Waters, Delmar, N.Y.: Scholars' Facsimiles & Reprints, 1976) fol. lxxixv, and John Davis, *The Seamans Secrets* (1607), in Albert Hastings Markham, ed., *The Voyages and Works of John Davis the Navigator* (London: Hakluyt Society, 1880), 256ff.

11. David Waters, "The Iberian Bases of the English Art of Navigation in the Sixteenth Century," *XXXVII Secção*

de Coimbra, Agrupamento de Estudos de Cartografia Antiga (Coimbra, 1970), 12.

12. Leonard Digges, *A Prognostication everlastinge* (1576; reprint, Norwood, N.J.: Walter J. Johnson, Inc., 1975), fol. Piv.

13. Purchas, "A true repertory of the wracke, and redemption of Sir Thomas Gates Knight," in *Hakluytus Posthumus*, 19:6. Shakespeare made use of this story in *The Tempest*.

14. Harold Gatty, *The Raft Book: Lore of the Sea and Sky* (New York: George Grady Press, 1943), 145.

15. James Clarke, *Atlantic Pilot Atlas* (London: International Marine, 1996).

16. Digges, *Prognostication everlastinge*, fol. 13v.

17. Alexandra Walsham, *Providence in Early Modern England* (Oxford: Oxford University Press, 1999), 178.

18. Purchas, "A true repertory," 6–7.

19. Ibid., 8.

20. James, *Strange and Dangerous Voyage*, 55.

21. Purchas, "A true repertory," 9–10.

22. Ibid., 11.

23. Peter Kemp, ed., *The Oxford Companion to Ships and the Sea* (Oxford: Oxford University Press, 1988), 744. See also Pablo E. Pérez-Mallaína, *Spain's Men of the Sea: Daily Life on the Indies Fleets in the Sixteenth Century*, trans. Carla Rahn Phillips (Baltimore, Md.: Johns Hopkins University Press, 1998), 242–5.

24. Purchas, "A true repertory," 12–13.

25. James, *Strange and Dangerous Voyage*, 31–2.

26. Purchas, "A true repertory," 13–14.

27. The story of the wreck of the *Sea Venture* has been told often. For a description of the circumstances, set against the context of the development of the Jamestown colony, see Wesley Frank Craven, *The Southern Colonies in the Seventeenth Century 1607–1689* (Baton Rouge: University of Louisiana Press, 1970), 97–110.

28. From E. Allde, *The Safeguard of Saylers, or great Rutter*, trans. Robert Norman (London, 1605), 12.

29. Purchas, "A true repertory," 15–16.

30. Ibid., 22–3.

31. Ibid., 41–2.

32. From "A Relation of the Voyage made to Virginia . . . Written by Master Thomas Canner . . ." in *Hakluytus Posthumus* 18:333–5; Ferdinando Yates' account of the voyage of the *Margaret* to Virginia from September–November 1619 as it appears in the Smyth of Nibley Papers, 13, reprinted in the *Bulletin of the New York Public Library* I, no. 3 (1897): 68–72.

33. Adapted from the Smyth of Nibley Papers, Smyth 3, no. 18: 97, reprinted in Susan Myra Kingsbury, ed., *The Records of the Virginia Company of London* (Washington, D.C.: U.S. Government Printing Office, 1906–35), 3:230.

34. John Dyos, *A Sermon preached at Paules Crosse the 19 of Juli 1579* (London, 1579), 14r.

35. Ibid., 14v.

36. Ibid., 30r–v, 31r, 33v.

37. Ibid., 34r.

38. Amir R. Alexander, *Geometrical Landscapes: The Voyages of Discovery and the Transformation of Mathematical Practice* (Stanford, Calif.: Stanford University Press, 2002), 21, 86ff; Wayne K. D. Davies, *Writing Geographical Exploration: James and the Northwest Passage 1631–33* (Calgary, Alberta, Canada: University of Calgary Press, 2003).

39. Jim Bennett, "Knowing and Doing in the Sixteenth Century: What Were Instruments For?," *British Journal for the History of Science* 36, no. 2 (June 2003): 140–1.

40. David Lambert, Luciana Martins, and Miles Ogborn, "Currents, Visions and Voyages: Historical Geographies of the Sea," *Journal of Historical Geography* 32 (2006): 487–8.

Glossary

NOTE: Readers interested in the language of the sea will delight in Dean King, *A Sea of Words*, 3rd ed. (New York, 2000), the most comprehensive lexicon of sea language in print. See also the entries under "Language" in John B. Hattendorf, ed. in chief, *The Oxford Encyclopedia of Maritime History* (Oxford, 2007), vol. 2, for a full background on the evolution of nautical language. *Voyage to Jamestown* acknowledges two important seventeenth-century sources of nautical language: Henry Mainwaring's *Sea-mans Dictionary* (London, 1644) and Captain John Smith's *A Sea Grammar* (London, 1627). Both provide the prime sources for nautical language in England in 1611.

A

abaft, aft Toward the stern of a ship (from "after").

altitude-distance method A method of determining distance traversed (δ) by taking the altitude (h) of the polestar (or the sun) on the meridian at starting point A and ending point B, and multiplying the difference by $16\,^2/_3$, the number of leagues believed to equal a degree of the meridian. The formula is $\delta = (hA - hB) \times 16\,^2/_3$.

angel An English gold coin valued at ten shillings.

armillary sphere A model of the Ptolemaic universe consisting of concentric rings that represented the reference circles of the celestial sphere, including the equator, zodiac, Tropics of Cancer and Capricorn, plus others. The sphere functioned as a demonstration tool or as an observational device, sometimes both. Further, the sphere could be used to derive mechanically solutions to some astronomical problems.

astrolabe In the medieval and Renaissance eras, a two-dimensional model of the universe in a stereographic projection with movable parts that enabled the user to perform calculations in timekeeping, astrology, and positional astronomy. One side of the astrolabe consisted of a rotating star chart that moved over an altitude scale, facilitating computations. The other side featured an alidade, or sighting arm, which permitted altitude measurements of celestial bodies, the measurements applied to calculations performed on the star chart side of the instrument. The mariner's astrolabe was a stripped-down version, a heavy disc suspended from a ring. This form of astrolabe, only one side of which was used for observation, included an alidade that moved over a scale of degrees marked on the limb. The mariner's astrolabe was used for altitude observations of the polestar and sun in order to compute the observer's latitude.

azimuth The arc of the horizon between a north–south meridian (a great circle intersecting the poles) and the vertical circle of a celestial object. Azimuth can be measured in degrees east or west of the north–south meridian.

azimuth circle An azimuth circle or azimuth compass was a combination of a mariner's compass with a sundial to help the user distinguish between true north and magnetic north.

B

backstaff An altitude-measuring instrument consisting of two graduated arcs, a movable sighting vane, and a movable shadow vane, permitting an observer to measure the sun's altitude indirectly, by sighting the horizon opposite the sun while the sun's shadow is made to fall on the horizon foresight.

beam The widest part of a ship.

beat To sail into an opposing wind by crisscrossing its path.

bilboes Padlocked shackles to confine the legs of prisoners (from Bilbao in Spain, a center of steel manufacturing).

binnacle, bittacle A small housing for the mariner's compass to protect it from disturbances (from Italian for "little house").

boatswain The officer in charge of sails, rigging, anchors, cables, and other equipment and supplies.

bonnet A strip of canvas added to a sail to increase the area exposed to wind.

bustian Cotton fabric; sometimes synonymous with fustian.

C

cable A very large hemp rope attached to the anchor; a unit of measurement of approximately 100 fathoms.

capstan A revolving barrel attached to the ship's deck to assist in hauling in and letting out cables.

card Another term for "carte" or chart; may sometimes refer to the card bearing the compass rose.

celestial pole The celestial extension of an earth's north or south pole on the celestial sphere.

celestial sphere An imaginary sphere of infinite radius onto which celestial bodies appear to be projected. For mapping and navigational purposes, the assumption is that all stars are located on this imaginary shell enclosing the earth.

chip log or **common log** A wooden board attached to a rope and thrown off the ship's stern to calculate the ship's speed. Once the small board or chip hits the water and trails astern, the rope is paid out. The number of knots in the rope (at measured intervals) that pass over the gunwale during a timed interval gives the ship's speed in knots.

chord Trigonometry, which dates to the fifteenth century, involved tables of functions used in calculations. A common table was that of chords. A chord is a straight line between two points on a sphere, whereby the line does not pass through the center of the circle. The chord represented an angle in early tables between the center of the circle and the end points of the chord. The chord had the same length as the radius of the circle.

circumpolar star A star that remains above the horizon during the entire night because of its proximity to the polestar; the star never rises or sets.

climates Renaissance cosmographers described the earth's latitude ranges as climates and zones where temperature, moisture, and the nature of the land determine the flora and fauna.

clyster An enema.

compass An instrument by which a ship may be steered on course, consisting of a magnetized piece of iron affixed to a card atop a pivot. The card, marked with thirty-two directions, floats atop the pivot and aligns with north.

complexion The individual combination of humors that constitutes the body of each organic being and governs its appearance, temperament, and abilities.

cosine A trigonometric function, in a triangle with a right angle (a right triangle), the ratio between the length of the side adjacent to an acute angle (less than 90 degrees) and the hypotenuse (the side opposite the right angle). (See also **secant**.)

cross-staff An altitude-measuring instrument consisting of a graduated staff and a sliding transom at right angles to it. The observer held one end of the staff to the eye while moving the transom closer to or away from the eye, trying simultaneously to view the bottom edge of the transom coincident with the horizon while viewing the upper edge coincident with the sun's disk.

D

dead reckoning Method of calculating a ship's position at sea by using courses and distances from the last known observed position; keeping a running track of a ship's direction, speed, and distance made good. Dead-reckoning tools include the compass, traverse board, sandglass, lead and line, and chip log.

declination The angular distance of a celestial object north or south of the celestial equator. Declination and right ascension are coordinate systems used on the celestial sphere. Declination is measured in degrees and minutes. Latitude, when projected onto the celestial sphere, is equivalent to declination, which measures the position of an object north or south of the celestial equator (measured in degrees, a positive number for objects north of the celestial equator and negative for those objects south of it). Tables of declination are therefore essential for latitude measurements. Solar declination tables for latitude calculations appeared as early as 1252, introduced by the Arabs to Christian Europe.

departure Usually refers to a ship's position in latitude and longitude at the beginning of a voyage and furnishes the datum for beginning dead reckoning. Also refers to movement away from a standard meridian.

diagonal scale An early measuring scale that consisted of two concentric, graduated arcs. In the space between them, a diagonal line extends from one graduated division to the *subsequent* division on the other line. By separating the two arcs and using diagonal lines between divisions, the diagonal lines themselves become easier to graduate than the arcs. Between the two bracketing arcs are other concentric arcs that intersect the diagonals at the divisions. This scale was used on multiple instruments, including the backstaff.

dip, magnetic The deflection of a magnetized needle in a vertical plane.

dipsie lead A lead weight of over 14 pounds used for sounding in deep water (100 fathoms or more). Its etymology is sometimes attributed to a shortened version of "deep sea lead," but there is no evidence for this. By contrast, a hand lead of approximately 7 pounds was used for shallower water.

doctrine of triangles Another name for trigonometry. The first treatise on trigonometry to appear in English was a translation from Latin of Bartolomeo Pitiscus' *Trigonometry: or The Doctrine of Triangles*, which appeared in 1614, the first mention of both terms in English. The first treatise in English on trigonometric functions, however, was Thomas Blundeville's M. *Blundeville His Exercises* (1594), which was used at sea.

E

ecliptic A great circle of the celestial sphere that represents the apparent path of the sun, moon, and planets against the background of stars known as the constellations of the zodiac.

elect A theological term that refers to the few thousand people predestined for eternal salvation.

epact The number of days' difference between a lunar year and a solar year. A solar year of 365 days is reckoned from successive returns of the sun to the same apparent place in the sky (background of stars). A lunar year has 354 days or 12 lunar months of 29 days, the time for one circuit about the sun. The epact was particularly important when almanacs were in common use to correlate lunar and solar calendars. Knowledge of the epact helps to predict the phase of the moon for a specific date and, hence, tidal highs and lows.

equal-altitude method By this method, the navigator observes and notes the sun at the same altitude in the morning when ascending, and in the afternoon when descending. Halfway between these two points, the sun crosses the meridian; therefore, halfway between the two points is a north–south line. This method can be used to gauge compass variation. The bearing of the sun is taken at both equal altitudes, and the compass bearing precisely at the midpoint denotes magnetic north. The difference between this bearing and the true meridian as due north–south gives variation.

equinoctial Otherwise known as the celestial equator; a projection of the earth's equator onto the celestial sphere. The celestial sphere assumes that all stars and planets are located on a sphere that encloses the earth, its north and south poles extensions of the earth's.

equinox The two points of intersection along the celestial sphere of the celestial equator (the projection of the earth's equator onto the celestial sphere) and the ecliptic. The sun crosses the equator at the equinox moving north on the first day of spring, and crosses it heading south six months later on the first day of autumn. On these two dates, around March 21 and September 23, daylight and darkness are of equal length.

F

fathom A unit of measurement equal to about six feet, based on the span between outstretched arms; used for measuring the depth of water. Also used ashore for some purposes, fathoms varied slightly by country because of differences in the length of a foot.

First Mover The First Mover (or Prime Mover, or *primum mobile*) on the Ptolemaic celestial sphere was God.

fly boat A fast, large, flat-bottomed coasting boat; corruption of the Dutch *vlieboot*.

forecastle The forward part of a ship where sailors live either below deck or in a compartment above the deck. On medieval ships, this compartment did indeed resemble a small wooden castle.

forestaff Another name for a cross-staff.

fundiment An early term for anus.

G

gear A generic term for rigging, line, and other paraphernalia.

gnomon The pointer on the face of a sundial whose shadow indicates the time.

great circle Any circle on a sphere with a center at the sphere's center. Great circles are found on the celestial sphere (the meridian, for example), or on the earth. Any great circle divides its sphere in half. "Great circle navigation" referred to one method of navigation of plotting a long-distance track across multiple meridians of longitude.

groat An English coin worth fourpence.

gunwale The part of a ship where deck and topsides meet; pronounced "gunnel."

H

halyard A rope for hoisting and lowering sails, flags, and so on.

horizon The horizon, from the seafarer's point of view, is where sea and sky meet in the distance, as far as one can see. With respect to the celestial sphere, it has a different definition. The celestial horizon is a great circle along the celestial sphere in the plane of the observer. Wherever the observer stands, the ground is a plane perpendicular to the observer's body, a plane that extends outward infinitely. The "poles" of the observer are the zenith and the nadir, also in a line perpendicular to the horizon plane. When we use a measuring instrument to determine our latitude or longitude (and therefore our position on earth), we measure the altitude of a celestial object. We measure altitude in degrees (from a point on the horizon upwards to the zenith is 90 degrees or a quarter of a circle). In navigation, multiple horizons exist for computational purposes; for the purpose of this book, the visible horizon is what is important.

humoral theory The idea that all organic bodies consist largely of four fluids (humors), with one of these predominating to influence that body's appearance, temperament, and abilities. The four humors are black bile, yellow bile, blood, and phlegm.

L

larboard The left side of a ship as one stands on the ship facing the prow. This term is now obsolete and has been replaced by "port." Opposite of starboard.

latitude East–west circles on the earth parallel to the earth's equator used for mapping purposes to produce a precise location when measured against longitude. A position along a line of latitude is measured in degrees and minutes. The Latin words for longitude and latitude, *longus* and *latus*, length and breadth, derived from the idea, dating to Democritus (fl. 450 BC), that the habitable part of the earth is broader east–west than north–south. Hipparchus (190–120 BC, regarded as the greatest astronomer of ancient Greece) referred to the latitudinal zones as *climata*, which to other writers became known as parallels of latitude. Some early literature uses the term "climates" for parallels of latitude. In 1611, the latitude zones of the world were viewed as climates, each characterized by distinctive flora, fauna, and human habitation. (See also **longitude**.)

lead and line A tool for measuring the depth of water underneath a ship and for sampling the sea floor. The lead, described by Captain John Smith as a "long plummet," about five to seven pounds, was secured to a line of rope with flags tied at various intervals of fathoms. Tallow was affixed to a shallow recess in the bottom of the lead and the lead was "heaved" into the sea. Particulate matter on the sea bed adhered to the lead. Mariners memorized their locations based on the water's depth and nature of the seabed. Both gave important navigational clues that signified the approach of land.

league A unit of measurement of about three miles used on land and at sea. During the early seventeenth century, many countries equated a degree of latitude on the earth's surface to be about 16 or 17 leagues. The equivalence was incorporated in departure tables.

leeward The direction opposite to that from which the wind is blowing.

leeway Movement forced on a ship by wind or tide to the lee, or opposite of the direction from which wind is blowing.

lodestone Magnetic ore rubbed on a piece of iron to magnetize it. The iron was affixed to a card showing compass directions and used to find north.

log reel The reel used to store and pay out line attached to a chip log.

longitude Circles about the earth running north to south parallel to the meridian, at right angles to lines of latitude. Longitude today is measured from the Prime Meridian that runs through Greenwich, England. Longitude is measured in degrees and minutes.

M

magnetic dip See **dip, magnetic.**

mariner's ring An offshoot of the mariner's astrolabe, also referred to as a sea or nautical ring. Developed for solar altitude observations, the wide mariner's ring enclosed an inner surface graduated in degrees. A conical hole in the ring allowed the sun's light to enter, the sunbeam illuminating a spot on the scale.

mark An English coin valued at thirteen shillings and fourpence.

meridian A reference circle on the celestial sphere that intersects the poles. An observer's meridian is a north–south circle passing directly overhead.

meridional distance A celestial object's distance in degrees from the meridian.

N

nadir The lowest point of the celestial sphere, directly below the observer (opposed to the **zenith**). An Arab word, nadir comes from *nazir*, "opposite."

neap tide A low tide occurring at the first and third quarters of the moon when the sun is at a right angle to the moon. At this lunar–solar configuration, the difference between high and low tides is minimal. Neap tides are opposed to spring tides.

nocturnal An instrument for telling the local time of night by observations of the circumpolar stars. The nocturnal features concentric, circular scales that represent the date and hour. In use, the user holds the nocturnal to the sky and then looks through a hole in the middle to see the polestar. Next, the observer swings an arm over the circular scales to align with the "pointer" stars of the Big Dipper, Ursa Major; the point at which the arm overlays the hour circle gives the local time.

O

oakum Twisted fibers of jute or hemp impregnated with tar and used to caulk the seams of a ship.

P

parallax An apparent change in the position of the sun, moon, or planets with respect to the background of stars because of a change in the position from which the sun, moon, or planets are observed.

pestifure The plague; or plague-bearing.

pinnace A small, light boat (either rigged or oared) used as a tender for a large ship. Pinnaces were also used for shallow-water exploration or to test conditions in uncertain waters before large ships proceeded.

poop An enclosed structure raised above the main deck at the rear of a ship.

predestination The theological doctrine that all events, particularly each person's eternal salvation or damnation, were foreordained by God at the creation of the universe.

prime The nineteen-year cycle required by the moon to perform its various motions.

Q

quarter(deck) The ship's quarter refers to an after part of the ship on one side of the centerline, as in starboard quarter. The upper deck abaft the mainmast is the quarterdeck.

R

right ascension One of the two coordinates (the other is declination) used to describe a celestial object on the celestial sphere. Right ascension is analogous to longitude on earth but is measured eastward in hours, minutes, and seconds.

right triangle A triangle containing an angle of 90 degrees.

road A protected place where ships may ride at anchor, but not as protected as a harbor.

room/roomer The maneuvering space for a ship; its clearance.

rummage To arrange or rearrange cargo on a ship.

rutter An English corruption of the French *routier*, a sailing handbook with piloting information.

S

sailing triangle A navigational reference consisting of the observer's zenith, the celestial pole, and the sun or other celestial body.

sandglass The chief mechanism for measuring time, or measuring any intervals at sea. Sandglasses consisted of two glass ampules joined together at their mouths, containing a quantity of fine sand. When inverted, the sand leaves the upper ampule for the lower one at a specific measure of time. Shipboard activities were regulated by sandglass.

secant In trigonometry, the reciprocal of a cosine; in a right triangle, the ratio of the length of the hypotenuse to the length of another side with reference to an enclosed angle. (See also **cosine**.)

sextant A modern navigational tool derived from the cross-staff and backstaff. The device uses mirrors attached to a frame and moving arc and allows the observer to simultaneously sight the horizon alongside an image of the sun or other celestial object, permitting a measurement of the object's height in degrees.

sine In trigonometry, in a right triangle the ratio between the length of a side opposite an acute angle and the length of the hypotenuse. In early sine tables, sines were expressed as lengths, not ratios.

solstice Along the sun's annual path, the ecliptic, the solstices represent the extreme positions north or south of the equator attained by the sun. The summer solstice, the longest day of the year, occurs about June 21; the winter solstice, the shortest day of the year, occurs about December 21.

soundings Refers to the measurement of the water's depth beneath a ship as measured by the lead and line.

spherical geometry A form of mathematics that involves the geometry of figures drawn upon a sphere as opposed to a plane.

spring tide The high tide which occurs at the new and full moons (opposed to neap tide), when the combined pull of the moon and sun (which are in alignment) produces the greatest tidal range.

starboard The right side of a ship as one faces the bow (as opposed to larboard).

stern The rear of a ship.

T

taffrail The rail at the stern of a ship.

tangent In trigonometry, in a right triangle, the ratio between the length of a side opposite an acute angle, and the length of an adjacent side.

ton/tonnne/tun Early tonnage referred to cargo capacity based on the number of tuns (casks) carried. A tun or cask of wine held about 250 gallons. The term *ton* later referred to weight or volume. In 1611, no international standard governed tonnage and its determination. A ton is now a metric ton of one thousand kilograms used as a measurement of displacement.

tops The platform at a masthead.

traverse board A device for recording a ship's traverse, a running record of a ship's speed and course made good. The board featured a compass rose with eight holes radiating outward along each compass direction. Eight small pegs were secured to cords, attached to the middle of the compass rose. At the end of each half hour of the ship's watch, a peg was placed in the innermost hole to represent the course made good during the preceding half hour. With each subsequent half hour through the end of four hours, a peg would be placed in an appropriate hole. The navigator then determined the mean course made good in four hours, recorded the information, and then removed all of the pegs to begin again. Many boards had pegs underneath the compass rose to indicate the ship's speed. A peg was placed next to the hole representing the number of knots as measured by a ship log.

trigonometry A mathematical system that uses the relationships among angles to determine the values of unknown angles or lengths of lines or arcs opposite or adjacent to angles.

V

variation The angular difference between magnetic and true north.

variation compass A magnetic compass designed for gauging the amount and direction of magnetic variation. Variation compasses took many forms, but during the sixteenth and seventeenth centuries, they usually consisted of a magnetic compass surrounded by a movable pair of vanes containing a string gnomon to compare true north (indicated by the sun's shadow) with the compass reading. The azimuth circle was a type of variation compass.

W

weigh anchor To raise anchor.

windward Refers to the direction from which the wind is blowing.

Y

yards Wooden spars attached to masts from which sails are set.

Z

zenith The point on the celestial sphere directly over the observer's head (opposed to the **nadir**). Zenith derives from the Arab *semt*, meaning "road" or "path."

Selected Bibliography

Primary Sources

Allde, E. *The Safeguard of Saylers, or great Rutter*. Trans. Robert Norman. London, 1605.

Barbour, Philip L., ed. *The Complete Works of Captain John Smith*. Chapel Hill: University of North Carolina Press, 1986.

Barlow, William. *Magneticall Advertisements*, 1616. Reprint, New York: Da Capo Press, 1968.

————. *The Navigators Supply*, 1597. Reprint, New York: Da Capo Press, 1972.

Blundeville, Thomas. *M. Blundeville His Exercises Containing Six Treatises*, 1594. Reprint, New York: Da Capo Press, 1971.

Borough, William. *A Discourse of the Variation of the Cumpas*, 1581. Reprint, Norwood, N.J.: Walter J. Johnson, Inc., 1974.

Bourne, William. *A Regiment for the Sea*, 1574. Reprint, introduction by E. G. R. Taylor. Cambridge: Cambridge University Press, 1963.

————. *The Treasure for Traveilers*, 1578. Reprint, Norwood, N.J.: Walter J. Johnson, Inc., 1979.

Cortés, Martín. *Arte of Navigation*, 1561. Reprint, introduction by David W. Waters. Delmar, N.Y.: Scholars' Facsimiles & Reprints, 1992.

Craven, Wesley F., ed. *Early Accounts of Life in Colonial Virginia 1609–1613*. Delmar, N.Y.: Scholars' Facsimiles & Reprints, 1976.

Crone, Ernst, E. J. Dijksterhuis, M. G. J. Minnaert, and A. Pannekoek, eds. *The Principal Works of Simon Stevin*. Vol. III. Amsterdam: C. V. Swets & Zeitlinger, 1961.

Cuningham, William. *The Cosmographical Glasse*, 1559. Reprint, New York: Da Capo Press, 1968.

Davis, John. *The Seamans Secrets*, 1633. Reprint, introduction by A. N. Ryan. Delmar, N.Y.: Scholar's Facsimiles & Reprints, 1992.

————. *The Seamans Secrets*, 1607, and *The Worldes Hydrographical Discription*, 1595. In Albert Hastings Markham, ed., *The Voyages and Works of John Davis the Navigator*. London: Hakluyt Society, 1880.

Dee, John. *General and Rare Memorials pertayning to the Perfect Arte of Navigation*, 1577. Reprint, New York: Da Capo Press, 1968.

————. *The Mathematicall Praeface to the Elements of Geometrie of Euclid of Megara*, 1570. Reprint, edited with an introduction by Allen Debus. New York: Neale Watson Academic Publications, Inc., 1975.

Dent, Arthur. *The Plaine Mans Path-way to Heaven*. 1601. Reprint, Norwood, N.J.: Walter J. Johnson, Inc., 1974.

Digges, Leonard. *A Prognostication everlastinge*, 1576. Norwood, N.J.: Walter J. Johnson, Inc., 1975.

Dyos, John. *A Sermon Preached at Paules Crosse the 19 of Juli 1579*. London, 1579.

Elyot, Thomas. *The Castell of Helthe*, 1541. Reprint, Samuel A. Tannenbaum, ed. New York: Scholars' Facsimiles & Reprints, 1937.

Flavel, John. *Navigation Spiritualized*. London, 1663.

Gilbert, William. *De Magnete*, 1600. Reprint, translated by Fleury Mottelay. New York: Dover, 1958.

Gray, Robert. *A Good Speed to Virginia*, 1609. Reprint, New York: Walter J. Johnson, Inc., 1970.

Gray, Todd. *Early-Stuart Mariners and Shipping: The Maritime Surveys of Devon and Cornwall, 1619–35*. New Series, vol. 33. Exeter, UK: Devon & Cornwall Record Society, 1990.

Hakluyt, Richard. *A Discourse on Western Planting*, 1584. Reprint, in Leonard Woods, ed., *Documentary History of the State of Maine*. Portland, Maine: Bailey and Noyes, 1877.

————. *The Principal Navigations Voyages Traffiques & Discoveries of the English Nation*. Second edition of 1600. Reprint (12 vols.), Glasgow: James MacLehose and Sons, 1903.

Hood, Thomas. *The use of the two Mathematicall instruments, the crosse Staffe . . . And the Jacobs Staff . . .* , 1596. New York: Da Capo Press, 1972.

James, Captain Thomas. *The Strange and Dangerous Voyage*, 1633. Reprint, Norwood, N.J.: Da Capo Press, 1968.

Kingsbury, Susan Myra, ed. *The Records of the Virginia Company of London*. Washington, D.C.: U.S. Government Printing Office, 1906.

Lamb, Ursula, ed. and trans. *A Navigator's Universe: The* Libro de Cosmographía *of 1538 by Pedro de Medina*. Chicago: University of Chicago Press, 1972.

Mainwaring, Henry. *The Sea-mans Dictionary*. London, 1644.

Marbury, Francis. *A Sermon Preached at Paules Crosse the 13. of June, 1602*. London, 1602.

Meyer, Virginia M., and John Frederick Dorman, eds. *Adventurers of Purse and Person, Virginia 1607–1624/5*. Richmond: Order of First Families of Virginia, 1987.

Norman, Robert. *The Newe Attractive*, 1581. Reprint, Norwood, N.J.: Walter J. Johnson, Inc., 1974.

Polter, Richard. *Pathway to Perfect Sayling*, London, 1605.

Price, Daniel. *Sauls Prohibition Staide. Or the Apprehension, and Examination of Saule*. London, 1609.

Purchas, Samuel. *Hakluytus Posthumus or Purchas His Pilgrimes*, 1625. Reprint (20 vols.), Glasgow: James MacLehose and Sons, 1905–7.

Recorde, Robert. *The Castle of Knowledge, 1556*. Reprint, Norwood, N.J.: Walter J. Johnson, Inc., 1975.

Stevin, Simon. *The Haven-Finding Art*, 1599. Reprint, New York: Da Capo Press, 1968.

Tapp, John. *The Sea-Mans Kalendar*. London, 1631.

Taylor, E. G. R., ed. *The Troublesome Voyage of Captain Edward Fenton 1582–1583*. Cambridge: Cambridge University Press, 1959.

Waghenaer, Lucas Jansz. *The Mariners Mirrour*, 1588. Reprint, introduction by R. A. Skelton. Amsterdam: Theatrum Orbis Terrarum, 1966.

Ward, John. *The Lives of the Professors of Gresham College*, 1740. Reprint, New York: Johnson Reprint Corporation, 1967.

Wiseman, Richard. *Of Wounds, of Gun-Shot Wounds, of Fractures and Luxations*, 1676. Reprint, introduction by John Kirkup. Bath, UK: Kingsmead, 1977.

Woodall, John. *The Surgions Mate*, 1617. Reprint, and introduction by John Kirkup. Bath, England: Kingsmead, 1978.

Wright, Edward. *Certaine Errors in Navigation; The Voyage of . . . George Earle of Cumberl. to the Azores*, 1599. Reprint, Norwood, N.J.: Walter J. Johnson, Inc., 1974.

Secondary Sources

Adamson, I. R. "The Administration of Gresham College and its Fluctuating Fortunes as a Scientific Institution in the Seventeenth Century." *History of Education* 9, no. 1 (1980): 13–25.

Akveld, L. M., ed. *VIth International Congress of Maritime Museums Proceedings*. Amsterdam & Rotterdam, 1987.

Albuquerque, Luís de. *Astronomical Navigation*. Lisbon: National Board for the Celebration of the Portuguese Discoveries, 1988.

Alderson, William T., and Shirley Payne Low. *Interpretation of Historic Sites*. Nashville, Tenn.: American Association for State and Local History, 1976.

Alexander, Amir R. *Geometrical Landscapes: The Voyages of Discovery and the Transformation of Mathematical Practice*. Stanford, Calif.: Stanford University Press, 2002.

Alpers, Svetlana. *The Art of Describing. Dutch Art in the Seventeenth Century*. Chicago: University of Chicago Press, 1983.

Andrews, Kenneth R. "Christopher Newport of Limehouse, Mariner." *William and Mary Quarterly*, 3rd ser., XI (1954): 28–41.

———. "The Elizabethan Seaman." *Mariner's Mirror* 68, no. 3 (1982): 245–62.

———. *Trade, Plunder and Settlement: Maritime Enterprise and the Genesis of the British Empire, 1480–1630*. Cambridge: Cambridge University Press, 1984.

———, N. Canny, and E. H. Hair, eds. *The Westward Enterprise: English Activities in Ireland, the Atlantic, and America 1480–1650*. Liverpool: Liverpool University Press, 1978.

Appleby, John C. "Abraham Jennings of Plymouth: The Commercial Career of a 'Western Trader,' c. 1602–49." *Southern History* 16 (1996): 24–42.

Armitage, David, and J. Braddick, eds. *The British Atlantic World, 1500–1800*. New York: Palgrave Macmillan, 2002.

Ash, Eric H. *Power, Knowledge, and Expertise in Elizabethan England*. Baltimore, Md.: Johns Hopkins University Press, 2004.

Atran, Scott. *Cognitive Foundations of Natural History*. Cambridge: Cambridge University Press, 1990.

Barbour, Philip L. "Captain John Smith's Sea Grammar and its Debt to Sir Henry Mainwaring's 'Seaman's Dictionary.'" *Mariner's Mirror* 58, no. 1 (1972): 93–101.

Bennett, Jim. "Catadioptrics and Commerce in Eighteenth-Century London." *History of Science* xliv (2006): 247–78.

———. *The Divided Circle: A History of Instruments for Astronomy, Navigation and Surveying*. Oxford: Phaidon-Christie's Limited, 1987.

———. "Knowing and Doing in the Sixteenth Century: What Were Instruments For?" *British Journal for the History of Science* 36, no. 2 (June 2003): 129–50.

Boxer, C. R. *The Dutch Seaborne Empire 1600–1800*. London: Hutchinson, 1965.

———. *The Portuguese Seaborne Empire 1415–1825*. New York: Alfred A. Knopf, 1969.

Brady, Thomas A., Heiko A. Oberman, and James D. Tracy, eds. *Handbook of European History 1400–1600: Late Middle Ages, Renaissance and Reformation*. New York: E. J. Brill, 1994.

Braudel, Fernand. *Civilization and Capitalism, 15th–18th Century: The Structures of Everyday Life: The Limits of the Possible*. Vol. 1. Trans. Siân Reynolds. New York: Harper & Row, 1981.

———. *Civilization and Capitalism, 15th–18th Century: The Wheels of Commerce*. Vol. 3. Trans. Siân Reynolds. New York: Harper & Row, 1979.

Brenner, Robert. *Merchants and Revolution, Commercial Change, Political Conflict, and London's Overseas Traders, 1550–1653*. Princeton, N.J.: Princeton University Press, 1993.

Broeze, Frank, ed. *Maritime History at the Crossroads: A Critical Review of Recent Historiography*. Research in Maritime History No. 9. St. John's, Newfoundland: International Maritime Economic History Association, 1995.

Brooke, John Hedley. *Science and Religion: Some Historical Perspectives*. Cambridge: Cambridge University Press, 1991.

———, Margaret J. Osler, and Jitse M. van der Meer, eds. *Science in Theistic Contexts: Cognitive Dimensions. Osiris*, special issue, 2nd ser., 16 (2001).

Burke, Peter, ed. *New Perspectives on Historical Writing*. Cambridge: Cambridge University Press, 1991.

Burstyn, Harold L. "Theories of Winds and Ocean Currents from the Discoveries to the End of the Seventeenth Century." *Terrae Incognitae* 3 (1971): 7–31.

Butel, Paul. *The Atlantic*. Trans. Iain Hamilton Grant. New York: Routledge, 1999.

Chapman, Allan. *Dividing the Circle: The Development of Critical Angular Measurement in Astronomy 1500–1850*. New York: Ellis Horwood, 1990.

———. "A Study of the Accuracy of the Scale Graduations on a Group of European Astrolabes." *Annals of Science* 40 (1983): 473–88.

Charlton, Warwick. *The Second Mayflower Adventure*. Boston, Mass.: Little, Brown, 1957.

Clark, Stuart. *Thinking with Demons: The Idea of Witchcraft in Early Modern Europe*. Oxford: Oxford University Press, 1997.

Clifton, Gloria. *Directory of British Scientific Instrument Makers 1550–1851*. London: Zwemmer, 1995.

Clucas, S., ed. *John Dee: Interdisciplinary Studies in English Renaissance Thought*. Dordecht, the Netherlands: Springer Verlag, 2006.

Cohen, Charles Lloyd. *God's Caress: The Psychology of Puritan Religious Experience*. Oxford: Oxford University Press, 1986.

Cohen, I. Bernard, ed. *Puritanism and the Rise of Modern Science: The Merton Thesis*. New Brunswick, N.J.: Rutgers University Press, 1990.

Coles, John. *Archaeology by Experiment*. New York: Charles Scribner's Sons, 1973.

Cormack, Lesley B. *Charting an Empire: Geography at the English Universities, 1580–1620*. Chicago: University of Chicago Press, 1997.

Cotter, Charles H. *A History of Nautical Astronomy*. New York: American Elsevier Publishing Company, Inc., 1968.

———. *A History of the Navigator's Sextant*. Glasgow: Brown, Son & Ferguson, Ltd., 1983.

Craven, Wesley F. *The Southern Colonies in the Seventeenth Century 1607–1689*. Baton Rouge: University of Louisiana Press, 1970.

Crosby, Alfred W. *The Measure of Reality: Quantification and Western Society*. Cambridge: Cambridge University Press, 1997.

Cumberlidge, Peter. *Bristol Channel and Severn Pilot*. London: Stanford Marine Ltd., 1988.

Cunliffe, Barry. *Facing the Ocean: The Atlantic and its Peoples 8000 BC–AD 1500*. Oxford: Oxford University Press, 2001.

Davids, Karel A. "Finding Longitude at Sea by Magnetic Declination on Dutch East Indiamen, 1596–1795." *The American Neptune* 50 (1996): 281–90.

Davies, Wayne K. D. *Writing Geographical Exploration: James and the Northwest Passage 1631–33*. Calgary, Alberta, Canada: University of Calgary Press, 2003.

Deacon, Margaret. *Scientists and the Sea 1650–1900: A Study of Marine Science*. Brookfield, Vt.: Ashgate Publishing Company, 1997.

Dear, Peter. *Revolutionizing the Sciences: European Knowledge and Its Ambitions, 1500–1700*. Princeton, N.J.: Princeton: Princeton University Press, 2001.

Dening, Greg. *Mr. Bligh's Bad Language*. Cambridge: Cambridge University Press, 1992.

Druett, Joan. *Rough Medicine: Surgeons at Sea in the Age of Sail.* New York: Routledge, 2000.

Duffy, Eamon. *The Stripping of the Altars: Traditional Religion in England 1400–1580.* New Haven, Conn.: Yale University Press, 1992.

Duffy, Michael, et al., eds. *The New Maritime History of Devon,* vol. I: *From Early Times to the Late Eighteenth Century.* London: Conway Maritime Press, 1992.

Dunn, Richard. "The True Place of Astrology among the Mathematical Arts of Late Tudor England." *Annals of Science* 51 (1994): 151–63.

Earle, Peter. *Sailors, English Merchant Seamen 1650–1775.* London: Methuen, 1998.

Ferguson, Eugene S. "The Mind's Eye: Nonverbal Thought in Technology." *Science* 197, no. 4306 (August 26, 1977): 827–36.

Fernando Oliveira and his Era. Humanism and the Art of Navigation in Renaissance Europe. Proceedings of the IX International Reunion for the History of Nautical Science and Hydrography, September 19–24, 1998. Cascais, Portugal: Patrimónia, 2000.

Findlen, Paula. *Possessing Nature: Museums, Collecting, and Scientific Culture in Early Modern Italy.* Berkeley: University of California Press, 1994.

Finney, Paul Corby, ed. *Seeing Beyond the Word: Visual Arts and the Calvinist Tradition.* Grand Rapids, Mich.: William B. Eerdmans Publishing Company, 1999.

Forty, Gerald. "Sources of Latitude Error in English Sixteenth Century Navigation." *The Journal of Navigation* 36 (1983): 388–402.

Fowler, Alastair. *Time's Purpled Masquers: Stars and the Afterlife in Renaissance English Literature.* Oxford: Oxford University Press, 1996.

Frake, Charles O. "Cognitive Maps of Time and Tide among Medieval Seafarers." *Man* 20 (1985): 254–70.

Fuller, Mary C. *Voyages in Print: English Travel to America, 1576–1624.* Cambridge: Cambridge University Press, 1995.

Fury, Cheryl A. "Elizabethan Seamen: Their Lives Ashore." *International Journal of Maritime History* X, no. 1 (June 1998): 1–40.

———. *Tides in the Affairs of Men: The Social History of Elizabethan Seamen, 1580–1603.* Westport, Conn.: Praeger, 2002.

———. "Training and Education in the Elizabethan Maritime Community." *Mariner's Mirror* 85, no. 2 (1999): 147–61.

Gatty, Harold. *The Raft Book: Lore of the Sea and Sky.* New York: George Grady Press, 1943.

Gaukroger, Stephen. *The Emergence of a Scientific Culture: Science and the Shaping of Modernity, 1210–1685.* Oxford: Oxford University Press, 2006.

Geneva, Ann. *Astrology and the Seventeenth Century Mind: William Lilly and the Language of the Stars.* Manchester: Manchester University Press, 1995.

Gethyn-Jones, Eric. *George Thorpe and the Berkeley Company: A Gloucestershire Enterprise in Virginia.* Gloucester, UK: Sutton, 1982.

Gingerich, Owen, ed. *The Nature of Scientific Discovery.* Washington, D.C.: Smithsonian Institution Press, 1975.

Gordon, Robert B. "Sixteenth-Century Metalworking Technology Used in the Manufacture of Two German Astrolabes." *Annals of Science* 44 (1987): 71–84.

Greenblatt, Stephen. *Marvelous Possessions: The Wonder of the New World.* Chicago: University of Chicago Press, 1991.

Gurevich, Aaron. *Historical Anthropology of the Middle Ages.* Chicago: University of Chicago Press, 1992.

Hair, E. H., and J. D. Alsop. *English Seamen and Traders in Guinea 1553–1565: The New Evidence of Their Wills.* Lewiston, N.Y.: Edwin Mellen Press, Ltd., 1992.

Hall, Marie Boas. *The Scientific Renaissance 1450–1630.* Reprint of 1962 edition. New York: Dover, 1994.

Hankins Thomas L., and Robert J. Silverman. *Instruments and the Imagination.* Princeton, N.J.: Princeton University Press, 1995.

Hattendorf, John B., ed. *Maritime History,* vol. 1: *The Age of Discovery.* Malabar, Fla.: Krieger Publishing Co., 1996.

———, ed. in chief. *The Oxford Encyclopedia of Maritime History,* 4 vols. Oxford: Oxford University Press, 2007.

Helm, Jürgen, and Annette Winkelmann, eds. *Religious Confessions and the Sciences in the Sixteenth Century.* Leiden: Brill Academic Publishers, 2001.

Higton, Hester. "Does Using an Instrument Make You Mathematical? Mathematical Practitioners of the 17th Century." *Endeavour* 25, no. 1 (2001): 18–22.

———. *Elias Allen and the Role of Instruments in Shaping the Mathematical Culture of Seventeenth-Century England.* Ph.D. diss., Cambridge University, 1996.

Hill, Christopher. *The World Turned Upside Down.* New York: Penguin, 1972.

Howse, Derek. "Some Early Tidal Diagrams." *Mariner's Mirror* 79, no. 1 (1993): 27–43.

Jacobs, Michael. *The Painted Voyage: Art, Travel and Exploration 1564–1875.* London: British Museum Press, 1995.

Jonkers, A. R. T. *Earth's Magnetism in the Age of Sail.* Baltimore, Md.: Johns Hopkins University Press, 2003.

Kassell, Lauren. *Medicine and Magic in Elizabethan London*. Oxford: Clarendon Press, 2004.

Kiely, Edmond R. *Surveying Instruments: Their History and Classroom Use*. New York: Bureau of Publications, Teachers College, Columbia University, 1947.

King, Dean. *A Sea of Words*, 3rd ed. New York: Owl Books, 2000.

Knudson, Douglas M., Ted T. Cable, and Larry Beck. *Interpretation of Cultural and Natural Resources*. State College, Pa.: Venture Publishing, Inc., 1995.

Kuhn, Thomas S. *The Copernican Revolution: Planetary Astronomy in the Development of Western Thought*. Cambridge, Mass.: Harvard University Press, 1976.

Kusukawa, Sachiko. *The Transformation of Natural Philosophy: The Case of Philip Melanchthon*. Cambridge: Cambridge University Press, 1995.

Lamb, Ursula, ed. *Cosmographers and Pilots of the Spanish Maritime Empire*. Aldershot: Variorum, 1995.

Lambert, David, Luciana Martins, and Miles Ogborn. "Currents, Visions and Voyages: Historical Geographies of the Sea." *Journal of Historical Geography* 32 (2006): 479–93.

Lane, Frederick C. "The Economic Meaning of the Invention of the Compass." *The American Historical Review* LXVIII, no. 3 (1963): 605–17.

Lavery, Brian. *The Colonial Merchantman* Susan Constant *1605*. Annapolis, Md.: Naval Institute Press, 1988.

Lestringant, Frank. *Mapping the Renaissance World: The Geographical Imagination in the Age of Discovery*. Los Angeles: University of California Press, 1994.

Lindberg, David C. *The Beginnings of Western Science: The European Scientific Tradition in Philosophical, Religious, and Institutional Context, 600 B.C. to A.D. 1450*. Chicago: University of Chicago Press, 1992.

Lloyd, G. E. R. *Demystifying Mentalities*. Cambridge: Cambridge University Press, 1990.

Loades, David. *England's Maritime Empire: Seapower, Commerce and Policy, 1490–1690*. London: Longman, 2000.

Lumley, Robert, ed. *The Museum Time-Machine*. London: Methuen, 1988.

Macdonald, Sharon, ed. *The Politics of Display: Museums, Science, Culture*. New York: Routledge, 1998.

MacMillan, Ken, and Jennifer Abeles, eds. *John Dee: The Limits of the British Empire*. Westport, Conn.: Praeger, 2004.

Mancall, Peter C. *Hakluyt's Promise: An Elizabethan's Obsession for an English America*. New Haven, Conn.: Yale University Press, 2007.

Marsh, Christopher. *Popular Religion in Sixteenth-Century England*. New York: St. Martin's Press, 1998.

May, W. E. *A History of Marine Navigation*. New York: W.W. Norton & Company, 1973.

McCary, Ben C. *John Smith's Map of Virginia*. Charlottesville: University of Virginia Press, 1981.

McGrail, Seán. *Ancient Boats in North-West Europe: The Archaeology of Water Transport to AD 1500*. London: Longman, 1998.

Merton, Robert K. *Science, Technology & Society in Seventeenth-Century England*. New York Howard Fertig, 2001.

Morgan, Irvonwy. *The Godly Preachers of the Elizabethan Church*. London: Epworth, 1965.

Morison, Samuel Eliot. *The European Discovery of America, The Northern Voyages A.D. 500–1600*. Oxford: Oxford University Press, 1971.

Mörzer Bruyns, W. F. J. *The Cross-Staff*. Zutphen, the Netherlands: Walburg Pers, 1994.

Muir, Edward. *Ritual in Early Modern Europe*. Cambridge: Cambridge University Press, 1997.

Nickerson, W. Sears. *Land Ho!—1620: A Seaman's Story of the* Mayflower, *Her Construction, Her Navigation, and Her First Landfall*. Lansing: Michigan State University Press, 1997.

Oatley, Keith. "Mental Maps for Navigation." *New Scientist* 64, no. 928 (December 19, 1974): 863–6.

Padrón, Ricardo. *Cartography, Literature, and Empire in Early Modern Spain*. Chicago: University of Chicago Press, 2004.

Parry, J. H. *The Age of Reconaissance*. New York: The World Publishing Company, 1963.

Pearce, Susan, ed. *Exploring Science in Museums*. London: Athlone Press, 1996.

Penrose, Boies. *Travel and Discovery in the Renaissance*. Cambridge, Mass.: Harvard University Press, 1952.

Pereira, José Manuel Malhão. "Experiências com Instrumentos de Navegação de Época dos Descobrimentos." *Mare Liberum* 7 (1994): 165–92.

———. *The Stellar Compass and the Kamal*. Lisbon: Academia de Marinha, 2003.

Pérez-Mallaína, Pablo E. *Spain's Men of the Sea: Daily Life on the Indies Fleets in the Sixteenth Century*. Trans. Carla Rahn Phillips. Baltimore, Md.: Johns Hopkins University Press, 1998.

Pope, Peter. "The Practice of Portage in the Early Modern North Atlantic: Introduction to an Issue in Maritime

Historical Anthropology." *Journal of the Canadian Historical Association* 6, new series (1995): 19–41.

Prown, Jules David. "Mind in Matter: An Introduction to Material Culture Theory and Method." *Winterthur Portfolio* 17, no. 1 (1982): 1–19.

Pumfrey, Stephen. *Latitude and the Magnetic Earth: The True Story of Queen Elizabeth's Most Distinguished Man of Science.* New York: MJF Books, 2002.

———, Paolo L. Rossi, and Maurice Slawinski, eds. *Science, Culture and Popular Belief in Renaissance Europe.* Manchester: Manchester University Press, 1991.

Quartermaine, Peter. *Port Architecture: Constructing the Littoral.* Chichester, West Sussex: John Wiley & Sons, 1999.

Quinn, David B. "Christopher Newport in 1590." *North Carolina Historical Review* XXIX, no. 3 (1953): 305–16.

———. *England and the Discovery of America.* New York: Alfred A. Knopf, 1974.

———, and A. N. Ryan. *England's Sea Empire, 1550–1642.* London: George Allen & Unwin, 1983.

Raban, Jonathan. *The Oxford Book of the Sea.* Oxford: Oxford University Press, 1992.

Randles, W. G. L. "The Emergence of Nautical Astronomy in Portugal in the XVth Century." *Journal of Navigation* 51 (January 1998): 46–57.

———, ed. *Geography, Cartography and Nautical Science in the Renaissance.* Burlington, Vt.: Ashgate, 2000.

Ray, Himanshu Prabha, and Jean-François Salles, eds. *Tradition and Archaeology: Early Maritime Contacts in the Indian Ocean.* New Delhi: Manohar, 1996.

Roche, John J. "Harriot's 'Regiment of the Sun' and its Background in Sixteenth-Century Navigation." *British Journal for the History of Science* XIV, part 3, no. 48 (November 1981): 245–62.

———. "The Radius Astronomicus in England" *Annals of Science* 38 (1981): 1–32.

Rodger, N. A. M. *The Safeguard of the Sea: A Naval History of Britain.* New York: W. W. Norton & Company, 1998.

Rolt, Peter. "Today's Bristol Channel Pilots." *Maritime Life and Traditions* no. 19 (Summer 2003): 2–13.

Russell-Wood, A. J. R. *The Portuguese Empire 1415–1808: A World on the Move.* Baltimore, Md.: Johns Hopkins University Press, 1998.

Sacks, David H. *The Widening Gate: Bristol and the Atlantic Economy, 1450–1700.* Los Angeles: University of California Press, 1991.

Samuel, Raphael. *Theatres of Memory,* vol. 1: *Past and Present in Contemporary Culture.* New York: Verso, 1994.

Sayers, William. "Some International Nautical Etymologies." *Mariner's Mirror* 88, no. 4 (November 2002): 405–22.

Scammell, G. V. "Manning the English Merchant Service in the Sixteenth Century." *Mariner's Mirror* 56, no. 2 (1970): 131–54.

Scammell, G. V. *The World Encompassed: The First of European Maritime Empires c. 800–1650.* Los Angeles: University of California Press, 1981.

———. *Ships, Oceans and Empire: Studies in European Maritime and Colonial History, 1400–1750.* Aldershot, Hampshire: Variorum, 1995.

Scott, Frank. "Speed, Navigational Accuracy and the 'Ship Log.'" *Mariners Mirror* 92, no. 4 (November 2006): 477–81.

Seaver, Paul S. *Wallington's World: A Puritan Artisan in Seventeenth-Century London.* London: Edwin Mellen Press, Ltd., 1985.

Sekula, Allan. *Fish Story.* Rotterdam: Richter Verlag, 1995.

VIIth International Congress of Maritime Museums Proceedings. Stockholm, 1990.

Sherman, William H. *John Dee: The Politics of Reading and Writing in the English Renaissance.* Amherst: University of Massachusetts Press, 1995.

Shirley, John W., ed. *Thomas Harriot, Renaissance Scientist.* Oxford: Oxford University Press, 1974.

Siraisi, Nancy G. *Medieval and Early Renaissance Medicine: An Introduction to Knowledge and Practice.* Chicago: University of Chicago Press, 1990.

Sloan, A.W. *English Medicine in the Seventeenth Century.* Bishop Auckland, Durham, South Africa: Academic Press, 1996.

Smith, Pamela H. "Art, Science, and Visual Culture in Early Modern Europe." *Isis* 97, no. 1 (March 2006): 83–100.

———, and Paula Findlen, eds. *Merchants & Marvels: Commerce, Science, and Art in Early Modern Europe.* New York: Routledge, 2002.

Sommerville, C. John. *The Secularization of Early Modern England: From Religious Culture to Religious Faith.* Oxford: Oxford University Press, 1992.

Souza, Philip de. *Seafaring and Civilization: Maritime Perspectives on World History.* London: Profile Books, 2001.

Springer, Haskell, ed. *America and the Sea: A Literary History.* Athens: University of Georgia Press, 1995.

Stafford, Barbara Maria, and Frances Terpak, eds. *Devices of Wonder: From the World in a Box to Images on a Screen.* Los Angeles: Getty Publications, 2001.

Steinberg, Philip E. *The Social Construction of the Ocean.* Cambridge: Cambridge University Press, 2001.

Stimson, Alan Neale, and Christopher St. J. Hume Daniel. *The Cross Staff, Historical Development and Modern Use.* London: Harriet Wynter, 1977.

Summers Claude J., and Ted-Larry Pebworth, eds. *Fault Lines and Controversies in the Study of Seventeenth-Century English Literature.* Columbia: University of Missouri Press, 2002.

Symons, Thomas H. B., ed. *Meta Incognita: A Discourse of Discovery, Martin Frobisher's Arctic Expeditions, 1576–1578.* Mercury Series Directorate Paper 10. 2 vols. Hull, Quebec: Canadian Museum of Civilization, 1999.

Taub, Liba, and Frances Willmoth, eds. *The Whipple Museum of the History of Science: Instruments and Interpretations, to Celebrate the Sixtieth Anniversary of R. S. Whipple's Gift to the University of Cambridge.* Cambridge: Cambridge University Press, 2006.

Taylor, E. G. R. *The Haven-Finding Art: A History of Navigation from Odysseus to Captain Cook.* London: Hollis & Carter, 1971.

———. "Instructions to a Colonial Surveyor in 1582." *Mariner's Mirror* 37, no. 1 (1951): 48–62.

———. "John Dee and the Nautical Triangle, 1575." *Journal of the Institute of Navigation* 8, no. 4 (1955): 318–25.

———. *Late Tudor and Early Stuart Geography 1583–1650.* London: Methuen & Co., Ltd., 1934.

———. *Mathematical Practitioners of Tudor & Stuart England.* Cambridge: Cambridge University Press, 1954.

———. *Tudor Geography 1485–1583.* London: Methuen & Co., Ltd., 1930.

Thomas, Keith. *Man and the Natural World: Changing Attitudes in England, 1500–1800.* Oxford: Oxford University Press, 1983.

———. *Religion and the Decline of Magic.* New York: Charles Scribner's Sons, 1971.

Turner, A. J. *Early Scientific Instruments, Europe 1400–1800.* London: Sotheby's Publications, 1987.

Turner, Gerard L'E. *Elizabethan Instrument Makers.* Oxford: Oxford University Press, 2000.

Unger, Richard W., ed. *Cogs, Caravels and Galleons: The Sailing Ship 1000–1650.* London: Conway Maritime Press, 1994.

———. *The Ship in the Medieval Economy 600–1600.* London: Croom Helm, 1980.

Vanes, Jean. *The Port of Bristol in the Sixteenth Century.* Local History Pamphlets No. 39. Bristol, UK: Bristol Branch of the Historical Association, 1977.

Walsham, Alexandra. *Providence in Early Modern England.* Oxford: Oxford University Press, 2001.

Warner, Deborah Jean. "What Is a Scientific Instrument, When Did It Become One, and Why?" *British Journal for the History of Science* 23 (1990): 84–6.

Waterman, Talbot H. *Animal Navigation.* New York: Scientific American Books, Inc., 1989.

Waters, David W. *The Art of Navigation in England in Elizabethan and Early Stuart Times.* New Haven, Conn.: Yale University Press, 1958.

———. "Columbus's Portuguese Inheritance." *Mariner's Mirror* 78, no. 4 (1992): 385–405.

———. "The Iberian Bases of the English Art of Navigation in the Sixteenth Century." *XXXVII Secção de Coimbra,* Agrupamento de Estudos de Cartografia Antiga. Coimbra, Portugal, 1970.

———. *Science and the Techniques of Navigation in the Renaissance.* Greenwich, UK: National Maritime Museum 1980.

Watson, Patty Jo, Steven A. LeBlanc, and Charles L. Redman. *Explanation in Archeology: An Explicitly Scientific Approach.* New York: Columbia University Press, 1971.

Westerdahl, Christer. "The Maritime Cultural Landscape." *International Journal of Nautical Archaeology* 21, no. 2 (1992): 5–14.

White, Lynn, ed. *Medieval Religion and Technology.* Los Angeles: University of California Press, 1978.

Williams, David M. "The Progress of Maritime History." *Journal of Transport History* 14, no. 2 (1993): 126–41.

Wingood, Allan J. "*Sea Venture*: An Interim Report on an Early 17th Century Shipwreck Lost in 1609." *International Journal of Nautical Archaeology and Underwater Exploration* 11, no. 4 (1982): 333–47.

———. "*Sea Venture* Second Interim Report—Part 2: The Artifacts." *International Journal of Nautical Archaeology and Underwater Exploration* 15, no. 2 (1986): 149–59.

Woodward, David, ed. *Art and Cartography: Six Historical Essays.* Chicago: University of Chicago Press, 1987.

Woodward, Donald. "Ships, Masters and Shipowners of the Wirral 1550–1650." *Mariner's Mirror* 63, no. 3 (1977): 233–47.

Yates, Frances. *The Art of Memory.* London: Pimlico, 1992.

Youings, Joyce. *Ralegh's Country, The South West of England in the Reign of Queen Elizabeth I.* Raleigh: North Carolina Division of Archives, 1986.

———. *Sixteenth-Century England.* London: Penguin Books, Ltd., 1984.

———, ed. *Privateering and Colonisation in the Reign of Elizabeth I.* Exeter Studies in History No. 10. Exeter: University of Exeter Press, 1985.

Index

Page numbers in *italics* indicate illustrations.

navigator: skills required of, 14–15, 106. *See also* ships' masters
Navigators Supply, The (Barlow), 40, 95, 132, 139
neap tides, 97
Newe Attractive, The (Norman), 1, 39, 72, 85, 93, 140, 156
Newport, Christopher, 13, 14
nocturnal device, 39–40, *82, 83*
Norman, Robert, 1, 39, 72, 85, 93, 140, 156
north pole, celestial: in calculating latitude, 27, 81, 116; proximity to polestar, 79, 80, 114–15; reckoning location of, 83
North Star, 80

O
ocean: in Christian imagery, 137. *See also* seascape
ocean color, as navigational clue, 125
oceanic motion, 67–68
octants, 110, 142
ocular parallax, 119

P
Paracelsus, 77
paradoxal compass, 73
parallax, 113, 119
passenger list, 33–34
Patience, 152
Perkins, William, 135
pilotage, 4, 6, 43, 45
pilots, 43
piracy, 24, 48, 55–56
plain meridian compass, 91
Plaine Mans Path-way to Heaven, The (Dent), 130, 138
plane geometry, in reckoning longitude, 143
Polaris, *80,* 81, 83
polestar, 81, 83; *altura* of, 27; equal-altitude method in observing, 114–15; quadrant in sighting, 109–10; sailing by altitude of, 27. *See also* Polaris
Port of Bristol, 28; smuggling around, 35
portolan chart, 59–60, 110
Portugal: latitude sailing developed by, 27; mathematical innovations in, 18
power projection, 8

predestination doctrine, 129–30
"Preface: Commendations of Navigation" (Purchas), 11
prime computation, 97, 98
Prime Meridian, 127, 142; selection of location of, 143
Principal Navigations Voyages Traffiques & Discoveries of the English Nation (Hakluyt), 3, 24, 37, 56, 86, 99, *126, 141*
privateering, 14, 24, 48, 55–56
Prognostication Everlastinge (Digges), 110
Protestant church, 131, 134. *See also* Christianity and Christian theology
Providence, relation to predestination, 129–30
provisioning of ship, 35–36
Ptolemaic cosmos, 68, *74, 75,* 132
Ptolemy, Claudius, 59, 143
Pumfrey, Stephen, 79
Purchas, Samuel, 3, 4, 11, 66–67, 132
Pythagorean Theorem, 143

Q
quadrant, *109,* 109–10

R
Ralegh, Walter, 27, 112
Recorde, Robert, 37, 66, 68, 133
refraction, 128; correction in cross-staff observations, 119; correction in sextant observations, 128; defined, 119
Regiment for the Sea, A (Bourne), 39, 80, 134, 144, *145, 147,* 156
Regiment of the North Star, 115
religion. *See* Christianity and Christian theology
rhumbs, *62*
right-angled triangle method, in distance measurement, 146–48
ritual, 10
Roanoke voyages, 27, 112
rode, 33
Rule to Raise or Lay a Degree of Latitude (Bourne), 144
running the latitude, 106
rutter, 45, 54, 100, 126

About the Author

Raised in an itinerant military and diplomatic family, Robert Hicks has lived throughout the United States and abroad. He has enjoyed multiple careers, including U.S. Naval cryptology, law enforcement, and interpretation at and management of museums and historic sites. His central interests in astronomy and history have informed his passion for telling stories about the material heritage of science.

He holds degrees in anthropology from the University of Arizona and a doctorate in maritime history from the University of Exeter, U.K. He is the director of the Mütten Museum and Historical Medical Library of The College of Physicians of Philadelphia.